1. desember 2001

Elsku Finnur

hjartanlegar hamingjuóskir
með glæsilegan fyrsta konsert
í Ameríku.

ástarkveðjur
pabbi og mamma

THE MASTER MUSICIANS

Series edited by Stanley Sadie

THE MASTER MUSICIANS

Titles Available in Paperback

Berlioz · Hugh Macdonald　　Rachmaninoff · Geoffrey Norris
Brahms · Malcolm MacDonald　　Rossini · Richard Osborn
Britten · Michael Kennedy　　Schubert · John Reed
Bruckner · Derek Watson　　Sibelius · Robert Layton
Chopin · Jim Samson　　Richard Strauss · Michael Kennedy
Handel · Donald Burrows　　Tchaikovsky · Edward Garden
Liszt · Derek Watson　　Vaughan Williams · James Day
Mahler · Michael Kennedy　　Verdi · Julian Budden
Mendelssohn · Philip Radcliffe　　Vivaldi · Michael Talbot
Monteverdi · Denis Arnold　　Wagner · Barry Millington
Purcell · J. A. Westrup

Titles Available in Hardcover

Bach · Malcolm Boyd　　Schumann · Eric Frederick Jensen
Beethoven · Barry Cooper　　Schütz · Basil Smallman
Chopin · Jim Samson　　Richard Strauss · Michael Kennedy
Elgar · Robert Anderson　　Stravinsky · Paul Griffiths
Handel · Donald Burrows

Titles In Preparation

Bartók · Malcolm Gillies　　Puccini · Julian Budden
Dvořák · Jan Smaczny　　Tchaikovsky · R. John Wiley
Musorgsky · David Brown

THE MASTER MUSICIANS

SCHUMANN

Eric Frederick Jensen

OXFORD
UNIVERSITY PRESS

2001

OXFORD
UNIVERSITY PRESS

Oxford   New York
Athens   Auckland   Bangkok   Bogotá   Buenos Aires
Cape Town   Chennai   Dar es Salaam   Delhi   Florence   Hong Kong   Istanbul
Karachi   Kolkata   Kuala Lumpur   Madrid   Melbourne   Mexico City   Mumbai
Nairobi   Paris   São Paulo   Shanghai   Singapore   Taipei   Tokyo   Toronto   Warsaw

and associated companies in
Berlin   Ibadan

Copyright © 2001 by Oxford University Press, Inc.

Published by Oxford University Press, Inc.
198 Madison Avenue, New York, New York 10016

Oxford is a registered trademark of Oxford University Press

All rights reserved. No part of this publication may be reproduced,
stored in a retrieval system, or transmitted in any form or by any means,
electronic, mechanical, photocopying, recording, or otherwise,
without prior permission of Oxford University Press.

Library of Congress Cataloging-in-Publication Data
Jensen, Eric Frederick, 1951-
Schumann / Eric Frederick Jensen.
p. cm. — (The master musicians)
Includes bibliographical references and index.
ISBN 0-19-513566-0
1. Schumann, Robert, 1810–1856.
2. Composers—Germany—Biography.
I. Title.   II. Master musicians series.
ML410.S4 J45 2000
780'.92—dc21   [B]   00-027866

Series designed by Carla Bolte

Portions of the text have been previously published and are reprinted by permission:
"Schumann at Endenich," *The Musical Times* CXXXIX (March and April 1998), pp. 10–19, 14–24;
"Explicating Jean Paul: The Program for Schumann's *Papillons*, Op. 2," *19th Century Music*,
Vol. 22, no. 2, pp. 127–44, © 1998 by The Regents of the University of California;
"Schumann, Hummel, and the Clarity of a Well-Planned Composition," *Studia Musicologica* XL (1999), pp. 59–70.

Photograph credits: photos 1–7, 9, 12–15, courtesy Robert-Schumann-Haus, Zwickau, Germany;
photos 8, 11, courtesy Wurlitzer-Bruck, New York;
photo 10, courtesy Henrich-Heine-Institut, Düsseldorf, Germany.

1 3 5 7 9 8 6 4 2

Printed in the United States of America
on acid free paper

THIS BOOK IS DEDICATED TO THE MEMORY
OF MY BROTHER, GROVER.

The songs I had are withered
Or vanished clean,
Yet there are bright tracks
Where I have been,

And there grow flowers
For others' delight.
Think well, O singer,
Soon comes night.

Ivor Gurney

Contents

Preface ix
List of Abbreviations xv

1   Childhood and Youth 1
2   University Years 17
3   Schumann and Literature 39
4   Commitment to Music 58
5   Schumann's Compositions Prior to 1834 80
6   The *League of David* 106
7   Courtship and Marriage 122
8   The Piano Compositions, 1834–39 141
9   Married Life in Leipzig 174
10 The Compositions, 1840–44 192
11 The Years in Dresden 217
12 Schumann's Dramatic Works 236
13 The Years in Düsseldorf 259
14 The Compositions, 1845–54 281
15 Endenich 312

Epilogue "The Poet Speaks": Schumann and Childhood 335

Appendices:
Calendar 345
List of Works 351
Personalia 364
Select Bibliography 368
Index 373

Preface

SCHUMANN'S CONTEMPORARIES WOULD BE ASTONISHED BY THE AMOUNT of interest in him today. To some, he was the composer of bizarre and often peculiar works for piano. To others, he was the composer of chamber music and symphonies too conventional and traditional in basis. To most, he was better known as a music critic than as a composer. Few would have considered him among the most significant composers of his day, preferring instead Mendelssohn or Spohr, Meyerbeer or Wagner.

Yet, Schumann is increasingly regarded not just as a composer of stature but as one of the leading figures of German Romanticism. The past decades have witnessed a phenomenal growth of interest in him and his music. A new scholarly edition of his compositions is in progress. A revised thematic catalogue of his work and complete editions of his correspondence and music criticism are being planned. A great number of scholarly articles and monographs have appeared, as well as recordings of virtually all of his music.

But Schumann's move to prominence has been a slow process. In 1854, he had a nervous breakdown (one of three over a twenty-year period), and at his own request was placed in a mental institution to recover. He died there two years later. Mental illness in the Victorian era was regarded with fear, suspicion, and abhorrence. Schumann was suddenly seen as a pathetic figure whose mental instability had marred much of his work. This attitude was one that lingered forcefully for much of the twentieth century. It was complemented by a maudlin view especially popular in the English-speaking world: Schumann the Romantic tone-poet, the sentimental creator of "Träumerei."

Conflicting perceptions of Schumann emerged during the first half of the twentieth century, primarily a result of social and political turmoil in Germany. When Schumann's private papers and journals (he maintained a copious series of diaries) became available for examination, they fell into the hands of Nazi scholars. Their studies, filled with fabrications and lies, presented Schumann as a model Aryan and devout anti-Semite.

During World War II, many of Schumann's personal documents were lost or displaced. A substantial portion of those that survived were in East Germany, and Marxist scholars then put them to use. Schumann became a courageous champion of "The People."

A more truthful view of Schumann only began to emerge in 1971, when the first of his diaries was published. The remaining diaries appeared sixteen years later; Schumann's household books (diaries of a sort) were published in 1982. A scholarly edition—still in progress—of Schumann's correspondence with his future wife, Clara Wieck, was begun in 1984. At last, nearly a century and a half after his death, it became possible to view him in his own words, and the picture that resulted differed substantially from those that previously had been available.

Rather than dreaming his life away at the piano, Schumann was an indefatigable worker driven by ambition. His compositions confirm it—well over 150 works, many of substantial length, during approximately twenty years. But more significant than their number is their variety. Throughout his career, Schumann challenged himself to explore new genres. He could easily have specialized in piano compositions or songs, as did many of his contemporaries. Instead, he made a point of attempting something new, whether in traditional forms such as opera or symphony, or in genres of his own creation, such as the choral ballads of his last years. In each case, Schumann's efforts were not the result of commissions—he often had no idea if his compositions would be performed—but were self-imposed.

Schumann seemed content only when he set new standards for himself. But, as the diaries and household books reveal, he was also concerned with the business of music. The music journal he founded and edited, the *Neue Zeitschrift für Musik*, was profitable and steadily increased in sales. Its success was almost entirely the result of Schumann's own efforts. In his compositions, Schumann reckoned on similar financial success. His move from piano compositions to songs, for example, was intended in part because of his hope to earn more money as a song writer.

What makes Schumann's accomplishments even more remarkable are the circumstances surrounding them. His success as a music critic was a mixed blessing. While he found much gratification as a writer (and helped to create a market for the new music of his day, often in the face of substantial opposition), he would have preferred to spend more of his time composing. Often work on compositions had to wait while a deadline was met for his criticism. Financial concerns were always present, and he earned more as a music critic than as a composer.

In addition, Schumann suffered from depression, so severe that at times work of any sort was impossible. But he was not the "madman" the nineteenth century created. By modern standards, it seems likely that his mental illness could have been managed, if not cured. The treatment he received only exacerbated his condition, making his final years an ordeal, and his confinement in a mental institution a nightmare come true.

Schumann's diaries and correspondence are often deeply personal, and bring him to life as no other source can. They reveal an exceptional human spirit, notable for its integrity and idealism, and steadfast in its devotion and dedication to music. Readily apparent are his great sensitivity and love for beauty, whether in nature (for which Schumann had a great appreciation) or in works of art. His friendships are consistently noted, and emphasize his ability to focus on what is best in human nature. Family life plays a large role as well. Surprising are the frequent references to his children, not, as might be expected, in the guise of a doting father but as a lover of childhood and a keen admirer of an idealized innocence.

In writing this study of Schumann, it seemed essential to use his diaries, household books, and letters as the primary source—not merely to create a more accurate representation of him, but to allow him to speak for himself. The diaries and household books are readily available in scholarly editions. But Schumann's correspondence—he was a prolific letterwriter—is scattered in more than a dozen books and periodicals published over the past century. None of these make any pretence of being complete, and the texts have frequently been heavily edited—in some cases, even altered and deliberately distorted. I have consulted all of them, but have used four most frequently: F. Gustav Jansen's *Briefe: Neue Folge* (Leipzig, 1904), Hermann Erler's *Robert Schumann's Leben: Aus seinen Briefen geschildert* (Berlin, 1887), Siegfried Kross's *Briefe und Notizen Robert und Clara Schumanns*, 2nd ed. (Bonn, 1982), and the correspondence of Schumann and his wife, *Briefwechsel: Kritische Gesamtausgabe* (Frankfurt am Main, 1984-).

For the letters of Schumann's youth, two often complementary editions are available: the *Jugendbriefe*, first edited by Clara Schumann in 1885, and *Der junge Schumann: Dictungen und Briefe*, edited in 1917 by Alfred Schumann. Although I have used both, the latter is more reliable and, whenever possible, I have used it in preference to the *Jugendbriefe*. I have also used as a primary source Georg Eismann's documentary study: *Robert Schumann: Ein Quellenwerk über sein Leben und Schaffen* (Leipzig, 1956; only the first volume: the second is a miscellany of Schumann's previously published music criticism).

It has been my intention to remove some of the mystery associated with Schumann and his music, and to present a more reliable representation of the man and his age. Common errors—such as the birthdate of Schumann's mother and even Schumann's true name—are corrected. And I have tried to provide lucid answers to a multitude of biographical questions that have long remained problematical, including Schumann's complicated relationship with his family, his literary skills and their effect on his compositions, the basis of his celebrated "hand injury," the sources of his *League of David*, the travails of his married life, and the nature of his mental illness.

In addition, a number of new points are presented concerning Schumann's compositions, particularly concerning his changing musical aesthetics. Much space has been devoted to literary influences, program music, and the significance of "hidden" musical quotations. I do not, however, perceive Schumann as a predominantly "literary composer," often a corollary to the perception of him as a sentimental "tone-poet." Early in his career (before 1832), and then again after his marriage in 1840, musical models strongly influenced his work, leading to the supposed dichotomy that has often been perceived between the piano compositions of the 1830s and his later work.

Schumann's compositions were often created in response to critical reaction and pressing financial needs—not, as has been frequently maintained, by following creative whim. Included is a reevaluation of all of his compositions, particularly from the latter part of his career (which are less known), as well as a comprehensive discussion of the works of his youth (that is, the compositions created before 1834, also lesser known). In exploring the programmatic tendencies of his music, an explanation is offered for the enigmatic program of *Papillons* op. 2 (including the significance of the quotation of the "Grossvater Tanz"), and the role of the "Sphinxes" in *Carnaval* op. 9. Part of the puzzle of Schumann's music has been not just its extramusical connotations but its unacknowledged association to the music of other composers; in that sense, new information is provided about the role of Schumann's musical borrowings, especially in the Second Symphony and String Quartets.

Of the sixteen chapters, five are devoted solely to a discussion of the music. But the biographical chapters have been conceived independently from those dealing with the music, and those who feel uncomfortable reading music analysis can skip the chapters on music without losing the thread of Schumann's life. With all primary sources, I have relied on the original (usually in German, but occasionally in French or Italian). The translations are my own, except in a few instances where I have preferred the work of another who seemed to capture the flavor of the nineteenth-century better than myself; these cases are noted in the footnotes. In order to reduce the number of footnotes, the two most frequently cited sources for Schumann's correspondence—Jansen's *Briefe* and the *Briefwechsel* between himself and his wife—are indicated in the text by dates.

My thanks to Stanley Sadie, and to Maribeth Anderson Payne, executive editor of music books at Oxford University Press, for their support, advice and encouragement. It has been a pleasure to work with Maureen Buja as she has guided this book through its final stages.

The brunt of the discomforts associated with this project fell on my family, and I am grateful to my wife, Allie, and son, Ben, for their understanding. As always, my wife has been my best critic. This book has been much improved by her suggestions.

List of Abbreviations for Frequently Cited Sources

Br   Robert Schumann, *Briefe. Neue Folge*, ed. F. Gustav Jansen (Leipzig, 1904).

Cl/Rob   Clara and Robert Schumann, *Briefwechsel*, ed. Eva Weissweiler, 2 vols. (Frankfurt am Main, 1984, 1987).

Eismann Georg Eismann, *Robert Schumann: Ein Quellenwerk über sein Leben und Schaffen*, 2 vols. (Leipzig, 1956). References are to the first volume only.

GS   Robert Schumann, *Gesammelte Schriften über Musik und Musiker*, ed. Martin Kreisig, 2 vols. (Leipzig, 1914).

HSHLT Robert Schumann, *Haushaltbücher, 1837–1856*, ed. Gerd Nauhaus, 2 vols. (Leipzig, 1982).

JgBr   Robert Schumann, *Jugendbriefe*, ed. Clara Schumann (Leipzig, 1886).

JS   *Der junge Schuman: Dichtungen und Briefe*, ed. Alfred Schumann (Leipzig, 1917).

Tgb I   Robert Schumann, *Tagebücher, I: 1827–1838*, ed. Georg Eismann (Leipzig, 1971).

Tgb II Robert Schumann, *Tagebücher, II: 1836–1854*, ed. Gerd Nauhaus (Leipzig, 1987).

W   Wilhelm Joseph von Wasielewski, *Robert Schumann: Eine Biographie* (Leipzig, 1906).

List of Abbreviations for Frequently Cited Sources

Br   Robert Schumann, *Briefe. Neue Folge*, ed. F. Gustav Jansen (Leipzig, 1904).

Cl/Rob   Clara and Robert Schumann, *Briefwechsel*, ed. Eva Weissweiler, 2 vols. (Frankfurt am Main, 1984, 1987).

Eismann   Georg Eismann, *Robert Schumann: Ein Quellenwerk über sein Leben und Schaffen*, 2 vols. (Leipzig, 1956). References are to the first volume only.

GS   Robert Schumann, *Gesammelte Schriften über Musik und Musiker*, ed. Martin Kreisig, 2 vols. (Leipzig, 1914).

HSHLT   Robert Schumann, *Haushaltbücher, 1837–1856*, ed. Gerd Nauhaus, 2 vols. (Leipzig, 1982).

JgBr   Robert Schumann, *Jugendbriefe*, ed. Clara Schumann (Leipzig, 1886).

JS   *Der junge Schuman: Dichtungen und Briefe*, ed. Alfred Schumann (Leipzig, 1917).

Tgb I   Robert Schumann, *Tagebücher, I: 1827–1838*, ed. Georg Eismann (Leipzig, 1971).

Tgb II   Robert Schumann, *Tagebücher, II: 1836–1854*, ed. Gerd Nauhaus (Leipzig, 1987).

W   Wilhelm Joseph von Wasielewski, *Robert Schumann: Eine Biographie* (Leipzig, 1906).

CHAPTER 1

Childhood and Youth

"You must have been such a strange boy!"
—Letter to Schumann from Clara Wieck (4 March 1838)

"AT SCHOOL HE WAS AN AVERAGE STUDENT," RECALLED EMIL Flechsig, a close friend of Schumann during his youth, "rather dreamy and inattentive. But what soon struck me about him was the absolute certainty in his own mind that one day he would become famous. In what he would be famous—that had yet to be determined—but famous whatever the circumstances."[1] The "dreamy and inattentive" side of Schumann's personality—Schumann, the romantic and impractical visionary—has been broadly affirmed by his biographers. His ambition has been all but forgotten. Zwickau, the small and tranquil town in Saxony where Schumann spent his childhood and youth, was an unlikely location for one bent on achieving fame in the world. Although he was only twelve years old when he first met Flechsig, by that age Schumann realized that his pursuit of fame would best be accomplished in the arts. Flechsig's query—"in what Schumann would be famous"—remained unanswered for some time. But in Schumann's mind there were only two possibilities: music or literature.

[1] Emil Flechsig, "Erinnerungen an Robert Schumann," *Neue Zeitschrift für Musik* CXVII (1956), p. 392.

Schumann's birth in Zwickau on 8 June 1810 and baptism six days later have been the source of confusion. In biographies and entries in dictionaries, lexicons, and encyclopedias, he is routinely given the middle name Alexander. But when baptized, Schumann was given no middle name at all—nor did he use one. On all official documents he is referred to as, simply, Robert Schumann. The middle name, Alexander, was mistakenly used by Schumann's first biographer, Wilhelm Joseph von Wasielewski, and has invariably been adopted since.

In the early nineteenth century, Zwickau had a population of only about four thousand. The surrounding countryside was beautiful and idyllic, and from an early age Schumann enjoyed walks in the fields and woods, a habit he was to continue throughout his life. His delight in the countryside was shared by his father who with obvious partiality described Zwickau as "one of the loveliest and most romantic regions of Saxony . . . On the whole, the entire area around Zwickau is so filled with natural beauty that it truly could be called a park."[2]

During the first years of Schumann's life, however, these idyllic charms were scarcely in evidence. In the summer of 1812, Napoleon was preparing to invade Russia, and he and his troops passed through Zwickau on their way to the Russian border. Saxony was an ally of France, and the disasters of the campaign filled Zwickau with the horrors of war. During the retreat, wounded French soldiers were quartered there; soon Cossacks of the victorious Russian army appeared outside the town itself. The theater of war moved to Saxony, and in 1813 the most significant battles of the campaign were fought in Dresden and Leipzig, each less than sixty miles from Zwickau. Food became scarce, sanitary conditions deteriorated, and a typhus epidemic broke out. Schumann's mother caught the disease and, to protect her son, he was sent to live with his godparents, the Ruppius family—a visit originally intended for only six weeks, but which (for reasons unknown) by Schumann's own account lasted for two-and-a-half years. It is not known how much contact Schumann had during this period with his own family, but his return at the age of six to his true home was probably an emotional one.

It could only have been a challenge during those difficult times for

---

[2] August Schumann, *Staats-, Post- und Zeitungslexicon von Sachsen*. Quoted in *Eismann*, p. 9.

Schumann's father to provide for his family. But August Schumann was a remarkable man who not only survived the turmoil but prospered during it. Schumann was forty at the time, having been born on 2 March 1773 in the small town of Endschütz near Gera. The eldest son of a Protestant minister, he early displayed unusual interest in literature and philosophy. Unfortunately, the comparative poverty of the family precluded a university education, and in 1787 he was apprenticed to a merchant.

During the next half dozen or so years, he worked as a clerk in a warehouse and in a grocer's shop, teaching himself bookkeeping in his spare time. But his interest in literature remained keen. He studied French and English, and avidly read contemporary works, including the then-popular *Night Thoughts* of the English poet Edward Young—a work imbued with a somber melancholy, which August Schumann later recounted had nearly driven him to madness. Because of his son's mental instability, this incident has been perceived as an indication of an inherent instability within the Schumann family itself. But to view August Schumann's infatuation with the *Night Thoughts* in such a light is to overlook both the power of Young's writing and the extraordinary sensitivity characteristic of the period. In an age fond of extravagant sentiment, readers longed to be swept away by their reading. As the title implies, Young's *Night Thoughts* focus on death and melancholy, as well as similar uncommonly gloomy topics relished by the public of the day. His reaction to it is best seen as proof of his passion for literature and deep sensitivity.

Schumann also tried his hand at writing, including a drama, "The Thalheim Family" (later turned into a story), and a novel, *Scenes of Knights and Tales of Monks*. For a short period of time he even enrolled as a student in the University of Leipzig but was unable to continue for lack of funds. His fortunes changed for the better when he was offered a position as bookkeeper in a bookstore in Zeitz owned by Gottlob Heinrich Heinse, an author of popular fiction. Schumann soon fell in love with Johanne Christiane Schnabel, his landlord's daughter. Before consent for the marriage could be obtained, however, it was stipulated that Schumann give proof of greater earning potential (an obstacle to marriage that Schumann's son was also to encounter).

Schumann's response was to write at a feverish pace more than a half dozen works, including fiction and mercantile publications, using the proceeds from their sale as the basis for opening a grocery store in Ronneburg in 1795. August Schumann and Christiane Schnabel were married that year. But he soon managed to favor his true interests by creating a lending library as part of the establishment, using his own library as the basis. In 1799, despite the objections of his father-in-law, Schumann abandoned the grocery and entered the book trade. It was a discerning move. The area around Leipzig had long been the book-publishing center in Germany, and the industry was growing. Schumann established a business devoted to both selling and publishing books. In 1808, with his brother Friedrich as partner, the firm was settled in Zwickau. An inexpensive pocket edition of literary classics—including works by Walter Scott, Friedrich Schiller, and Miguel de Cervantes—became highly profitable. Translations of Byron undertaken by Schumann himself were also offered, including *Beppo* and portions of *Childe Harold*. In 1810, Friedrich Schumann left to establish his own publishing business in Gera. By that time August Schumann was one of Zwickau's most notable citizens, and publisher of the local newspaper.

Emil Flechsig's primary recollection of August Schumann was of his industry: "I never saw him do anything but work."[3] It took its toll. Although Schumann created a publishing firm that was a resounding financial success and that was to survive his death by fourteen years, ill health plagued him, including abdominal complaints, gout, and occasional spells of giddiness. When he died in 1826, Schumann left 60,000 talers, a sum ample enough to assure financial security to his family for many years. From his inheritance Robert Schumann received funds to travel, to attend college, and a sizable bequest as well. It was his father's success as a publisher that ultimately provided the financial means for Schumann to study music, marry, and begin a career as a composer.

Throughout his life Robert Schumann expressed a deep love and veneration for his father. In Robert's student years, August Schumann's portrait (along with that of Napoleon, Jean Paul Richter, and, later, Beethoven) was prominently displayed by his writing desk—men who in his youth served as models and sources of inspiration. In the months

---

[3] Flechsig, p. 392.

after his father's death, Schumann's diary contains poignant references to his loss. As an adult, the memory of his father did not fade. "This is the date on which my good father died," he noted in his diary in 1842, "about whom I often think."[4] Schumann's attitude toward his mother differed considerably. Both love and solicitude were present, but she was never placed on the pedestal reserved for his father. She was six years older than her husband, having been born on 28 November 1767. After their marriage, she worked for a while in her husband's grocery store, but it is apparent that much of her time was devoted to raising an ever-growing family: Eduard (born 1797), Carl (born 1801), Julius (born 1805), and Emilie (born 1807).

The Schumann household was one in which literature and music played an important role. Like her husband, Christiane Schumann had a lively interest in literature (a poem by her, "To Napoleon Bonaparte," was included by her son in one of his earliest literary efforts). Both she and August Schumann sang; and, in addition to Robert, Eduard and Julius received piano lessons. Because of her reluctance later to support Robert in his decision to make a career in music, she has routinely been portrayed as stolidly middle class, narrow-minded, and insensitive to the talent and the wishes of her son. That was clearly not the case. She took understandable pride in the fact that she was the first to suggest music lessons for Robert. And it is possible that Schumann's maternal ancestry was the source for some of his musical gifts: two members of the Schnabel family (Schumann's maternal great-grandfather and great-greatuncle) earned their living as musicians in the eighteenth century.

Schumann's formal schooling began at the age of six-and-a-half in the private school of Hermann Döhner. This is an indication not only of the importance given to education in the Schumann family but of the financial success of August Schumann's firm. In the spring of 1820 Schumann entered the Lyceum. The study of music began when he was seven, with piano lessons under the direction of Johann Gottfried Kuntsch. The instruction probably stemmed from Schumann's singing ability—he was a gifted soprano as a boy. Kuntsch, the most knowledgeable and most prominent musician in Zwickau, taught at the Lyceum and was organist at the Marienkirche, the largest church in

---

[4] Entry of 10 August in *Tgb II*, p. 237.

Zwickau. When Schumann started his study with him, Kuntsch was forty-two years old. Of his musical background and ability, little is known. There is no indication that he himself had received any musical training in depth; quite probably, to a great extent he was self-taught. He made a name for himself in the area by organizing concerts and recitals, including, on 11 March 1802 (only two years after the publication of the score), the first performance in Zwickau of Haydn's *Creation*.

Virtually nothing is known of the nature of Schumann's study with Kuntsch. One former student described Kuntsch as "a very good, but strict teacher."[5] Music theory and harmony apparently were not taught by him, piano alone being the focus. As for Kuntsch's skill at the piano, Schumann himself later described him as being only a "tolerable" player.[6] All in all, biographers of Schumann have not treated Kuntsch kindly, emphasizing the obvious fact that the student was far more gifted than the teacher. Many have taken their cue from Schumann's wife, who in 1889 bluntly stated that Kuntsch had not been "distinguished enough to be my husband's teacher."[7] But Kuntsch was clearly the best that Zwickau had to offer. And in many ways, he may have been an ideal teacher for Schumann. He perceived his extraordinary ability, fostered it, provided an outlet for its development, and offered constant support. Schumann was grateful, and throughout his life held Kuntsch in high regard. They exchanged letters, scores, and gifts.

By the time of Schumann's entry into the Lyceum, his family had purchased a new Streicher grand piano for his use. He began playing duets with a friend, and soon was participating in an amateur concert series founded in 1819 and supported by Kuntsch. This series, the *Deklamatorisch-musikalischen Abendunterhaltung* (Poetic and Musical Evening Entertainment), provided an ideal means for displaying Schumann's growing ability. In addition to music, there were dramatic readings, and for a period of seven years (1821–1828) he participated in both areas.

Schumann's abilities were prominently displayed: on the program for

---

[5] E. Herzog quoted in *Br*, p. 528.

[6] Eismann, p. 12.

[7] Letter of 28 May 1889 to Frederick Niecks in Frederick Niecks, *Robert Schumann* (London, 1925), p. 32.

25 January 1828, he both recited a monologue from Goethe's *Faust* and performed an arrangement of Friedrich Kalkbrenner's Piano Concerto op. 61. In the midst of these activities Schumann found time to study briefly both cello and flute. And he participated in the larger-scale performances organized by Kuntsch. In 1821, there was a presentation of the then-popular oratorio by Friedrich Schneider, *The Last Judgment*, an event Schumann remembered fondly and with some amusement, having served as accompanist for the performance while *standing* at the piano. Schumann also organized occasional informal recitals at his home, including a memorable performance of the overture to Vincenzo Righini's *Tigrane* (1800) with a pair of violins, two flutes, a clarinet, and two horns (Schumann himself filled in the rest of the orchestral parts at the piano). Such informal concerts at the Schumann home could be extensive, comprising nearly a dozen pieces—a reflection of the extravagant length typical of concerts of the time.

Schumann's musical experiences were not limited to performing. He probably heard performances of Weber's *Der Freischütz* and *Preciosa*, Cherubini's *Les deux Journées*, Méhul's *Joseph*, and Mozart's *Entführung aus dem Serail*. And he attended recitals regularly, one that he heard with his mother in Carlsbad in 1819 being, by his own account, of special significance. Ignaz Moscheles, probably the most distinguished piano virtuoso of the time, was seated behind them. Schumann kept as a precious memento a concert program that Moscheles had touched. Years later when Moscheles dedicated one of his compositions to Schumann, Schumann wrote to thank him, mentioning as well the concert of 1819: "At that time," he wrote, "I never dreamed that I would be honored in this manner by so celebrated a master" (20 November 1851).

Much of Schumann's repertory during these years consisted of fashionable works of composers highly regarded at the time, but little known today: Ignaz Pleyel, Johann Nepomuk Hummel, Bernhard Anselm Weber, Ferdinand Ries, Moscheles, Carl Czerny, and—later to become one of Schumann's *bêtes noires*—Henri Herz. But he also studied works of Haydn and Mozart, often in arrangements for four hands. It appears likely that he did not become familiar with the music of Beethoven until 1826 or 1827. Much time was spent as well in improvising at the piano, as Schumann later remembered, "for many hours each day."[8] Improvisation was important to him. Not only was he later to make a considerable name for himself with it, many of his early compositions are clearly improvisatory in origin.

"Even in my youth," Schumann recalled in 1846, "I felt the urge to create, if not in music, then in poetry."[9] He began composing dances for the piano not long after he had started lessons on the instrument. His first complete composition of length was created in 1822—a setting of Psalm 150 for chorus and orchestra—a work that he later dismissed as a childish effort. The grandiose seemed to hold special appeal for him, for at about the same time he began work on several overtures and sketches for opera. These attempts reveal more about Schumann's ambition than about his musical abilities. He knew little of music theory, harmony, or instrumentation.

Despite his musical accomplishments during these years, much of Schumann's energy was directed toward literature. In 1823, he assembled in a sketchbook a literary miscellany including poetry by himself and his parents, anecdotes, biographies of composers, a fragment for a tragedy, and references to musical performances. It was given the fanciful title *Blätter und Blümchen aus der goldenen Aue: Gesammelt und zusammengebunden von Robert Schumann, genannt Skülander* (Leaves and Little Flowers From the Golden Meadow: Collected and Assembled by Robert Schumann, known as Skülander). In format, it had much in common with the literary albums and annuals popular at the time. Two years later Schumann devised a similar project that he entitled *Allerley aus der Feder Roberts an der Mulde* (A Miscellany From the Pen of Robert on the River Mulde). Both undertakings can be seen as precursors of the diaries and household records Schumann was to keep intermittently for much of his life. Although diaries and literary albums were much in vogue during the first half of the nineteenth century, Schumann took particular pleasure in noting—no matter how tersely—daily events, while at the same time maintaining a record of his artistic interests and development.

In December 1825 his love for literature led to the creation of a literary society. The group, composed of about a dozen school friends,

---

[8] *Eismann*, p. 18.

[9] *Tgb II*, p. 402.

met thirty times and was in existence for more than two years. Their intentions were to broaden their literary knowledge and—at the same time—promote German literature, an object very much a reflection of growing German nationalism, as well as that of the Rektor of the Lyceum, Gottfried Hertel. Schumann provided the spirit and energy for much of the group's activities. Goals of the society included the reading of literary masterpieces and biographies of celebrated writers, discussions of obscure passages from their readings, and the presentation of original poetry by the members. Although classical poets such as Anacreon were included in their discussions, most of their attention was focused on popular German writers of the Enlightenment and early nineteenth century.

There can be little doubt that at this time Schumann was giving serious consideration to becoming a writer. He took an active role as researcher, writer, and proofreader in two ambitious publishing ventures of his father: *Bildnisse der berühmtesten Menschen aller Völker und Zeiten* (Portraits of the Most Celebrated People of All Time) in 1823, and a new edition of Egidio Forcellini's monumental *Totius latinitatis Lexicon* (1771; issued in four volumes by the Schumann firm, 1831–35). He also held an exalted view of the mission of a poet, a not uncommon stance for the time. In a student essay written in September 1827, "The Life of the Poet," Schumann rhapsodized: "Is not the entire life of the poet a happy, pure and spiritual one, devoted to what is most noble and most high?"[10] In 1826, he wrote without success to a newspaper, the Dresden *Abendzeitung*, asking them to publish some of his poetry.

It is not difficult to see the hand of August Schumann in these endeavors. In many ways, his son was being encouraged to accomplish what the father had not. In 1826, he attempted to arrange for Carl Maria von Weber—at the time Kapellmeister in Dresden, not far from Zwickau—to become Robert's teacher. But on 16 February 1826 Weber left for England to arrange performances of his recently completed opera, *Oberon*. Already suffering from tuberculosis, he died in London on 5 June. August Schumann's desire to retain Weber as a teacher confirms the earnestness with which he viewed his son's ability. But it was

---

[10] *GS II*, p. 182.

in many ways an impractical choice. Weber had few pupils. His students in general tended also to be considerably more advanced in their study than Robert was. It would have been unusual if he had taken Schumann on. But August Schumann must have realized that the selection of Weber as a teacher—assuming he would have consented—would probably have set Robert firmly on the path of making music his profession.[11]

August Schumann's plans never came to fruition. He died unexpectedly on 10 August 1826, probably of a heart attack. The only contemporary account of his death attributes it to "nervenübel."[12] It is a comparatively useless diagnosis—perhaps best translated as "nervous disease"—but used in the nineteenth century as a catch-all to cover a broad array of illnesses, including heart ailments. It is important to note that "nervenübel" is not associated with a nervous breakdown or mental illness, for in studies of Schumann the word is consistently mistranslated (and in German studies, often misunderstood). As a result, August Schumann's death has been erroneously presented as a portent of his son's mental collapse.

What made the sudden loss of August Schumann all the more difficult for the family was the recent death of Robert's sister, Emilie. It appears that she took her own life, an act of particular significance given Schumann's own suicide attempt in 1854. Little information about her is available. From her childhood she had suffered from a disfiguring skin disease that led to fits of depression. This resulted in what one contemporary source described as a "quiet madness," an apparent reference to the fact that she was not violent and did not require either restraint or, what was more common at the time, confinement.[13]

It is alleged that Emilie drowned herself in 1825 in a feverish state resulting from typhus. Her death certificate lists the cause of death as a "nervous stroke,"[14] but again this imprecise term is not helpful. That

---

[11] Our only source for the claim that August Schumann considered Weber as a teacher for Robert is found in the correspondence of his son (see particularly the letter of 20 August 1831 from Schumann to Hummel in *Br*, p. 31.) According to Wasielewski, the correspondence between August Schumann and Weber was destroyed after Weber's death.

[12] *Eismann*, p. 28.

[13] Eugenie Schumann, *Ein Lebensbild meines Vaters* (Leipzig, 1931), p. 61.

[14] Nancy B. Reich, *Clara Schumann. The Artist and the Woman* (Ithaca, NY, 1985), p. 58.

this much is known concerning Emilie's state is an indication that her condition was common knowledge in Zwickau. Schumann does not refer to her in his diaries or letters (though the letters of his youth have been edited and references to her might have been deleted). Christiane Schumann recalled, in a letter to her son in 1828, that he used to play dances for Emilie's pleasure.

The deaths of friends and members of his family affected Schumann deeply. There are later references in his diary to the deaths of his brothers and a beloved sister-in-law, all of which profoundly distressed him. It is strange, then, that Schumann never referred in writing to Emilie's madness, nor to the manner of her death. That he did not reveals a good deal. In his youth, Schumann was fascinated with madness, and was particularly intrigued by poets, writers, and musicians who had been insane or taken their own lives. According to Flechsig, the instance of Franz Anton Sonnenberg (1779–1805), a poet who committed suicide, "made a great impression upon him."[15] In a similar manner Schumann was interested in the poet Friedrich Hölderlin, who spent the final thirty-six years of his life as a recluse living in a garret and calling himself "Scardenelli."

In the nineteenth century, madness was romanticized; in some instances, a tinge of it was regarded as a necessary ingredient for creativity. But in Schumann's case, the condition of Emilie must have brought him in touch with the painful reality of depression and mental illness. That he made no mention of her condition or death in his correspondence or diaries indicates that rather than successfully confronting what must have disturbed him, he attempted to ignore it. When in the 1830s Schumann began to display unusual concern for his own mental health, his interest no longer appears detached, and his fascination has been augmented by fear and anxiety.

It is fortunate that the grieving for the loss of his father and sister was tempered by close friendships with classmates and a more active social life. His best friend remained Emil Flechsig. Flechsig, two years older than Schumann, was a year ahead of him in school, but the difference in age and grade level was no hindrance to what became a remarkably enduring association—one that continued when Schumann

---

[15] Flechsig, p. 396.

went to college and even lasted, though with infrequent contact, through Schumann's professional career.

Schumann and Flechsig shared common interests, both literary and social. In company with Flechsig, Schumann made trips to neighboring villages, sampled the local beer and wine, and met girlfriends. Striking a pose characteristic of the day, he sentimentalized his relationships with girls, portraying them as peerless creations whom he venerated and idolized. But one incident revealed much about Schumann's temperament and anticipated similar reactions while he was a student in Leipzig and Heidelberg. In his diary, Schumann noted meeting with a girlfriend, Flechsig, and others one Sunday. Describing his reaction to what occurred that day (the actual events are not related), he wrote (and later crossed out): "It was a terrible day. Such days shorten one's life: when sensual pleasure comes too strongly forward, man becomes a beast. And I was a beast. Enough. I am ashamed of myself."[16]

By nature Schumann was attracted to sensual pleasure; beautiful girls—references to them are frequent in his diary—delighted him, as did champagne, good wine, Bavarian beer, and cigars. He feared overindulgence, felt degraded by it, and over the years the diary offers evidence both of what he sensed as his overindulgence and his attempt to chastise and change himself. There was within Schumann an intense struggle between a spiritual idealism and what he perceived as a base sensuality. When he surrendered to purely physical pleasure, Schumann not only felt degraded, he felt a sense of guilt as well. No doubt a major reason for this guilt was Schumann's belief in the purity and transcendent spirituality of the creative artist. But yet another source can be traced to the strict and often hypocritical morality representative both of the Victorian era and Biedermeier Germany.

Of all his friendships, most important for Schumann's development as a musician was his association with the Carus family. In 1827, he met Dr. Ernst August Carus, director of the mental institute in nearby Colditz. Carus's wife, Agnes, was a beautiful young woman and a gifted, sensitive musician. Schumann soon became a regular visitor to the Ca-

---

[16] *Tgb* I, p. 30. Peter Ostwald's psychobiography, *Schumann: The Inner Voices of a Musical Genius* (Boston, 1985), makes frequent reference to Schumann's supposed homosexual tendencies. On the contrary, Schumann's diary presents consistent indication of his overwhelming attraction to the opposite sex.

rus home, developed a marked infatuation for Agnes, and wrote poetry for her. When the Carus family later moved to Leipzig (during Robert's student days there), Schumann's infatuation intensified. In his diary he revealed his deep attachment to her: "I will go to bed and dream of her, of her. Good night, Agnes . . . beautiful, beautiful dreams of A." And (crossed out): "heavenly dream about A."[17]

What served to strengthen the friendship between Agnes Carus and Robert was their mutual admiration for the music of Franz Schubert. Schumann's first encounter with it had a profound effect on him. He studied what was then available of Schubert's lieder and piano works, and Schubert soon became Schumann's favorite composer. Schumann even wrote a letter to Schubert but was too timid to send it. "There was a time," Schumann recalled with effusion, "when I spoke unwillingly of Schubert, who should only be spoken of at night in the midst of the forests and the stars."[18] Early in December 1828, when he learned of Schubert's death, Schumann noted in his diary: "*Schubert is dead*—dismay and confusion."[19] Flechsig, Schumann's roommate at the time, recalled that Schumann wept all night.

Schumann's discovery of Schubert's music coincided with a broadening and refining of his musical interests in general. As a composer, he began to branch out and composed several lieder, as well as sketches for a piano concerto in E flat major. His attention became focused not just on popular composers for the piano, like Pleyel and Herz, but on the work of composers of greater complexity and challenge. The music of Mozart and Haydn was studied. Johann Sebastian Bach is first mentioned in Schumann's diaries in 1827 (as yet, there is no indication of the exalted position Bach was to hold in Schumann's eyes).

While his musical interests and knowledge were expanding, in the summer of 1827 Schumann discovered the writings of Jean Paul Richter. They were a revelation to him, comparable in their effect to his discovery of Schubert. The work of Jean Paul tends to elicit strong reactions from his readers. His style is distinctive and original, with abrupt changes in mood and plot, full of whimsy, humor, outrageous

---

[17] Entries of 13 July 1828, and 22 and 23 February 1829 in *Ibid.*, pp. 94, 175, 176.
[18] Review published in 1838 of Schubert's *Grosses Duo* op. 140 in *GS I*, p. 328.
[19] *Tgb I*, p. 151.

metaphors, and overweening sentiment. Schumann was captivated by Jean Paul, and recommended him to all his friends. "Get *Titan* [Jean Paul's most famous novel] from the nearest library so that we can discuss it together," he advised Flechsig. "You will thank me when you have read it."[20]

Because Schumann's fame rests on his work as a composer, the intensity of his literary interests can be easily underestimated. Schumann at age seventeen revealed greater attraction to literature than to music. "What I truly am," he wrote in his diary on 24 January 1827, "is not at all clear to me. I believe I possess imagination. . . . I am not a deep thinker. . . . Whether I am a poet—one can never become one—posterity shall determine."[21] Schumann's use of the word "poet" is intended in a general sense (as the equivalent of "artist"). But his diary contains numerous references to books and authors; music is scarcely mentioned until 1828. Still, Schumann's literary pretensions need to be placed in perspective. At that time youthful infatuation with contemporary literature was far from unusual. To become a poet or writer was a dream of countless adolescents. In that sense, Schumann's diary emphasizes in many ways how unexceptional he was. Even more common than reflections on the arts are self-centered musings about himself, social outings, and girls. It would require a reader of prodigious sensitivity to discern in Schumann's diary at this stage any indication of musical genius.

In the spring of 1828, Schumann passed his final examinations at school, receiving the grade "worthy in all aspects." On 29 March, he traveled to Leipzig to enroll in the university; the term began in May. Flechsig had been studying there for a year. Although the matter may have been discussed, serious consideration was not given to Schumann becoming either a writer or a musician. It was his mother's decision (supported by Schumann's brothers) that he study law—a profession, it was hoped, that would provide a stable income. By contemporary social standards, the decision to study law was a decided move up for the Schumann family.

---

[20] Letter of 29 August 1827 in *JS*, p. 115.
[21] *Tgb* I, p. 30.

As a graduation present, before commencing his studies at the University of Leipzig, Schumann took a short trip through Bavaria with a new friend, Gisbert Rosen. Rosen, two years Schumann's senior, was also a student of law at Leipzig. He and Schumann had met during Schumann's visit in March and had got along well together, foremost being a mutual love of Jean Paul. But Rosen was now transferring to the University of Heidelberg, so it was decided that Schumann should accompany him part of the way, and then return by himself to Leipzig to begin his studies.

Although Schumann had traveled a little before, his previous trips had been limited to Saxony and locations not too distant. This was to be his most extensive trip, and the first to Bavaria. Rosen and Schumann first stopped at Bayreuth, the small town where Jean Paul had spent much of his life. "I am living," Schumann wrote to his brother Julius, "among blessed memories of Jean Paul."[22] The pair then traveled via Nuremberg to Augsburg where Schumann spent nearly a week with the family of Dr. Heinrich Wilhelm von Kurrer, who had been a close friend of his father. It was through the Kurrers that Schumann was able to arrange what became one of the highlights of the trip: a meeting with Heinrich Heine in Munich. Carl Krahe, an actor engaged to Kurrer's daughter Clara, knew Heine and presented Schumann with a letter of introduction.

On 5 May, Schumann and Rosen arrived in Munich for a four-day stay. On the 8th, they met Heine. His *Reisebilder* (two volumes had appeared in 1826 and 1827) and *Buch der Lieder* (1827) were growing in popularity. Heine in 1828 was already a poet of considerable fame; unable to earn enough from his writing, however, he was hopeful of gaining a professorship in Munich. Because of the irony and sarcasm characteristic of much of Heine's work, Schumann viewed their meeting with trepidation. But he was charmed by him. "I had imagined Heine to be sullen and misanthropic," Schumann later wrote to the Kurrers, "but he was completely different from what I had thought. He greeted me in a friendly manner ... and escorted me around Munich for several hours." Schumann seemed pleased to note "a bitter, ironical

---

[22] Letter of 25 April 1828 in *JS*, p. 122.

smile—but a lofty smile at the trivialities of life, disdainful of the pettiness of mankind."[23]

In Munich, Rosen and Schumann parted. Schumann returned home, on the way stopping once again in Bayreuth. This time he visited Jean Paul's residence and met his widow (who gave him the portrait of Jean Paul that was displayed by his desk). On 14 May, Schumann arrived in Zwickau. But to his family's dismay, he remained only a few hours to pack his bags, and then left for Leipzig, eager to begin life as a university student.

After graduating from the Zwickau Lyceum, Schumann had mused (much in the manner of Jean Paul) on his prospects:

> School is now done with and the world lies before me. I could hardly refrain from tears on coming out of school for the last time; but the joy was greater than the pain. Now the inner, true man must come forth and show what he is: thrust out into existence, flung into the world's night, without guide, teacher, and father—here I stand, and yet the whole world never appeared to me in a lovelier light than now as I confront it and, rejoicing and free, smile at its storms.[24]

The start of an independent life provided Schumann with excitement and a sense of elation. But his exhilaration and lack of maturity were to create unexpected difficulties and complications at home. Schumann's move to Leipzig in 1828 was the beginning of what was to become an unusually stressful and troubling two-year period for his family.

---

[23] Letter of 9 June 1828 quoted in *Eismann*, p. 35. The meeting must have inspired Schumann. His diary notes that in August he was reading the *Buch der Lieder*.

[24] Letter of 17 March 1828 to Flechsig (*JS*, p. 118), translated in Niecks, p. 40.

CHAPTER 2

University Years

> *Every man, however brief or inglorious may have been his academical career, must remember with kindness and tenderness the old university comrades and days. The young man's life is just beginning: the boy's leading strings are cut, and he has all the novel delights and dignities of freedom.*
> —Thackeray, *Pendennis*

SCHUMANN'S EAGERNESS TO LEAVE ZWICKAU WAS DUE NOT TO the specific attractions of Leipzig, but rather to his yearning for independence and a change of scene. Leipzig—with a population ten times that of Zwickau—provided him with his first extended contact with urban life. It was a bustling, mercantile center, noted for its publishing industry (its book fairs attracted buyers from all over Europe). Music publishing flourished as well: two of the most prestigious publishers in Europe, Breitkopf & Härtel and Hofmeister, were located there.

Musical life in Leipzig was unusually rich. The venerable Gewandhaus concerts, created in 1781, were among the earliest and most eminent in Europe. At the time of Schumann's residence in Leipzig, the series comprised twenty concerts per season. Other concert series included the Euterpe (orchestral concerts founded in 1824), as well as a chamber music series featuring the Matthäi Quartet. The Thomas-schule, with which Johann Sebastian Bach had been associated, presented regular choral concerts. For opera there was the Leipzig Theater—the weak link in Leipzig's musical life—supplemented with regular visits from the Italian Opera in Dresden. To someone who loved music, the opportunities must have appeared irresistible. Yet, surprisingly, Schumann's letters and diary at first made little reference to them. As a student of law, it is perhaps understandable that his attention should have been directed less toward the musical attractions of the city, and more toward his studies and classwork. But Schumann found both the study of law and Leipzig itself distinctly distasteful.

"Leipzig," he wrote to Gisbert Rosen not long after his arrival, "is an infamous hole. . . . I am wretched here and student life strikes me as too coarse to plunge into" (5 June 1828). At the time, social activities for students at German universities were dominated by the *Burschenschaften*, organizations similar to fraternities. They had long been associated with liberal political tendencies, including the dream of a united Germany bound by a more democratic form of government. Schumann had come to Leipzig with a naive perception of the *Burschenschaften*, and was disappointed to discover in them a preoccupation with drinking, fencing, and duels. Missing was a sense of idealism. "Ah! what models I had of students, and how wretched I found most of them!," he lamented.

Other aspects of life in Leipzig disappointed Schumann as well. "Nature—where can you find it here?" he wrote to his mother. "All has been disfigured by man. There are no valleys, no mountains, no woods where I can immerse myself in my thoughts."[1] While it is true that the landscape near Leipzig lacked the variety and contrast of Zwickau, it seems that at least some of Schumann's disappointment was a result of being homesick. With Rosen now settled in Heidelberg, Schumann had few close friends except for Emil Flechsig. Unfortunately, his association with Flechsig was not as rosy as Schumann had hoped. Schumann complained that he was dull and prosaic. Instead of the lively and stimulating life Schumann had hoped to find, he described himself leading a life "monotonous and *devoid of all pleasure*. I'm lucky that I don't live alone. I could easily become melancholy."[2]

---

[1] Letter of 21 May 1828 in *JS*, pp. 124–25.
[2] Letter to his mother of 31 August 1828 in *JgBr*, p. 34.

Lengthy visits home (15–22 July, 12 September to 21 October, as well as three weeks during the Christmas holidays) seem to have improved his outlook, but the study of law offered no consolation. From the start, Schumann not only showed no inclination for it but revealed a decided prejudice against it. Since his father's death, Schumann's guardian—working in association with Christiane Schumann—had been Gottlob Rudel, a cloth and iron merchant in Zwickau. Rudel was regarded as an inflexible businessman, and for the next two years his association with Schumann would be a severe trial for them both. Writing on 4 July 1828, Schumann assured Rudel that he would work "industriously," but described the study of law as "ice-cold and dry."

Schumann's dislike of law may have owed something to his fondness for Jean Paul, whose novels rarely portray lawyers favorably. In *Flegeljahre*, one of Schumann's favorites, an unemotional and eminently practical lawyer named Knoll serves as the embodiment of Philistinism, expressing disdain for all poetry—except that in Latin. "Cold jurisprudence," Schumann reported to his mother, "overwhelming from the beginning with its ice-cold definitions, cannot please me. Medicine I will not and theology I cannot study. I find myself in an eternal inner struggle, and search in vain for an advisor who could tell me what to do. And yet—there is no other way. I must study law, no matter how cold or dry it may be. I will triumph: if a man but *wills* it, he can do everything."[3]

Schumann's determination was admirable, but short-lived. According to Flechsig, he "never set foot in a lecture room."[4] Flechsig's statement is complemented by that of another friend, Moritz Semmel, who noted that Schumann "nearly never" attended law classes. "But it must be noted," Semmel concluded, "that for Schumann self-instruction was of great importance."[5] It is quite true that Schumann excelled in teaching himself; much of what he was to learn about composition was the result of his own efforts. But there is no indication that Schumann devoted much time to teaching himself law. In later years when questioned

---

[3] Letter of 21 May 1828 in *JS*, p. 125.
[4] Emil Flechsig, "Erinnerungen an Robert Schumann," *Neue Zeitschrift für Musik* CXVII (1956), p. 393.
[5] Quoted in Wilhelm Joseph von Wasielewski, *Schumanniana* (Bonn, 1883), pp. 86–87.

about his law study, Schumann would smile and note that he had gone to the doors of the lecture rooms and "had eavesdropped there for a bit."[6]

While Schumann had no hesitation in telling his family of the tedious and tiresome nature of studying law, they were never informed of the irregularity of his class attendance. On the contrary, they were frequently advised of his hard work and regular attendance. During these months Schumann was devoting far more energy to music than to law. He was contemplating making music his career, but remained uncertain what steps next to take. In the previous year Schumann had come across a collection of songs by Gottlob Wiedebein, and had been much impressed by them. Wiedebein, a modest man who composed little, was Kapellmeister in Brunswick. Schumann now decided to write to Wiedebein, both to praise Wiedebein's work and, by enclosing a half dozen of his own lieder, to seek Wiedebein's advice and criticism.

The letter, deferential in tone and highly respectful, was written on 15 July 1828: "Be lenient with the youth who, uninitiated in the mysteries of tones, was incited to create with unsure hand his own work and to lay before you these first attempts for your kind, but strictly impartial criticism."[7] Wiedebein's reply was a model of its kind. His criticism was brief; what faults he discovered he attributed to Schumann's youth and inexperience. Much of the letter is fatherly in tone (Wiedebein was forty-nine at the time) and filled with advice, hope, and encouragement for the young composer.

> Above all else, seek truth. Truth of melody, of harmony, of expression—in a word, poetic truth. Where you do not find this, or where you find it even threatened—discard it, even if you cherish it. . . . You have received much, a great deal from nature; use it, and the esteem of the world will not pass you by.[8]

Four days later (5 August 1828) Schumann replied, offering heartfelt thanks for Wiedebein's advice. He wanted to make clear as well the limitations of his musical education:

[6] *W*, p. 45.
[7] *Eismann*, p. 39.
[8] *Ibid.*, p. 40.

> I believe that in my earlier letter to you I forgot to say that I know nothing of harmony, or thoroughbass, etc., or of counterpoint. Rather I am a pure and artless pupil following the direction of nature. . . . But now I shall begin the study of composition.

Implicit in Schumann's letter was the hope that Wiedebein would take the time to write to him yet again. It is unfortunate that he did not, for over the next few years Schumann could have used more of Wiedebein's advice and support.

Schumann's assertion to Wiedebein that he was now going to study composition is indicative of a change in direction. Despite his talent and love for music, Schumann remained a gifted dilettante. Now, with the praise of a composer he greatly admired providing the impetus, at the age of eighteen Schumann appears to have acknowledged his deficiencies and determined to remedy them. But inaction and indecision persisted for two more years. To some extent, Schumann's lack of decisiveness resulted from the opposition he anticipated from his family should he select music as a career. But his situation was further complicated by his continued attraction to literature, and his interest in the possibility of becoming a writer. In the end, Schumann did nothing because he was confused. With the death of his father, there was no one as sympathetic to Schumann and as familiar with his situation to provide the guidance he needed.

During these years Schumann never revealed frustration, desperation, or a sense of urgency in determining his career. Even when he eventually decided to abandon law, he retained it as a possible future option. He seems to have felt that it would all work out in the end, and, as his diary reveals, for much of the time he was too busy enjoying himself to worry about it. Although Schumann began by finding life in Leipzig to be dull and dismal, within a few months he had found in the outskirts a romantic spot which he enjoyed and where he wrote poetry. He began, too, to lead a more social life. The frequent references in his diary to hangovers give an indication of the results of these new activities. Schumann had broad tastes: Champagne, Burgundy, Bordeaux, Tokay, domestic wines, or beer. "Worst hangover of my life—as if I were dead" (27 April 1829). "Very drunk" (3 May 1829).[9] He noted

---
[9] *Tgb I*, pp. 192, 194.

in a nearly scientific manner the effect of stimulants on his creative spirit. "If I have been drunk or have vomited, then on the next day my imagination soars and is enhanced. While I am drunk, I can't do a thing—but afterward I can. Black coffee also makes me drunk."[10]

The diary also documents Schumann's continued interest in the opposite sex. Beautiful girls—even those glimpsed in the street—always seem to have merited an entry. Flirtations were common. In fact, much of Schumann's diary presents him as a fairly typical college student. Drinking—often to excess—was an all-too-common part of German student life. And, like his fellow students, Schumann also was frequently in debt. At college, he was constantly short of funds, and became quite skillful at pestering his mother, brothers, and Rudel for more. Who would deny the urgency of the following appeal: "I would be much obliged to you, most honored Herr Rudel, if you would send me as soon as possible as much as possible!" (26 March 1830). As late as 1838 Schumann was to acknowledge that he was still far from overcoming his "great indifference" to financial matters.[11]

But not all of Schumann's time was taken up by student affairs. Within a week after settling in Leipzig, he renewed his friendship with the Carus family (Dr. Carus had accepted a position as professor of medicine at the university). Their home was a meeting place for many of the musicians in Leipzig, and it was probably at the Carus home on 31 March 1828 that Schumann first met Friedrich Wieck and his eight-year-old daughter, Clara.

In many ways Wieck was a character whom only E. T. A. Hoffmann could have created: opinionated, domineering, impassioned, rude, irascible, and eccentric. He made his living primarily as a teacher of piano, and he perceived his daughter to be his greatest accomplishment. Although only a child, her precocity, as well as the skill of her father's training, were well known. From her birth, it had been Wieck's intention to produce in her a concert pianist without peer. Clara had begun her formal study of piano at the age of five, and was soon exposed to her father's sense of discipline; by 1828, she had an hour lesson daily, and was practicing three hours each day. At the time of Schumann's

---

[10] Entry of July 1828 in *Ibid.*, p. 97.

[11] Letter of 12 February 1838 to Clara Wieck in *Cl/Rob I*, p. 102.

meeting with them, Clara was preparing for her initial appearance that October at a Gewandhaus concert (as an assisting artist).

Wieck seemed to live through his daughter, controlling her life and basking in her glory. Much the same could be said of his relationship with Clara's mother, a gifted singer and pianist twelve years younger than Wieck. But she found life with him to be unbearable, and filed for divorce when Clara was five. Like Schumann, Clara maintained a diary, but hers was written under her father's supervision. A number of the entries were actually written by Wieck, under the pretense they were his daughter's words. "Father arrived by express coach at seven in the evening," reads one entry in Wieck's hand, "I flew into his arms and took him right to the Hotel Stadt Frankfurt."[12] Just nine days after Clara's successful debut at the Gewandhaus, she (if not at Wieck's dictation, then under his watchful eye) wrote in the diary: "My father, who long had hoped for a change of disposition on my part, observed again today that I am just as lazy, careless, disorderly, stubborn, disobedient, etc. as ever, and that I am the same in my piano playing and my studies."[13] Had this been a tale by Hoffmann, Clara would have been exposed as an automaton with Wieck as her demented creator. In actuality, Wieck was to become Schumann's piano teacher and, after years of struggle to gain her hand, Clara was to become Schumann's wife.

From the start, Schumann was very much impressed with Wieck and his gifted pupil. By August he was taking occasional piano lessons from Wieck and visiting his home regularly. It was a valuable opportunity to come into contact not only with the leading musicians of Leipzig—many of whom frequently met at Wieck's—but with important musicians visiting Leipzig as well. Wieck was forty-three when he and Schumann met. He had been settled in Leipzig for about a dozen years, and was owner of a piano store and music shop. Primarily self-taught as a musician, he was fascinated by the many piano instruction courses and methods fashionable at the time. Unfortunately, the precise nature of Wieck's approach is not known. To his pupils he emphasized the close

---

[12] Entry of 17 June 1834 quoted in Nancy B. Reich, *Clara Schumann: The Artist and the Woman* (Ithaca, New York, 1985), p. 43.

[13] Entry of 20 October 1828 in *Ibid.*, p. 55.

connection between good piano playing and singing (bel canto). The ultimate goal for his students was for them to attain "pure, precise, equal, clear, rhythmical, and, finally, elegant playing"[14]—an approach that would appear to owe more to the eighteenth century than to the flamboyant virtuosity of the 1830s and 1840s.

It is not certain how frequently Schumann studied piano with Wieck; the diary only lists about a half dozen lessons from mid-August 1828 until early May 1829 (at which time Schumann left Leipzig). It is quite likely that not all of his lessons with Wieck were noted, but, as in his study of law, Schumann's attendance was far from regular. What is clear about the course of study is that Wieck began with elementary instruction. Flechsig, Schumann's roommate at the time, recalled that Schumann "had to work on finger exercises again like a beginner."[15] But time was spent as well studying specific compositions, including challenging works such as the first movement of Hummel's Piano Concerto op. 85.

Although Wieck's approach must have been discouraging at first, Schumann continued to broaden his knowledge of music by learning more of the repertory. In November 1828 he formed a chamber group with himself as pianist and other students playing violin, viola, and cello as needed. Wieck and Dr. Carus often attended the performances of the group, which continued until March 1829. According to Schumann's diary, there were seventeen meetings in all. In November much time was spent on the chamber music of Prince Louis Ferdinand, including the Piano Quartet op. 6 and the *Notturno* op. 8. In December, they played through Schubert's Piano Trio op. 100. In all, thirty works were examined.

These performances provided stimulus for Schumann to compose, a sight not easily forgotten. Flechsig recalled:

> I still see him. . . . Since he continually smoked a cigar, the smoke always got in his eyes. So with his mouth and the cigar pointing upwards as much as possible, he squinted downward at the keyboard, making truly extraordinary grimaces. The cigar was an additional annoyance. He liked to whistle

---

[14] Frederick Niecks, *Robert Schumann* (London, 1925), p. 65.
[15] Flechsig, p. 393.

or hum the melody he was composing, and to do this with a cigar in one's mouth is pretty much impossible.[16]

In March 1829, Schumann completed his most ambitious work to date, a Piano Quartet in C minor (WoO 32). As he neared the end of his first year of study in Leipzig, it remained his most notable accomplishment. Study of law was only a pretense, but one that it would have been disastrous to abandon. From the time of his arrival in Leipzig, Schumann had expressed interest in transferring to the University of Heidelberg in Baden. The university's primary attraction to Schumann was the presence there of Gisbert Rosen. But Schumann's mother—convinced by her son's reference to the distinguished law faculty in Heidelberg—agreed to the change. If Schumann were to practice law in Saxony, he would need to complete his study in a Saxon university. It was decided that he would study in Heidelberg for one year, beginning in May 1829.

In April, Schumann prepared for the move, returning to Zwickau on the 15th. Plans for the trip itself became more elaborate, and it was decided to visit Frankfurt and explore for a week the Rhine, before traveling on to Heidelberg. Amid details of a round of parties and balls, he informed Rosen that he had performed as part of a concert in Zwickau (probably performing Moscheles's *Alexander Variations* op. 32 and the first movement of Hummel's Piano Concerto op. 85).

Schumann arrived in Frankfurt on 13 May, and spent several days there, examining the sights. He then traveled to Wiesbaden and through the Rheingau, including stops in Cologne, Mainz, and Mannheim. Above all, he reveled in the beauties of the Rhine, which he described as "very romantic."[17] On first nearing it, he closed his eyes in order better to be overwhelmed by the sudden spectacle of its splendor: "It lay before me—calm, peaceful, stern, and proud, like an old German god, and with it the magnificent, green Rheingau with its mountains and valleys in blossom and the whole paradise of vineyards."[18] It goes without saying that fruit of the vineyards was sampled, Schumann professing a strong inclination for Rudesheimer.

---

[16] *Ibid.*, p. 394.
[17] Entry of 17 May in *Tgb I*, p. 48.
[18] Letter to his mother of 25 May 1829 in *JS*, p. 150.

In addition to the scenic splendor, Schumann took delight in several of his fellow travelers. He was much taken with a jovial major who claimed to have been an adjutant for one of Napoleon's most colorful marshals, Joachim Murat. More significant was Schumann's association with Wilhelm Häring, whom he met on the way to Frankfurt. Häring wrote under the pseudonym Willibald Alexis, and was a well-known author of both fiction and poetry. *Walladmor*—a novel that he published in 1824 under the guise of it being a translation of Walter Scott—had been his first successful work. When Alexis revealed himself as the author (and followed it with another in Scott's style—*Schloss Avalon*, 1827), his popularity was assured.[19] Alexis was traveling to Paris, and despite the difference in age (he was twelve years Schumann's senior), he and Schumann got along extremely well. They saw Frankfurt and much of the Rhine together, before separating at Coblenz. In writing home, Schumann made a point of describing his new friend, clearly flattered by both his celebrity and literary accomplishments.

The trip concluded in what was to become the usual manner for trips undertaken by Schumann during his youth. Arriving in Mannheim, Schumann realized that he had overspent and did not have enough money left to purchase the coach fare to Heidelberg. As a result, he was obliged to walk to Heidelberg (about twelve miles), arriving there on the 21st, where he was welcomed by Rosen "with open arms."[20]

Heidelberg is a city closely associated with German Romanticism. In the first decade of the nineteenth century, it had been home to Clemens Brentano and Achim von Arnim—both were authors admired by Schumann—and much of their *Youth's Magic Horn (Des Knaben Wunderhorn)* had been edited there. Joseph von Görres and Brentano's sister,

---

[19] Ironically, *Walladmor* became so popular that there was demand for it in England as well. Thomas De Quincey was paid to prepare a translation of it, but he was convinced that Scott could not be the author of what De Quincey considered to be a wretched work. De Quincey expressed his disdain for the project by noting on the title page that his edition of *Walladmor* was " 'Freely translated into German from the English of Sir Walter Scott' and now Freely translated from the German into the English."

[20] *Tgb* I, p. 49. Schumann's friendship with Rosen—a more lively and worldly companion than Flechsig—became close during Schumann's residence in Heidelberg. But it was not an enduring one. Unlike the association with Flechsig, Schumann and Rosen drifted apart after Schumann left Heidelberg.

Bettina, had been part of this literary circle, whose most fascinating creation had been the short-lived *Zeitung für Einsiedler* (*Newspaper for Hermits*). In addition to its literary associations, Heidelberg was a city of elegance and charm, not far from the Rhine, and situated on the Neckar River with magnificent views of neighboring hills. No complaints are heard from Schumann on the ugliness of the countryside. "Here," he wrote to his mother, "it is as if one were living in Provence—the air seems scented and filled with music."[21]

His correspondence gives the impression that at first Schumann benefited from the change. He soon reported to his mother that his law classes were excellent and that he "now appreciated the true value of law, in that it promoted all venerable and noble interests of humanity."[22] For the first time, there seemed to be a commitment to his studies, and throughout his stay in Heidelberg Schumann continued to affirm his industry. To his brother Carl, he offered his daily schedule: he rose each day at four and studied law until eight. From eight to ten he played the piano, followed by one segment of classes until noon, and another from two to four. He was strong as well in his praise of Rosen with whom he quickly reestablished a rapport. This led in the spring of 1830 to an invitation from Rosen's brother to visit him in England, a trip Schumann wanted very much to take, no doubt envisioning it as a kind of grand tour similar to that which was part of a gentleman's education at the time. Schumann did not make the trip—emphasis surely was placed on the need for him to complete his education—but later in life he contemplated visiting England on several occasions. He was charmed by the English, briefly studied the language, and willingly admitted a fascination for English ladies.

But Schumann's assertions to his family of hard work and dedication to study were far from the truth. Although it appears that he was more regular in attending law classes, extracurricular activities consumed much of his time. There were trips to nearby towns, including a four-day trip to Baden-Baden in July where Schumann's friends (not himself, so he claimed) enjoyed themselves at the roulette table. And he not infrequently drank to excess, culminating in a period in February 1830

---

[21] Letter to his mother of 17 July 1829 in *JS*, p. 161.
[22] Letter of 17 July 1829 in *JgBr*, p. 62.

that he referred to as the "most debauched week of my life."[23] Such conduct was not a matter of pride with Schumann, and on occasion he made a point of noting his disgust: "My loathsomeness—drunk out of boredom—very high—my longing to plunge into the Rhine."[24] His need for more money remained a problem as well, yet he refused to accept responsibility for his spendthrift ways. University life and the resulting high cost of living were, Schumann maintained, the basis of his financial difficulties.

The ambition that had struck Flechsig so forcefully seven years earlier was little in evidence. Delighted by his freedom and the opportunity to determine his own conduct in life, for a time Schumann simply wanted to enjoy himself, and evidently was in no mood to be concerned with the future. Yet it seems likely that after settling in Heidelberg Schumann made a sincere, though rather short-lived, attempt to devote himself to the study of law. Heidelberg possessed two outstanding jurists on the faculty, Karl Joseph Mittermaier and Anton Friedrich Justus Thibaut. Thibaut's reputation extended throughout Germany; he had worked consistently against the reactionary spirit of the day and had advocated significant changes in civil law supportive of individual rights. Schumann registered for classes with both Mittermaier and Thibaut, but Thibaut became a favorite. His classes were known for being lively and interesting. When they first met on 25 May (Thibaut was fifty-seven at the time), Schumann noted his "friendliness."[25]

It was not Thibaut's expertise in law, however, which drew Schumann closer to him. In 1825, Thibaut had published a small book, *Purity in Music*. It became a popular work, and one that Schumann regarded highly. It is strongly opinionated: the work of a dilettante and amateur, but one with a deep love of and reverence for music. Thibaut championed music of the past—particularly compositions of the Renaissance and Baroque, works for the most part unknown at the time to the general public. To Thibaut the finest types of music were those in a

---

[23] *Tgb I*, p. 226.
[24] 18 March 1830 in *Ibid.*, p. 236.
[25] *Ibid.*, p. 50.

"strict church style, compositions in the oratorio style . . . and . . . select national songs [folksongs] of all lands."[26] Contemporary music he found contrived and mannered, and criticized it relentlessly, describing it as "sensational, ill-formed, absurd, and vile."[27] Bach—whose chromaticism was not to Thibaut's liking—was chastised for his "florid part-writing."[28] Schumann acknowledged the flaws in Thibaut's approach—what he described as Thibaut's "narrow-minded" and "pedantic view"[29]—but recognized as well his noble intentions.

For his mother, Schumann had nothing but praise for Thibaut: "Thibaut is a splendid and excellent man. The hours I have spent with him have been my most enjoyable."[30] But the hours that Schumann was referring to were probably not those spent in the classroom, but rather those spent in Thibaut's home where Schumann occasionally attended performances of works that Thibaut prepared and conducted. The compositions selected included little-known works by Durante, Leo, Marcello, Palestrina, and Vittoria, among others. Handel was a particular favorite; Bach—as might be expected given Thibaut's criticism of him—was performed infrequently.

Schumann was by no means a regular visitor to Thibaut's home. And he admired not so much the accuracy and precision of the performances—Thibaut was not an accomplished musician—but the spirit imparted to them:

> When he performs a Handel oratorio at his home [Schumann is referring to a performance he attended of the first part of *Samson*] . . . and in a rapture accompanies at the piano, two big tears roll down from the fine, large eyes beneath his beautiful, silvery hair. Then he comes to me filled with joy and delight, and presses my hand and is silent from sheer emotion. I often don't understand how a beggar like myself has the honor to be admitted to listen in such a sacred house.[31]

---

[26] A. F. Thibaut, *Purity in Music* (London, [1882]), p. 102.
[27] *Ibid.*, p. 5.
[28] *Ibid.*, p. 11.
[29] Letter to Wieck of 6 November 1829 in *JgBr*, p. 81.
[30] Letter of 24 February 1830 in *JS*, p. 191.
[31] *Ibid.*, pp. 191–92.

Franz Brendel, who knew Schumann well in the 1830s and 1840s, described Schumann's association with Thibaut as having "the first substantial and persistent effect on his inner life."[32] Perhaps Brendel was unaware of the intensity of Schumann's earlier interest in Jean Paul and Schubert. Still—and despite the fact that the influence of Thibaut diminished in time—his effect on Schumann was considerable. Although he acknowledged the danger of Thibaut's narrow conservatism, he came to represent—in Schumann's eyes—both the vitality of tradition in music and a transcendent love for music itself. Thibaut could have become as well an example of how devotion to music and the law could exist alongside one another; but Schumann perceived that Thibaut lacked technical music expertise, which may have indicated to him that mastery in music could not be attained if it were treated as little more than a hobby.

Heidelberg's proximity to Switzerland and Italy tempted a number of the students at the university to travel there when classes were not in session. Schumann was eager to make the trip. To his mother, he wrote of the ideal opportunity the trip would afford to improve his grasp of foreign languages, essential knowledge, Schumann claimed, to get ahead in the world. In a skillful attempt at manipulation, should the money for the trip not be available, Schumann threatened to borrow it himself at 10 percent interest, though he hoped that "it would not come to that."[33]

The itinerary included stops in Switzerland (Basel, Zürich, Lucerne, Interlaken, Thun, and Bern) as well as northern Italian cities, such as Milan, Brescia, Verona, Vicenza, Padua, and Venice. As preparation for the journey he read Petrarch and Alfieri. Schumann had intended making the trip with Rosen and another friend, Moritz Semmel (a fellow student at both Leipzig and Heidelberg whose sister, Therese, was married to Schumann's brother, Eduard), but in the end was obliged to travel by himself. Although no notable fellow traveler such as Willibald Alexis was encountered, Schumann had a marvelous time. He reveled in the grandeur of the Alps:

---

[32] Franz Brendel, "Robert Schumann's Biographie von J. W. von Wasielewski," *Neue Zeitschrift für Musik* XXIV (1858), p. 160.

[33] Letter to his mother of 3 August 1829 in *JS*, p. 165.

> From Zürich I went on foot over the Albis to Zug. I wish you had a map in hand while reading all my descriptions, so as in a way to travel along with me. My walk was splendid, and, because of the ever-changing beauty of nature, not at all tiring. I wandered on alone, my knapsack on my back ... constantly stopping and looking around in order to impress indelibly upon my memory this Alpine paradise.[34]

Mindful of his role as a tourist, he saw a variety of sights, including Leonardo's *Last Supper* (a disappointment to him), and the battlefield of Marengo, site of Napoleon's victory over the Austrians in 1800. Nearly everything about the trip appeared to enchant him. Italian girls he found beautiful. The Italian language itself he described as "unending music"(16 September 1829). Inspired, he continued reading his Petrarch and bought an edition of Dante.

Schumann was not an admirer of Italian music, but to Wieck he reported a highlight of the trip: hearing the great soprano, Giuditta Pasta, at La Scala in an opera by Rossini. "In the Leipzig Concert Hall I have sometimes thrilled with rapture and awe in the presence of the genius of music; but in Italy I learned to love it; and there is just one evening in my life when it seemed to me as if God stood before me and let me look openly and hushed upon His face—that was in Milan when I heard Pasta and Rossini."[35] A wonderful experience—but perhaps just a figment of Schumann's imagination. His diary makes no reference to the event, and Pasta does not appear to have performed in Milan during Schumann's visit. It would not have been out of character for him to have concocted the incident to impress Wieck.

Schumann ran out of money during the trip and had to borrow both in Italy and from the Kurrers in Augsburg in order to have enough to return to Heidelberg. He arrived there on 20 October, excited and tired from the trip. Perhaps he felt somewhat disappointed as well. Compared to Italy, Heidelberg had little to offer musically. "There is much love for music here," Schumann wrote to Wieck not long after his return, "but little talent."[36] That in itself could be to Schumann's advantage. In the active and competitive musical environment in

---

[34] Letter to his mother of 31 August 1829 in *Ibid.*, pp. 167–68.

[35] Letter of 6 November 1829 in *JgBr*, p. 81. Translated in Niecks, pp. 89–90.

[36] Letter of 6 November 1829 in *Ibid.*, p. 79.

Leipzig, Schumann's skills had appeared inconsequential. In Heidelberg, he soon developed a reputation as one of the finest pianists in the area.

Despite assurances to his mother that he played "seldom and very poorly," he continued to practice.[37] A concentrated period commenced in late December 1829 as preparation for a public performance of Moscheles's virtuosic *Alexander Variations* for the Heidelberger Musik-Verein, a primarily student-managed organization. By Schumann's own account, it was overwhelmingly successful. More important, the acclaim for his performance provided stimulus for his work as a composer. During his residence in Heidelberg, Schumann contemplated adapting his Piano Quartet into a symphony, and sketched a number of works for piano, including an early version of what would later be published as the Toccata op. 7, dances that would become part of *Papillons* op. 2, and portions of his first published work, the *Thème sur le nom "Abegg" varié pour le pianoforte* op. 1.

It was around this time that Schumann made an attempt at self-evaluation, striving for objectivity by referring to himself in the third person:

> I would not reckon him among ordinary men. . . . His temperament is melancholy, more sentimental than contemplative, more subjective than objective. . . . A powerful imagination. . . . needing external stimulus. . . . Discernment, wit, reflective thought—not strong. More emotional than intellectual—leaning towards the artistic rather than the speculative. Distinguished in music and literature. Not a musical genius. His talent as musician and poet are on an equal level.[38]

The portrait is that of the Romantic *par excellence*—original, melancholy, emotional, imaginative, subjective, neither a logician nor a rationalist. That Schumann perceived himself in that manner is not surprising. What is surprising is the statement: "Not a musical genius." In contrast to the achievements of Schubert and Prince Louis Ferdinand—probably the two composers whom he most admired at this time—

---

[37] Letter to his mother of 11 November 1829 in *JS*, p. 182.

[38] *Tgb I*, p. 242. Schumann assigned no particular date to this entry. It probably dates from the spring or summer of 1830, or possibly to late 1829.

Schumann may have felt that he had accomplished little. Of particular interest is Schumann's continued reference to his literary abilities. But again—because he rated his abilities as both poet and musician equally—he appears to have believed that he lacked genius as a writer as well.

While concerning himself with music in both Leipzig and Heidelberg, Schumann's interest in literature and in writing had remained keen. The diary that he began at the commencement of his college study he entitled *Hottentottiana*, an arcane and whimsical title in the manner of Jean Paul. *Hottentottiana*, while containing a record of many of his daily activities, was perceived by Schumann as a literary exercise, and contained thoughts and observations, as well as excerpts for his *Juniusabende* and *Selene*—both works of fiction in the style of Jean Paul. But while Schumann displays in his writings facility and skill, one looks in vain for the originality that was beginning to make its appearance in the works he was composing for piano.

Schumann felt the need to evaluate himself at a time when it was becoming necessary to think about the future. He must have realized that his situation was precarious. The pretense of law study could not be maintained indefinitely; his deception would end if he were unable successfully to complete his study in Heidelberg. In the spring of 1830, he wrote to his mother asking that his stay there be extended for six months, a request that she granted. Two events, however, directed Schumann toward adopting music as his profession.

On the day before Easter Sunday 1830, he traveled to Frankfurt to hear the violinist Niccolò Paganini. Paganini, without question the most flamboyant virtuoso of his day, was then at the height of his success. His technique dazzled and astounded those who heard him, including seasoned musicians. For Schumann, Paganini's performance on 11 April was a revelation. Although disturbed by Paganini's showmanship—the beginning of Schumann's questioning of the role of virtuosity—he was enthralled by his artistry and musicianship. Paganini's performance had a profound effect on him. At about the same time the German violin virtuoso Heinrich Wilhelm Ernst came to Heidelberg as part of his first concert tour. According to one of Schumann's friends at the time, Ernst and Schumann got along well (Schumann was actually four years older than Ernst), leading to a relationship that—coupled with Schumann's own recent success as a performer—seems to have prompted him seriously to consider music as a career.

For a while during the summer there was a return to the old way of life, including requests for more money and a complaint about the cold study of law. Then, on 30 July, he rose early and wrote a letter to his mother—a letter intended not just for her eyes, but probably written with studied deliberation for the eyes of posterity as well:

Heidelberg, July 30, 1830
5 o'clock
Good morning, Mother!

How can I describe to you my happiness at this moment! The coffee is brewing, and the sky is pure and golden enough to kiss—and the whole spirit of the morning is calm and fresh. There is sufficient sunshine and blue sky in my life at present . . . still, sometimes I get truly concerned when I think about myself. My entire life has been a twenty-year struggle between poetry and prose, or call it music and law. . . . In Leipzig I gave little thought about a plan for my life, but dreamed and dawdled, and in essence accomplished nothing substantial; here I have worked more, but in Leipzig and here I have always felt myself more fervently and more ardently attached to Art. Now I stand at the crossroads, and I am startled by the question: what direction shall be taken? If I follow my genius, it directs me to Art, and, I believe, the right path. But truly (do not take offense, and I say it to you softly and only with affection) it always seemed to me that you were obstructing my way there, for which you had your good, motherly reasons—reasons which I also understood quite well, and which you and I called the "precarious future and uncertain means of support" . . . [But I] am certain that, since the whole of piano playing is pure mechanics and dexterity, with diligence and patience and the guidance of a good teacher, within six years I will be able to compete with any piano player; now and then, I also have imagination and perhaps talent to create my own works. . . .

If I continue to study law, it is essential that I remain here one more winter, in order to study pandects with Thibaut—which every lawyer must study with him. If I were to continue with music, then unquestionably I have to leave here and return to Leipzig. Wieck in Leipzig—to whom I wholly and willingly entrust myself, and who knows me and is able to judge my ability—would then have to train me further. Later I would have to go to Vienna for a year and, if at all possible, study with Moscheles. Now a request, my good mother, which perhaps you will willingly grant me. *Write to Wieck at Leipzig and ask candidly what he thinks of myself and my plans for the future. . . .* If you wish, *enclose this letter with your letter to Wieck.* . . .

You can see that this letter is the most important one I have written and will ever write. For that very reason, grant my request not unwillingly and answer me soon. There is no time to be lost.[39]

It is unfortunate that no preliminary drafts for the letter have survived, for it is a letter that Schumann probably labored over. On the surface, it appears remarkably frank and open—particularly the reference to having "dreamed and dawdled" while in Leipzig. But did Schumann actually believe that piano playing consisted solely of "pure mechanics and dexterity," or was he more interested in deceiving his mother? Had Wieck been consulted in advance about Schumann's idea? The implication is that he was not, and that he was now being called upon to serve as an impartial judge of Schumann's ability. But not to have sought Wieck's opinion on the matter would have been foolhardy, if for no other reason than to determine whether he had the time to work with Schumann.

Schumann's letter created consternation at home. His brothers and Rudel strongly opposed the change of career, and their position is understandable. Schumann had been pampered, humored—in many ways, spoiled. The only member of his family to attend a university, he had been fully supported financially not just in his studies but in travels in Germany, Switzerland, and Italy. None of these privileges had been granted to his brothers. Now he was willing to discard what was perceived as years of work and what appeared to be a sure means of earning a livelihood in order to pursue an uncertain career in music.

Christiane Schumann was alone in supporting her son, although it is clear that she felt he was making a mistake. To abandon law at this stage of his career was not in her mind either a mature or rational mode

---

[39] *JS*, pp. 200, 201, 202, 203.

of behavior. But—more than anything else—she wanted to see him happy. Since music seemed of such importance to him, she did not want to stand in his way. She wrote to Wieck with considerable apprehension, enclosing her son's letter.

> Ah, I can't tell you how overwhelmed and melancholy I am when I think of Robert's future. . . . Now he suddenly wants to adopt a profession which he should have taken up ten years ago. . . . My other three sons are dissatisfied and insist that I should not give in. I am the only one who does not want to force him in a direction where his own feelings do not lead him. . . . Everything depends on your decision—the peace of mind of a loving mother, the entire happiness of a young, inexperienced person who lives purely in higher spheres and does not wish to enter into the practical matters of life.[40]

Wieck replied quickly, eager to set her mind at ease. In his usual manner, he wrote bluntly, and with more than a touch of arrogance:

> Let your son leave Heidelberg—his imagination becomes heated there—and return to cold, flat Leipzig. . . . I pledge within three years, by means of his talent and imagination, to make your son Robert into one of the greatest pianists now living—with more warmth and spirit than Moscheles, and more nobility than Hummel. Proof of this I present to you with my eleven-year-old daughter.[41]

But Wieck also expressed serious reservations, and made his acceptance of Schumann as a pupil conditional. To begin with, Wieck asked that Schumann study with him for one year, although six months might be sufficient to determine Schumann's resolve. For Schumann's resolve—his commitment to hard work and dedication to learning—was what Wieck doubted.

> Has our charming Robert changed and become more sensible, firmer, forceful and, may I say it, more practical and mature? From his letters, this does not appear to be the case. . . . My dear friend—do not worry. In such

---

[40] Letter of 7 August 1830 in *Eismann*, p. 62.

[41] Letter of 9 August 1830 in *Ibid.*, p. 63.

matters, compulsion is of little use. We want to do what we can as parents; God does the rest . . . let him go in peace and give him your blessing.[42]

Wieck's support was enough to convince Christiane Schumann to permit her son to begin study with him. When he received word of the decision, Robert was elated and wrote to his mother to justify her decision: "Think of my father who early on understood me and intended me for Art or Music. . . . Mother, look deeply both within yourself and myself, and ask yourself whether I could endure such deadly monotony [the practice of law] for my entire life. Can you picture me sitting in my office from seven in the morning until seven in the evening?"[43] And to his guardian, Rudel, he expressed his willingness to return to the study of law if need be ("If Wieck has the slightest doubt after the six months, nothing will have been lost in the study of law, and I am fully prepared to take my examinations within a year"), but added: "Believe me, I was born to dedicate myself to Art, and will remain true to it" (21 August 1830).

To Wieck, Schumann wrote in a humble manner—as disciple to master—and expressed his eagerness and determination to begin study: "The path of Knowledge lies over the Alps and is a truly frigid one; the path of Art has its mountains, but they are Indian, and full of flowers, hopes, and dreams. . . . I am brave, patient, trustworthy, and eager to learn. I trust you completely and place myself in your hands. Take me as I am, and in all matters be patient with me" (21 August 1830). While Wieck may have been pleased with his pupil's willingness to begin study, he could not have failed to notice that youthful idealism and exuberance—not maturity and reason—remained predominant.

Despite her decision, Christiane Schumann remained concerned, hopeful for the success of her son's new venture, yet anxious and hesitant to believe that all would turn out well: "Take a look at how you have acted since the death of your good father. You must agree that you have lived only for *yourself*."[44] There was justification for her concern. While she and Wieck were consulting about her son's future, he was enjoying a four-day visit to Baden-Baden and Strasbourg. In

---

[42] *Ibid.*, pp. 64, 65.

[43] Letter of 22 August 1830 in *JS*, pp. 205, 206.

[44] Letter of 12 August 1830 in *Eismann*, p. 65.

Baden-Baden he once again met Ernst, and did not seem to be all that concerned about the deliberations concerning his future. "Good food; splendid sleep," he noted in his diary on 7 August.[45] Even after the decision had been made for Schumann to return to Leipzig and study with Wieck, he procrastinated. He finally left on 24 September, but not for Leipzig. As if to enjoy one last fling before settling down to work, he traveled for the remainder of the month, with stops in Cologne and Münster, as well as a visit with Rosen in his home in Detmold. It was not until late in October that Schumann moved into the Wieck house as a boarder and began instruction.

Bitterness over the entire episode lingered. Although he remained friendly with his brother, Carl Schumann so strongly opposed the change to music that over the years he refused to permit any musical instruments in his home. In giving her consent, even Christiane Schumann had been unable to conceal her distress: "Your brothers [and other people in Zwickau] do not approve of your ideas on this matter. So now you are left to handle the situation *entirely on your own*. May God give you his blessing!!! That is my prayer and supplication for you."[46]

But Schumann did not stand alone as he made preparations to begin his study of music. When he learned from Christiane Schumann of her son's new choice of career, Johann Gottfried Kuntsch—Schumann's boyhood piano teacher—wrote to express his support:

> When I think of your splendid talent, your ardent love of music which displayed itself so strongly from your earliest days, your lively imagination, as well as the earnestness, zeal, and tenacity with which you tirelessly pursue your goal . . . there can be no doubt that with such a splendid union of qualities only the finest results can be expected. In you, the world will number a great artist, and this Art—to which you dedicate your life—will most certainly bring you fame, honor, and immortality. This, honored friend, is my firm conviction.[47]

---

[45] *Tgb I*, p. 291.

[46] Letter of 12 August 1830 in *Eismann*, p. 65.

[47] Letter of 9 December 1830 in Wolfgang Boetticher, ed., *Briefe und Gedichte aus dem Album Robert und Clara Schumanns* (Leipzig, 1981), p. 102.

CHAPTER 3

Schumann and Literature

The greatest pleasure in life is that of reading, while we are young.
—Hazlitt, "Whether Genius is Conscious of Its Powers"

FOR MUCH OF THE NINETEENTH CENTURY, THE INTEREST OF composers not just in music but in all the arts was truly extraordinary. An interrelationship among the arts was commonly recognized. "The well-educated musician," wrote Schumann, "can study a Madonna by Raphael, the painter a symphony by Mozart, with equal benefit. Yet more: in sculpture the actor becomes a silent statue while he brings the sculptor's work to life—the painter transforms a poem into an image, the musician sets a painting to music."[1] Coupled with a broad interest in the arts was a preoccupation with the "extramusical" properties of music itself. It was a literary age, and program music flourished. That may, to a certain extent, help explain the interest many composers had in literature. Not a few were distinguished writers themselves: Berlioz as critic, essayist, and autobiographer; Liszt as critic and essayist; Wagner as dramatist, essayist, and theoretician; and Weber as critic and author of an unfinished novel.

[1] "Aus Meister Raros, Florestans und Eusebius' Denk-und Dichtbüchlein," (*c.* 1833) in *GS* I, p. 26.

Yet Schumann's passion for writing and his enthusiasm for literature set him distinctly apart. Until he was twenty, he was considering writing as a career. His diary and letters confirm his intentions and reveal a deliberately cultivated literary style. What makes Schumann's literary interests particularly intriguing is the close association in his mind of word with music. While still a student at the Lyceum in Zwickau, Schumann wrote an essay: "On the Intimate Relationship between Poetry and Music." Although a juvenile effort with little original thought, it indicates where his sympathies lay. In his diary for 1828, he wrote: "Tones are words, but on a higher level. . . . Music is the higher power of poetry; angels must speak in tones, spirits in words of poetry. . . . Every composer is a poet, only at a higher level."[2] It probably appeared natural to Schumann to associate composers with writers. "When I hear music by Beethoven," he noted, "it is as if someone were reading to me a work of Jean Paul. Schubert reminds me of Novalis."[3] Distinct similarities did not serve as the basis of Schumann's reactions; the resemblance between Schubert and Novalis, for example, is hardly striking. It was because of his enthusiasm for particular authors and composers that he was eager to couple them. This linking of poets and composers, however, was subject to change: "When I play Schubert," he wrote to Wieck on 6 November 1829, "it is as if I were reading a novel by Jean Paul."[4]

During the 1820s, music and poetry (word and tone) were interwoven for Schumann. It was a concept that, to a certain degree, he retained for years: one of the titles considered for the *Fantasie* op. 17 (1836) was *Dichtungen* (Poems). Believing himself gifted both as a writer and composer, the confusion and frustration he experienced in determining a choice of career could only have been compounded by the intimate association he perceived between the two arts. "If only my talents for poetry and music were concentrated in but *one* point," he confided to his mother.[5] It reveals much about Schumann that, in eventually choosing music as a career, in his own mind he was selecting an

---

[2] *Tgb I*, pp. 96, 41.
[3] *Ibid.*, p. 97.
[4] *JgBr*, p. 82.
[5] Letter of 15 December 1830 in *JS*, p. 213.

art that he believed to be more elevated—"at a higher level"—than poetry.

Schumann's love of the arts, and of literature in particular, owed much to his father, particularly August Schumann's work as a writer. Although he was a part-time writer, August Schumann was astonishingly prolific. It is possible to assign to him the authorship of nine substantial works of fiction—well over four thousand pages—between 1793 and 1800. Publications after 1800 are more difficult to trace, but at least three other novels appeared. His writings are representative of the popular literature of the day, for which there was a growing demand in the latter decades of the eighteenth and early nineteenth centuries. Preferred settings were the Middle Ages, or exotic locales such as India; there were inevitable struggles between good and evil, with often colorful villains and, working behind the scenes, secret societies reminiscent of freemasonry. With their fantastical settings and fanciful themes, novels of this type provided inspiration to writers such as Tieck, Arnim, Hoffmann, and Jean Paul.

There are no references in Schumann's diary and published correspondence to his father's work. Of the leading writers of popular literature—such as Christian August Vulpius, Christiane Benedicte Naubert, Heinrich Zschokke, or Carl Friedrich Grosse—mention is made only of Zschokke. But it is inconceivable that Schumann was unfamiliar with this more popular literature, including the work of his father. Insatiable reader that he was, he would have encountered popular literature at an early age, probably during adolescence. That may explain why his diary is silent on the matter: he did not begin keeping a diary until 1827, at which time his interests were directed toward more "serious" literature. That he was familiar with the popular literature of the day is best seen both in the style and content of his own writings, and by his admiration for Jean Paul—of all contemporary German writers perhaps the one most strongly indebted to popular literary styles.

Schumann's first efforts as a writer were poems. He began creating them in his early teens, and included examples in the two anthologies he assembled, *Blätter und Blümchen aus der goldenen Aue* (Leaves and Little Flowers from the Golden Meadow) (1823) and the *Allerley* (Miscellany) (1825–28). Yet another collection, *Einzelgedichte* (Detached Poems), primarily 1825–30, contained additional poetry, "polymeters" (poetic aphorisms in the style of Jean Paul), and notes about composers. " 'Melancholy at Evening' was a poem where I first felt myself to be a poet," Schumann confided to his diary in 1828, "and tears came from my eyes as I wrote it."[6] Schumann's poetry from the time, however, is surprisingly stiff and conventional.

Although he continued to write poetry sporadically during his life—including the ballad "The Bell of Ivan Veliky" in 1844 during a visit to Moscow—he wrote far more prose. His early prose attempts are also derivative, and owe much to Jean Paul. The diary for August 1828 contains fragments from *Juniusabende und Julitage*, which he enthusiastically described as "my first work, my truest, and my most beautiful."[7] That autumn, excerpts from *Selene* as well as ideas for its content appear in the diary.[8] Both works are in the style of Jean Paul (who also wrote a *Selena*), and they bring to mind *The Invisible Lodge*, a work that itself is much indebted to the popular literature of the day. Schumann worked on *Selene* in November 1828 and had some unusual ideas for it: both Jean Paul and Prince Louis Ferdinand were to appear as characters.

Drama interested Schumann as well. He wrote "robber plays" (a popular genre of the time, owing much to the success of Schiller's *Die Räuber* (The Robbers), and he acted in them. There are also references in Schumann's diary to the creation of two tragedies, one based on the life of Coriolanus and another on the political struggles of the Montalti family in fourteenth-century Genoa. As late as June 1831, he completed the first scene of a projected drama based on the story of Abelard and Heloise.

In the 1830s, much of Schumann's writing was music criticism, especially for his own paper, the *Neue Zeitschrift für Musik* (New Journal for Music). But he still managed to find time to write fiction, although his attempts remained unpublished and incomplete. In 1831, he began work on a tale, "The Philistine and the Rascal King"; its title brings to

---

[6] May 1828 in *Tgb I*, p. 76.

[7] 29 July 1828 in *Ibid.*, p. 98. Nineteen pages of the work survive.

[8] Only about six pages of this work (much of it strongly autobiographical in nature) are extant.

mind fairy tales by Hoffmann or Eichendorff. Of particular interest is an eight-page fragment for a novel Schumann began at about the same time: *Die Davidsbund* (The League of David). This appears to be the same work referred to in his diary as "Wunderkinder," whose characters were to include Paganini, Hummel, Wieck, and Clara, among others.

In many ways, Schumann's writing was a natural outgrowth of what he read. His passion for reading—no doubt encouraged by his father—began early. Over the years his diary, household books, and a special "reading notebook" attest to the breadth of his reading. It is truly astonishing. His knowledge of European literature was comprehensive and included not just poetry, drama, and fiction, but history and biography. Of foreign literature, nearly all was read in German translation. Although in school and on his own he studied Latin, Greek, French, Italian, and English, Schumann's grasp of foreign languages was limited.

From his study in school, Schumann acquired the expected familiarity with Roman and Greek classics, particularly Aeschylus, Euripides, and Sophocles; in 1825 he tried his hand at translating Anacreon, Homer, and Horace. Among European writers, Schumann read Calderón, Dante, Petrarch, Cellini, Pellico, Alfieri, Racine, Rousseau, Ponsard, Hugo, Sand, and Sue—although contemporary French writing tended to disturb him with what he perceived as its cheap sensationalism. Like his father, he was fond of English writers, Byron in particular. Other English writers with whom he was familiar include Goldsmith, Fielding, Burns, Shelley, Moore, Macaulay, Scott, and Bulwer-Lytton. American literature does not seem to have interested him greatly; he read *Uncle Tom's Cabin* and *Bracebridge Hall*, but Cooper—an author extremely popular in Europe at the time—is surprisingly absent.

Contemporary German writers held the greatest attraction for Schumann. References to the works of Immermann, Grillparzer, Goethe, Humboldt, Friedrich and August Wilhelm von Schlegel, Schiller, Tieck, Hauff, Arnim, Brentano, Geibel, Mörike, Uhland, Novalis, Platen, and Chamisso, as well as lesser-known writers, such as Hölty, Droste-Hülshoff, Ernst Schulze, Heinse, Seume, Herwegh, and Gutzkow, are found in Schumann's diary and household books. Frequently what he read influenced his musical direction. His fondness for the poetry of Justinus Kerner inspired his first songs (and in 1840 also served as the basis for the *Zwölf Gedichte* op. 35). In fact much of Schumann's reading of German poetry was with an eye toward its suitability for setting to music.

Friedrich Rückert was an early favorite, reverently described by Schumann as a "beloved poet, a great musician in words and thoughts."[9] Schumann set more than four dozen of Rückert's poems to music. His translations from Hariri (Rückert was an orientalist) served as inspiration for the collection of Schumann's four-hand piano pieces, *Bilder aus dem Osten* (Pictures from the East) op. 66; poems from his *Liebesfrühling* (The Springtime of Love) were selected and set to music by Schumann and his wife as a poetic and symbolic statement shortly after their marriage in 1840 (published as op. 37). A copy of the songs was sent to Rückert, who responded with a poem that delighted Schumann.

Of the many poets whose work he set to music, Rückert may have been Schumann's favorite. But because of the popularity of Schumann's *Liederkreis* op. 24 and *Dichterliebe* (A Poet's Love) op. 48, the poetry of Heinrich Heine is probably most closely associated with him. When Schumann and Heine met in Munich in May 1828—their only meeting—Schumann had not set any of Heine's poetry and had yet to make music his career. In May 1840—the year in which Schumann wrote most of his lieder—he wrote to Heine in Paris (where Heine had moved), enclosing several of his settings of Heine's poetry. Schumann was hoping not only for a favorable reaction from Heine but to draw closer to him. But Heine never responded, and Schumann was offended. Although he continued to read Heine's new works, he was disgusted by Heine's *Romanzero*—probably by what he perceived as the excessively personal and often depreciative nature of the poetry in the collection.

Also closely associated with Schumann is the poetry of Josef von Eichendorff. Schumann's setting of selected poems by Eichendorff in the *Liederkreis* op. 39 is one of remarkable sensitivity. Schumann described it as his "most Romantic" song cycle, a reference not to any love interest within the poetry, but to the emotional and dramatic in-

---

[9] Review published in 1840 of H. Esser's *Lieder* op. 6 in *GS I*, p. 496.

tensity of many of the texts.[10] He always seemed eager to meet those poets whose writings he admired, curious to determine the association between the artist and his work (the two, Schumann felt, were closely related). He met Eichendorff on several occasions in January 1847. Eichendorff was twenty-two years older than Schumann, recently retired, and with musical interests (he played the violin). But although he professed "delight" with Schumann's settings of his poems, no intimacy resulted.

Schumann's meeting with Hans Christian Andersen—another writer he greatly admired—was more engaging, and it was one they both remembered fondly. Andersen's reputation today is that of a writer of fairy tales. During the nineteenth century, he was greatly esteemed not just for his tales but for his novels, travelogues, and poetry. Schumann seems to have read everything by Andersen he could get his hands on, invariably with great enjoyment. By nature, Andersen was open and kindly. He was fond of music, and counted among his friends several composers. In 1842 Schumann dedicated and sent to Andersen a copy of his *Fünf Lieder* op. 40 (which included in German translation four settings of Andersen's poetry). Andersen was an inveterate traveler (he never owned a home of his own), and in 1844, while traveling through Germany, made a point of visiting Schumann in Leipzig. A memorable evening resulted with performances of Schumann's Andersen songs as well as readings by the poet. Schumann later wrote to Andersen describing the experience as "unforgettable" (14 April 1845), a response shared by Andersen in his autobiography.

Just as Schumann was naturally drawn while reading poetry to thoughts of a musical setting, his reading of dramas (and fiction in general) often led to thoughts about the work's suitability as a basis for opera. He completed but one opera, *Genoveva*, based on dramas dealing with the Genoveva legend by Tieck and Friedrich Hebbel. The more psychological setting of Hebbel particularly appealed to him. At first, unsure of how to proceed, he wrote to Hebbel anxious for him to collaborate on the libretto. Hebbel was three years younger than

---

[10] Letter to Clara Wieck of 22 May 1840 in Wolfgang Boetticher, *Robert Schumann in seinen Schriften und Briefen* (Berlin, 1942), p. 340.

Schumann. Like Schumann, he had studied at the University of Heidelberg and had been befriended by Thibaut. But Hebbel's career had been one of constant struggle. *Genoveva* was completed in March 1841, but not published until 1843 and not performed until six years later.

Schumann's diary reveals his great admiration for him and his work. Unfortunately, Hebbel did not respond in a similar manner. His knowledge of music was limited, and conservative (Mozart was his favorite composer). When they met, he found Schumann to be quiet and excessively introverted. There was no collaboration. They kept in touch, however, and in 1853 when Schumann dedicated and presented to Hebbel his setting of Hebbel's *Nachtlied*, he responded with gratitude and dedicated to Schumann his play *Michael Angelo*, sending him the manuscript of it.

What appeared to be of particular attraction to Schumann was the distinctive individuality of Hebbel's thought, often pervaded with a dark pessimism and somber melancholy (a reflection perhaps of the extreme poverty and depressing circumstances of much of Hebbel's life). Not long after the completion of *Genoveva* in 1848, Schumann turned again to Hebbel's work for the piano pieces, *Waldszenen* (Forest Scenes) op. 82. For one of the pieces in the set, "Cursed Place," Schumann set the mood by prefacing it with a short poem by Hebbel. It is a gruesome text, describing flowers "pale as death," with a single, dark red flower among them, its color the result of having been nourished on human blood.

Those characteristics that attracted Schumann to the work of Hebbel were traits that he found intriguing in literature in general. He was intrigued by works of marked originality, and fascinated by those that contained elements of the bizarre and unusual. That was particularly true of Schumann's youthful interests. In 1828, during his first year of university study at Leipzig, he discovered the controversial plays of Christian Dietrich Grabbe. Although an admirer of Grabbe's skill as a writer, Heine dryly noted in his work "a lack of good taste, a cynicism, and a wildness that surpass the maddest and most abominable things conceived by the human mind"—precisely those traits that Schumann probably found of interest.[11]

---

[11] Quoted in Alfred Bergmann, ed., *Grabbe in Berichten seiner Zeitgenossen* (Stuttgart, 1968), p. 24.

Schumann's curiosity about Grabbe extended both to his life and work. The diary includes references to Grabbe's *Marie und Nannette; Comedy, Satire, Irony, and Deep Meaning; Marius und Sulla; Herzog Theodor von Gothland* (all read in 1828); and *Hannibal* (read in 1846). *Gothland* made an unusually strong impression on Schumann, so much so that nearly an entire page in his diary was devoted to thoughts about the work. He discussed at length the plot, and concluded it was a "tragedy without parallel, unique. . . . It often brings to mind those bizarre traits of Heine's Lieder, that burning sarcasm, that *great* despair."[12] Schumann's fascination with Grabbe led him in November 1828 to write to Gisbert Rosen—who lived in Detmold, where Grabbe was then residing—to ask for information about him. Grabbe's life was in many ways a counterpart to the "wildness" noted by Heine in his writings. After Grabbe's death in 1836, Schumann read with interest Karl Immermann's recollections of the dramatist.

Similar eccentricity—in life, work, or a combination of the two—attracted Schumann to three other writers: Friedrich Hölderlin, Heinrich von Kleist, and Nikolaus Lenau. Hölderlin's popularity as a poet was broadened by both the intensity of his writing and the sensationalized circumstances of his mental illness. Schumann knew Hölderlin's work well; as a mark of his esteem, several excerpts from Hölderlin's writings were used as the mottos Schumann placed at the head of each issue of the *Neue Zeitschrift für Musik*. He knew as well of his madness and, according to Emil Flechsig, in the 1820s "spoke about it with fear and awe."[13] Although Hölderlin had been diagnosed as being incurably insane in 1807, Schumann's interest in him was no doubt stimulated by the fact that a collected edition of Hölderlin's poems had only recently appeared in print for the first time (1826).

Kleist, too, was a tragic figure. He belonged to a distinguished Prussian military family, and his suicide in 1811 (at age thirty-four) had created scandal not just in literary circles but in the upper society of which he had been a part. His writing is unsettling, with characters

---

[12] Entry for 31 October 1828 in *Tgb I*, p. 129.

[13] Emil Flechsig, "Erinnerungen an Robert Schumann," *Neue Zeitschrift für Musik* CXVII (1956), p. 396. From 1828 to 1835 Schumann kept a book of literary extracts suitable for mottos (including those by Hölderlin); it was nearly 250 pages in length.

seeming to be always at the mercy of the whims and caprices of fate. Schumann described Kleist's stories as "monstrous, but nonetheless very interesting," and considered one of them ("Michael Kohlhaas," a remarkable tale of justice gone awry) as the basis for a possible opera libretto.[14] For Kleist's play, *Kätchen von Heilbronn*, perhaps his most idyllic and conventional work, Schumann contemplated writing an overture.

Like Hölderlin and Kleist, Nikolaus Lenau suffered from depression and mental instability. The last six years of his life were spent in an asylum. Lenau's poetry is often pervaded by profound melancholy, a trait that seemed to have particular appeal to Schumann. In 1838, through a mutual friend, Schumann attempted to obtain some verse from Lenau for the *Neue Zeitschrift für Musik*. No new poetry by Lenau appeared in the journal, but perhaps he never received Schumann's invitation. It is unlikely that he would have turned down the opportunity: his interest in music—particularly that of Beethoven—was considerable.

Later that year when visiting Vienna (where Lenau resided), Schumann wanted very much to meet him, but was shy about doing so. "I saw Lenau in a cafe, but did not speak to him," he noted in his diary.[15] When Schumann was later presented to Lenau, he seemed pleased to detect "a melancholy, very gentle and captivating look about his mouth and eyes."[16] Shortly after Lenau's death in 1850, Schumann offered as a tribute his op. 90: settings of six of Lenau's poems with a brief requiem added, all published with an unusually elaborate cover including depictions of a cross and funereal wreath.

Of the many German writers who interested Schumann, it was E. T. A. Hoffmann and Jean Paul Richter who had the most profound effect upon his work. Once again, it was the distinctive nature of their writing—both in style and content—that appear to have prompted his initial attraction. The first extended reference to Hoffmann in Schumann's diary occurs in 1831, but at that point he had been familiar with Hoffmann's writings for a number of years, having previously noted

---

[14] 27 and 30 August 1852 in *Tgb II*, p. 436.
[15] Entry of October 1838 in *Ibid.*, p. 74.
[16] Entry of December 1838 in *Ibid.*, p. 83.

resemblances between Hoffmann's work and Schubert's. His reading of Hoffmann found him in a strange frame of mind. 5 June 1831: "In the evening read that damned E. T. A. Hoffmann. Klein Zaches [one of Hoffmann's tales] and an ugly, loathsome idea as basis. . . . Concept for a poetical biography of Hoffmann. . . . One can scarcely breathe while reading Hoffmann. . . . Reading Hoffmann unceasingly. New worlds. The Mines at Falun [another Hoffmann tale]. Opera text which greatly inspires me."[17]

Hoffmann and Schumann had much in common. Both were gifted in literature and music. Like Schumann, Hoffmann had been obliged to study law. After completing his law study, attempts to make his living as a writer, composer, and conductor were unsuccessful, and influential friends secured for him a position as a judge. Although he never achieved comparable recognition for his music, Hoffmann was a composer of considerable skill. It is worth noting that Schumann thought enough of it to examine in manuscript the score for his opera, *Aurora* (1812).

As a composer, Hoffmann's indebtedness to the music of others (particularly Mozart) is unmistakable. His short stories and novels, on the other hand, are strikingly original: highly imaginative, visionary, and often grotesque (which helps explain Schumann's reference to "an ugly, loathsome idea" in "Klein Zaches"). In his use of the *Märchen*—the cultivated, German version of a fairy tale for adults—Hoffmann was particularly adept, and created a world with a constant and dizzying shift between fantasy and reality.

Hoffmann's most famous literary creation was the eccentric musician Johannes Kreisler—gifted, temperamental, and at odds with the prosaic life of his time, a personality not unlike that of Hoffmann himself. Kreisler appears in two major works by Hoffmann: *Kreisleriana* (a collection of essays and tales), and *Kater Murr*, a novel left unfinished at Hoffmann's death in 1822. Schumann, like a number of nineteenth-century musicians, was particularly fond of Kreisler, in many ways the Romantic musician *par excellence*. In an unusual indication of his regard for the work, excerpts from *Kreisleriana* were published in the *Neue Zeitschrift für Musik* in 1834 and 1836.

---

[17] Entries of 5 and 6 June 1831 in *Tgb I*, pp. 336, 337.

Inspired by Hoffmann's work, Schumann published his own *Kreisleriana* for piano (subtitled *Fantasies*) in 1838 as op. 16. It is likely as well that Hoffmann's first published work—a collection of tales entitled *Fantasiestücke in Callots Manier* (Fantasy Pieces in the Manner of Callot)—led to Schumann's title for his op. 12: *Fantasiestücke*.[18] The *Nachtstücke* (Night Pieces) op. 23 may similarly have been inspired by Hoffmann's collection of stories, *Nachtstücke*—although in this instance the word was not unique to Hoffmann. In the 1830s, Hoffmann consistently provided Schumann with a source of inspiration that led him to designate compositions as musical counterparts to Hoffmann's work. One senses as well that they were intended as homage to a writer whom he regarded with unusual affection.

Despite the measure of pride Hoffmann derived from the singularity of his work, he willingly acknowledged the influence of one contemporary author: Jean Paul Richter. "Your works," he wrote to Jean Paul, "have inspired my innermost being and influenced my development."[19] It was a sentiment with which Schumann would have concurred. In Schumann's eyes, no writer had so great an influence on his own life and work.

Johann Paul Friedrich Richter—Jean Paul was his pen name—was born in 1763, the son of a clergyman (who was, incidentally, a talented musician). Like August Schumann, from an early age he showed a great love for literature, becoming a voracious and not always discriminating reader. At the age of fifteen, he began keeping a series of notebooks filled with arcane material he had encountered in books, excerpts from which invariably later found their way into his own writing—often as amusing, erudite, and generally irrelevant footnotes to the text.

In 1781, Jean Paul entered the University of Leipzig as a student of theology. But he had little money, did not enjoy his course of study, and devoted much of his time to reading on his own. He remained for only one semester. Determined to become a writer, he published anonymously his first book, *Greenland Lawsuits*, in 1783. It attracted little

---

[18] The bizarre creations of the artist Jacques Callot (c.1592–1635)—particularly those in his *Caprici di diverse figure* (1617)—enjoyed renewed popularity during the nineteenth century.

[19] Letter of 30 January 1822 in Johanna C. Sahlin, ed. & trans., *Selected Letters of E. T. A. Hoffmann* (Chicago, 1977), p. 321.

attention, and it wasn't until ten years later with the appearance of *The Invisible Lodge* that he began to make a name for himself. Widespread fame followed with *Hesperus* (1795), *Siebenkäs* (Flower, Fruit, and Thorn Pieces) (1797), and *Titan* (1803). A year after the publication of *Titan*, Jean Paul settled in the small town of Bayreuth, where, despite the rather peculiar nature of his writings, he led by all accounts a solidly middle-class existence. One of the major attractions Bayreuth held for him was the superior quality of its local beer. Before his death in 1825, two additional novels appeared (both unfinished): *Flegeljahre* (Walt and Vult) (1805) and *The Comet* (1822).

Today, Jean Paul is all but forgotten. During his life, and for about a half century after his death, he was a writer of enormous popularity. His fame extended well beyond Germany. To a great extent, the extreme sentimentality and emotional excess of his writings were a major attraction. But his unique prose style—tangled, prolix, and discursive—had many admirers. Thomas Carlyle, Jean Paul's most vocal partisan in England, characterized it as "a perfect Indian jungle . . . nothing on all sides but darkness, dissonance, confusion worse confounded. Then the style of the whole corresponds, in perplexity and extravagance, with that of the parts. . . . That his manner of writing is singular, nay in fact a wild, complicated Arabesque, no one can deny."[20]

Within Jean Paul's novels—each typically nearly a thousand pages in length—scenes of sentiment and emotion of an astonishing extravagance are commonplace. The beauties of nature are a frequent subject, one in which Jean Paul gives free rein to exuberant, at times incomprehensible, descriptions teeming with fanciful metaphor. Jean Paul had studied piano as a youth, and was particularly fond of music. It plays an important role in his novels, frequently as a means of transporting his characters beyond themselves:

> Clotilda without any hesitating vanity consented to sing. But for Sebastian, in whom all tones came in contact with naked, quivering feelers, and who could work himself into sadness at the very songs of the herdsmen in the fields—this, on such an evening, was too much for his heart; under cover of the general musical attentiveness, he had to steal out of the door. . . .

[20] *The Works of Thomas Carlyle* (New York, 1897), XIV, p. 13. Carlyle's essay on Jean Paul (from which this quotation is taken) was originally published in the *Edinburgh Review* in 1827.

> But here, under the great night-heaven, amidst higher drops, his own can fall unseen. What a night! Here a splendor overwhelms him, which links night and sky and earth all together; magic Nature rushes with streams into his heart, and forcibly enlarges it. Overhead, Luna fills the floating cloud-fleeces with liquid silver, and the soaked silver-wool quivers downward, and glittering pearls trickle over smooth foliage, and are caught in blossoms, and the heavenly field pearls and glimmers. [. . .] He glowed through his whole being, and night-clouds must cool it. His finger-tips hung down, lightly folded in one another. Clotilda's tones dropped now like molten silver-points on his bosom, now they flowed like stray echoes from distant groves into this still garden [. . .] But it seemed to him as if his bosom would burst, as if he should be blest could he at this moment embrace beloved persons, and crush in the closeness of that embrace in a blissful frenzy his bosom and his heart. It was to him as if he should be over-blessed, could he now before some being, before a mere shadow of the mind, pour out all his blood, his life, his being. It was to him as if he must scream into the midst of Clotilda's tones, and fold his arms around a rock, only to stifle the painful yearning.[21]

The passion and sentiment displayed in Jean Paul's novels often appear alongside sinister and foreboding elements, including violence and extravagant eroticism. In *Titan*, for example, the villainous Roquairol assumes the identity of his best friend, Albano, in order to seduce Albano's fiancée. Roquairol then publicly reveals his act during the presentation of a play that he has written, at the conclusion of which he kills himself on stage—the audience casually dismissing it all as an entertaining part of the drama itself. What contributes to the distinctiveness of Jean Paul's style—Carlyle's "perfect Indian jungle"—is the unpredictable association of macabre, often frightening occurrences with scenes of overweening sentiment and sublime emotion.

As an additional means of disorienting the reader, there is Jean Paul's singular sense of humor. He was a great admirer of Laurence Sterne, in whose whimsy and caprice he discovered a kindred spirit. The first

---

[21] Jean Paul, *Hesperus*, 2 vols., trans. Charles T. Brooks (Boston, 1865), I, pp. 118–120. I have used, whenever possible, nineteenth-century translations of Jean Paul, because these capture—with unusual success—his often convoluted imagery and syntax.

chapter of *Titan*—called, incidentally, a "Jubilee" by Richter (chapters as such rarely exist in his works)—is fifty-six pages in length. It is followed by what should have preceded it: a thirteen-page "Introductory Program to *Titan*." It is this juxtaposition of humor, sentiment, and the bizarre, and the abrupt and unpredictable movement between them that makes his work so disconcerting. Coupled with Jean Paul's numerous asides and footnotes, a dualistic structure often results: the plot itself, and the author's digressions, comments, and reaction to it.

Schumann's enthusiasm for Jean Paul first became apparent in the summer of 1827. (Here again, the influence of his father is evident. Jean Paul had been one of August Schumann's favorite writers.) In his diary, his literary attempts, and in his letters, he imitated the style of Jean Paul, emphasizing the excessive sentimentality and emotional extravagance characteristic of him. The following example—found in both his diary and in a letter to Flechsig—is a typical tirade à la Jean Paul, and representative of Schumann at his most sentimental:

> Oh friend! Were I a smile, I would want to hover about her eyes; were I joy, I would skip lightly through her pulses; Yes!—were I a tear, I would weep with her; and if she then smiled once again, gladly would I die on her eyelash, and gladly—yes, gladly—be no more.[22]

Schumann's source of inspiration—in this instance he surpassed his mentor—can be traced to a passage in one of his favorite novels by Jean Paul, *Flegeljahre*:

> Were I a star ... I would shine upon thee; were I a rose, I would bloom for thee; were I a sound, I would press into thy heart; were I love, the happiest love, I would dwell therein.[23]

Throughout 1828 and 1829, Schumann avidly read Jean Paul. He was a sensitive and impressionable reader, and his diary documented the often potent effect his reading had on him. 18 January 1829: "Bedtime reading: Jean Paul's Gianozzo [*Comic Appendix to Titan*] and his life and death—poor sleep." 25 January 1829: "Bedtime reading:

---

[22] *Tgb* I, p. 69 and letter of July 1827 to Flechsig in *JS*, p. 109.
[23] Jean Paul, *Walt and Vult, or The Twins*, 2 vols. (Boston, 1846), II, p. 32.

Diocha from Nikolaus Marggraf [*The Comet*] by Jean Paul—voluptuous sleep."[24] Schumann's reaction to *Siebenkäs* bordered on frenzy: "Siebenkäs is frightful, but I would like to read it a thousand times more. . . . [After reading it] I sat completely enraptured among the trees and I heard a nightingale. But I didn't cry—and I struck out with my hands and feet, because I felt so happy. But on the way home I felt as if I had taken leave of my senses. I was in my right mind, but I still thought I was not. I was actually crazy."[25] "If the entire world were to read Jean Paul," Schumann concluded, "it would become a better place, but unhappier. He has often nearly driven me mad, but the rainbow of peace and of the human spirit always hovers gently above all tears, and one's heart is marvelously exalted and gently transfigured" (5 June 1828).

At times, Schumann felt and acted as if he were living in a novel by Jean Paul. In his diary he wrote: "[Moritz Semmel] said again how much he would like to die. He was beside himself, and it was a scene from Jean Paul."[26] When during his visit to the Rhine in 1828, Schumann closed his eyes at the approach of the river in order to enjoy all at once the magnificent spectacle, he was imitating the character Albano in *Titan* who acted similarly when about to behold the beauty of Isola Bella. And when in 1829 Schumann visited Italy, the sight of Isola Bella was inextricably interwoven with thoughts of *Titan*. "Gran albergo al lago—bliss—Albano!," he wrote in his diary.[27]

Over the years Schumann's devotion to Jean Paul remained strong. Selections from his writings were published in the *Neue Zeitschrift für Musik*, and excerpts frequently appeared as mottos for individual issues. His exceptional interest in Jean Paul attracted attention. In 1839, the composer Stephen Heller, also a devoted admirer of Jean Paul, enthusiastically wrote to Schumann: "Your compositions are Jean Paulish Fruit, Bloom, and Thorn pieces, and Siebenkäs, Schoppe-Leibgerber (Euseb-Florestan), Lenette, Pelzstiefel, etc. are found note for note in them. And because I love Jean Paul so deeply, I love you as well."[28]

---

[24] *Tgb I*, pp. 168, 170.
[25] Entry of 29 May 1828 in *Ibid.*, p. 83.
[26] July 1828 in *Ibid.*, p. 93.
[27] 7 September 1829 in *Ibid.*, p. 255.
[28] Letter of 18 September 1839 in Stephen Heller, *Briefe an Robert Schumann*, ed. Ursula

To his fiancée, Schumann wrote expressing his delight that she was reading *Flegeljahre*. But he warned her that on first reading all might not be clear to her: "It is in its way like the Bible" (20 March 1838). Within six weeks of their marriage, Schumann was reading Jean Paul's *Life of Fibel* with her so that "for the first time she could better understand" Jean Paul.[29] It was as if Schumann felt everyone should be familiar with Jean Paul, and was genuinely astonished when he learned that was not the case. Emilie Steffen, a friend of the family in the 1840s and a piano student of his wife, recalled that "one day Schumann asked her if she were studying Shakespeare and Jean Paul diligently, and whether she knew *Coriolanus* and *Siebenkäs*. On receiving a negative answer, he looked at her with such surprise and at the same time so kindly that she at once began to read, and was grateful to him ever after."[30]

Although Schumann's affection for the work of Jean Paul remained constant, over the years his admiration for another author whom he had discovered during his youth—William Shakespeare—grew. By the 1850s, as maturity supplanted the enthusiasm of his youth, Shakespeare became his favorite author. Schumann's admiration for Shakespeare coincided with a rediscovery and reevaluation of Shakespeare's work during the first half of the nineteenth century.

The interest of German Romanticism in Shakespeare did much not only to broaden his international reputation but to place him on a pedestal as possibly the greatest of all writers. During the eighteenth century, Shakespeare had been perceived as at times tasteless and a bit of a barbarian. But it was precisely his emotional "excess" and profusion of lively action that appealed to nineteenth-century audiences. In Germany, the criticism and translations of Tieck and August Wilhelm von Schlegel did much to promote Shakespeare's popularity. For the first time, his works became available in uncut and truly poetic translations.

Schumann read Shakespeare throughout his life, singling out for

---

Kersten (Frankfurt, 1988), p. 142. Siebenkäs, Schoppe, Leibgeber (not "Leibgerber"), Lenette, and Pelzstiefel are all characters in *Flower, Fruit, and Thorn Pieces*. Heller later wrote a work for solo piano inspired by Jean Paul's novel (published as op. 82, and usually referred to by the French title, *Nuits blanches*).

[29] Entry for 25–31 October 1840 in *Tgb II*, p. 118.

[30] Frederick Niecks, *Robert Schumann* (London, 1925), p. 250.

praise his universality. But Shakespeare's skill at character development probably provided a major source for Schumann's attraction. The first mention of Shakespeare in Schumann's diary is of *Hamlet*. On 25 October 1828, Schumann saw the play, prompting a reading of it two days later. The melancholy figure of Hamlet was one with particular appeal in the nineteenth century, and in 1831 and 1832 Schumann considered an opera on the subject, writing sketches for a "Sinfonia per il Hamlet."[31]

Schumann's knowledge of Shakespeare's plays was extensive. In 1831, he compiled (for reasons unknown) a listing of the female characters in his dramas. Nine years later, while in negotiation to receive an honorary doctorate from the University of Jena, Schumann, as an indication of his accomplishments, offered to send to the university a study of Shakespeare and music. He received the degree shortly thereafter, and, except for a four-page sketch, the study was not written. But it was an idea that Schumann returned to later in the year, when in October he marked passages in Shakespeare's works intending to use them as the basis for an article on Shakespeare and music, probably for the *Zeitschrift*.

The direct influence of Shakespeare on his own compositions was not inconsiderable. Schumann intended as a motto for the third Intermezzo (*Rasch und wild*) of the *Novelletten* op. 21 (1838) the opening lines from *Macbeth*: "When shall we three meet again?/In thunder, lightning, or in rain?". And he set to music the concluding song of the clown in *Twelfth Night*. During his extensive search for a suitable subject for an opera, Schumann considered *The Tempest* and *Romeo and Juliet* (in 1846 and 1850, respectively). Toward the end of his career, inspired by Shakespeare's *Julius Caesar*, he wrote a concert overture on the subject.

But probably the most intriguing of Shakespeare's influences on Schumann is for a work never, as far as is known, even begun. On 4 July 1832, Schumann noted in his diary: "Why are there no operas without texts; that would quite certainly be dramatic. There is much for you in Shakespeare."[32] Later in the month (or possibly in August),

---

[31] Although the work was never completed, thematic material was later incorporated into Schumann's Symphony in G minor.

[32] *Tgb I*, p. 411.

there is the cryptic entry: "The opera without a text."[33] It was an idea he returned to in December of that year in a letter to the music critic, Ludwig Rellstab. But what Schumann meant remains unclear. Could he have had in mind a programmatic, instrumental composition? Or would singers have been involved? And, most interesting, how had this idea been developed by Schumann from his reading of Shakespeare?

Beginning in April 1852 Schumann commenced a concentrated and systematic rereading of Shakespeare's plays. The study took one year, a time when he composed little and seemed particularly interested in literary pursuits; during this same period he put together in book form his music criticism. Schumann's reading of Shakespeare was part of a larger project that was to occupy him intermittently until his death. It necessitated rereading many of his favorite books, including a great deal of Jean Paul in the summer and autumn of 1853. What Schumann had in mind was an anthology of writings from celebrated authors from antiquity to the present, an anthology devoted solely to excerpts from their work that dealt with music. It was to be called *Dichtergarten* (A Poet's Garden). The possibility of finding a publisher for the work was not great. Schumann had recently experienced considerable difficulty in finding a publisher for his collected music criticism, for which there would surely have been a broader market than for a specialized, literary anthology. Yet, he worked extensively on the project, completing nearly three hundred pages in manuscript. It was a labor of love, and the final testament not just of Schumann's passion for literature but of his long-abiding interest in the relationship between word and music.

---

[33] *Ibid.*, p. 412.

CHAPTER 4

Commitment to Music

> *This is ultimately what it is like to be alone: you spin yourself into the silk of your soul, you become a pupa and await the metamorphosis, which is certain to come. While waiting, you live on your past experiences and telepathically you live the lives of others. Death and resurrection; being reared and trained for something new and strange.*
>
> —Strindberg, *Alone*

There was no more crucial time in Schumann's life than the three-and-a-half years from October 1830 until the spring of 1834—the period of his apprenticeship as a musician. During that time, he acquired what was to serve as the foundation for his skills as a pianist and as a composer. But as his mother had noted to Wieck, these were skills Schumann should have learned much earlier. He was twenty years old and just beginning seriously to study music—an unusually late start. In addition, he had received only grudging consent to begin his new career. In time, his life became exceptionally stressful, often because of his determination to accomplish as much as possible in as short a time as possible. There were frequent personal crises and setbacks as well. As a result, these years were among the darkest and most challenging of Schumann's life.

He began his new career in a depressed and morose humor, the lingering effect of the far from wholehearted support of his family. "My heart," he wrote to his mother, "is dead and empty, like the future."[1] Schumann eventually became a boarder at Wieck's home, where he was to live for about a year. But the move to Wieck did not improve his mood. To his mother, he described himself as often bored and feeling little pleasure in life: "Of the old warmth and enthusiasm, only cinders remain."[2]

But despite his low spirits—some of which may have been an attempt to gain sympathy—there is no indication that Schumann initially felt pressured by the six-month trial period that had been agreed to. Heinrich Dorn, who was shortly to become Schumann's theory and harmony teacher, remembered him at the time as "a very handsome young man, whose blue eyes squinted a bit [Schumann was nearsighted], but when he laughed, with roguish dimples."[3] Unfortunately, there is no diary to document Schumann's activities for the period from October 1830 until May 1831. In later years he claimed to have practiced "more than six or seven hours daily."[4] But his correspondence reveals hardly strenuous activities. Piano practice does not appear to have had a significant role. During his instruction with Dorn, he felt that Schumann was "neglecting his piano playing."[5]

There is no reason to doubt, however, that at the commencement of his study with Wieck, piano practice was a priority. It is unlikely that Wieck would have tolerated any neglect of the instrument on Schumann's part. Their relationship at the start appears to have been cordial. But within weeks Schumann became dissatisfied and decided to seek a new teacher: Johann Nepomuk Hummel, Kapellmeister in Weimar. Compared to Hummel's—one of the most distinguished musicians of his day—Wieck's credentials admittedly were inferior. But the intended leap from Wieck to Hummel, although an ambitious move on Schumann's part, was, given his own inexperience and anonymity, unrealistic. Schumann's dissatisfaction with Wieck could also be

---

[1] Letter of 27 September 1830 in *JS*, p. 209.
[2] Letter of 15 November 1830 in *Ibid.*, p. 210.
[3] From a letter of 7 September 1856 to Wasielewski, in *Eismann*, p. 74.
[4] No date given. *Ibid.*, p. 77.
[5] *Ibid.*, p. 74.

perceived not as an indication of ambition but of fickleness. Prior to accepting Schumann as a pupil, one of Wieck's major concerns had been Schumann's irresponsibility and lack of commitment. By wanting to leave when the trial period agreed to had hardly begun, Schumann seemed to be both confirming Wieck's apprehensions and justifying what Schumann's family had perceived as an immature and scatter-brained decision.

At the time, Hummel was nearing the end of an illustrious career. He was regarded as the most gifted of Mozart's pupils. In 1804 (at the age of twenty-six), he had become Kapellmeister to the Esterházy family—a distinguished position formerly held by Haydn. Fifteen years later he assumed the musical direction at the court of Weimar, a post that he retained until his death in 1837. Although active as a teacher of piano, in the last eight years of his life Hummel cut back on the number of his pupils (a fact of which Schumann was probably unaware).

Despite his age and what was perceived as his old-fashioned style, Hummel continued to perform in public to acclaim. He was known for the purity and clarity of his playing, characteristics he tried to instill in his students. Wieck, on the other hand, preferred the style of John Field (whom, incidentally, he had never heard). Field's compositions (especially his nocturnes, which were very popular)) are characterized by an expressive touch, rich in sonority. Wieck was preoccupied with a bel canto approach to piano-playing as demonstrated in the title of his only work on the subject, *Klavier und Gesang* (Piano and Song, 1853). Wieck's text, however, is a disappointment: chatty, padded, intended to be controversial (but, by 1853, dated). Little of a technical nature is presented. Given his emphasis on bel canto, his preference for Field's approach—and dislike for what he perceived as Hummel's antiquarian stance—is not surprising.

Compared to Hummel, Field's method was more in sympathy with the changing musical perceptions of the day; Chopin, for example, was among the admirers of Field. In selecting Field as a model, Wieck revealed his progressive tendencies. One would have thought that such an approach would have found favor with Schumann. But to Schumann, Hummel's greatest attraction was neither his skill as a performer—he never heard him perform—nor skill as a composer, but his celebrity.

Over time, Schumann's relationship with Wieck continued to deteriorate. There can be little doubt that he felt neglected. Clara, as Schumann was well aware, was Wieck's primary concern. Perfecting her technique and establishing a career for her occupied much of his time and energy. On 25 September 1831, Wieck took Clara on an extended concert tour that included more than a half dozen German cities, as well as a two-month stay in Paris. They did not return until 1 May 1832, and during those seven months Schumann was on his own. That may have been the primary reason why, for a year-and-a-half, Schumann never really abandoned the idea of having Hummel as his teacher.

From January 1831 until May 1832, in letters to friends and family Schumann referred to his intention of studying with Hummel. During that time, he had taken up the study of Hummel's *Anweisung zum Pianofortespiel* (1828), a practical guide to developing piano technique. It was a text he had used previously (in February 1829 and later while a student in Heidelberg). In July 1831, he completed his study of it, copying exercises from it into a sketchbook for more ready reference. While busy studying them, he finally wrote to Hummel. In his letter (20 August 1831), Schumann sketched his background, mentioned "the passionate love for music" he had had since a child, and related that he had spent entire days improvising at the piano. Mention was made as well of August Schumann (and his plans for his son to study with Weber), Schumann's university years, the difficult decision to abandon law, and present study with Wieck.

At that point Schumann expressed his dissatisfaction with Wieck in some detail. According to Schumann, Wieck appeared to be uninterested in touch or fingering, and paid little attention to whether Schumann played well or poorly. What mattered to Wieck, Schumann wrote, was that the performance be "spirited and in the style of Paganini." As a result, what was lacking was a focus on the rudimentary mechanics of piano playing. Schumann felt that he was being misdirected, was allowed little opportunity to develop, and consequently had little to show for his study. He concluded by asking Hummel to be his teacher, and as an example of his work enclosed a solo selection from a piano concerto in F major that he had been composing.

How valid was Schumann's criticism of Wieck? From what is known of Wieck's teaching, that he ignored the mechanics of piano technique appears doubtful—remember that he initially had Schumann practicing simple finger exercises. But because Schumann was now a more advanced student and because Wieck was an admirer of Field's "singing tone," perhaps bel canto had assumed priority at the expense of "mechanics." Curiously, what Schumann singled out as being emphasized by Wieck—"spirited" performances—was more characteristic of the imagination and lively temperament of Schumann that Wieck was attempting to curb. The reference to Paganini is also somewhat suspicious. Schumann admired Paganini; he was within a few years to base two of his own compositions on Paganini's *Caprices*. It is difficult to believe, then, that in 1830 Schumann would not have been elated to have been able to perform "in the manner of Paganini." But Hummel, as the leading representative of an older school, would have sympathized with Schumann's complaints. Much of Schumann's letter is best seen in that light.

One would imagine that Hummel would have been pleased to accept that rare pupil, eager to work on the comparatively dry aspects of technique, and in no hurry to emulate Paganini. But Schumann received no response from Hummel, and wrote to him again on 25 April 1832, enclosing copies of his first two published compositions, the *Abegg Variations* op. 1 and *Papillons* op. 2. Hummel finally responded with a brief critique of the works in a letter dated 24 May 1832. Two days later Schumann wrote to his mother, and gave her Hummel's reaction to his compositions: "I have examined your two recent works with interest," Schumann quoted Hummel as writing, "and am delighted with your lively talent. Let me point out in particular that at times there is a too rapid change of harmony, etc. Also you seem somewhat too often to surrender yourself to your distinctive originality. I would not like, out of habit, for this to become your style, for it is not compatible with the beauty, freedom, and clarity of a well-planned composition."[6] Schumann did not mention to his mother that he had sent the compositions to Hummel, preferring to have her believe that his fame was growing and that Hummel's comments were unsolicited.

---

[6] Letter to Christiane Schumann of 26 May 1832 in *JgBr*, p. 179.

But in his letter Schumann presented to his mother a version of Hummel's criticism that had been both edited and altered, in the process creating a far more favorable impression than Hummel had intended. Added by Schumann was Hummel's supposed reference to "your distinctive" originality, and omitted from it was Hummel's observation that he had found Schumann's originality to be "somewhat bizarre."[7] The "etc." strategically placed by Schumann replaced a statement by Hummel in which he explained that the rapid harmonic changes in Schumann's compositions would make them less "intelligible."[8] Although to his mother Schumann presented himself as thoroughly content with Hummel's response, the alterations to the letter reveal that he did have misgivings. At this stage of his career, nothing could have been further from his mind than Hummel's ideal of the "clarity of a well-planned composition." On the contrary, in works such as *Papillons* Schumann seemed to revel in mystification.

No additional mention is found in Schumann's correspondence of studying with Hummel. But that did not deter him from considering teachers other than Wieck. In the same letter to his mother in which he presented to her his expurgated account of Hummel's criticism, Schumann discussed his preference—without giving any reason—of now going to Vienna to study. In his diary he noted with enthusiasm: "To Vienna, to Vienna, where my Schubert and Beethoven are at rest: the decision is made."[9] This was an idea that he had had earlier, and one to which he was to return to as late as December 1832—a year of study in Vienna (supposedly with Ignaz Moscheles) in order to add the finishing touches to his skills as a pianist. But this was even more far-fetched than studying with Hummel. Moscheles had few pupils. Moreover, since 1825 he had been living not in Vienna, but in London.

Despite his preferences, Schumann now attempted to make the best of his situation with Wieck. On his birthday in June 1832, Schumann informed Wieck that although he was now entering his twenty-third

---

[7] Wolfgang Boetticher, ed., *Briefe und Gedichte aus dem Album Robert und Clara Schumanns* (Leipzig, 1981), p. 91.

[8] *Ibid.*

[9] Entry of 27 May in *Tgb I*, p. 399.

year, in reality it was "only my second"—a flattering reference to the supposed significance of his study with Wieck.[10] But despite Schumann's honeyed words, he increasingly was viewing Wieck in a hostile manner. He came to believe that Wieck's relationship with Clara was motivated not by either love for Clara or love for music, but rather by love for money. "Meister Allesgeld [Master Moneyhungry]" is the name Schumann created for him in his diary.[11] At one point after seeing Wieck lose his temper, throw his son Alwin to the floor and pull his hair (Alwin had not played well during a lesson with his father), Schumann asked himself: "Am I living among human beings?"[12] "Each day," Schumann wrote in May 1832, "Wiek [sic] seems to me to be duller, more insipid, and more arrogant."[13] As Schumann became dejected both by his relationship with Wieck and slow progress, for a time music itself lost its attractiveness to him. "Music," he wrote in the diary, "how loathsome you are! I hate the very sight of you!"[14]

Schumann's study of music theory was not progressing much better than his study of the piano. This aspect of Schumann's instruction was required by Wieck; he viewed a background in music theory as essential to the development of a musician. Schumann chose to study with Heinrich Dorn, only four years older than Schumann, but music director of the Hoftheater. Study with Dorn began in July 1831 and lasted until the spring of 1832. In later years, Dorn had nothing but praise for Schumann's industry: "An indefatigable worker; if I gave him a single example to work on, he would always do more."[15] But Dorn felt that Schumann had a great deal to learn: "The first four-part chorale—which he had to do for me as an indication of his knowledge of harmony—broke all the rules of part-writing."[16]

Schumann's initial impression of Dorn was not favorable: "I will

---

[10] Letter of 8 June 1832 in *JgBr*, p. 181.
[11] Entry of 13 October 1831 in *Tgb I*, p. 371.
[12] Entry of 21 August 1831 in *Ibid.*, p. 364.
[13] Entry of 15 May 1832 in *Ibid.*, p. 389.
[14] Entry of 5 June 1831 in *Ibid.*, p. 336.
[15] Letter of 7 September 1856 to Wasielewski in *Eismann*, p. 74.
[16] *Ibid.*

never become any closer to Dorn. He has no feelings."[17] Schumann was impatient, and exasperated by all the rules he was obliged to follow in his exercises. Its dryness must have brought to mind his earlier reaction to the study of law. "I will never be able to get along with Dorn," he wrote in January 1832. "Music to him is a fugue, and he wants me to think the same way. God!"[18] By February, Schumann had progressed to the study of three-voice fugues (their lessons ended prior to the study of canon).

But the relationship between them was not as strained as Schumann had feared. He and Dorn shared similar tastes in music. To both Wieck and Christiane Schumann, he acknowledged that study with Dorn had been helpful and had led to more reflection. It also had led to greater self-confidence. But despite Dorn's later praise of Schumann's hard work, it appears that it was he who broke off the lessons with Schumann, probably because of what he perceived as lack of commitment. If Dorn's later assertions are to be believed—known for his dry sarcasm, he may have been having fun at the expense of Schumann's biographers—it is likely that Schumann's "indefatigable" work was primarily directed toward his compositions. "I think of you nearly every day, often somewhat sadly," Schumann later wrote to Dorn. "I learned in too disorderly a fashion. But I am always thankful; in spite of it all, I learned more than you think" (14 September 1836).

Schumann's primary source of knowledge during this time was what he taught himself. He perused the works of Chopin with care, studying as much as eight hours a day. Bach, some of whose preludes and fugues he had played in Heidelberg, became of increasing importance, and Schumann examined his work in depth. To Kuntsch, he wrote that Bach's *Well-Tempered Clavier* had become his "grammar, and moreover the best."[19] As a continuation of his theory study, after lessons with Dorn had ended Schumann on his own worked in theoretical treatises of Gottfried Weber and Friedrich Wilhelm Marpurg.

But despite Schumann's efforts, personal problems continued to

---

[17] Entry of 30 July in *Tgb I*, p. 358.
[18] Letter of 11 January 1832 to Wieck in *JgBr*, p. 162.
[19] Letter of 27 July 1832 in *Ibid*, p. 187.

complicate his life. As had been the case during the university years, he seemed to be in almost constant need of more money. And his fondness for wine and beer remained keen. The references in his diary to drinking and hangovers greatly diminish after the college years, but Schumann was concerned enough about his reputation to write to his family to state that he had nearly given up drinking beer. He began to perceive some of his past behavior in a different light. No longer was it a question of studying the inspirational effects of inebriation: "I believe that the greatest happiness exists in the purest sobriety. You can not become drunk drinking nectar."[20]

Schumann's friends from both the university years and the early 1830s invariably testified to his good character and upright, moral behavior. To Emil Flechsig, Schumann was "of an altogether noble nature, spotless and pure as a Vestal virgin."[21] But Schumann was not as virtuous as Flechsig maintained. In Schumann's diary for February 1830—not long after what he described as "the most debauched week of my life"—there is a reference to "the whore and Anderson and Braun."[22] On 7 May 1829, the diary reads: "The whores—embraces—lust—my innocence saved by a major coup."[23] Such references testify to Schumann's sexual curiosity and interest, and not explicitly to his experience. But in mid-May 1831 there began to appear in Schumann's diary curt and sometimes cryptic references to "Chr."(whom Schumann later referred to in the diary as "Charitas"). Her true name was Christel (full name not known), and for at least a year, but probably longer, she and Schumann were lovers.

From May until the autumn of 1831, Schumann's diary recounts in a dry manner, but with surprising detail, their physical relationship and his guilt and remorse concerning it. From the autumn of 1831 until November 1838, Schumann did not maintain his diary in the usual detail. For that reason, it is not possible to follow the continuing rela-

---

[20] Entry of 11 May 1831 in *Tgb I*, p. 329.

[21] Emil Flechsig, "Erinnerungen an Robert Schumann," *Neue Zeitschrift für Musik* CXVII (1956), p. 394.

[22] 22 February 1830 in *Tgb I*, p. 228.

[23] *Ibid.*, p. 195.

tionship between Christel and Schumann, nor is it possible to determine when it ended. There are references to her until July 1832, but with less frequency. In the summer of 1834 Schumann was attracted to and in the process of becoming engaged to Ernestine von Fricken, a student of Friedrich Wieck. For him to have continued his relationship with Christel at that time would have been unlikely; in fact, the affair probably ended no later than 1833.

Christel is first mentioned in Schumann's diary on 12 May 1831, but it is clear that their association is not recent. From that time until August she is mentioned at least once and often several times each week. Allusions to their sexual encounters are plain. Schumann was disturbed by the relationship, both by its moral implications and by the physical pleasure he derived from it. There is no mention of Christel's thoughts or her interests; no indication of her personality or temperament. From the diary, it appears that the relationship in Schumann's eyes was one solely of physical attraction. What came to dominate Schumann was a sense of guilt and disgust with himself. "Only guilt gives birth to Nemesis," he wrote in the very first diary entry concerning their relationship.[24] In having an affair he was defying the social and religious standards with which he had been raised. But the artistic implications were perhaps of even greater significance to Schumann. His illicit sexual relationship was not compatible with his artistic idealism.

The following weeks repeatedly revealed Schumann's remorse as the affair continued: "I can hardly be pure/holy anymore"; "I am sinking, sinking back into the old slime. Will no hand come from the clouds to hold me back? I must become that hand"; "Evil days—may God and my heart forgive me!"[25] He tried to find distraction in work: it was during this period that he devoted himself so intently to a study of Chopin. When he had no contact with Christel, Schumann appeared relieved and declared the week "beautiful and nearly completely pure."[26] His despair culminated in an emotional outburst at the end of October: "God! I want to change myself, I swear it to You. Give me

---

[24] 12 May 1831 in *Ibid.*, p. 330.

[25] Entries of 7 June, 20 June, 30 June in *Ibid.*, pp. 338, 344.

[26] 14 August 1831 in *Ibid.*, p. 360.

just one person—only one—on whom I can lay my heart—a sweetheart, a beloved, give me a feminine heart—a feminine heart! I can then become reconciled to myself, to everything!"[27]

To complicate matters, at the time of his tormented relationship with Christel, Schumann developed an irrational fear of contracting cholera. The outbreak of cholera had started in India in the late 1820s and then spread to Russia. In 1831, it arrived in Germany. All of Europe appeared mesmerized by its appearance. Although its devastation was hardly comparable, allusions were made to the Black Death of the Middle Ages. For a time, Schumann was overwhelmed by his fear. Early in September he mentioned fleeing to Rome or Paris—"I have a distressing, somewhat childlike fear of cholera. . . . The thought of dying now, after having lived for twenty years and done nothing but spend money, overwhelms me . . . in short, I am in such a disagreeable state of uneasiness and indecision, that I would prefer to put a bullet in my head."[28] By the end of the month Schumann reported to his mother that he was no longer anxious, but, as late as May 1832, reference was still made to the disease. By then the epidemic had moved further west, and there was little cause for concern.

All of the problems facing Schumann contributed to his condition. He had to contend not just with his fear of cholera, but with his frustrating and, to his mind, mostly profitless study with Wieck. There was as well the dry and forbidding study of music theory, and his tortuous, guilt-ridden relationship with Christel. When he had begun his study with Wieck he could hardly have conceived that so many problems would beset him and that in his own mind so little progress would have been made. Within three years, Wieck had promised to make Schumann into another Moscheles. Instead, Schumann must have felt a sense of desperation as time quickly passed, problems mounted, and a hopeless feeling of isolation increased. "The artist," wrote Schumann in January 1832, "must maintain a sense of balance with the outside world. Otherwise he will go under—like myself."[29]

It was in this state of mind that the most devastating blow of all

---

[27] *Ibid.*, p. 375.

[28] Letter to Julius Schumann in *JgBr*, pp. 148–49.

[29] 5 January 1832 in *Tgb I*, p. 378.

occurred. On 5 April 1833, Schumann wrote to a friend from Heidelberg, Theodor Töpken, describing a problem that had developed: "I have a numb, broken finger on my right hand. . . . I can hardly use the hand at all for playing." Schumann had been aware of the serious nature of the injury for more than a year. But the problem itself had been present even prior to study with Wieck. A diary entry for 26 January 1830 made reference to "my numb finger."[30] Eight months later, in a letter to Dr. Carus, Schumann complained that as a result of practicing, one finger now felt "as if it were broken."[31]

Throughout the month of May 1832, Schumann's diary documented the deteriorating condition of the third (middle) finger. On the 22nd, he pronounced it "incorrigible," and in mid-June, "completely stiff."[32] A visit was made with Wieck to a doctor in Dresden. Herbal bandages were applied and, in an archaic attempt at a cure, Schumann's hand was placed for periods of time into the thoracic or abdominal cavity of a freshly slaughtered cow. In June 1833, as a last resort, a homeopathic cure was attempted, and his diet was regulated. Even an electrical treatment of some kind was adopted in an attempt to cure his condition.

There was no improvement. As a result, in August 1832 Schumann wrote to his mother informing her that there was no longer any reason for him to contemplate continuing piano study in Vienna. He suggested that he would return to the university, this time to study theology. When there was no change in his condition, he wrote in early November to tell her that he was "completely resigned" to his condition, which he now felt was incurable.[33] He announced as well his intention to rest his hand, and take up the study of the cello, which he felt would add another dimension to his musicianship and be valuable in the composition of symphonies. The idea he had previously expressed to her of studying theology he now dismissed as a momentary aberration.

Schumann's hand injury has always been a matter of controversy. How serious was it? What might have caused it? Schumann later stated

---

[30] *Ibid.*, p. 222.

[31] Letter of 25 September 1830 to Dr. Ernst August Carus in Siegfried Kross, ed., *Briefe und Notizen Robert und Clara Schumanns*, 2nd ed. (Bonn, 1982), p. 28.

[32] *Tgb I*, pp. 394, 410.

[33] Letter of 6 November 1832 in *JS*, p. 234.

that the problem first became apparent in October 1831; he attributed it to excessive practicing in the early 1830s when he played the piano "more than six or seven hours a day. A weakness in my right hand, which worsened, obliged me to break off these studies."[34] In 1839, writing to his friend Simonin de Sire, Schumann attributed the problem both to excessive writing and piano playing. Traditionally, however, Schumann's problem has been attributed not to excessive practice but to a mechanical device he himself had constructed and used while practicing. Its purpose was to immobilize one or more of his fingers, in the expectation of creating greater dexterity and strength. Friedrich Wieck appears to have been the original source for this theory; in *Klavier und Gesang* he made reference (Schumann was not mentioned by name) to: "the finger torturer thought up by a famous pupil of mine to the just outrage of his third and fourth fingers, which he fashioned against my wishes and used behind my back."[35] When questioned after her husband's death, Clara Schumann had no recollection of a mechanical device but attributed the problem to excessive use of a dumb keyboard.

Recently discovered contemporary documents—as well as Schumann's diary from the period—have resolved the matter. Schumann's hand injury was clearly a result of the abuse to which he subjected his right hand (according to Schumann's own observations, already weaker than his left) by the use of a mechanical device. It was not an uncommon practice at the time for pianists to use such contraptions. Numerous devices to support the wrists, hands, and fingers were available for purchase. Schumann evidently made his own. In his diary for May 1832, reference is made to a "Cigarrenmechanik," probably Schumann's homemade device (which may have been made from a cigar box).[36] Apparently Schumann had been using either this device or another for years, and was well aware of its possible harmful effect. In writing to Dr. Carus in the autumn of 1830, he traced his nearly "broken" finger to use of a mechanical apparatus, but he continued to use the device long after the problem developed.[37]

---

[34] *Eismann*, p. 77. No date is given for these observations by Schumann.

[35] Friedrich Wieck, *Klavier und Gesang*, trans. and ed. H. Pleasants as *Piano and Song* (Stuyvesant, NY, 1988), p. 73.

[36] 7 May 1832 in *Tgb I*, p. 386.

[37] Letter of 25 September 1830 in Kross, p. 28.

In 1841, during a physical examination to determine his suitability for military service, Dr. Moritz E. Reuter (a good friend of Schumann) concluded that the middle and index fingers of the right hand were damaged, and attributed the problem—presumably based on information supplied by Schumann himself—to a mechanical device that had been intended to strengthen them and that "held these fingers strongly towards the back of the hand."[38] As a result Schumann could not use the middle finger when playing the piano, "the index finger somewhat, and cannot grasp an object firmly."[39] In fact, this condition may help explain why later in life Schumann had difficulty holding a baton while conducting.

After November 1832—the point at which Schumann claimed to be "completely resigned" to his injury—no further consideration was given to becoming a virtuoso. Nor was any mention made, as had been previously agreed, of returning to the study of law if his piano study did not work out. By this time his family, too, had become resigned—resigned to whatever course of action Schumann might prefer. Emotionally and physically drained by the vicissitudes of Schumann's career, at times they reacted with indifference. At one point, Schumann even asked his mother to write to Wieck, who had expressed surprise at never receiving from Schumann's family any inquiries concerning his progress.

Throughout the entire episode, Schumann exhibited unusual coolness and composure. The full implications of his loss only appeared to strike him later when, little known as a composer, he felt frustrated by his inability to perform his own compositions in public: "Often I have cried to heaven and asked, 'My God, why have you done this to *me*?' "[40] But at the time of his injury, noticeably absent was the sense of panic or despair that—given his previous behavior—might have been expected. Schumann may very well have felt relieved. The injury to his hand simplified matters considerably. Now he could focus his attention on writing music. Schumann's hand injury merely provided him

---

[38] Report quoted in Arnfried Edler, *Robert Schumann und seine Zeit* (Bonn, 1982), p. 297.

[39] *Ibid.* The injury did not actually prevent Schumann from playing the piano. Reuter no doubt exaggerated the extent of Schumann's disability in order to present as convincing a case as possible of Schumann's inability to serve in the military.

[40] Letter of 3 December 1838 to Clara Wieck in *Cl/Rob I*, p. 307.

with the excuse to do what he had long desired. In that sense, it was a blessing. Quiet and introverted by nature, it would have been a challenge for him to promote himself. Dorn even commented that Schumann "lacked the boldness" for public performances.[41]

Beginning in April 1832, Schumann had been trying with little success to establish independence and promote himself as a composer. In November 1831, his op. 1, the *Abegg Variations*, appeared in print. The pride he felt in its appearance he shared with family and college friends. During the winter of the same year, he started work on what was intended as the first movement of a sonata for piano to be dedicated to Moscheles (later published as the Allegro op. 8). During 1832 Schumann devoted his attention to composing as he never had before; he completed two substantial works: the Paganini Etudes op. 3 and the *Intermezzi* op. 4. And he discussed his compositions with those whom he felt were influential in the musical world, including Ludwig Rellstab, editor of the music journal *Iris im Gebiet der Tonkunst* (1830–41), Ignaz Castelli, editor of the Viennese *Allgemeiner Musikalischer Anzeiger* (1829–40), and Gottfried Weber, editor of *Cäcilia* (1824–39).

Most significant of all at this time was Schumann's determination to compose a symphony. With the exception of about a dozen songs composed prior to going to college, all of Schumann's previous works had focused on the piano. Writing a symphony would accomplish a great deal, Schumann hoped, in establishing a name for himself as a composer. He worked on the symphony from October 1832 until May 1833, and found it to be challenging. Most frustrating was the orchestration, for Schumann's knowledge of it was limited. Eventually he contacted Christian Müller, conductor of the Euterpe concert series, for assistance. It had become a matter of some urgency: a performance of the first movement was arranged for 18 November in Zwickau, at which Clara Wieck was also to play (as part of a small concert tour including visits to Zwickau, Altenburg, and Schneeberg). Here was an opportunity that Schumann as a youth had probably dreamed about—his own symphony performed before friends and family in the community in which he had been raised. It was as well an opportunity publicly to exhibit both his ability and the results of the past two years, in its way a justification of

[41] *Eismann*, p. 74.

his abandonment of law. But it did not turn out as Schumann had hoped. While Clara was a success, the symphony was not; according to Wieck, the audience simply did not understand it.

Schumann used the experience to make changes in the first movement and work on a second movement, all in preparation for other performances, first in Schneeberg (probably 18 February) and then in Leipzig (29 April). But these performances were not successful either. To his mother, Schumann wrote that discerning critics had praised the symphony—but in truth there had not been enough praise, and there was no interest in performing the work again. He laid the symphony aside, and never completed it. The symphony's failure—coupled with the many personal and professional complications of the previous two years—might have convinced one less determined to abandon music as a career. There is no indication that such a thought occurred to Schumann. He continued to write music: not long after the performance of his symphony he composed the *Impromptus* op. 5. But there can be little doubt that these difficulties discouraged him and may have taken their toll on his health. His diary reveals that for much of July and August he was disconsolate and ill with an intermittent fever (possibly malaria).

By nature Schumann was soft-spoken, quiet, and reserved. Writing in 1856 to their mutual friend Emil Flechsig, Eduard Röller (a friend from Schumann's university years) recalled that it was difficult to say much about Schumann: "He wasn't open or outspoken enough totally to reveal himself."[42] It was a temperament that lent itself well to solitude. During these years in Leipzig Schumann had few close friends, and spent much time alone. The idea of solitude as a source of inspiration was deeply ingrained in the public mind during the nineteenth century, and one with which Schumann was familiar. In an essay from his last years at the Lyceum, Schumann had proclaimed: "Solitude nurtures all great spirits."[43]

Christiane Schumann was well aware of her son's fondness for solitude, and more aware than he of its dangers. "I hope you are associating with people," she wrote in January 1832. "You can not and must not

---

[42] Quoted in Wilhelm Joseph von Wasielewski, *Schumanniana* (Bonn, 1883), p. 80.

[43] From the essay, "Einfluss der Einsamkeit auf die Bildung des Geistes und die Veredelung des Herzens." Excerpt included in *Tgb I*, p. 77.

isolate yourself."[44] But all too often Schumann disregarded her advice, resulting in the lack of a "sense of balance with the outside world" that he had noted in his diary that same month. As a result, Schumann's perception of himself and perspective of the world around him were prone to distortion. He was inclined as well to worry about the state of his health, at times—as has been seen with his obsession with cholera—to the point of irrationality. His sense of isolation, anxiety over the future, and increasing frustration with the lack of recognition accorded his work all contributed in the autumn of 1833 to what he described as "torment from the most frightful melancholy . . . the idea that I was going mad became an obsession."[45]

Events came to a head during the night of 17/18 October. Schumann remembered it as "the most frightful night of my life."[46] What actually happened remains unclear. Schumann's account of the incident lacks detail, and was written five years after the event. But even with the lapse of time, his fear and horror of what occurred remain striking. At the same time, his reaction contains a curious sense of detachment, as if the horrors of that night had occurred to a character in a work of fiction by Jean Paul or Hoffmann, where visions of madness are common enough. Schumann's first biographer, Wilhelm Joseph von Wasielewski, reported that in a fit of despair Schumann wanted to hurl himself out of a window, but others informed him that was not the case. Whether true or not, after this event Schumann exhibited a fear of heights. He soon moved from the fourth floor, which he "could no longer bear," to the first.[47]

What appeared to have precipitated the incident was the imminent death of Schumann's brother Julius (from tuberculosis: he died on 18 November at the age of twenty-eight), coupled with the death of Schumann's sister-in-law, Rosalie (Carl's wife). She had been ill for much of the summer apparently from malaria and died on 17 October. Schumann had been very close to Rosalie, a trusted confidante with whom

---

[44] Letter of 3 January 1832 in Eugenie Schumann, *Robert Schumann. Ein Lebensbild meines Vaters* (Leipzig, 1931), p. 143.
[45] Recollected in November 1838. *Tgb I*, p. 419.
[46] Ibid.
[47] Ibid.

he often shared his plans for the future. He had also been godfather to Rosalie and Carl's son, Robert, born in 1831 (and whose death on 4 June 1832 may also have contributed to Schumann's state). He described Rosalie as "unforgettable... we were of the same age [Rosalie was actually two years older]. She was more to me than a sister, but it was not a question of us being in love" (11 February 1838).

To Clara (to whom he was then engaged), he recounted not what had happened the night of 17/18 October, but how he had felt during it: "During the night of October 17 to 18, 1833 the most terrifying thought that anyone can have—the most frightful punishment of heaven—'losing one's mind.' It took possession of me with such intensity, that all consolation, all prayer were powerless" (11 February 1838). He confessed that he had thought of suicide, and visited a physician (probably his friend, Reuter).

The effects of the night lingered, and his condition worsened. Now in a state of severe depression, he informed his mother that he would be unable to travel to Zwickau. The death of Julius had affected him so that

> I was hardly more than a statue, without coldness, without warmth. Only by means of hard work did life return again, bit by bit. But I am still so fearful and upset, that I can not sleep alone... I don't have the courage to travel to Zwickau alone out of fear that something could happen to me. Violent congestion of my blood, unspeakable fear, shortness of breath, and fainting fits alternate rapidly, although less now than in the preceding days. If you had any idea of how deeply melancholy has taken hold of me, you would surely forgive me for not having written to you.[48]

To his mother, he presented what he felt was the cause of his malady: "I have never known sorrow [presumably, the deaths of Julius and Rosalie]. Now it has come to me, but I could not bear it, and it has crushed me a thousandfold."[49] But Schumann had "known sorrow" before—the deaths of his father and sister. Although he may not have realized it at the time, he was later able to describe to Clara the true reason for his collapse. He attributed it both to the lack of recognition for his

---

[48] Letter of 27 November 1833 in *JS*, pp. 242–43.
[49] Letter to his mother of 4 January 1834 in *Ibid.*, p. 243.

compositions, and to the injury to his hand. But in addition it was the loss (in the death of Rosalie) of someone whom he loved deeply and who had become an essential support. Discouraged and exhausted by the struggle to achieve success first as a pianist and then as a composer, Schumann's collapse was a reaction to what had become a despairing and seemingly hopeless situation.

The one consolation afforded to Schumann was the support of friends. And by a stroke of good fortune, in December 1833 Schumann met Ludwig Schuncke, a young musician recently arrived in Leipzig. The beneficial effect of Schuncke on Schumann cannot be overemphasized. He was to become, in an uncommonly short time, not only Schumann's closest friend but probably the closest friend he was ever to have. Schuncke was a pianist and composer, at the time attempting to make a name for himself as a virtuoso. He possessed the training and background that Schumann lacked, including study in both Vienna and Paris. Schuncke was extremely gifted and at the outset of a promising career (his Piano Sonata op. 3—dedicated to Schumann—is, in fact, an extraordinary work), and Schumann felt he had discovered in him a kindred spirit. They lived in the same house and spent much time together, going for walks, ice-skating, and performing and discussing music.

It was through Schuncke that Schumann soon came to know the Voigts, Carl and Henriette. They were both music lovers, and their home became a popular meeting place for musicians in Leipzig. Schumann later wrote: "Merely to step into their house made an artist feel at home. Hanging above the piano were portraits of the great masters, and a select musical library was at your disposal. It was as if the musician were master of the house, and music the supreme goddess of it."[50] Carl Voigt admired Beethoven to such an extent that he made an anonymous donation to the Gewandhaus Orchestra to assure performances of the Ninth Symphony. Henriette was a gifted pianist who took lessons from Schuncke, and in Berlin had studied with Ludwig Berger, who had also taught Mendelssohn. Her diary—excerpts from which Schumann published after her death—reveals her to have been a passionate and sensitive musician. Schumann soon came to refer to her as "Eleonore" (a

---

[50] "Erinnerung an eine Freundin" (1839) in GS I, p. 446.

reference to the heroine of Beethoven's *Fidelio*) and his "Soul in A flat Major." In many ways, Henriette Voigt became to Schumann what Agnes Carus had been earlier. And although there are no references in his diary to romantic dreams about her, it would be surprising if at times he did not think of her in a similar fashion. She felt a particular attraction to Schumann's music, later writing poetry inspired by the *Fantasiestücke* op. 12 and the *Kinderszenen* op. 15.

If friends provided the support and distraction Schumann needed during this difficult period in his life, none was of greater personal significance to him than Clara Wieck. At first simple and direct, the relationship between them developed into one of considerable complexity. From the beginning, Schumann appears to have been enchanted with her, and fascinated by what he perceived as her dual nature: the child, and the mature, gifted musician. He would tell her ghost stories and go on walks with her.

> [Clara] is just the same—wild and enthusiastic—she runs and jumps and plays like a child and then all at once says the most thoughtful things. . . . As we were coming home together from Connewitz the other day (we take walks for two or three hours nearly every day) I heard her say to herself: 'Oh, how happy I am! How happy!' Who would not enjoy hearing that! On the same road there are a great many rocks in the middle of the footpath. As it often happens that when I am talking with someone I have a tendency to look up rather than down, she always goes behind me and tugs gently on my coat at each stone so that I don't fall. Meanwhile she stumbles over them herself.[51]

It was in music that their relationship first began to take on greater significance. Schumann was one of the earliest champions of Chopin, and both he and Clara were particularly fond of Chopin's *Variations on Mozart's 'La ci darem'* op. 2. Schumann composed a set of studies based on it; Chopin's op. 2 was an important piece in Clara's repertory. Schumann made the following suggestion:

> Tomorrow precisely at eleven o'clock I will play the adagio from Chopin's Variations and at the same time I shall think of you very intently, exclusively

---

[51] Letter to Christiane Schumann of 28 June 1833 in *JS*, p. 238.

of you. Now my request is that you should do the same, so that we may see and meet each other in spirit. The place will probably be over the Thomaspförtchen, where our doubles will encounter one another. (13 July 1833)

The mention of "doubles" ("doppelgänger") was a reference to the tales Schumann used to entertain the Wieck children, some of which had as a basis the doppelgänger stories of Hoffmann and others. But the whimsical humor in Schumann's letter—humor that appears to have been added as an afterthought in an attempt to diminish the romantic tone of his suggestion—should not detract from the seriousness of purpose. Schumann at the time was twenty-three; Clara had not yet turned fourteen. Despite the disparity in their ages, the early nineteenth century offers a number of celebrated romances of a similar nature (often ill-fated), in particular Novalis's love for the twelve-year-old Sophie von Kühn and Hoffmann's love for the fourteen-year-old Julia Marc.[52]

Most symbolic of all was Schumann's reaction to one of Clara's compositions, the *Romance varié* op. 3, a work dedicated to him. Early in August Clara sent a copy of her newly printed *Romance* to Schumann. In acknowledging the dedication, he wrote (rather formally, but with clear intent): "I would like to speak to you of the hope I have that the union of our names on the title page, may become a union of our views and ideas at a later time" (2 August 1833). Schumann further responded with a composition of his own, the *Impromptus sur un thème de Clara Wieck* op. 5, using as its basis the theme from Clara's *Romance*. To the theme itself, Schumann added his own bass line, and the result was a series of variations on both the theme and the bass. It was dedicated to Clara's father and presented to him on his birthday, 18 August 1833. Nine months earlier, during the performance in Zwickau of Schumann's symphony, Clara had found herself with Christiane Schumann as her son passed by. "Someday you must marry my Robert," she reportedly told Clara.[53] In Schumann's mind, perhaps unknowingly

---

[52] In an early biography of Schumann published in 1882, Philipp Spitta wrote that a "special affection [between Robert and Clara] first was apparent in the spring of 1836." In her copy of the biography, Clara corrected the statement: "Already in 1833." Nancy B. Reich, *Clara Schumann: The Artist and the Woman* (Ithaca, NY, 1985), p. 66.

[53] Litzmann I, p. 54.

at first, it is clear that Clara was becoming the ideal, the "feminine heart" which he had been desperately seeking. "I often think of you," Schumann wrote to her on 11 January 1832, "not as a brother thinks of a sister, nor as a boyfriend thinks of a girlfriend, but as a pilgrim before a distant shrine."

CHAPTER 5

Schumann's Compositions Prior to 1834

> Let all that is marvelous fly neither as a bird of the day nor as one of the night, but as a butterfly at twilight.
> —Jean Paul, *Introduction to Aesthetics*

According to his own recollections, Schumann began to compose when he was seven or eight (not long after beginning to study the piano). None of these earliest works, which he described as dances, is known to have survived. A setting for voices and orchestra of Psalm 150 followed at the age of twelve. On an elaborate, handmade title page in childish handwriting, Breitkopf & Härtel is listed as its publisher. In 1850, Schumann described it as his "oldest, completely finished work," but dismissed it as a juvenile attempt.[1] Not long after the psalm, Schumann began work on an opera, but composed only an overture and a peasant chorus.

Schumann's first work of substance was a collection of about a dozen songs (two of them incomplete) composed in 1827 and 1828 and not published during his lifetime. Eleven of them have since appeared in print. Three have texts by Schumann: "Lied für ★★★" (c. 1827), "Sehnsucht" (June 1827), and "Hirtenknabe" (August 1828), the latter two using the pseudonym Ebert (not "Ekert," as erroneously published). In

---

[1] *Tgb* II, p. 402.

addition, there are individual settings of Byron, J. G. Jacobi, Goethe, and five of Justinus Kerner.

Several of the Kerner lieder were sent to Gottlob Wiedebein in July 1828 in order to provide him with a basis to evaluate Schumann's ability as a composer. Wiedebein's tactful response revealed both a kind and generous spirit, for there are enough inept and cumbersome passages in the songs for him to have written a fairly uncharitable evaluation. The melodic line of Kerner's "Kurzes Erwachen" (29 June 1828), for example, is simplistic, and not idiomatic for the voice. Problems also occasionally occur with the piano accompaniment (the ungainly modulation from D flat major to F major in Kerner's "An Anna"; 31 July 1828).

These are flaws attributable to Schumann's inexperience. More disturbing are indications of his inability, or lack of interest, in tailoring the music to the sentiments of the text. "Sehnsucht" provides a notable instance. The work itself—with a Schubertian melody and simple arpeggios in the piano accompaniment—is pleasing. But the introductory four measures of block chords are crude. Their sole function seems to be to establish the tonality. There are aspects of the songs that are effective, particularly when Schumann's lack of formal training is taken into account. His setting of Byron's "Die Weinende" (July 1827; "I Saw Thee Weep" from the *Hebrew Melodies*) is perhaps the best of the series. The introduction, beginning on a V 6/5 of ii and moving to a diminished seventh, is adventurous, admirably setting the scene for Byron's poignant text.

The songs were composed at the start of Schumann's infatuation with Jean Paul. Although he did not set any of Jean Paul's texts to music, he felt no hesitation in admitting the significant effect Jean Paul had on him as a composer. In the 1840s, looking back on his earlier compositions, he wrote to a friend that the two greatest influences on his work had been Bach and Jean Paul, an influence so obvious in Schumann's mind that he added: "which you would probably notice without my pointing it out to you" (5 May 1843). From Jean Paul, Schumann claimed to "have learned more about counterpoint than from my music teacher" (15 March 1839)—a remark to which Dorn would not have taken kindly, but one that reveals much about Schumann's view of musical academicism. In the compositions created prior to 1834, the influence of Bach is not yet a predominant element, but the influence of Jean Paul is profound.

There are four distinctive traits in the music composed by Schumann during the 1830s, which appear to owe much to his reading of Jean Paul. Several of these concepts—the last one in particular—are expanded and used with greater frequency in the piano compositions of the latter 1830s:

1. The use of brief, almost aphoristic musical statements. Much of Jean Paul's work reveals a fondness for short, pithy statements, whether within the text itself or as asides in footnotes. This was an aspect of Jean Paul's style—at times he referred to them as polymeters—that particularly appealed to Schumann.
2. A love for mystery and concealed meaning. This is a notable characteristic of Jean Paul, and one frequently encountered in his novels, whether it be the long-concealed true identity of characters (such as Albano in *Titan*) or mysterious machinations within the plot (such as that of the Death's Head Monk, also in *Titan*). In Schumann's music, this has its counterpart in the enigmatic Countess Abegg of op. 1, the concealed programs behind works such as *Papillons*, the fondness for musical puzzles (such as spelling words with pitches), and the "borrowings" from Beethoven, Clara Wieck, and other composers, which often served as a cryptic form of communication.
3. The quotation of musical ideas from previous compositions in new ones. There are two notable instances: the quotation of a theme from *Papillons* in *Carnaval* (its appearance marked by Schumann in the score) and, in a similar manner, the quotation of the A-B-E-G-G theme from op. 1 in the *Intermezzi* op. 4 (but not noted in the score). Related to these is the quotation of a folk tune (the "Grossvater Tanz") in opp. 2, 4, and 9 (indicated solely in the score of op. 9 as a "Thème du XVIIème Siècle"). Schumann seems to be taking his cue from Jean Paul; in totally unrelated novels, offhanded references to the plots and characters of earlier works are common. This was an attempt by Jean Paul, as it probably was by Schumann, on the one hand to bind his oeuvre together, and on the other hand, by means of romantic irony to shatter the illusion of reality created by the work.
4. The often abrupt juxtaposition of grotesque humor with elements of

profound sentiment. Humor fascinated Jean Paul; a substantial part of his *Introduction to Aesthetics* (1804; revised edition, 1813) was devoted to it. Jean Paul explored an "annihilating or infinite idea of humor," describing "humor as inverse sublimity."[2] And he pointed out that such instances of humor were present in music. Schumann was familiar with Jean Paul's text; his diary shows he was reading the *Aesthetics* in September 1828. In Schumann's music, humor is often created by contrast—startling and dramatic.

Schumann was able to justify as well his fondness for improvisation by reference to Jean Paul. "In improvisation music brings together all that is sublime.... It is the same in Jean Paul's polymeters.... Freedom is always more original and spirited than constraint."[3] Schumann's ability in improvisation attracted attention. In Heidelberg, this contributed considerably to his musical reputation. Theodore Töpken, a student at Heidelberg who played occasional duets with Schumann, recalled that while improvising "ideas would flow out of [Schumann] in an abundance without end."[4] At the time, improvisation was essential to Schumann as a composer. Writing to his mother in March 1834, he dismissed concern for his hand injury, pointing out that it did not prevent him from composing, nor did "it bother me while improvising."[5]

Schumann's improvisational skills took more tangible form in the music he composed in the late 1820s and 1830s, especially in dances for piano. After the completion of the lieder, in August and September of 1828 he composed eight *Polonaises* for piano four hands (WoO 20). With the exception of the fourth in the set, there were *galant* titles for each: "La douleur," "La belle patrie," "Paix et douleur," "La réconciliation," "L'aimable," "La fantaisie," and "La sérénade." Their inspiration can be found in the four-hand polonaises (particularly *Sechs Polonaisen* op. 61 D. 824, c. 1825, and *Vier Polonaisen* op. 75 D. 599, c. 1818) of Schubert—Schumann's favorite composer at the time. They were performed privately on several occasions with Töpken while in

---

[2] Jean Paul Richter, *Horn of Oberon. Jean Paul Richter's School for Aesthetics*, trans. Margaret R. Hale (Detroit, 1973), p. 91.
[3] 13 August 1828 in *Tgb I*, p. 113.
[4] From a letter of 30 September 1856 by Töpken to Wasielewski in *Eismann*, p. 55.
[5] Letter of 19 March 1834 in *JS*, p. 248.

Heidelberg. At their best, they are successful Hausmusik: light, enjoyable, and unpretentious.

After completion of the *Polonaises*, in December 1828 Schumann began work on his most ambitious composition to date: a Piano Quartet in C minor (WoO 32). It was inspired by the music of Prince Louis Ferdinand, whose chamber music Schumann's college chamber group was examining at the time. Before beginning the quartet, Schumann composed a set of piano variations (four hands) using as a basis a theme of Louis Ferdinand, a work now lost. Louis Ferdinand's own Piano Quartet op. 6 served as a model for Schumann's quartet.

He worked on the quartet until 21 March 1829, and as he did so, movements were performed by the chamber group to a select audience, including Wieck. It is a modest accomplishment, displaying the limitations of his musical knowledge and a resulting lack of craftsmanship. The sonata structure of the first movement is as painfully evident as if it were taken from a textbook. The third movement (Andante) seems archaic, and is in an almost *galant* style, decorative and ornamented. In all, there is a striving for dramatic effects—a grandiose fortissimo opening, tremolos in the development of the first movement, a heroic close from minor to major in the concluding fourth movement.

Perhaps most successful is the second movement, a scherzo. It was a movement to which Schumann attached particular significance. Writing in 1846 he described the trio of the scherzo—unusually lyrical—as "*romantic* . . . a new poetic life appeared to disclose itself to me."[6] But too much meaning should not be attached to Schumann's words. His diary reveals that he reacted in a similar manner to his unfinished F major Piano Concerto.

Beginning in the winter of 1828, Schumann turned from chamber music to music for solo piano, and sketched and completed several works: a *Fantasie on "An Alexis"* (probably the *Canon on "An Alexis"* WoO 4) and *Variations on Weber's Invitation to the Dance* (both December), an early version of what was to become the Toccata op. 7 (December and January 1829), as well as what he later described as "short pieces" (probably dances) and "etudes" (both 1829).[7]

---

[6] *Tgb II*, p. 402.
[7] From the project book in *Eismann*, p. 81.

In 1830, as his adoption of music as a career became firm, he turned to compositions of greater dimension. While a student at Heidelberg, he began a Piano Concerto in F major and continued work on it over the next two years. It was not his first attempt at writing a concerto. A diary entry for 16 December 1828 makes reference to a piano concerto in E flat major (sketches for this, as well as for one in C minor, undated, have survived). The F major concerto, however, was of particular significance to Schumann. A sketchbook reveals that he intended dedicating the work to Hummel, with whom at the time he hoped to study. The concerto remained unfinished, some work being done on all three movements, but only the solo part of the first movement was completed.

A number of other piano works from the early 1830s either remain as sketches, or, when completed, were regarded by Schumann as unsuitable for publication: *Exercice fantastique* (January and July 1832; originally conceived in April 1829), *Etude fantastique en double-sons* (May 1830 and July 1832),[8] Variations on an Original Theme in G Major (1831), Studies Based on Chopin's op. 2 (1831–2), *Fandango* (also referred to by Schumann as *Fantaisie rhapsodique* and *Rhapsodie musicale*, August and September 1832; portions were later included in the first movement of the First Piano Sonata op. 11), Variations on the *Sehnsuchtswaltz* (1833),[9] Etudes on the Allegretto from Beethoven's Symphony No. 7 (WoO 31, 1833), and Variations on Chopin's Nocturne op. 15 no. 3 (*c.* 1835). These compositions reveal an increasing concern both with virtuosity and with the theme-and-variation principle—interests expected in pianists of the day. Schumann's originality is seen in the reference to the imaginative ("fantastique"), and in the not particularly fashionable composers selected for the variations: Schubert, Beethoven, and Chopin. Of significance in light of the path Schumann was to adopt later is the reliance on musical rather than literary models. Stylistic associations can be traced to the work of composers admired by Schumann (such as Louis Ferdinand, Beethoven, and Schubert), and

---

[8] Probably the same work listed in Schumann's diary as an *Exercice en doubles sons* (*Tgb I*, p. 418). This (and the *Exercice fantastique*) appears to refer to the work that later became the Toccata op. 7.

[9] As early as March 1829, Schumann's diary notes improvisation on the *Sehnsuchtswaltz* (*Tgb I*, p. 177). The waltz (D. 365) was composed by Schubert in 1816.

thematic material is often borrowed to serve as the basis and provide inspiration for Schumann's own work.

Schumann considered a variety of projects. In 1831, he contemplated writing separate sets of variations for piano, based on Paganini's "bell" theme (from the B minor Violin Concerto) and the march from Weber's *Preciosa*. But it was in 1832, at a time of increased problems with his right hand, that a large number of ideas for piano works were conceived, including the *Fandango*, Three Satirical Fugues (probably intended as a comment on his study of music theory), Eight Pictures Based on Beethoven's Symphonies (*Florestaniana*; perhaps the Etudes on Beethoven's Symphony No. 7 were part of this scheme), a *Burla* (later revised and published as no. 12 in op. 124), and an *Idyll*.

Given the many pieces Schumann sketched or contemplated writing (and taking into consideration the tribulations of his personal life), the actual number of pieces completed to his satisfaction during the years 1830 to 1833 is impressive: the *Abegg Variations* op. 1, *Papillons* op. 2, two sets of Paganini etudes (op. 3 and op. 10), the *Intermezzi* op. 4, the Allegro op. 8, the Toccata op. 7, and the *Impromptus* op. 5.

Schumann's first published work, the *Abegg Variations* op. 1, appeared in November 1831. Paris was both the musical capital of Europe and the center of piano virtuosity, so it is appropriate that Schumann's title was in French: *Thème sur le nom "Abegg" varié pour le pianoforte*. Theme and variations were the standard production of piano virtuosos, whether technically demanding for their own concert performances, or simplified to satisfy the public's demand for pleasing melody. More than likely, the theme would be a well-known tune from an opera by Rossini, or another popular composer of Italian opera or opéra-comique. It was in the choice of theme that from the start Schumann revealed both his originality and the direction much of his music was to take in the 1830s.

Rather than choosing a theme from Italian opera (for which, in general, Schumann had little regard) or from German opera (one of Weber's works, which he admired, would have been a possibility), Schumann went against the grain by selecting a theme of his own composition. Even more curious was the nature of the theme itself (Ex. 5.1), fragmentary, not at all lyrical, and based on the letters of the alphabet, spelling the name A-B-E-G-G (sounding in the German musical system as A-B flat-E-G-G). The idea of using musical pitches to

EX. 5.1

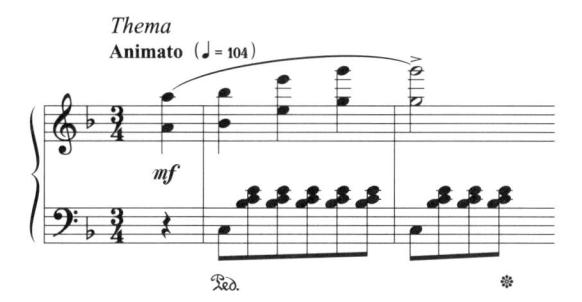

Thema
Animato (♩ = 104)

spell words was not Schumann's invention. The most notable previous instance was probably Bach's introduction into the *Art of Fugue* of a subject using B-A-C-H (H is B natural in the German system). But the approach greatly appealed to Schumann, probably because it permitted him to combine his love of literature (letters becoming sounds) with that of music (sounds becoming words). At the same time it allowed him to indulge in his love of mystification.

Schumann took unusual care with the *Abegg Variations*, requesting that the work appear before 18 November, the birthdate of the dedicatee, Countess Pauline von Abegg. But there was no countess. As Schumann confessed to Töpken, he had created her: "I had reasons for this mystification, which I will share with you later" (5 April 1833). To his mother's inquiry concerning the mysterious countess, he jokingly ruled out any possibility of a romantic attachment, describing the countess as "an old maid of twenty-six, clever and musical, but sharp and ugly."[10] Schumann's perception of the whole affair is best seen in an entry he made in a friend's album prior to leaving Heidelberg. He wrote the Abegg theme, and underneath it the words: "Je ne suis qu'un songe"("I am but a dream")—a quotation from Jean Paul's *Titan* in which Liana obliquely informs Albano that she is but a copy of Idoine, the woman whom he eventually will love.

While the countess might have been a creation of Schumann, the name was not. Meta Abegg (1810–34) was a beautiful and accomplished pianist whom Schumann had met in Mannheim in 1830 while a student

---

[10] Letter of 25 November 1831 in *JS*, p. 224.

in Heidelberg. Töpken later stated—presumably using as a basis Schumann's explanation to him of the "mystification"—that Schumann's interest was not in Meta Abegg but rather in the musical possibilities of her name. But it would not be surprising if there were more to Schumann's "mystification" than the simple musical play of the name itself—perhaps some symbolic association with the theme or a more elaborate connection to Jean Paul.

Schumann had begun work on the *Abegg Variations* while still a student in Heidelberg. After attending a masked ball on the previous evening, the diary for 22 February 1830 records: "Abegg 'waltzes'."[11] According to his recollections, the work was completed in July and August of that year. It is significant that, if not originally, then not long afterwards, a version was contemplated for piano and orchestra (for which sketches survive), no doubt in the manner of Moscheles's popular *Alexander Variations*.

The *Abegg Variations* is a fairly short work, less than a dozen pages in length. In addition to the theme (also presented in retrograde), there are three variations, a one-page *cantabile* section, and a finale (the improvisatory *cantabile* section serving as a transition to the finale). The most original aspect of the piece is the unusual word/theme used as the basis for the work. The theme itself is presented as a waltz, and a dancelike character serves as a backdrop for the work. Schumann's indebtedness to other composers is apparent (notably Weber and Moscheles in the figuration of the third variation). There are reminiscences of Chopin as well, seen in the ornamentation of the *cantabile* section. As would be expected, a glittering virtuosity is not neglected—especially rapid passagework in the upper register, a hallmark of the virtuoso style of the day.

But the virtuoso element is far from dominant, so that the work could also have been purchased by talented pianists to play at home. Overall, the *Abegg Variations* are considerably more comprehensible than Schumann's later piano compositions. The music does not disturb or startle with rapid changes of mood or texture, nor is there much use of dissonance. It is clear that Schumann intended the work to be com-

[11] *Tgb I*, p. 228.

paratively conventional, entertaining, and pleasing—goals that, as time passed, increasingly he abandoned.

Despite the fact that Schumann's next published work, *Papillons* op. 2, contains musical material dating to 1828, it reveals not only more originality than his first opus, but technical growth as well. With the *Abegg Variations*, the conventions and predictability of contemporary works that served as his models seem frequently to be present; with *Papillons*, we enter a strikingly original world of Schumann's own creation. The music in *Papillons* was composed over a period of several years. Nos. 1, 5, 6, and 7 were written during his residency in Heidelberg (nos. 1, 6, 7, and 9 appear as waltzes in a sketchbook). Work was completed in two primary stages in April 1830 and in January 1831. But *Papillons* nos. 5 and 11 are based on melodic material from three of Schumann's *Polonaises* for four hands (nos. 7, and 4 and 3, respectively) from 1828.

As with the *Abegg Variations*, there is a mystification involved, both with the title and with the program associated with the work (never publicly revealed). On the surface, the title *Papillons* (Butterflies) is an innocuous one. It was a common practice of the day for musical compositions—particularly those for piano—to contain associations to the beauties and charms of nature in the title. *Papillons* is a completely undistinguished title in that vein. Yet—although the musical content of several of the *Papillons* (such as the second in the set) could be perceived as being evocative of the butterfly—those were not Schumann's intentions. He sent a review of *Papillons* to Töpken, in which the work was described as an accurate depiction of the nature of butterflies: "The Papillons," Schumann informed Töpken, "are something else entirely. In my next letter, you will receive the key to their comprehension" (5 April 1833). Schumann's explanation to Töpken, if sent, has not survived, but he gave a good idea of his intentions in a letter to Henriette Voigt: "a bridge to the Papillons: because we can readily imagine the psyche floating above the body turned to dust.—You could learn a good deal from me about this, if Jean Paul had not explained it better" (22 August 1834).

Butterflies occur in virtually every major work of Jean Paul (usually as symbols of the soul), and frequently associated with transformation and attainment of an ideal. In a musical sense, the butterfly could more literally be transformed. Perhaps that is why the ascending theme Schumann created for *Papillons* uses all the possible letters associated with the musical scale (A, B, C [sharp], D, E, F [sharp], and G). Each succeeding piece can then be seen as a transformation (or rearrangement) of the pitches of the original theme (Ex. 5.2).

Jean Paul provided the inspiration for the program as well as the title for *Papillons*. "Read as soon as possible the last scene from Jean Paul's *Flegeljahre*," Schumann wrote to his family. "Papillons is an attempt truly to set to music this masked ball. Ask them [his sisters-in-law, to whom the work was dedicated] if perhaps reflected in the Papillons there is not something of Wina's angelic love, of Walt's poetic soul, and of Vult's mordant temperament."[12] To Ludwig Rellstab, editor of *Iris im Gebiete der Tonkunst*, Schumann wrote: "Bring to mind the last scene in *Flegeljahre*—the masked ball—Walt—Vult—masks—Wina—Vult's dancing—the exchange of masks—avowals—anger—revelations—hurrying off—the final scene, and then the brother going away.—Often I turned over the last page, for the end seemed to me actually to be a new beginning—almost unaware of what I was doing, I found myself at the piano, and thus one Papillon after another was created."[13]

Ex. 5.2

---

[12] Letter of 17 April 1832 in *JS*, p. 228.

[13] Letter of 19 April 1832 in *JgBr*, pp. 167–8. In a manuscript of *Papillons* now in the Bibliothèque Nationale, Paris, Schumann placed at the head of it the final sentence from *Flegeljahre*: "Noch aus der ferne hörte Walt entzückt die fliehenden Töne reden: denn er merkte nicht, dass mit ihnen sein Bruder entfliehe."

Jean Paul's *Flegeljahre* deals with twin brothers, Walt and Vult, long separated, but recently reunited. The two are uncommonly dissimilar. Walt is poetic, naive, thoughtful, and contemplative. Vult is passionate and intense, sarcastic and opinionated. The primary plot of the novel deals with sixteen outlandish stipulations that Walt must fulfill in order to gain possession of a substantial inheritance. Schumann was concerned with the conclusion of the novel: the love of Walt and Vult for Wina. Wina is in love with Walt, but neither brother has confessed his love for her. The final scene is a masked ball attended by all three. While dancing with Wina, Vult, disguised as his brother, learns from her that she is in love with Walt. His hopes dashed, he writes a farewell letter, and in the early morning hours—as his brother drifts off to sleep—Vult leaves, playing his flute as he departs. Walt hears the flute's tones, not realizing that as the sounds of the flute diminish, Vult is vanishing from his life.

Masked balls were an extraordinarily popular form of entertainment during the first half of the nineteenth century. Schumann was fond of them, and even wrote a poem about one. As his letter to Rellstab revealed, *Papillons* was intended as a musical representation of the masked ball and subsequent events in *Flegeljahre*. In his own copy of *Flegeljahre*, Schumann amplified the general association and indicated in the text eleven specific passages, assigning them to the first ten of the twelve pieces comprising *Papillons*.[14] They are brief excerpts, several only consisting of a sentence.

In creating *Papillons*, Schumann's initial inspiration was the very end of *Flegeljahre* (Wina's avowal of love and Vult's departure), scenes represented in the final two pieces in *Papillons*. But the composition did not come into existence in the spontaneous manner Schumann recounted to Rellstab. It seems likely that he next marked in his copy of the novel additional passages of interest in the last chapter, composing and adapting music to suit them. The chronological order of the novel was not retained in the music; musical effect and contrast remained of primary significance, so the order of several passages was switched.

A comparison of the music with the marked texts reveals a strong

---

[14] For further details, see my article, "Explicating Jean Paul: Robert Schumann's Program for *Papillons* Op. 2," *19th-Century Music* XXII (1998–99), pp. 127–44.

connection. After a brief introduction, the first piece, a short waltz in D major, introduces the primary theme associated with the work. The corresponding passage in *Flegeljahre* refers to Walt in a mock-heroic manner as he prepares for the ball (and in an insightful reflection of Walt's temperament by Schumann, his heroism is rendered "dolce"). Schumann intended the next *Papillon*, only twelve measures in length, to describe Walt's confusion as he entered the ball. In the music, the abrupt change to rapid sixteenth notes (Prestissimo), followed by the ungainly hesitancy created by the numerous sixteenth-note rests, are an apt musical counterpart. For the third *Papillon*, Schumann selected a peculiar image: a costume of a "giant boot, sliding around and dressed in itself." His wonderful attempt at illustration begins with ponderous octaves (the "giant boot"), cleverly leading to a brief canon ("dressed in itself"; Ex. 5.3).

Similar discoveries can be made by examining each of the pieces. The dramatic change in register and tonality in the middle of the eleventh *Papillon* (m. 32) would appear to be a musical counterpart to Wina's avowal of love for Walt. In a delightful poetic touch, the *Papillon* itself is a *Polonaise*—for during their dance Vult and Wina speak in

Ex. 5.3

Ex. 5.4

Polish, her native language. The final *Papillon* describes both Vult's reaction and his departure. The piece begins by quoting the "Grossvater Tanz," a somewhat banal folk melody, square and predictable, and strikingly different from Schumann's own music (Ex. 5.4).

Although it was several hundred years old at the time Schumann used it, the "Grossvater Tanz"—both text and music—remained well known. Traditionally, it was performed near the conclusion of wedding festivities. The text describes a grandmother and grandfather transformed and rejuvenated by dance into a youthful bride and groom—transformed, that is, until the arrival of the next day. Schumann has quoted the melody as a commentary (much in the sardonic, self-reflective manner of Vult) on Vult's hopeless predicament. Like the grandfather, Vult's wishful transformation to youthful bridegroom is displaced by his encounter with reality: in this instance, Wina's true feelings. As the clock strikes the early morning hour in the upper register of the piano, both the "Grossvater Tanz" and the main *Papillon* theme become quieter, and during the diminuendo the melody representing Vult's flute playing becomes fragmented. Silence (one measure of notated rest, with a fermata) marks the departure of Vult, followed by a brief, quiet codetta—concluding pianissimo.[15]

Schumann's program is complex. But with knowledge of it, *Papillons* makes greater sense. Prior to its publication, dances were published in sets, often of a dozen. Typically they were light, at their best unpretentious, and intended as simple entertainment. No program was associated with them. *Papillons* is a mixture of dances and short, character pieces. Anyone purchasing *Papillons* at the time could only have been perplexed by the format created by Schumann. But by knowing the program associated with the work, *Papillons* becomes more than a conglomeration of charming and, at times, bizarre dances and character pieces. It is unfortunate that Schumann never revealed the program in more detail, or drew attention to the pertinent passages from *Flegeljahre*. On the one hand, he was always reluctant to admit the presence of programs in his music, and may have feared the ridicule one as elaborate as this might have provoked. But he seemed to believe that anyone familiar with Jean Paul—a vast number of people, in Schumann's eyes—would have little problem understanding his intentions. "I have a question," Schumann wrote to Henriette Voigt. "Aren't the Papillons self-evident to you? I am interested in learning if they are" (22 August 1834). Schumann expected a great deal from his friends.

In his diary in May 1832, Schumann expressed interest in creating a second collection of *Papillons*, an idea he returned to as late as June 1833 in a letter to the publisher Friedrich Kistner. But he also must have realized that *Papillons* was not the kind of composition on which to establish fame as a piano virtuoso. Its format was too unusual, and, from a technical point of view, it offered insufficient virtuosity. It was for that reason that Schumann turned to the Piano Concerto in F major, and to a challenging work originally intended as the first movement for a piano sonata to be dedicated to Moscheles. Neither the concerto nor the sonata was completed. But the first movement of the sonata was later published separately as the Allegro op. 8.

Schumann was working on it in December 1831 and January 1832, but composition continued sporadically for some time. It was not pub-

---

[15] The sentences found on the final page of many current editions of *Papillons*—"Das Geräusch der Faschingsnacht verstummt. Die Turmuhr schlägt sechs"—are not Schumann's and were added after his death.

lished until 1835. Schumann described it to Töpken as an "Allegro di bravura," a reference to the technical difficulties the work possessed and to its grandeur (the piece begins in B minor and concludes buoyantly in B major). In addition to its virtuoso characteristics, however, it was Schumann's longest piece to date for solo piano and his first attempt at writing a movement in sonata form for solo piano. Its structure is neither dry nor academic (the three fortissimo unison chords in the opening serve as its structural pivots). Although there is an ungainly move in the exposition to the second theme (in the relative major, so one would think that the modulation should have presented little difficulty), there is engaging tonal variety in the recapitulation, where the second theme reappears in the unexpected key of G major. The Allegro is definitely a showpiece—but by the time Schumann completed it to his satisfaction, other compositions had his attention, and the concluding movements of the projected sonata were never composed.

In April 1832, Schumann began work on a series of six etudes intended as transcriptions for piano from Paganini's *24 Caprices* op. 1 for solo violin. Because Paganini's *Caprices* were regarded as the embodiment of transcendent virtuosity, Schumann's project can be perceived not just as a mark of his admiration for the composer but as an attempt to make a name for himself as a virtuoso for piano in the manner of Paganini. The principle problem for Schumann lay in the nature of Paganini's compositions: being conceived for solo violin, by necessity they are primarily melodic in nature, often with implied harmony. In adapting them for piano, Schumann had a difficult time determining what he felt would be the appropriate harmonic accompaniment. He described his work on the project to Gottfried Weber as "Herculean" (11 January 1834).

Despite the efforts involved, the Etudes were complete in all essentials in June, and published in December 1832 as his op. 3. Schumann supplied them with a lengthy introduction, including suggestions for performance, as well as original finger exercises—focusing primarily on flexibility and independence—to improve technique. The six *Caprices* he selected for his Etudes reveal much about his perception of virtuosity. The third Etude (based on Paganini's eleventh *Caprice*) is a short intermezzo, in many ways a charming character piece. The bravura display associated with Paganini has been discarded.

Several of the pieces—especially the continuous, running sixteenth-notes of the *agitato* section in the first etude and the *minore* section of the fifth etude—sound, if not Bach-like, then distinctly Baroque (Schumann included a reference to and recommendation of the *Well-Tempered Clavier* in the introduction to the set). There is also an interesting programmatic connection. Schumann had recently seen a grotesque caricature of Paganini by the musician-artist, Johann Peter Lyser, in which were included skeletons, ghosts, and a representation of Paganini's murdered wife (colorful legends circulated around Paganini, including, among others, that he had made a pact with the devil to acquire his skill, and that he had killed his wife). Schumann was haunted by these images, and while composing the *minore* section of the fourth etude, noted in his diary that Lyser's picture "often floated before me. I believe that the conclusion strongly brings it to mind."[16]

The Etudes emphasize Schumann's concern to remain as faithful as possible to the original. Perhaps for that reason, in adapting the *Caprices* for the piano he avoided the flamboyant virtuosity of which the piano was capable. For the second etude—based on Paganini's ninth *Caprice*—he used straightforward octave doublings (Ex. 5.5). Liszt's 1838 transcription of the same passage in his Paganini Etudes reveals a grandiose virtuosity and a rhetoric of which Schumann was incapable (Ex. 5.6).

Schumann later observed that in his op. 3 he had "copied the original nearly note for note—perhaps to its detriment—and only enlarged on the harmony."[17] He undoubtedly felt as well that there were virtuoso

Ex. 5.5

[musical notation: Allegretto, 2/4 time]

[16] 4 June 1832 in *Tgb I*, p. 404.
[17] Review published in 1836 of his op. 10 in *GS I*, p. 212.

Ex. 5.6

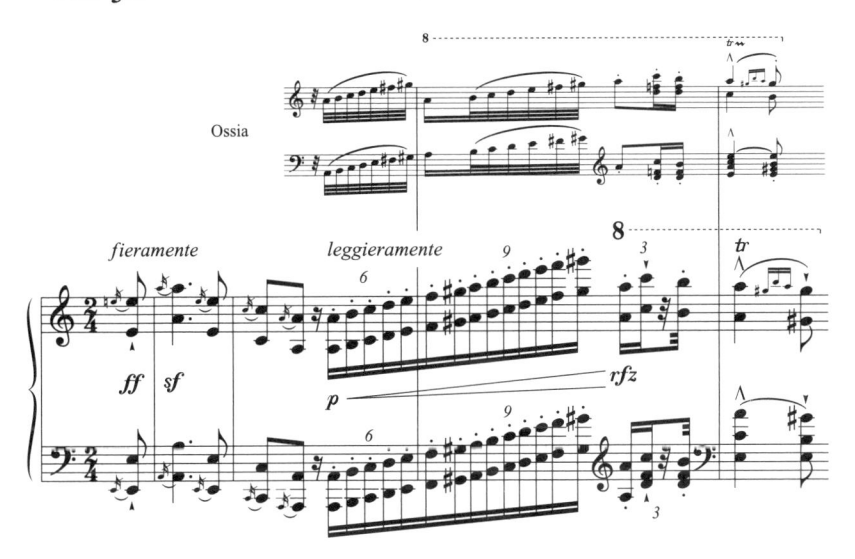

elements in the *Caprices* that he had not explored. In 1833, he prepared a second set of six etudes. The title in this instance shows the intended differences between these etudes and those of op. 3: the new pieces are entitled *Etudes de concert*, that is, works suitable for concert performance. The six new etudes, published as op. 10 in 1835, use Paganini more as a point of departure. The original is not altered, but occasional additions are presented—the arpeggiated chords, for example, to the opening of the last etude (only octaves in Paganini's third *Caprice*). Greater technique is demanded, but the glittering virtuosity of Liszt is rarely present.

While working on the Paganini Etudes, Schumann also composed music more in the style of *Papillons*: the *Intermezzi* op. 4, composed from April to July 1832 and published in 1833. He described them to Töpken, as "longer Papillons" (5 April 1833), an apt description. Both in spirit and content they bring to mind op. 2, but with the distinction that each piece is usually two to three times the length of each of the *Papillons*. As with the Allegro op. 8, Schumann was clearly making an effort to write more extended compositions. But he also was determined that the *Intermezzi* be distinct from the *Papillons*. "The *Intermezzi*," he wrote in his diary, "should be something—each note shall be weighed and balanced"—this at a time, incidentally, when he was still studying Marpurg on his own.[18] In his sketchbook, the fifth intermezzo was entitled "Pièce fantastique." The only precise programmatic connection revealed by Schumann for the set, however, concerns the second intermezzo. In the slower, middle section, printed above the melody are the words "Meine Ruh' ist hin . . ." ("My peace of mind has vanished")—a quotation from the well-known song of Gretchen in Goethe's *Faust, Part I.*[19] Given the turmoil in his personal life, the words were applicable as well to Schumann's perception of his own situation.

The *Intermezzi* provide evidence of astounding growth. Of the six, only one, the fourth, is short. The increased length of the others is achieved by combining what Schumann would previously have published as several pieces. It was a major challenge to join these sections together with effective bridges. In the "alternativo" transition of the first intermezzo, he achieves this with great simplicity. Effectively using silence and dynamic contrast, he moves from A major (forte) to D major (pianissimo) in only three measures. The rhythmic inventiveness is striking. Syncopation, rhythmic displacement (using dynamic contrast), and hemiola all serve to startle and jostle the listener with unexpected variety and contrast (Ex. 5.7).

The *Intermezzi* also provide tantalizing insights into Schumann's compositional approach. He regularly drew on earlier compositions, both published and unpublished, for his work. A major source were five sketchbooks (dating from 1829 to 1833), currently in the Bonn University library. These are not sketchbooks in the usual sense, for they did not necessarily serve for the elaboration of musical ideas. Rather, they often became sourcebooks to preserve musical thoughts already in a fairly finished state. Many of these, dancelike in character, probably resulted from his improvisations.

The melody from an unpublished song, *Hirtenknabe* (August 1828), appears in the fourth intermezzo in the original key (A minor). But it now sounds distinctly pianistic (and *Papillons*-like), with the use of octaves in the right and left hands, and sparse accompaniment (Ex. 5.8,

---

[18] 22 May 1832 in *Tgb I*, p. 394.

[19] Akio Mayeda in *Robert Schumanns Weg zur Symphonie* (Zürich, 1992) notes as well a connection to Wiedebein's setting of "Gretchens Klage."

Ex. 5.7

5.9). Schumann adapted the remainder of the musical material in the piece from the sketchbooks, using an idea originally considered for *Papillons*, but with the meter now changed from 3/8 to 12/8. An unpredictable juxtaposition of musical ideas has resulted, creating precisely the sense of humorous discontinuity (in the Jean Paul sense) that Schumann often strove to create in his music at this time. The *Intermezzi* are also rich with musical allusions to Schumann's previously published work—yet another indication of his indebtedness to Jean Paul. A

Ex. 5.8

Kindlich und innig

Bin nur ein ar-mer Hir-ten-knab, das Hüft-horn ist mein gan-zes Hab,

Ex. 5.9

Allegretto semplice (♩. = 50)

fragment from the "Grossvater Tanz" is found in the fifth intermezzo. And near the end of the final piece, the ABEGG theme from op. 1 makes a surprising appearance.

Schumann placed greater reliance on his skill as a composer than on his skill as a performer. After the hand injury, he decided to attempt to make a name for himself not just as a composer of works for piano—of which there were many—but as a composer on a grander scale, more in the tradition of Beethoven. It was for that reason that he began work in earnest on a symphony. The idea of writing a symphony was not a new one for him, but in the past he had done little more than think about it. In January 1830, his diary contained references to turning the Piano Quartet into a symphony (sketches survive). And, in a sketchbook from 1831–2, there are orchestral sketches for an Allegro in E flat, marked "Sinfonia per il Hamlet"; in fact, two themes from these sketches were later incorporated into what was to become his Symphony in G minor (WoO 29).

What may be interpreted as the first indication of Schumann's symphonic intentions is found in a letter of 27 July 1832 to Kuntsch, where he stated that he was about to study orchestral scores and instrumentation. Schumann had attempted composing for orchestra before, notably with the Piano Concerto in F major, and the orchestral versions of the Piano Quartet and *Abegg Variations*. But probably the primary reason why these projects had not been completed was his inexperience in writing for the orchestra. According to Schumann, he worked on the G minor Symphony from October 1832 until May 1833, but it appears likely that some work was done earlier in the late summer and autumn of 1832.

Only the first two movements were finished, with sketches existing for the third and fourth. There were performances, only of the first movement, in Zwickau on 18 November, in Schneeberg four months later, and, most important of all, on 29 April 1833 at the Gewandhaus in Leipzig. None of the performances met with the wholehearted endorsement for which Schumann hoped. Wieck commented that the audience in Zwickau had not "understood" the work; his own evaluation was that the Symphony was well written, but "too meagerly orchestrated."[20] There is no doubt that the orchestration created difficulties for Schumann. He admitted as much to the publisher Hofmeister in a letter of 17 December 1832, asked several more experienced musicians to examine his score, and continued to tinker with the orchestration after each performance.

But, in addition to the instrumentation, Schumann experienced problems with the structure of the work. The piece begins with a dramatic statement of forte dominant and tonic chords, probably intended as an oblique reference to the opening of the "Eroica." The remainder of the first movement (in sonata form) resembles a mosaic, each section clearly delineated. It is perhaps here that Schumann's inexperience is most clearly evident. Despite some typical Schumann touches (abrupt dynamic contrast in the second theme of the first movement, rhythmic inventiveness in the surprisingly lengthy development), the work appears labored, with few resemblances to his distinctive piano compositions, such as the *Intermezzi*.

Despite the symphony's failure, within a short time Schumann was again writing music, completing at the end of May the *Impromptus sur une Romance de Clara Wieck* op. 5. Impetus was probably provided by

---

[20] *Eismann*, p. 78.

the associations the work had with Clara, whom he was increasingly regarding in a more romantic manner. The *Impromptus* are a response to Clara's *Romance varié* op. 3, dedicated to Schumann. The melodic motive of the *Romance* was composed by Schumann in 1830 (unacknowledged in the publication—Clara may actually have been unaware of the connection, but, more likely, it served as a secret bond between them). The *Impromptus* use that same theme (now solely attributed to Clara) with a new bass line (first conceived by Schumann in May 1832) for a series of variations.

In later years Schumann associated the *Impromptus* with his study of Bach, and expressed the belief that "a new form of variation" was evident in them.[21] What he may have been referring to was the use of both the bass and the theme itself, separately and together, as the basis of the variations. In addition to variations in pitch, attention is focused on variation of rhythm, particularly in the second, sixth, and seventh of the twelve pieces comprising the set. But the connection to Bach is not as apparent as in Schumann's later piano compositions. The last piece contains a fugue on the bass theme—certainly not a common approach for the time—but it appears academic and contrived (and Schumann seems ill at ease with it).[22]

In the variations, for the most part the themes are kept readily recognizable; that is, the variations do not depart radically from the melodic or harmonic basis of the theme to create what might be perceived as markedly new musical material. In that sense, the approach is contrary to that employed by Schumann in another piano work, the Etudes on the Allegretto from Beethoven's Symphony No. 7 (actually a series of free variations), completed in 1833. Perhaps the inspiration for this work stemmed from Schumann's score-study preparatory to the writing of his own symphony. Two of his sketchbooks contain studies of the *Leonore* Overture No. 3 and the second movement of the Fourth Symphony. But Schumann did not think highly of the Etudes, later describing the motive that serves as its basis as "very unpleasant"; it may not

---

[21] *Ibid.*, p. 77.

[22] From the sketchbooks, it appears that a fugal finale using the same theme was considered for the finale for the Symphony in G minor.

be as unpleasant as he believed, but its regular recurrence is exceedingly monotonous.[23]

The final work completed in 1833 was the Toccata op. 7, a piece first started three years earlier. This early version was monothematic and only about half the length of the work as published; to Töpken, who had heard the earlier version, Schumann characterized the completed work as being "not as wild, and much more polite" (18 August 1834). The title itself was unusual; toccatas were a rarity in 1830. While it may have been intended in part as a tribute to Bach, the only significant element it shares with the Baroque toccata is a concern with virtuosity, a characteristic also found to a lesser degree in two toccatas by contemporary composers (Charles Mayer and Carl Czerny) studied by Schumann. In fact, there are several incongruities: it is in sonata form, and resembles more an etude than a toccata. It was Schumann's most virtuoso work to date, and in many ways the most demanding technically that he was to write for piano. Ludwig Schuncke was the dedicatee, at least in part because of his magnificent rendering of it.

Schumann worked diligently to promote his compositions, sending copies of them, (and, when appropriate as with *Papillons*, providing insights into their creation) to the editors of leading German-language musical journals. The most flattering notice appeared in a review of opps. 1 and 2 in the 28 June 1832 issue of the *Allgemeine Musikalischer Anzeiger*, in which Schumann's originality was commended: "he belongs to no school . . . [and] has created a new world of the ideal."[24] In a similar manner, Gottfried Weber in *Cäcilie* and Ernst Ortlepp in *Der Komet* praised the new and original in Schumann's music. But those same distinctive characteristics were often what repelled others. While creating *Papillons*, Schumann had felt that a "certain *independence*" had become manifest, but, he noted, that same independence "mostly confused the critics."[25]

He seemed particularly interested in winning over Ludwig Rellstab,

---

[23] Entry of 28 November 1838 in *Tgb I*, p. 421. One of the etudes later appeared as the second piece ("Leides Ahnung") in the *Albumblätter* op. 124.

[24] *Eismann*, p. 82.

[25] Letter to his mother of 3 May 1832 in *JS*, p. 230.

the editor of *Iris*; conservative in taste, Rellstab had a reputation for integrity, independence, and modest discernment. Yet despite (or perhaps because of) his correspondence with Schumann, Rellstab found little to praise in his music. He made fun of the letters/pitches basis of the *Abegg Variations* (finding the theme monotonous), thought the program for *Papillons* unnecessary, and completely misunderstood the nature of op. 3 by describing Schumann as simply "the arranger."[26] By the time of the *Intermezzi*, he had had enough: "We believe and in all frankness tell [the composer] that he is following the completely wrong path ... This type of modulation, these chopped-up rhythms ... all do violence to the authority of Nature.... It is our wish that the composer not take offense at what we have written, but rather become resolved to strike out on another path."[27] Schumann's concern led him to write to his mother whom he suspected would learn of the review: "Opposition makes one stronger. Everyone should follow their own path."[28]

Gottfried Wilhelm Fink (1783–1846), editor of the influential *Allgemeine Musikalische Zeitung* from 1828 to 1841, also became in time an inveterate opponent of Schumann (similar to the opposition of François-Joseph Fétis to Berlioz). It was not until September 1833, after Schumann had written asking why nothing of his had been reviewed in the journal, that a review of Schumann's compositions appeared—a fairly lengthy critique of opp. 1, 2, 3, and 5. It showed neither understanding nor sympathy for his music. After that, his works were ignored.

In order to gain recognition, the support of influential journals such as *Iris* and the *Allgemeine Musikalische Zeitung* was essential. In addition, because of Schumann's hand injury, other pianists were needed to champion his work. Clara Wieck began gradually to perform them, but even among friends his music could be viewed with incomprehension. After a private performance of *Papillons* (with Wieck, Dorn, and the Caruses present) Schumann noted in his diary that "[they] looked at one other shocked, and were unable to grasp the rapid changes."[29]

Their reaction might have been more favorable had they been aware

---

[26] *Tgb* I, p. 428.
[27] *GS* II, p. 451.
[28] Letter of 19 March 1834 in *JS*, p. 248.
[29] 28 May 1832 in *Tgb* I, p. 399.

of the program associated with it. Schumann's reticence concerning it makes clear that *Papillons* as he conceived it was not intended for the masses, but rather for a select audience—those who, like Stephen Heller, could discover Jean Paul "note for note" in Schumann's music. Perhaps there were others who Schumann felt might grasp at least his general intentions or who would search for the music's meaning, prompted by the correspondence between title and music, or by the distinctive nature of the music itself. What seems particularly revealing about Schumann's approach was his enjoyment of it. The mystification, and the game and playfulness associated with it, were one measure of the originality he so actively sought as a composer. The bewildered reaction to *Papillons* that he noted among friends and associates contained, for him, a certain mark of distinction.

As time passed Schumann came to acknowledge that his early compositions were truly unconventional. In 1840, he described them as "too short and rhapsodic"—probably he had *Papillons* particularly in mind.[30] But, in 1834, he was unable to adopt such an objective stance. There were at the time too few people able to recognize the originality and beauty in much of his music. Acknowledgement of his predicament must only have served to heighten his sense of isolation.

---

[30] Quoted in Wolfgang Boetticher, *Robert Schumann in seinen Schriften und Briefen* (Berlin, 1942), p. 23.

CHAPTER 6

The League of David

> *It was my good fortune to be part of a great event: to be a member of the League, and to be permitted to participate in that unique journey with them. What wonder it had at the time, like a meteor flashing through the heavens!*
>
> —Hermann Hesse, *The Journey to The East*

"Today," Schumann wrote on 1 July 1831, "completely new characters make their appearance in the diary. Two of my best friends—although I have never seen them: Florestan and Eusebius."[1] Schumann's whimsical announcement concealed his intentions. His new friends were to become the two most famous characters in a larger creation of Schumann: the *Davidsbund* ("League of David"). During the 1830s, the *League* seemed to take on a life of its own, presenting his ideas about the musical life of his day and the direction he wanted it to pursue.

The idea for the *Davidsbund* was born on Schumann's birthday in 1831: "From today on, I want to give my friends more beautiful and appropriate names."[2] Wieck became "Master Raro," Clara became "Cilia," Dorn became "the Music Director," and Christel became

---
[1] *Tgb I*, p. 344.
[2] Entry of 8 June in *Ibid.*, p. 339.

"Charitas," among others. It seems that Schumann's original intention was to use these characters as the basis for a novel, tentatively entitled *Die Wunderkinder*, a work that would have included Paganini and Hummel, as well as Florestan, "the Improvisatore."[3] From these poetic effusions, the association of a group of people, real and imaginary, formed in Schumann's mind. They were united in their determination to raise the musical standards of their day, and adamantly opposed to mediocrity. But rather than using them in a novel, Schumann introduced those he considered most important into his music criticism. To the group, he eventually gave the name *Davidsbund*, a reference to the biblical King David and his musical ability, as well as to the war the *Davidsbund* intended to wage on the Philistines of the 1830s—the narrow-minded arbiters of public taste.

The *Davidsbund* attracted considerable attention. Who were the mysterious Florestan and Eusebius? Schumann added to the mystery by publishing his *Davidsbündlertänze* op. 6 and First Piano Sonata op. 11 not under his own name, but under those of Florestan and Eusebius. Friends added to the confusion. Stephen Heller dedicated his *Rondo-Scherzo* op. 8 to Florestan and Eusebius. Franz Otto's *Phalènes* op. 15 was dedicated to them as well. In 1840, a chapter in Julius Becker's novel *The New Romanticists* was entitled "Florestan and Eusebius." The mystification delighted Schumann. But privately he explained that the *League* was only a "spiritual, romantic" creation (14 September 1836) for which he alone was responsible, and that for the most part its members—some living (such as Berlioz), some dead (such as Mozart)—were unaware of their membership in it.

The name of the *League* and its musical function was Schumann's creation; the idea for it was not. Drawing upon the growth of secret societies such as freemasonry, German popular literature of the late eighteenth and early nineteenth century reveled in mysterious, secret organizations, whether political or cultural in basis. These leagues routinely battled evil barons or political reactionaries, at the same time often striving for the improvement of mankind. From popular literature it became a part of the more "serious" literature of the day, in works such

---

[3] Entry of 15 June in *Ibid.*, p. 342. This led to the six-page fragment of a novel, entitled *Die Davidsbündler*.

as Goethe's *Wilhelm Meister's Apprenticeship* (1796) and Arnim's *The Guardians of the Crown* (1817).

As his letters and diaries reveal, from his youth Schumann was fond of perceiving the musical world of his day as a kind of League (or *Bund*), one with mysterious religious and occult overtones. In writing to Gottlob Wiedebein in 1828, Schumann had addressed him in the style of an initiate, referring to Wiedebein as a "holy priest, standing amidst the mysteries of the World of Tone" (5 August 1828). Writing to Wieck from Heidelberg, Leipzig became the "Olympus of Music ... [and Wieck] the priest who softly and powerfully removed the veil from the eyes of the dazzled disciple."[4] In 1830, Schumann decided to present an analysis of himself in his diary; he did so as if it were the report of an unknown, mysterious third person. "S.," the report began, "is the young man whom I long have loved and observed"[5]—all of which brings to mind the secret societies found in the literature of the day, whose primary purpose, it seems, was to observe and guide the destiny of gifted, young men who had proven themselves worthy of the society's interest.

Schumann discovered the idea for the *Bund* readily enough in contemporary literature. He borrowed the idea for Florestan and Eusebius from Jean Paul. Florestan and Eusebius resemble two brothers, each with strongly contrasting temperaments: Florestan, wild and impetuous; Eusebius, quiet, introverted, and more reflective. Pairs of contrasting characters (such as Walt and Vult in *Flegeljahre*) are frequently encountered in Jean Paul's work. The selection of the names Florestan and Eusebius was a curious one, and emphasizes yet again Schumann's love of mystification. Both names are unusual. Florestan, however, was associated with two well-known works of the time: he appears as a memorable and rootless character in Ludwig Tieck's novel *Franz Sternbald's Travels* (1798), and he is also the hero of Beethoven's opera *Fidelio* (1805).

There may have been a literary association for Eusebius as well. Eusebio is the name of a fascinating character in Clemens Brentano's novel *Godwi* (1801). But it seems more likely that Schumann selected the

---
[4] Letter of 6 November 1829 in *JgBr*, p. 79.
[5] *Tgb I*, p. 242.

name from the church calendar of saints' feast-days. That for 12 August is Clara; the 14th is Eusebius. It was yet another way for Schumann to emphasize a connection to Clara, and one to which he was later to draw attention. The other most important fictional character he created for the *Davidsbund*—Master Raro—possesses an equally distinctive name. His role is one of a knowledgeable and mature artist who often helps to resolve the contrary opinions of Florestan and Eusebius, and in that sense he brings to mind Hoffmann's creation, the good friend of Kreisler, Master Abraham. Given his love for puzzles and word play, Schumann may have created the name Raro from an amalgamation of his own name and that of Clara: CLA**RARO**BERT.

The first public appearance of Florestan, Eusebius, and Master Raro was, oddly enough, in the *Allgemeine Musikalische Zeitung*, the staunchly conservative music journal. Schumann's great admiration for Chopin's music led in the summer of 1831 to his writing a review of Chopin's *Variations on 'La ci darem'* op. 2. But his review (which appeared in the 7 December 1831 issue) was unlike any other, giving the appearance not of a work of criticism but of an excerpt from a novel or short story. It begins:

> Eusebius quietly entered the room the other day. You are familiar with his pale features, and the ironical smile which arouses curiosity. I sat with Florestan at the piano. Florestan is, as you know, one of those rare musicians who seems to sense in advance all that is new and extraordinary. Today he was in for a surprise. With the words, "Hats off, gentlemen—a genius!", Eusebius put down a piece of music.[6]

The review (which appeared erroneously as the work of "K. Schumann") was enthusiastic in its praise. But in an attempt to counteract its extravagant tone, it was not published in full, and a more critical and conventional review of Chopin was included in the issue as well.

Schumann's excitement over the appearance of the review was equaled only by the excitement he had experienced a month earlier with the publication of his first composition. Although no further writing of his was published in the *Allgemeine Musikalische Zeitung*, with self-assurance Schumann continued to write, finding an outlet elsewhere.

[6] *GS I*, p. 5.

He knew that he wrote well, and was convinced of the significance of the ideas he wanted to communicate. At a time when his piano study was progressing poorly, writing provided him with an opportunity to gain recognition.

The *Davidsbund* reappeared in another journal, *Der Komet* (in three issues in December 1833 and January 1834). Schumann informed his mother that it had created "some sensation," and that he hoped to write a book with the *Davidsbund* in it, possibly to be published by his brothers.[7] His criticism for *Der Komet* led its editor, K. G. R. Herlosssohn, to request contributions by Schumann for the *Damen-Konversationslexikon* in 1834. Sixty-eight items by Schumann were published in the lexicon, including short biographies of composers and definitions of musical terms.

By the summer of 1834, a project that had long interested Schumann had finally come to fruition: the creation of a music journal devoted to new music, the *Neue Zeitschrift für Musik*. To understand the need for such an enterprise, it is necessary to recognize the impoverished state of music criticism at that time. Nearly all of the leading music journals of the day were produced by music publishers. Works that they published were given priority and invariably received favorable reviews. The musical taste exhibited in the journals generally ranged from the innocuous to the deplorable. Vapid, salon music was assured of praise, there being a consistent market for it. The reviewers displayed a markedly conservative taste, and found little to recommend in the compositions of Chopin, Schumann, and others. From the reviews of his own works, Schumann had experienced firsthand the obstacles facing a composer who departed from convention. But he was fortunate in having friends who not only shared his perceptions but were willing to work for them. The time was ripe for change.

On 28 June 1833, Schumann wrote to his mother that plans were underway to create a new music journal to be published by Hofmeister and that a prospectus for it would shortly appear: "Its tone and color will be more lively and diverse than others."[8] Later in the summer he confirmed to his friend Franz Otto that a new music journal was in

---

[7] Letter of 4 January 1834 in *JS*, p. 244.
[8] *Ibid.*, p. 237.

the making, scheduled to be published in October, but in his enthusiasm for the project Schumann failed to take into consideration both the financial costs and the need to deal effectively with a number of diverse temperaments. From the outset, work on the journal was to be a team effort.

In addition to Schumann, those most closely associated with the project at this stage included Friedrich Wieck and Ernst Ortlepp (a writer and music critic, ten years Schumann's senior). But progress on the journal must have come to a halt as a result of Schumann's depression and breakdown in October. When the project was next mentioned to Schumann's mother—on 19 March 1834—the inner circle now comprised, in addition to himself and Wieck, Ludwig Schuncke, Ferdinand Stegmayer, and Julius Knorr. Stegmayer was a composer, Knorr a pianist and music teacher (and friend of Schumann since 1828). Stegmayer, notoriously unreliable, ended up leaving the venture, leaving Wieck, Schumann, Schuncke, and Knorr as editors.

There was no shortage of energy for the project, but problems soon developed in locating a publisher (in addition to Hofmeister, the firm of Schumann's father, now managed by Eduard, was considered). Eventually, C. H. F. Hartmann became the publisher. Knorr became editor-in-chief, but he soon fell ill, and Schumann assumed many of the duties. The first issue, four pages in length, appeared on 3 April 1834, the journal being published biweekly. The title at that time was the *Neue Leipziger Zeitschrift für Musik*, but *Leipziger* was dropped with the 2 January 1835 issue (at which time Schumann became sole editor).

Schumann's role in the publication was extremely active. He wrote to his mother on 2 July that with Wieck away, Knorr ill, and Schuncke's lack of skill with a pen, he needed to devote his full energy to the journal. But he was unable to spend all of his time in Leipzig guiding the journal and, as a result, a major crisis developed in December 1834. Schumann's absence, coupled with Wieck's lack of interest and Knorr's increasing unreliability, provided the basis for dissatisfaction on Hartmann's part, leading to an attempt to take over the journal. "We could not have selected a greater rascal as our publisher," Schumann concluded.[9]

---

[9] Letter to Joseph Fischhof of 14 December 1834 in *JgBr*, p. 264.

Hartmann's coup attempt came at a disastrous time. Ludwig Schuncke had died on 7 December from tuberculosis. Ill for months, in the final stages he had been cared for by Henriette Voigt. "May Heaven give me the strength to bear his loss!," Schumann had written to her on 25 August 1834 on hearing that it was not expected for Schuncke to survive the winter. Four days after Schuncke's death, an emotional tribute by Schumann appeared in the *Zeitschrift*.

Despite the loss of his closest friend, in his dealings with Hartmann Schumann acted promptly and with resolution. To settle the dispute at the journal, he bought the rights to the *Zeitschrift* outright for 350 talers, and selected J. A. Barth as the new publisher. Schumann was now both editor and proprietor. But there was trouble with Knorr, who, as previous editor-in-chief (and one of the signatories to the original contract), felt slighted by Schumann's action and sought restitution for his duties. It was not until July that a payment by Schumann to Knorr resolved the matter.

Content of the journal varied. In addition to music criticism (including reviews of both published works and concerts), there were reports of the musical life in European cities (with an emphasis on Germany), discussions on both the theoretical and historical aspects of music, and occasional biographical sketches of composers and performers, as well as short stories and poetry. An important adjunct was occasional musical supplements. Under Schumann's guidance, the editorial content and musical mission of the *Zeitschrift* became strengthened. In time the list of contributors grew considerably, with Heller, Lyser, Dorn, and Töpken, among others. In keeping with the idea of the *Davidsbund*, many of them at first used pseudonyms or numbers in signing their work (Schumann used the numbers 2, 12, 22, 32, 13, and 39). The *Davidsbund* had a significant recurring role. Their first appearance was on 10 April 1834 (signed "FN"), with another four days later (signed "Euseb"). Over the next three years, members of the *Bund* appeared fairly frequently; but from 1838 their presence is less noticeable. They did not appear in 1840 or 1841; Florestan made the last appearance in the journal for the group on 3 May 1842. By that time, not only had the *Bund* served its purpose, but with marriage and a growing family, for the time being Schumann had lost interest in the more Bohemian days of which the *Bund* was a reminder.

The reputation of the *Zeitschrift* was made by the controversial nature of its criticism. Its thrust was keen and candid but at the same time idealistic and poetic. While there were those who considered the entire approach both arrogant and extravagant, to others it became its major attraction.

> The editors of this journal have been reproached with cultivating the poetical side of music at the expense of its scholarly and practical side. They have been accused of being young visionaries who know nothing of Greek or other music [that is, the dry and academic], etc. This reproach contains precisely those points that are intended to distinguish this paper from others. We do not care to inquire into whether this or that approach will more quickly benefit art. But to speak frankly, the finest criticism is that which itself creates an impression similar to that awakened by its subject.[10]

The idea of creating "an impression similar to that awakened by its subject" was a concept dear to Schumann. In his eyes, an objective stance served little purpose. To create in its way a work of art inspired by the work of art under consideration appealed to his literary sense. His criticism for the journal was invariably the most distinctive, frequently employing members of the *Davidsbund*. Florestan would often expose the weaknesses of the composition under discussion; Eusebius would discuss its attractions. Occasionally, Master Raro would be present to prepare a more balanced summation. It was an ideal approach, useful in avoiding platitudes and at the same time a unique way to express differing points of view. Both a more comprehensive, more entertaining, and more insightful critique of the work was offered. Perhaps Schumann received the idea for this distinctive type of criticism from Jean Paul, who, in his *Introduction to Aesthetics* wrote: "Ultimately, I should like two completely different journals for the works of genius. The first would need only to censure a masterpiece . . . [and] a second . . . whose holy soul would contemplate in the work of art . . . nothing but the beauty or the god whom it resembles."[11]

Over the years, Schumann reviewed the works of hundreds of

---

[10] Review published in 1835 of Ferdinand Hiller's *Etudes* op. 15 in *GS I*, p. 44.

[11] Jean Paul Richter, *Horn of Oberon. Jean Paul Richter's School for Aesthetics*, trans. Margaret R. Hale (Detroit, 1973), pp. 243–44.

composers. Some, such as Schubert and Mendelssohn, were already fairly well established. For others, including Chopin, Berlioz, and Norbert Burgmüller, Schumann was among the first to champion their work. His ability to discern merit was extraordinary. In time, a surprising number of young composers at the outset of their careers would write to Schumann, seeking his advice—a clear indication of his reputation for being fair, forthright, and encouraging.

Just as he was quick to praise music of uncommon value, he did not hesitate to castigate music of little worth. There was no shortage of it, frequently music for piano by budding or established virtuosos. Much of it sold well, and other music journals regularly singled it out for praise. What resulted was a war against much of the "popular" music of the day. Composers such as Henri Herz, Franz Hünten, and Alexander Dreyschock came to exemplify to Schumann the low musical standards of the time.

It was not merely wretched piano works that provoked his wrath. Schumann also displayed a profound contempt for the music of Giacomo Meyerbeer, probably the most popular composer of the day. Starting with the extravagant success of his *grand opéra, Robert le diable*, in 1831, Meyerbeer's works were performed with regularity throughout Europe. Schumann saw him as both a musical charlatan and a traitor. In his eyes, Meyerbeer, who had received a thorough musical training from Abbé Vogler (Weber had been a friend and fellow student), had sacrificed his musical talents by creating music in a style intended solely to please the public. There was some substance to Schumann's criticism, but greater quality to Meyerbeer's music than he acknowledged.

Schumann was distrustful of the standards preferred by the masses, and he seemed to believe that their tastes were frequently directed by the press towards music simplistic, light, and ephemeral in nature. Such a view could easily have led to pretentious criticism with a strongly didactic and moralistic tone. But that did not occur. His caustic reviews—there was usually no need to bring in the *Davidsbund* for these—have lost none of their bite:

Alexander Dreyschock, *Grosse Phantasie* op. 12
   This is the first substantial work by the young hero of the piano whom the papers speak so much of. Unfortunately, we are obliged to confess that

it has been a long time since we have encountered a work so insipid. What poverty of imagination and melody, what expenditure in attempting to impose lack of talent upon us, what affectation over hackneyed platitudes! Did the young virtuoso have no friend near to tell him the truth, no one who, overlooking his facility at the keyboard, could draw his attention to the barren emptiness of the music? . . . the *Phantasie* discloses not so much the work of a pupil, as a truly innate incapacity to create. This might be expressed more mildly; but when impotence steps forth so pretentiously, it is impossible to stand by quietly.[12]

Schumann expressed indignation over pretension of any kind, even if associated with a composer whom he greatly admired. He did not hesitate to ridicule the beatific ecstasy of those who had begun to deify Beethoven. "waxing lyrical and rolling your eyes in rapture, you rave about Beethoven's freedom from earthliness, his transcendental flight from star to star."[13]

Despite the success of the journal and its growing influence, by today's standards the number of sales seems surprisingly small. In 1837, Schumann referred to a readership of about five hundred. Three years later, he remarked that he felt the paper to be stable enough so that even the loss of one hundred subscribers would not harm it. But the success of the journal cannot be measured in sales. It set a new standard for music criticism of the day, a standard—gradually adopted by many other music journals in Europe—that was receptive to different musical styles and more candid in its criticism. Schumann's association with the *Neue Zeitschrift für Musik* brought him the fame and recognition that had eluded him as a composer. On the one hand, this fame worked against him, for by many he was perceived not as a composer, but as a music critic who occasionally wrote music. But to his advantage, his work on the journal brought him into contact with a number of musicians who became both his supporters and his friends.

In the autumn of 1835, Mendelssohn settled in Leipzig to assume

---

[12] Review published in 1841 of Alexander Dreyschock's *Grosse Phantasie* op. 12 in *GS II*, pp. 24–25.

[13] Review published in 1835, "Die Mut über den verlornen Groschen: Rondo von Beethoven [op. 129]," in *GS I*, p. 101. Adapted from the translation of Fanny Raymond Ritter in Robert Schumann, *Music and Musicians: First Series* (New York, 1895), p. 13.

duties as conductor of the Gewandhaus Orchestra. Schumann had met Mendelssohn in August, the introduction having been provided by the Voigts. Because of the *Zeitschrift*, he was able to meet him not as a struggling composer who had recently abandoned plans for a career as a virtuoso, but as the editor and owner of a distinctive music journal whose popularity was growing. Unfortunately, in Mendelssohn's eyes, this was not necessarily to Schumann's advantage. Mendelssohn was suspicious of critics, many of whom he regarded as inept dilettantes. The perception of Schumann as a dilettante was one that, to a certain extent, Mendelssohn probably always retained. But to Schumann, Mendelssohn soon became the contemporary musician whom he most highly regarded. He delighted in Mendelssohn's skill as a performer, whether as pianist or conductor. The *Zeitschrift* regularly praised Mendelssohn's compositions, extolling both their craftsmanship and the inspiration animating them. Yet, Schumann was not unstinting in his praise. While commending Mendelssohn, he could still be critical—as if always expecting more from him.

Although only one year older then Schumann, Mendelssohn in 1835 had in the musical world attained an eminence that during his lifetime Schumann would never achieve. It is characteristic of Schumann that there was no evidence of envy. "Mendelssohn is the one," Schumann wrote, "on whom I gaze upward as if to a high mountain. He is a true god" (1 April 1836). In the 1830s, Mendelssohn and Schumann spent a good deal of time together, and established a friendship that, with some strain, lasted until Mendelssohn's death in 1847.

Mendelssohn's move to Leipzig helped to raise the musical standards of the city, and led as well to an increase in prestige. Distinguished musicians, many of them his friends and associates, were attracted to Leipzig, and it became an ideal opportunity for Schumann to become better acquainted with them. In October 1835, Ignaz Moscheles, Mendelssohn's teacher and good friend, visited the city. At Mendelssohn's instigation, Ferdinand David, a gifted violinist Schumann's age, became in February 1836 the new leader of the Gewandhaus Orchestra. And that autumn, the young English composer William Sterndale Bennett arrived in Leipzig, attracted by Mendelssohn's fame. During the time of his visit, which lasted about eight months, he and Schumann became good friends. Bennett was six years younger than Schumann and at the beginning of his career. The *Neue Zeitschrift für Musik* did much to help establish his reputation. In Schumann's estimation, Bennett was "English through and through, a splendid artist, a beautiful, poetic soul" (15 November 1836). Not long after his return to England, Bennett pressed Schumann to pay him a visit. The idea of visiting England was one that Schumann cherished, but it remained unfulfilled.

Chopin also visited Leipzig briefly in September 1835 and for a more extended stay a year later. To Dorn, Schumann related his "great joy" at meeting Chopin. Deeply moved at the opportunity to hear a number of Chopin's most recent compositions, Schumann described them as "all incomparable" (14 September 1836). Unlike those who seemed merely charmed by Chopin's compositions, Schumann recognized the audacity in the midst of their elegance: "Chopin's works are cannons," he wrote in a review of Chopin's two piano concertos, "concealed in flowers."[14]

During this same time, friendships developed with two other pianist composers: Stephen Heller and Adolph Henselt. Heller and Schumann never met, but through their correspondence they discovered their similarities. The impetus for their friendship was provided by their mutual affection for the writings of Jean Paul; Heller went so far as to dedicate his *Trois Impromptus* op. 7 to Liane de Froulay, a character in *Titan*. Both Heller and Henselt were, like Schumann, introverted. Henselt wrote little and, plagued by stage fright, performed infrequently. He and Schumann first met in January 1838. "We were like two brothers," Schumann wrote of the occasion.[15] It was not long before he and Henselt addressed one another using the less formal "du"—an intimacy rarely extended by Schumann.

The growing number of friendships, the work on the *Zeitschrift*—all seemed to provide a new sense of direction to Schumann. On 18 August 1834, he wrote to Töpken that he was "now living a novel such as perhaps never existed in any book." At times, it must have seemed to Schumann as if his fortune had finally changed for the better. But

---

[14] Review published in 1836 of Chopin's Second Piano Concerto op. 21 in *Ibid.*, p. 167. Chopin, incidentally, was far from enthusiastic about Schumann's compositions.

[15] Letter to Clara Wieck of 2 January 1838 in *Cl/Rob I*, p. 65. Schumann dedicated the *Novelletten* op. 21 to Henselt in 1839.

what made his situation even more extraordinary was his romance with a pupil of Friedrich Wieck, Ernestine von Fricken.

The Wiecks had met Ernestine and her father early in April 1834 at a concert in Plauen. Arrangements were made for her to study and board with Wieck, and she arrived in Leipzig on 21 April. Three years older than Clara, Ernestine was a talented pianist who, like Schumann, had considered studying with Hummel. She and Schumann got along well with one another, and matters progressed quickly. He wrote breathlessly to his mother in July: "Ernestine, daughter of a rich Bohemian—Baron von Fricken, her mother is a Countess Zettwitz, a splendid, pure, child-like nature, delicate and thoughtful, attached with the most heartfelt love to myself and to all that is artistic, extraordinarily musical—in short exactly what I wish for in a wife—and I whisper in your ear, my dear mother: if the question were put to me—whom would you choose—I would firmly answer: this one."[16] It was as if the mysterious Countess Abegg had come to life—noble, beautiful, rich, and musical.

Henriette Voigt became the confidante of the two lovers, and in late August was told of their engagement. Schumann gave Ernestine a ring and his portrait. All that was lacking was the consent of her family. Wieck, aware of the relationship, wrote to Ernestine's father: "Between Ernestine and Schumann there is—I do not say an intimate—but a great attraction . . . they have not exchanged a kiss, nor held one another's hand, but rather have taken a great *interest* in each another. That reflects Schumann's nature. How much I would need to write in order to describe Schumann to you—somewhat droll and headstrong, but noble, excellent, fanciful, highly gifted—a composer and writer of deep feeling and exceptional talent."[17] Ernestine's father wrote to her on 23 August, concerned about the propriety of the relationship, and advised her to avoid any actions that could be interpreted by others to her disparagement. He himself went to Leipzig later in the month to learn firsthand of the situation, met Schumann (whom he liked), but left with his daughter on 6 September, for their home in Asch.

Although approval for their engagement was not received, neither

---

[16] Letter of 2 July 1834 in *JgBr*, p. 243.
[17] Quoted in *W*, p. 141.

was it denied, and Ernestine and Schumann exchanged letters regularly. Schumann also began work on a piano composition, the *Etudes symphoniques* op. 13, a set of variations that use a theme by Ernestine's father (who was an amateur musician) as the basis. In addition, after noting the letter/pitches possibilities of her home, A–S (the pronunciation of E flat in German)–C–H (B natural in the German system), Schumann received the idea for the musical mottos that serve as the basis for *Carnaval* op. 9. In both October and December he visited Ernestine in Asch. In November he joyfully informed Henriette Voigt that Ernestine's father had given his consent. Four months later the Allegro op. 8 appeared, dedicated to "Mademoiselle la Baronne Ernestine de Fricken."

It is at that point that details of Schumann's relationship with Ernestine become sketchy. A letter in early June 1835 to his mother gives the impression that the association between Schumann and Ernestine had not altered. But at some time, possibly during a visit to Asch that next month, Schumann learned that Ernestine was not who she had claimed. She had been christened Christiana Ernestine Franziska, and was the illegitimate daughter of a sister (Countess Caroline Ernestine Louise von Zedtlitz) of Fricken's wife. The Frickens were childless, and Ernestine had been raised in their house as their daughter, but not formally adopted until 13 December 1834—after permission had been granted for the marriage to Schumann. With this knowledge, what Schumann the previous September had described as a "summer novel . . . the most remarkable of my life" abruptly came to an end.[18] In January 1836, by mutual agreement, the engagement was broken off.[19]

Our primary source for Schumann's reaction to the affair is found in a letter he wrote to Clara on 11 February 1838, the same letter in which he described his depression and the frightful night of 17/18 October 1833. During that episode he had visited a physician and told him he feared he might take his own life, but

---

[18] Letter to his mother of 5 September 1834 in *JgBr*, p. 256.

[19] Schumann met her for the last time in August 1837 and returned her letters to her. He later told Clara that the engagement had not been "*definite*" (letter of 13 July 1838). This statement does not ring true and is contradicted by Schumann's assertion to Henriette Voigt.

The doctor comforted me kindly, and finally said with a smile: 'Medicine is of no help here. Find a wife for yourself; she will soon cure you.' . . . Then came Ernestine—as good a girl as ever there was—She, I thought, is the one who will save you. I wanted to cling with all my power to some woman. I felt better—she loved me, that was clear—You know all—the separation, that we wrote to each other. . . . But now that she was away, and I began to think of how it might end, when I learned of her poverty, that I myself, no matter how industrious I might be, earned little, I felt enchained—I saw no end, no relief—then in addition I heard of unfortunate family complications which involved Ernestine, and for which I naturally blamed her, because she had long concealed it from me. All this taken together—cursed me—I must confess that I grew colder.

The two reasons given by Schumann as the basis for breaking off the engagement—her poverty and the "unfortunate family complications" (presumably her illegitimacy)—should have provided no obstacle had he actually loved her. At that time, Schumann saw no great earning potential for himself, evidently not enough to support a wife and family in the style he desired. Ernestine's supposed wealth had been intended by Schumann to serve as the basis for their household. He was not prepared to abandon music and adopt another profession in order to gain a more stable income. If it were necessary to choose between Ernestine and his career in music, Schumann's choice was clear. He was troubled as well by her illegitimacy, but seemed particularly concerned that she had not told him about it earlier. In fact, the hurried adoption in December 1834 could have been interpreted as a means of concealing it. This lack of openness and trust disturbed him.

But it was the realization of his love for Clara—not Ernestine's illegitimacy and her comparative poverty—that had been the deciding factor for him. During much of 1834, Clara had been on tour. When she returned, she seemed different. "You were no longer a child with whom I could laugh and play," he wrote to her. "You spoke so intelligently, and in your eyes I saw a secret love" (11 February 1838). During the summer and autumn of 1835, they spent much time together. The diary records: "Clara's eyes and her love . . . the first kiss in November."[20] Clara, too, remembered the first kiss. It occurred one

---

[20] Recollected in 1838. *Tgb I*, p. 421.

evening while leaving the Wieck house, as Clara guided him with a light down the stairs. "When you first kissed me," she recalled, "I thought I was going to faint. Everything turned black before my eyes. I could scarcely hold the lamp to show the way" (16 December 1838). Although it was not until 1835 that they professed and acknowledged their love for one another, the special relationship uniting them had been apparent to others—not least to Ernestine. "I have always thought," she wrote when she learned of their engagement, "that you could only love Clara."[21]

---

[21] Letter from Schumann to Clara of 26 October 1838 in *Cl/Rob I*, p. 276.

CHAPTER 7

Courtship and Marriage

> *Yet in these thoughts myself almost despising,*
> *Haply I think on thee, and then my state,*
> *Like to the lark at break of day arising*
> *From sullen earth, sings hymns at heaven's gate;*
> *For thy sweet love rememb'red such wealth brings*
> *That then I scorn to change my state with kings.*
> —Shakespeare, *The Twenty-ninth Sonnet*

WITH THEIR LOVE FOR ONE ANOTHER NOW ACKNOWLEDGED, and his association with Ernestine formally broken off, Schumann undoubtedly felt it would be a simple matter to gain the consent of Clara's father, and that their marriage would take place within a reasonable period of time. But Schumann was to find in Friedrich Wieck a stubborn, persistent, cunning, and often unethical opponent who would stop at nothing to prevent his daughter's marriage to Schumann. Why did Wieck react in such a manner? Writing to Baron von Fricken, he had described Schumann as "noble, excellent, fanciful, highly gifted—a composer and writer of deep feeling and exceptional talent"—admirable characteristics for a prospective son-in-law. Yet, within a few years, Wieck was publicly vilifying both his daughter and Schumann. Probably the deciding factor for Wieck was his conviction that all of the efforts he had made on his daughter's behalf would ultimately be wasted. There was not a single, notable instance of a female pianist—no matter how gifted—continuing her career with any regularity after marriage.

Wieck, who had noticed the attraction between Schumann and Ernestine, did not fail to perceive the growing relationship between his daughter and Schumann. He decided on a course of action that he was to use with some regularity: to separate them. Wieck and Clara left for Dresden in January 1836, but on 7 February Wieck returned to Leipzig on business. Schumann heard of his return and, accompanied by a friend, went to Dresden where he met secretly with Clara over a three-day period. He later described them as "holy, unforgettable" days.[1] Wieck learned of the meetings and was furious. Schumann's secretive visits had been improper, and he must have appeared shamefaced. Clara was only sixteen at the time; Schumann was twenty-five. Still, Wieck's reaction was extreme. He supposedly threatened to shoot Schumann and banned him from his home. Wieck and Clara soon left on a concert tour, and did not return until April.

There had been a sense of urgency to Schumann's visit to Dresden in February. His mother had died on the 4th. Distraught, Schumann did not attend the funeral. He had most recently spoken with her in December, and discussed with her the end of his relationship with Ernestine. Clara must have been discussed as well, and it is likely that Christiane Schumann, who was fond of Clara, gave her blessing to their love and encouraged their marriage. It must have been a source of profound distress for Schumann at the time of his bereavement to encounter Wieck's unexpected resistance.

Schumann and Clara were not to meet again for nearly eighteen months. During that time, Clara was frequently on tour. There was no communication between them. When Schumann sent to Clara a copy of his First Piano Sonata op. 11—published on Schumann's birthday in 1836 and "Dedicated to Clara by Florestan and Eusebius"—Wieck

---

[1] Gerd Nauhaus, " 'Schwere Abschiede'—Neuentdeckte autobiographische Dokumente Schumanns aus den Jahren 1836 und 1838," in *Schumann-Studien* 5, ed. Gerd Nauhaus, (Cologne, 1996), p. 21.

refused to allow her to acknowledge receipt of it. Shortly afterwards, he demanded that Clara return to Schumann all of the letters he had written to her.

At the same time, despite the growing success of the *Zeitschrift*, Schumann was meeting increasing difficulty and frustration in his professional life. There were few reviews of his music. He confided to Moscheles (whom he had befriended): "Music publishers want to know nothing of me" (8 March 1836). Additional proof of the instability of his career was provided later in the year when he felt it necessary to borrow money from his brothers, Carl and Eduard. Looking back on this period of his life, Schumann described it to Clara as

> The darkest time when I knew absolutely nothing about you and wanted forcibly to forget you. . . . I became resigned. But then the old pain broke out once again—then I wrung my hands—in the night I often said to God—"mercifully, only let this pass without me going mad." I thought at one time that I found your engagement announced in the newspapers. . . . I was a poor, beaten man unable for eighteen months either to pray or weep. (3 January and 6 February 1838)

In his despair, Schumann confessed: "[I] wanted to cure myself by making myself fall in love with a woman who nearly had me entrapped." Her identity remains unknown. But in his diary (in a synopsis of these years written in November 1838) there are the cryptic remarks: "Gloomy year 1836 . . . looked for Charitas and following thereof in January 1837."[2] Did Schumann reestablish his relationship with Christel? There has been speculation that in January 1837 a child was born to Christel; Schumann's diary for January 1837 contains the entry: "A little girl (on the fifth, I believe)."[3] With the lack of conclusive evidence, only conjecture is possible. But, given Schumann's despair and his fear that his engagement with Clara was over, resumption of his affair with Christel might have occurred. During this time, he appears not to have led the most virtuous life. In a letter of 11 October 1837, Clara expressed outrage over what she had heard of Schumann's recent conduct, and threatened to leave him if he did not control his "passions."

[2] *Tgb* I, p. 422.
[3] *Tgb* II, p. 31.

As Schumann's sense of discouragement and anxiety about the future increased, so did his need for female companionship. In the early 1830s, he had turned to his sister-in-law Rosalie for solace and comfort. He now turned to another sister-in-law, Therese (Eduard's wife), and she became a valued confidante. "In this deadly anxiety which sometimes comes over me, I have no one but you," he wrote to her on 31 December 1836.[4]

The initiative to reestablish his relationship with Clara was undertaken by Clara herself. On 13 August 1837, she performed three of Schumann's *Etudes symphoniques* at a concert in Leipzig. It was, she later wrote to him, the only way she could reveal her feelings to him. At about the same time, through their mutual friend, Ernst Becker, Clara asked Schumann to give back to her the letters he had previously written to her and that her father had demanded that she return. Schumann refused—and asked if she would like new ones in their place. He wrote to her on the 13th. On the 14th (Eusebius's saint's day), they became engaged. "An eternal union," Schumann wrote in his diary.[5] A year and a half had passed since they had first determined on an engagement, and both Clara and Schumann seemed to believe that now her father would relent.

Schumann had never written to Wieck formally asking for his daughter's hand. On Clara's birthday (13 September), he did so, telling Wieck of their mutual love and of his commitment to her. The exact nature of Wieck's response is not known. What is clear is that he did not forbid the marriage outright, but demanded they wait for two years and that Schumann amass sufficient funds to provide for them both. Further correspondence was not permitted, and all meetings between them would need to be public. In despair, Schumann wrote to Clara of Wieck's "coldness, this ill-will, this confusion, these contradictions— he has a new way to kill: he thrusts both blade and hilt into the heart" (18 September 1837).

The primary obstacle Wieck placed before Schumann was his

---

[4] After the death of Eduard, Schumann contemplated having Therese move in with himself and Clara; Clara for a time believed that Therese was in love with Schumann (*Cl/Rob II*, pp. 452, 462).

[5] Recollected in November 1838 in *Tgb I*, p. 422.

comparative poverty. But Schumann was convinced that Wieck was preoccupied with the financial aspects of marriage, and only interested in finding a rich husband for Clara. Despite Wieck's injunction, Clara and Schumann continued to correspond, secretly using her maid as an intermediary. On 26 September, he received Clara's response to her father's stipulations: "My spirit is strong, my heart constant and unchanged."

Some of the letters that they sent to one another during the next two years are among the most beautiful ever written. Schumann was eloquent and eager to display his love. Clara was inspired by his passion. During this first year of correspondence they were captivated by the sheer romance of their situation. For Schumann in particular it was as if he were once again living a novel: two lovers of extraordinary gifts destined for one another but thwarted by a reprehensible father. Many of his letters appear to be knowingly directed not just to Clara but to future readers.

Their constancy would be put to the test with regularity. In October 1837, Clara and her father left for a concert tour to Vienna, where they remained until May 1838. Her success was extraordinary. As a mark of honor, the position of Royal and Imperial Chamber Virtuoso was conferred on her. The post was without salary, but it was a distinction that had previously been conferred on two other great virtuosos of the day, Paganini and Thalberg. For Schumann, however, there were no triumphs. Early in November, he received a cold letter from Wieck, the contents of which are known only from Schumann's reference to it. To Clara, he contemptuously described Wieck as "a good businessman," and paraphrased Wieck as writing: "Hearts? what do I care about hearts?" (8 November 1837).

Schumann thought longingly and frequently of her, but somber considerations seemed to obsess him. On New Year's Eve as the clock struck twelve he wrote: "Alone and sober with thoughts of Clara . . . but I can not pray with as full a heart as I used to—why? Am I then so great a sinner?"[6]

Their separation proved a great trial for Clara as well. Through it all, she showed much strength and independence, but it was difficult

---

[6] *Tgb II*, p. 49.

for her to balance her duty as a daughter with her love for Schumann. Wieck spared no effort to undermine her resolve. He intimated that Schumann did nothing to support her artistry. Why, she asked Schumann in December, was there not more frequent mention of her in the *Neue Zeitschrift für Musik*? Schumann replied that he felt it was necessary to exercise restraint in referring to Clara in the journal lest Wieck believe Schumann was attempting to curry his favor.

There were additional misunderstandings. In her first letter from Vienna, Clara told Schumann that she had been thinking about their future *"very seriously"* (24 November). Marriage would not be possible, she informed him, unless their situation changed dramatically. Her musical career could not flourish if burdened by financial concerns. Schumann was filled with dismay. All he could offer was his determination to improve their lot, and a dry assertion that in several years he would be able to support "one or even two wives" (28 November).

Schumann laid great value on the symbolic meaning of rings. In 1828, he had received one from his mother: "I venerate in the ring not the ring itself, but you, dear mother, and the sentiment which led you to give it to me. May it be a magic ring, and a talisman against all sin, and may it lead me like a magic wand to good fortune."[7] The ring he had given to Clara was special to him, but when he wrote to her of it, she responded incredulously: "You put your trust in the ring? My God, that is only an external bond. Did not Ernestine also receive a ring from you? . . . And yet you broke the bond with her. So the ring is no help at all" (24 November 1837). Schumann was deeply offended: "You say somewhat harshly that I *broke* the bond with Ernestine. That is not true. It was approved and dissolved by both parties in suitable form. . . . And now that you care so little for my ring, I no longer care for yours and stopped wearing it yesterday. I dreamed I was walking by some deep water and it suddenly struck me to throw the ring into it—then I had an immense longing to plunge in after it" (28 and 29 November 1837). Now realizing the extent of his belief in the ring, Clara in later letters made a point of referring to it as a cherished symbol of their union.

It was a time of great loneliness for Schumann—separated from Clara, denied her hand, and denied as well recognition for his com-

---

[7] Letter of 29 June 1828 in *JgBr*, p. 27.

positions. "It sometimes pains me," he wrote, "that I hear so little said about them" (22 April 1838). He felt that Clara was the only one to whom he could speak about his art. But there were a few others with whom he could speak, if not as confidingly as with her. In January he received a letter from a devoted admirer, Simonin de Sire, and responded gloomily. "My path," he replied, "is, I know, a fairly lonely one—with no hurrahs from the crowds to stimulate my work" (8 February 1838). Four months later, Schumann received a letter from Franz Liszt, filled with praise. "Of those compositions that greatly interest me, there are only Chopin's and yours," Liszt wrote.[8] Unlike that of de Sire, the support of Liszt had a practical advantage: he could perform Schumann's music, and it was only by public performance that it could gain a wider audience.

Liszt's letter could not have come at a better time. Despite the turmoil in his personal life (or, as he seemed at times to believe, because of it), Schumann had been writing a great deal of music, all of it for solo piano: the First Piano Sonata op. 11 (completed in 1835), the *Fantasie* op. 17 (1836), the *Concert sans orchestre* op. 14 (1836), the *Fantasiestücke* op. 12 (1837), and the *Davidsbündlertänze* op. 6 (1837). In 1838, he completed the *Novelletten* op. 21, the *Kinderszenen* op. 15, the Second Piano Sonata op. 22, and *Kreisleriana* op. 16: in all, more than 250 pages of music. Liszt, in an insightful review (published in November 1837 in Paris in the *Revue et gazette musicale*) had singled out for praise the *Impromptus*, the Sonata op. 11, and *Concert sans orchestre* op. 14.

Despite Liszt's support, they did not meet until mid-March 1840, when Schumann traveled to Dresden to hear Liszt perform. A short time later, he came to Leipzig. "[Liszt] said to me yesterday, 'It is as if I had known you for twenty years'—and I feel the same way"—but despite being awed by Liszt's phenomenal musical ability, Schumann was put off by what he described as the "tinsel"—Liszt's showmanship.[9] He was to be disappointed as well in his hope of broader recognition as a result of Liszt's support. Unfortunately, on those occasions when

---

[8] Quoted in Wolfgang Boetticher, ed. *Briefe und Gedichte aus dem Album Robert und Clara Schumanns* (Leipzig, 1981), p. 109.

[9] Letter to Clara of 18 March 1840 in *Litzmann I*, p. 413.

Liszt did perform Schumann's music in public, audiences did not comprehend it and vastly preferred more conventional, virtuoso showpieces.

With the return of Clara from Vienna in May 1838, she and Schumann met frequently in secret. But Wieck kept a watchful eye on her, even conducting occasional searches for letters from Schumann. Two years earlier at the outset of their struggles, Schumann had described Wieck as "an honorable man, but a hothead" (1 March 1836). Now he saw him as a Philistine—materialistic, unfeeling, and concerned only with finding a rich husband for his daughter. It was at this point that Wieck's conduct became clearly malicious. In July, Clara reported that he had contacted Ernestine von Fricken in an attempt to stir up trouble. Matters were not helped by the presence of the composer Louis Rakemann who, six years younger than Schumann, was in love with Clara and doted on her. Clara found his presence annoying, but Wieck encouraged his visits.

The uncertainty and seemingly unending struggle took its toll. In his diary that August, Schumann described one episode—an anxiety attack of fearful proportions—that brings to mind the dreadful night of 17/18 October five years earlier. "Tuesday the entire day and night, the most frightful of my life. I thought I must burn up with anxiety and fear. In the afternoon a good letter from Clara arrived, the first in two weeks—but it did not help—all came together—that we must soon part, the fear, whether I would be able to succeed, alone in a large city—for a moment in the night I thought I could bear it no longer ... an unending, painful, tormenting music—God preserve me from dying in such a manner."[10]

Schumann's anxiety stemmed from his recent decision to travel to Vienna and publish the *Zeitschrift* there. Wieck had never wavered in his insistence that the primary obstacle to their marriage was Schumann's limited income. "It is settled," Wieck wrote in Clara's diary, "that Clara can never live in poverty and obscurity—but must have over 2,000 talers a year to spend."[11] Leipzig, Wieck asserted, would never be able to supply Schumann with the requisite income. Clara

---

[10] 7 August 1838 in *Tgb II*, p. 61.

[11] Quoted in Nancy B. Reich, *Clara Schumann: The Artist and the Woman* (Ithaca, NY, 1985), p. 83. 2,000 guilders (according to Clara, 1,600–1,800 talers) seems to be meant here.

interpreted his remarks to mean that if Schumann were to settle in a larger city and succeed there, Wieck would support their marriage. The idea of moving to Vienna strongly appealed to her. She had been charmed by her stay there, and described the city to Schumann as possessing a stimulating and elevated musical life.

When he received word from Clara that a successful move to Vienna would resolve the concerns of her father, Schumann reacted with enthusiasm. But he had some reservations. "I am a Saxon through and through," he noted, and he felt it would be difficult to leave his family and be far from his homeland (19 March 1838). Schumann also wondered if the move had been devised by Wieck as an ideal means of getting Schumann out of Leipzig and away from Clara. But because of Clara's influence, Schumann began seriously to consider moving to Vienna as early as March 1838. He tentatively set the date for their marriage—Easter 1840—and left Leipzig on 27 September. It was, his diary noted, "*my first step as a man.*"[12]

Schumann's primary concern in Vienna was convincing the Austrian censors to permit publication of his journal. Censorship in Austria was severe, a result of the policy of repression initiated by Metternich after the fall of Napoleon in 1815—even Schumann's copies of Jean Paul and Byron were retained at the border. Schumann, whose *Zeitschrift* had no political tendencies, hoped to encounter few difficulties. In addition, Count Joseph Sedlnitzsky, the powerful director of censorship, had been a supporter of Clara during her earlier visit to Vienna and, it was hoped, would prove receptive.

Schumann arrived in Vienna on 3 October, and six days later met with Sedlnitzsky (whom he described as friendly toward him). He was told that, because he was a foreigner, it was first of all necessary to find an Austrian publisher willing to publish the journal. Initially, Tobias Haslinger—who, in addition to publishing the *Allgemeine musikalischer Anzeiger*, had published Schumann's opp. 13, 14, and 16—was approached, but he made excessive demands. Schumann then turned to the publisher, Carl Gerold. Formal government application for publication was initiated.

"You will regret ever having come here," Haslinger had told Schu-

---

[12] *Tgb II*, p. 68.

mann not long after his arrival (25 October 1838). It is not clear whether his statement was meant as a threat or as a comment on Schumann's naivete. But Schumann soon became frustrated with the situation. As time passed, it became apparent that he was dealing with a large and omnipotent bureaucracy. All of Schumann's efforts—including asking Clara to write to a lady-in-waiting of the Empress whom she knew from her earlier visit—were without effect. As the process dragged on, it began to resemble a nightmarish episode by Kafka. By mid-October, Schumann was considering other cities (Paris and London) as possible sites for the *Zeitschrift*. "Believe me, Therese," he wrote to his sister-in-law in December, "if it depended on me alone, I would return to Leipzig tomorrow. Leipzig is not as small a place as I thought. Here there is as much gossip and provincialism as in Zwickau" (18 December 1838). What Schumann was gradually discovering was that small-mindedness and pettiness could present obstacles even more formidable than censorship.

Disheartening news was received from Clara not long after his arrival. Wieck told her that he would "never give [his] consent" to their marriage, even if Schumann were to meet with success in Vienna (1 October 1838). That month he wrote directly to Schumann (the contents are not known). Clara was astounded by the letter; Schumann felt insulted. His diary and correspondence reflected his profound depression.

For months, Schumann persisted in his attempt to gain official sanction from the authorities. He still remained hopeful. To Oswald Lorenz, managing the *Zeitschrift* in his absence, Schumann wrote that publication of the journal in Vienna might now be delayed until July 1839. But even Clara became disgusted with the delays and obstacles, and advocated returning to Leipzig, where she now felt they would be better off. Finally, early in March, Schumann received word that permission to publish the *Zeitschrift* in Vienna had been denied. The reason for the decision is not known, but there are several possibilities. Most plausible is that the censor received malicious reports about Schumann, possibly from the editors of rival journals. Schumann speculated that Wieck had written directly to Sedlnitzsky in an attempt to undermine his position; there is no evidence for this assertion, but at one point Clara did inform Schumann that Wieck had written to Haslinger, among others.

Schumann strongly suspected that, fearful of the competition the *Zeitschrift* would provide, Haslinger may have had a hand in the decision.[13] But even if no damaging reports had been received, it is quite possible that the Austrian censors would have been disturbed by what they perceived as the revolutionary tendencies of the *Zeitschrift*. At a time when secret and prohibited political societies such as the Carbonari were flourishing, the *Davidsbund* itself might have been suspect.

In mid-March, Schumann wrote to Clara, announcing that he would leave early in April. But he was reluctant to accept defeat and hesitant to abandon plans for moving to Vienna. He suggested that before their marriage Clara return to Vienna to perform and that they settle there—if possible publishing the *Zeitschrift* in Vienna starting in 1841. A few days before his departure, an additional complication arose. Schumann informed Clara that Haslinger had now expressed his willingness to publish the *Zeitschrift*, if Schumann served as editor in Germany. But Schumann was suspicious of the offer, and then, when he appeared to believe that Haslinger was sincere, failed to follow up on it before leaving Vienna.

Despite his assertions to Clara, Schumann had had his fill of Vienna. His struggle with censorship had been exasperating, but even more disturbing had been the musical life in the city. He had not found the musical Arcadia that Clara had described. Instead, in his eyes the general musical perception of Vienna, with its fondness for light, entertaining music, had been confirmed. Schumann had been surprised both by the number of musical cliques and their pettiness. Vienna is a city, he wrote in the *Zeitschrift* in 1838, where "they are afraid of everything new, of everything that strays from the beaten track. Even in music they want nothing revolutionary"—a comment that in itself must have endeared him to the censors.[14] "The Viennese," he confided to Carl Kossmaly on 1 September 1842, "are an ignorant people, and actually know little of what occurs outside their city."

Schumann left Vienna on 5 April (his departure hastened by news he had received that his brother Eduard was seriously ill). But despite

---

[13] See the letter to Clara of 4 February 1839 in *Cl/Rob II*, p. 381. After Schumann's departure from Vienna, Haslinger disappears as a significant publisher of Schumann's works.

[14] Review of Berlioz's compositions in 1838 in *GS I*, p. 31.

his disappointment, the six months spent in Vienna had not been wasted. By attending regularly concerts and performances of opera, Schumann had come into contact with a good deal of music (some of it, such as Donizetti's *L'elisir d'amore*, not at all to his liking). He also had been active as a composer, completing in all essentials four works (the *Arabesque* op. 18, *Blumenstück* op. 19, *Nachtstücke* op. 23, and *Humoreske* op. 20), and beginning work on three others (the *Faschingsschwank aus Wien* op. 26, Four Pieces for Piano op. 32, and a Piano Concerto in D minor). Because of his admiration for Schubert, he had made a point of looking up Schubert's brother, Ferdinand. Ferdinand possessed a number of his brother's manuscripts, both musical and literary. As a result, Schumann arranged to have several of Schubert's letters and the autobiographical "My Dream" published in the *Zeitschrift*. Schumann also examined a group of unpublished compositions by Schubert, writing to Breitkopf & Härtel to aid their publication.

Most significant of all had been Schumann's discovery of Schubert's last symphony (No. 9. "The Great," in C major). Schumann took an active role in arranging its publication by Breitkopf, leading to its successful premiere by Mendelssohn and the Gewandhaus Orchestra on 21 March. He was enthusiastic about his find—"a magnificent work, somewhat long, but extraordinarily full of life, and *completely new* in character"[15]—and wrote a lengthy and laudatory review of the work for the *Neue Zeitschrift für Musik*. To write it, he used what he felt was a precious relic discovered in Vienna. Not long after his arrival, Schumann had visited Beethoven's grave and found a pen-nib near it. His diary took note of the "strength and happy thoughts" it imparted.[16] Schumann used it in writing the review of Schubert's symphony, concluding: "I only use it on festive occasions, such as today."[17] Two years later, he used the pen-nib to write the Symphony in B flat major op. 38, his first major orchestral composition.

During Schumann's residence in Vienna, Clara had been preparing a concert tour to Paris, with the possibility of following it with a trip to London. The journey was to be made without Wieck, who did not

---

[15] Letter to Kossmaly of 8 January 1842 in *Br*, p. 212.
[16] October 1838 in *Tgb II*, p. 73.
[17] Review of Schubert's C major Symphony published in 1840 in *GS I*, p. 464.

disguise his hope of its failure in order to emphasize her continued dependence on him. From the beginning, he had made a point of telling Clara that he would do nothing to help her earn any money that could be used as a basis for achieving the financial security he had stipulated as a requirement for her marriage to Schumann.

Despite her father's refusal to accompany her, Clara remained determined to make the trip. Her independence was extraordinary. Not just her concert tours but much of the day-to-day existence of her life had been controlled by her father. Now she would to a great extent be on her own, and would be responsible not just for performing brilliantly but for arranging all aspects of the tour—including mundane but essential matters such as accommodations, rental of the concert hall, locating a suitable instrument to perform on, having it tuned, tickets, reimbursement for any assisting musicians, and so on. At the time, it would have been expected for a man—husband, father, or manager—to handle those aspects of the journey. Clara's tour to the musical capital of Europe was an emphatic confirmation of her determination, courage, and ambition.

She left on 8 January 1839, accompanied by a salaried companion (a Frenchwoman by the name of Claudine Dufourd selected by Wieck) whom she disliked and distrusted, and whom she was relieved to dismiss in March. The itinerary included several concerts in Germany, and, in the midst of her performances, she received some welcome news: in November Ernestine von Fricken had been married to Count Wilhelm von Zedtwitz. No time was lost in writing to Schumann about it, who also appeared relieved. He had felt some guilt for his conduct toward her. Now that Ernestine was married (and, as she reported to Clara, extremely happy), his guilt lessened, as did his concern that Ernestine would supply Wieck with malicious information to be used against him. There had actually been no cause for Schumann's concern. Both before and after her marriage, Ernestine was steadfast in her support of them.[18]

On 6 February, Clara arrived in Paris, where she was to remain for more than six months. In her father's absence, she felt increasingly iso-

---

[18] The remainder of her life was unfortunate: after less than eight months of marriage, her husband died intestate in 1839. Ernestine received no financial support, and later wrote to both Clara and Schumann despairingly. She died of typhus in 1843.

lated and low in spirits. Schumann responded with his unwavering support. But it was late in the concert season, and despite playing well, Clara was not satisfied. She had hoped for a triumph similar to what she had experienced in Vienna, but that had not been the case. Although she met many of the notables in Paris, including Meyerbeer and Heine, she was sensitive and quick to take offense, seeming to believe at times that nearly everyone was working against her. Schumann's friends and associates in Paris had been counted on for their support. But Clara became highly critical of the two from whom the most had been expected: Hector Berlioz—whose *Symphonie fantastique* Schumann had praised with remarkable discernment in the *Zeitschrift*—and Stephen Heller. Both, Clara mistakenly believed, were hostile to her. Schumann offered constant praise, and enthusiastically encouraged her to continue her tour by traveling to London. But she thought it best to remain in Paris for the year, and to play again in the next concert season.

Not long after her arrival, Clara had renewed contact with a good friend now living in Paris, Emilie List. Emilie (whom Schumann also knew) was the daughter of Friedrich List, who had fled Germany as a result of political repression. After emigrating to the United States, he had returned in 1833 as American consul in Leipzig. Emilie and Clara had been particularly close (they had been in the same confirmation class), and Clara, taking advantage of their presence in Paris, decided to live with the List family.

While Clara attempted to focus her attention on gaining entry into Parisian musical circles, her father once again began to show interest in her. Late in February he wrote to Clara, suggesting that she perform in Amsterdam where he would meet her, and then follow that with a brief tour in Germany. Clara declined, but she seemed brightened by the possibility of renewed contact with her father. When Schumann learned of Wieck's overtures, he bluntly advised her to renounce all hope of gaining consent for their marriage from Wieck. Now convinced that it might become necessary to go to court in order to gain approval for their marriage, Schumann contacted an attorney for advice.

Early in April, Wieck wrote to Emilie List—with the obvious intention of having the information passed on to his daughter—and expressed his continued dissatisfaction with the relationship between Clara and Schumann. He threatened to disown her, deprive her of her inheritance, and bring a lawsuit against the pair should they continue in their folly. It was Wieck's most threatening stance thus far, and Clara must have been both frightened and perplexed by it. Then, on 1 May, Emilie List received a second letter from Wieck, but this time a letter that spoke of his love for Clara and her misunderstanding of him, a letter that was intended to appeal to Clara's heart and her sense of responsibility as a daughter. In her desire to appease what she felt were his wounded feelings, Clara anxiously replied to her father on the same day. Although she remained firm in her support of Schumann—"if only I could convince you of his kindheartedness!"—she promised not to marry until they were assured of a more secure financial future.[19] At the same time she mentioned the possibility of a concert tour to Belgium, Holland, and England, and suggested that Wieck come to her in Paris.

The next day she wrote to Schumann presenting her father's concerns in the best possible light. She emphasized the need for "a worry-free future," maintained that the marriage must be postponed, and expressed her concern that by her actions she might very well be guilty of driving her father to an early grave. With a secure financial basis, she assured Schumann, her father's consent for their marriage would be readily given. Mention was also made of Wieck coming to Paris and the possibility of the extended concert tour. At the same time, Emilie List wrote to Schumann. She told him of the most recent letter she had received from Wieck—not the hotheaded one that had threatened to disown Clara if she and Schumann married. Every attempt was made to calm Schumann and to convince him of Wieck's good intentions. "On the contrary," she wrote, "[Wieck] would like to see Clara married to you"—but simply desired "a more secure, worry-free future" for his daughter.[20] She added that for some months Clara had not been well.

Schumann's reaction to the letters was one of shock and anger. It must have seemed to him that after years of struggle, Clara's resolve was weakening and that Wieck, now with the assistance of her best friend,

---

[19] Letter of 1 May 1839 in *Litzmann I*, p. 316.

[20] Letter of [2 May 1839] in Clara Schumann, *"Das Band der ewigen Liebe": Briefwechsel mit Emile und Elise List*, ed. Eugen Wendler (Stuttgart, 1996), p. 62.

was putting forth the same old excuses, continuing to delay the marriage, while still giving no indication when, if ever, he would support it. This latest crisis came at a time of turmoil. Schumann's brother, Eduard, had died on 6 April. Coupled with his disappointment concerning the trip to Vienna, Schumann's spirits were unusually low.

With Eduard's death, the firm created by August Schumann became available for purchase, and Schumann seriously considered buying it. He felt that the firm could expand by publishing music. As it turned out, the cost of the firm was, in Schumann's eyes, excessive, so nothing came of the plan. At the same time, he was considering another short-lived project: a collaboration to produce a *Klavierschule*. In the preface to his op. 3 etudes, Schumann had already taken steps toward writing a piano school of sorts. In this new venture, he was to provide the text, Henselt the exercises, and Ernst Ferdinand Wenzel (a collaborator on the *Zeitschrift*) the pedagogical material. Schumann later offered to let Clara contribute as well, but she was not enthusiastic about the venture. Both projects were hastily conceived, no doubt as a result of the failure to move the *Zeitschrift* to Vienna.

Schumann's response to Clara's and Emilie List's letters (as well as a second letter from Clara) were later destroyed, so the precise nature of his reaction is not known. Schumann himself described his letter to Clara as a "spirited protest,"[21] while Clara later characterized his letter to Emilie as "too harsh, too rude" (23 May 1839). It seems clear that he expressed forcefully his anger and exasperation. On 13 May, Clara wrote to Schumann, eager to restore their relationship to what it had been. From now on, both appear to be united in their distrust and suspicion of Friedrich Wieck. Their wedding, they agreed, would take place on Easter Sunday 1840 (19 April).

Now once again reconciled with Schumann and in harmony with their plans for the future, Clara wrote to her father, painting a rosy picture of their financial state and asking for his permission for the marriage. Wieck responded with a ten-page letter in June, and offered his consent, but made his support contingent on the acceptance of a number of outrageous stipulations: neither Clara nor Robert could live in Saxony during Wieck's lifetime; Schumann's statement for his income

---

[21] *Tgb II*, p. 496.

would be audited and examined by an attorney of Wieck's choice; Clara would receive no inheritance; Wieck would retain Clara's previous concert earnings for five more years before turning them over to her. Clara was horrified by Wieck's insistence that she sign a statement agreeing to his terms.

At Clara's request on 24 June Schumann wrote to Wieck in a final attempt to come to terms with him. But Wieck, using his wife as intermediary, responded curtly, and severed all connections with Schumann. Six days later, Schumann contacted Wilhelm Einert, an attorney in Leipzig, in order to take legal means to gain approval for the marriage. Einert was instructed to negotiate with Wieck, if possible. If unsuccessful, the matter was to be brought before the Court of Appeal. On 16 July, Schumann and Clara began court proceedings to invalidate Wieck's opposition.

On 27 July, the court ruled that an attempt should first be made to come to a friendly understanding between the two parties. Clara reluctantly left Paris during the second week of August in order to attend this meeting, fearful of confronting her father face-to-face. She was no longer welcome in Wieck's home. In July, Schumann traveled to Berlin to meet Clara's mother, Marianne Bargiel (now re-married), in order to gain her consent to the marriage. It was quickly given, and Clara now moved in with her mother. She did so with hesitancy, however, feeling uncomfortable with a mother with whom she had had only limited contact.

The stress of the court proceedings exacted a severe toll. From the start, Schumann felt oppressed by his role in the proceedings, and confessed to Clara that he was deeply disturbed that he was separating her from her father. As time passed and delays were encountered, his spirits sank. The death of Henriette Voigt on 15 October (like Schuncke, from tuberculosis) was an additional source of anguish. During this time of crisis, Schumann found solace in the music of Bach. "I save myself again and again with Bach," Schumann wrote, "and derive joy and strength to work and love" (11 August 1839). Bach had become, he told Dorn on 5 September, his "daily Bible."

At first, Wieck appeared anxious to avoid bringing the matter to court, and on Clara's birthday she received a letter from him asking her to meet him in Dresden. Einert, however, suspected a trap and advised Clara to meet in the more friendly and familiar environment of Leipzig, where they met on 25 September. But once again Wieck was willing to give his consent only if certain conditions were met. As before, the stipulations were outlandish, including requiring her to pay 1,000 talers for her belongings and piano, giving her previous earnings as a concert artist to her brothers, and the settlement of 8,000 talers on her by Schumann in the event of a separation. Wieck's demands knew no bounds. He later attempted to charge her for the lessons he had given her.

On 2 October, the first meeting of the Court of Appeal (*Appellationsgericht*) was held. Wieck did not appear, and petitioned for postponement. A new hearing date was scheduled for 18 December. At that time, he presented a lengthy list of charges against Schumann. He attacked Schumann's skill as critic and composer, claimed that he was unable to support Clara and wanted to live off her earnings, asserted that he could not speak or write clearly (Schumann's handwriting was notoriously poor), that he lied about his income, and that he was a drunkard. It was a ludicrous and in many ways a pathetic attempt to discredit Schumann. Each of Wieck's charges could be refuted, and Schumann and Clara remained confident, hoping to be married before May.

On 4 January 1840, the court announced the dismissal of all of Wieck's accusations except for the one accusing Schumann of being a drunkard. It was a serious charge, and Wieck was given additional time to validate his assertion. Schumann was somewhat vulnerable to Wieck's allegation—his fondness for beer and wine was no secret—but to depict him as a drunkard was spiteful, and Schumann prepared to line up a series of witnesses, including Mendelssohn, to testify to his sobriety. On 1 June, Schumann brought a suit against Wieck for defamation of character.[22]

During this period, Wieck behaved abominably. He was the author or instigator of several malicious "anonymous" letters sent to Clara. When Clara gave a series of concerts in Berlin and northern Germany,

---

[22] The case was not decided until 1841; Wieck lost and was sentenced to eighteen days in jail.

he attempted to undermine them, writing to associates describing her as "a fallen, abominable, wicked girl."[23] Friends of Wieck were used to distribute copies of his charges against Schumann in cities in which Clara performed. The strain on Clara was overwhelming. Prior to a concert on 25 January 1840, she fainted.

The court proceedings dragged on through the spring and summer of 1840 (a result of extensions granted to Wieck), producing a time of continued stress. For Schumann, a private and reserved man, the increasingly public nature of the spectacle could only have appeared humiliating and demeaning. But Clara, despite her father's malicious conduct, remained torn by her love for him. In March 1840, she was distressed to learn that Liszt, when performing in Leipzig, had neither visited her father nor sent him complimentary tickets—actions she attributed to Liszt's friendship with Schumann.

On 6 July, unable to offer support for his charge, Wieck withdrew his assertion of Schumann's drunkenness. On 1 August 1840, the court ruled in Schumann's and Clara's favor. Wieck still had ten days to appeal the decision, but no further attempt was made to delay the settlement. Wieck, however, continued to retain money from Clara's earlier concert appearances, a matter that was only settled later by an intermediary. On 12 August, the final decision of the court was announced, and on the 16th the banns were published. Schumann wrote to Ernst Becker—whose mutual friendship had led three years earlier to their engagement—announcing the date of the marriage, but asked him to tell no one about it. Schumann still feared the possibility of some malicious action. On Saturday, 12 September—the day before Clara's twenty-first birthday—in a ceremony limited to only the closest friends and family, she and Schumann were married in Schönefeld, a small town near Leipzig. In her diary—on a date that she described as the "most beautiful and most important" of her life—Clara observed that after days of oppressively cloudy weather, the sun appeared, as if to bless their union.[24]

---

[23] *Litzmann I*, p. 409.

[24] Entry of 12 September 1840 quoted in Clara Schumann, *"Band,"* p. 20.

CHAPTER 8

The Piano Compositions, 1834–39

> *To a pure mind, especially, the carnival appears like the return of man to primitive innocence and joy, like the realization of the loveliest legends from the time of the minnesingers and troubadours, or even like a new Paradise, vouchsafed to us for one week in every year. Then are laid aside all strict social forms, because the evil they are meant to restrain seems to have been banished from the earth.*
>
> —M. Goldschmidt, *Homeless; or, A Poet's Inner Life*

THE PIANO COMPOSITIONS CREATED BY SCHUMANN DURING the 1830s remain among his most popular works. Many of them are of unparalleled exuberance, impetuosity, and intensity—all characteristics that have assured a devoted following, but that initially proved an obstacle to their comprehension. Schumann himself was aware of the distinctive nature of this work, an aspect that he later attributed to his youth and to the "turbulent and agitated" life he was leading. "The man and the musician always attempted to express themselves at the same time," he wrote (5 May 1843). But it is also evident that Schumann made a conscious effort to create music unlike that of any of his contemporaries.

His compositions, Schumann felt, were a reflection of his life. His love for Clara, pain at their forced separation, anger, despair, and dismay over their struggle to marry, as well as hope for their future together—all could be found in his work. "Everything in the world has an effect upon me," he wrote to Clara on 13 April 1838. "Politics, literature, people: I think about it all in my fashion, and my feelings find their expression in music." The hardship and anguish Schumann experienced as a result of Wieck's implacable resistance at times led him to despair, but, as he revealed to Clara, they could also serve as inspiration: "I have discovered that there is no more powerful stimulus to imagination than tension and longing for something" (19 March 1838). At times during these difficult years the ease with which musical ideas presented themselves seemed miraculous. But during the summer and autumn of 1839, burdened by concern over the trial, Schumann found himself unable to compose at all, and lamented over his condition both to Clara and in his diary.

Schumann perceived much of the music he composed during these years as in its way a musical record of his life, and as one strongly emotional in content. These were not views, incidentally, which he retained later in life. He explained to Moscheles in 1837 that the program associated with *Carnaval* was of less significance than the soul-states created by the music, that is, the distinct emotions or moods (reflective of the soul) that could be portrayed in sound. Schumann even went so far as to find programs and specific emotions in purely instrumental compositions of other composers. "Most" of Bach's fugues, he once wrote, were "character pieces."[1]

But Schumann remained skeptical of music's ability to transmit with accuracy a comprehensive and detailed program (such as that for Berlioz's *Symphonie fantastique*). He was dubious as well of the ability of music alone—absolute music—to transmit with precision the emotional state intended by the composer. It was for that reason that the use of titles in his compositions invariably took on special significance to Schumann. In selecting a title, he attempted to direct the listener with greater precision to the program (if present) or the soul-state intended for the piece. To those who maintained that titles were unnecessary, he replied that a composition was not harmed by having one, and gained the

---

[1] Review in 1838 of Czerny's *Schule des Fugenspiels* op. 400 in *GS I*, p. 354.

distinction of preventing "obvious and gross misunderstanding of the character [of the piece]."[2] "A title selected with care," he concluded, "increases the impression produced by a piece of music."[3]

Yet, he always remained sensitive to criticism of his use of titles, and made a point on several occasions of emphasizing that, in his compositions, titles were supplied only after the music had been created (which in truth was not always the case). In numerous instances Schumann never revealed his programs. He did not want to be perceived as excessively literary, that is, more concerned with the program than with the music itself. And he also was hesitant to disclose his personal feelings, not just because of his private nature but because in some instances he feared he was leaving himself open to possible ridicule.

Schumann was convinced that the two most significant influences on his compositions during the 1830s were Jean Paul and Johann Sebastian Bach. But he never thought of himself as an imitator, and took great pride in his originality. When Clara attempted to flatter him by referring to him as a second Beethoven, he responded irritably: "Never refer to me again as Jean Paul II or Beethoven II. For the length of a second I could truly hate you. I am willing to be ten times less than these others, and only *something to myself*" (25 January 1839). That his compositions were distinctive and original—even if it hindered their comprehension—was of great importance to him. During the latter half of the 1830s, the specific influence of Jean Paul is less striking. That of Bach, however, increased in prominence.

It is often thought that Bach was "rediscovered" as a result of Mendelssohn's performance of the *St. Matthew Passion* in 1829. If by use of the term "rediscovery" the exposure of Bach's music to a wider audience is meant, then there is some justification for its use. Mendelssohn's performance (and others that followed) introduced Bach's music to far more people than had known it during his lifetime. But "rediscovery" implies "forgotten," and that had not at all been the case with Bach. "You will find that a great many organists, cantors, etc., etc., in Germany possess one or more pieces by S. Bach," wrote Johann Nicolaus

---
[2] Review in 1838 of Moscheles's *Charakteristische Etuden* op. 95 in *Ibid.*, p. 361.
[3] Review in 1839 of Henselt's *Etudes de salon* op. 5 in *Ibid.*, p. 390.

Forkel (Bach's first biographer) in 1801, "which these gentlemen consider a musical treasure solely because of reputation."[4] Bach's music increasingly became available during the late eighteenth and early nineteenth centuries, and the keyboard works—especially *The Well-Tempered Clavier* and the *Goldberg Variations*—were held in great esteem.

It would not be surprising if Schumann's initial contact with Bach's music was a result of his study with Kuntsch. Kuntsch's musical tastes were expansive and progressive enough to include the music of Prince Louis Ferdinand. In addition, as an organist, he would probably have been familiar with Bach. When, in the 1830s, Schumann wrote to Kuntsch of his increasing study of Bach, the inference seems clear that Kuntsch was familiar with it. It is likely, then, that Schumann came into contact with Bach's music well before 1827. But it is misleading to interpret Schumann's reference to Bach's influence on him solely as a reference to Bach's polyphony, and to trace Bach's presence in predominantly contrapuntal compositions such as the Studies for Pedal Piano op. 56, or the Six Fugues on the Name "Bach" op. 60.

In the works of the 1830s, passages of fugue, canon, or elaborate counterpoint are not common. There is the fugal conclusion to the *Impromptus* op. 5 a conspicuous and not particularly successful Bach influence. But after the completion of op. 5, Schumann benefited from a more detailed and exhaustive study of Bach's music. From February 1837 until the autumn of that year, he examined the *Art of Fugue*, somewhat critically, for he was disdainful at times of what he felt to be its excessively cerebral nature. Over the next two years, he described Bach as his "daily bread" and "daily Bible," and from the diaries it seems these doses of Bach consisted of repeated study of the *Well-Tempered Clavier*.[5] Pieces such as the *Fughette* from Schumann's op. 32, although light in nature, bear witness to the contrapuntal influence of Bach, as do the *Scherzo* and *Gigue* from the same opus.

To understand the extent of Bach's influence on Schumann, it is essential to recognize that he meant far more to Schumann than con-

---

[4] Letter of 4 December 1801 in *The Forkel-Hoffmeister and Kühnel Correspondence: A Document of the Early 19th-Century Bach Revival*, ed. George B. Stauffer (New York, 1990), p. 13.

[5] Letters to Clara of 19 March 1838 and to Dorn of 5 September 1839 (*Cl/Rob I*, p. 126; *Br*, p. 171).

trapuntal mastery. "What art owes to Bach," Schumann wrote in 1840, "is to the musical world hardly less than what a religion owes to its founder."[6] It was Bach's chromaticism, rhythmic drive, and melodic structure that particularly appealed to Schumann.

Schumann's use of chromaticism (particularly the extensive use of secondary dominants) owes much to Bach. It often leads not just to striking dissonance, but to tonal distortion. Also present are a drive and intensity (derived from well-defined, repetitive, rhythmic cells) resulting in distinctly Bach-like configurations (Ex. 8.1).

Rather than relying on a lyrical, "singing" melodic line—a type of tunefulness preferred during much of the first half of the nineteenth century—in the 1830s Schumann often used a more motivic melodic basis recalling that of Bach. By doing so, and by supplementing it with occasional use of imitation, the melodic structure became more complex. Schumann noted with pride this change in his compositional approach, commenting that he was no longer satisfied with the "lyric

Ex. 8.1

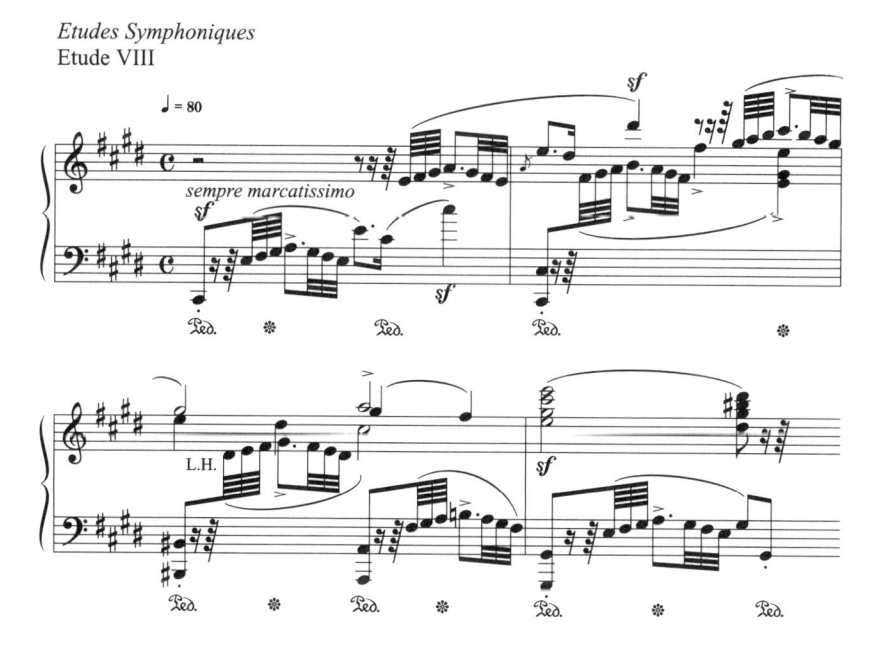

Etudes Symphoniques
Etude VIII

[6] Review in 1840 of Mendelssohn's "Organ Concert" in GS I, p. 492.

Ex. 8.2

Kreisleriana

simplicity" of his earlier works, and attributing the change to his study of Bach and Beethoven (14 June 1839; Ex. 8.2).

Schumann's reverence of Bach made his own compositions more complex and distinctive, and at the same time served to make them appear less intelligible to audiences of his day. Clara felt that by creating such original and at times abstruse compositions, he was severely limiting both his audience and his potential income. She advised him to compose something "brilliant, easy to understand," without a program and titles—"not too long and not too short . . . perhaps some variations or a rondo" (2 April 1839). It was well-intended advice, and in his way Schumann complied with the *Arabesque* op. 18 and the *Blumenstück* op. 19, but it was a token effort.

Although the specific influence of Jean Paul was not as strong during these years, the general effect of Schumann's admiration for his work continued to express itself in his compositions. The love for mystery and concealed meaning remains, and, more than ever, the juxtaposition of humor and sentiment. This continued interest gives many of Schumann's works a marked literary basis, that is, literary models (rather than musical) often predominate, and frequently influence compositional design.

The piano compositions of the 1830s fall into two broad categories: (1) large-scale works, three to five movements in length, traditional in genre (such as the sonatas and fantasie), and (2) multimovement compositions similar in approach to the *Intermezzi* op. 4, frequently with programmatic implications (such as *Carnaval* op. 9). In both categories, there is much variety of structure. Traditional musical forms are encountered, such as sonata form (the first movements of the Second Piano Sonata op. 22 and Third Piano Sonata op. 14) and sonata-rondo (the finale of the Second Piano Sonata), but always with individual touches. In the multimovement works, ternary form is the norm. But there are numerous instances of truly unique musical structures (the finale of the First Piano Sonata op. 11 is a notable instance)—an indication of Schumann's inventiveness and a matter of pride to him.

Substantial variety is found as well in Schumann's thematic material (and his use of it). The most conventional melodic structures are found in slow movements, movements that he often intended to be songlike and tuneful. In general, however, his melodies are not vocally oriented, but idiomatic for the piano. Much about them is unpredictable. Their movement can be disconcerting, with surprising leaps and rapid runs, often creating a soaring effect. Schumann displays much ingenuity in their construction. Symmetrical four-bar phrases are encountered less frequently than in his work of the 1840s. In compositions such as the sonatas (which he regarded as more grandiose), he displayed considerable interest in melodies motivic in basis—not necessarily with an eye for their development within the movement itself, but, for their restatement (and transformation) in other movements, as a means of unifying the composition.

For its time, Schumann's harmony is quite adventurous. Hackneyed chords such as the diminished seventh (often used by other composers for dramatic effect) are used sparingly. Most effective is his distinctive juxtaposition of chords, resulting in harmonic progressions that frequently go against textbook models and even today can be abrasive in their effect. He became increasingly adept at avoiding statements of the tonic key, increasing tension in the process (the first movement of the Fantasie op. 17 does not make a full statement of the tonic until the final measure). But prolonged chromaticism, such as that found in the music of Liszt, appears infrequently.

Schumann's inventive use of rhythm is frequently overlooked, yet it is one of the hallmarks of his style. In addition to driving, impetuous motor rhythms, there is extensive use of syncopation, hemiola, and cross-rhythms. In an era when little interest was displayed in rhythmic complexity, Schumann's resourcefulness is truly astonishing.

Of Schumann's compositions of the 1830s, an admirer recalled that "the circle that comprehended them was at first confined to the limits of a club."[7] Not just the general public but experienced musicians as well were confused by them. In the summer of 1838, Schumann played several of his compositions for the theorist Moritz Hauptmann (exactly what he played is not known). Hauptmann later described them as "pretty, curious, little things . . . there was no real central point in them, but they were better in other respects."[8] Dorn frankly admitted to Schumann his inability to comprehend some of his works. Both Dorn and Hauptmann were somewhat conservative in taste, and what they probably missed in Schumann's compositions was the thread that connected his works to the classical tradition with which they were familiar. What the public found wanting was the simplistic brilliance and tunefulness that provided light entertainment. To enjoy and understand Schumann's music, a mind open to innovation and new, often startling ideas was essential.

The *Etudes symphoniques* op. 13 and *Carnaval* op. 9

Both works stem directly from the fanciful life Schumann was leading in 1834—what he described as his "summer novel"—and both are closely related to his attachment to Ernestine von Fricken. Schumann originally intended them to appear not under his own name, but as the work of fictional members of the *Davidsbund*: *Carnaval* as the work of Florestan, and the *Etudes symphoniques* as the joint work of Florestan and Eusebius.

The *Etudes* consist of a theme and twelve variations (Schumann pri-

---

[7] Louis Ehlert, *From the Tone World* (New York, 1885), p. 219.

[8] Letter of 13 February 1839 in Moritz Hauptmann, *Letters of a Leipzig Cantor*, 2 vols. (New York, 1972), I, p. 198.

vately described them as "Variations symphoniques," 12 December 1835). On separate manuscripts, he also referred to them as "Variations pathétiques" and "Fantaisies et Finale." When a new edition was issued in 1852, they were titled *Etudes en forme de Variations*, and notable changes were made in the music (including the omission of the second and ninth variations).

Despite the rapid arpeggios (vivace, thirty-second notes) in the third etude and the frequent octave chords in the tenth, etude-like qualities seem overshadowed by concern with the variation principle. The original title is misleading. Except for variety of texture, there is not much evidence of a "symphonic" quality to the music or an attempt to experiment with timbre. In fact, the *Etudes* are distinctly pianistic. It is likely that the title was suggested by the publisher, Haslinger (it appears that he was responsible for the title of the *Concert* op. 14, also a misnomer), in the expectation that calling them "Etudes symphoniques" would attract more attention to them.

Schumann's *Etudes* are free variations, often of strongly contrasting character. There is a march for the first, a bel canto aria for the second, and, for the finale, a lively rondo (the longest of the set, ending triumphantly in D flat major, but seeming excessively grandiose). For the opening of the finale, Schumann used an excerpt from the Act 3 romance "Wer ist der Ritter hochgeehrt" in Heinrich Marschner's *Der Templar und die Jüdin* (1829). Marschner's opera was based on *Ivanhoe*, the "Ritter" being Richard-the-Lionheart. Schumann intended the quotation as a tribute to the dedicatee of the *Etudes*: his good friend the English composer William Sterndale Bennett. The theme itself (in C sharp minor) is somber in mood, and, as was often the case with themes selected by Schumann as the basis for a set of variations, it is prosaic, somewhat stiff, and conventional. What made the theme of particular interest to him was that it was the work of Ernestine's father, an amateur flutist.

Schumann's other major composition from this time, *Carnaval*, is linked to Ernestine in a more direct manner. He began work on it in December 1834, after permission had been received for their engagement. He wrote to Henriette Voigt (the confidante of both Ernestine and Schumann during their relationship), noting that Ernestine's place of residence, Asch, was a "very musical" name (13 September 1834).

Schumann had discovered that the letters of the town had equivalent musical pitches. He ingeniously arranged them in three patterns, spelling the town as well as the musical letter possibilities in his own name: (Ex. 8.3). All but two of the twenty-one pieces in *Carnaval* use either the second or third motto (the first does not appear). The mottos themselves appear between the eighth and ninth pieces of the set and are designated "Sphinxes" by Schumann. But although he chose to reveal the motivic basis of *Carnaval*, he made no reference in the score to its autobiographical association.

Ex. 8.3

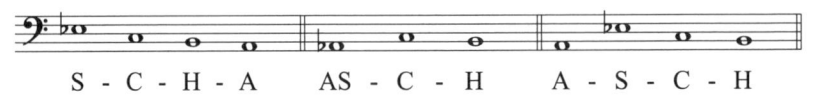

S - C - H - A   AS - C - H   A - S - C - H

That Schumann decided to call the mottos "Sphinxes" is puzzling. The Sphinx proposed riddles, not the solution to them. The key to Schumann's choice of wording seems once again to point to his reading of Jean Paul. In 1812 Jean Paul published an essay, "Twilight Butterflies or Sphinxes." In it he makes reference to three species of butterflies: "Day (Papilio), Evening (Sphinx), and Nightbird (Phalaena)."[9] The butterfly, as has been seen, was used frequently by Jean Paul, often appearing as a symbol of the soul and of transfiguration. Schumann now discovered an ideal counterpart to the papillons in op. 2—the evening papillon, Sphinx. Like the papillon in op. 2, the Sphinxes can be seen as providing the musical basis for most of the pieces in op. 9.

Each of the pieces comprising *Carnaval* has a title, the whole being a musical representation of an elaborate and imaginative masked ball during carnival season (Schumann at one point referred to the pieces as "masked dances," 23 August 1837). The association with Jean Paul and *Flegeljahre* lingers. To Moscheles, whom he was anxious to gain as a supporter, Schumann affirmed on two occasions that the titles and overall organization of the piece occurred only after the music had been created. He may have been concerned that Moscheles, of an older generation that in general was suspicious of program music, should not

---

[9] Jean Paul, *Sämtliche Werke*. Vol. XIV, *Politische Schriften*, ed. Wilhelm von Schramm (Weimar, 1939), p. 252.

misunderstand his intentions and perceive *Carnaval* as more program than music. But to understand the piece, it is essential to understand at least in a general manner the significance of the titles. For that reason, it would be surprising if, despite his assertion to Moscheles, a general program had not been in Schumann's mind before the music was composed—as had been the case with *Papillons*. Prior to selecting "Carnaval" as a title, Schumann rejected "Fasching" (a German word for carnival with slang connotations) and "Fasching. Schwänke auf vier Noten" ("Pranks on Four Notes"), the latter even appearing as a pre-publication advertisement in the *Zeitschrift*.

Both the music and program for *Carnaval* recall *Papillons*, notable differences being the length (*Carnaval* is more than twice as long) and the addition of titles for each piece. A number of the pieces refer to dances during the masked ball, such as No. 4, "Valse noble", and No. 16, "Valse allemande." Others allude to events within the ball, and it is not difficult to associate them directly with Schumann. No. 14, "Reconnaissance" ("Recognition"), refers to the identification during the ball of, presumably, Schumann and Ernestine (who appeared in the previous piece, entitled "Estrella"). No. 18, "Aveu" ("Avowal"), would be his confession of love—both instances seem to be indebted to the masked ball in *Flegeljahre*.

But the majority of pieces in *Carnaval* are musical portraits, often of a fantastical nature. In that sense, there seems to be a direct association with the novel planned by Schumann in 1831, *Die Davidsbündler*. There are characters from the *commedia dell'arte* whose costumes were frequently represented at masked balls (No. 2, "Pierrot"; No. 3, "Arlequin"; No. 15, "Pantalon et Columbine"), composers whom Schumann admired but had not met (No. 12, "Chopin"; No. 17, "Paganini"), and friends of Schumann (No. 11, "Chiarina" [Clara]; No. 13, "Estrella" [Ernestine]), No. 5, "Eusebius"; No. 6, "Florestan"). The *Davidsbund* appears en masse in the final piece ("March of the 'Davidsbündler' against the Philistines"), in this instance the Philistines being represented by yet another appearance of the "Grossvater Tanz" (identified by Schumann in the score as a "Theme from the 17th Century," and intended as representative of old-fashioned and outdated ideas).

Schumann cut and pruned *Carnaval*. There is less reliance on repeated, rhythmic dance figurations, no need for slight introductions to set the scene for each piece, a more extensive use of dissonance, and a conscious effort to bind the pieces with a related key structure (focusing on A flat major). To Kistner (whom he was attempting to interest in publishing the piece), Schumann mentioned that he had enough material for a second set, but no sequel appeared.[10] No doubt the public found one set of *Carnaval* confusing enough. To those unfamiliar with Schumann's *Davidsbund*, the titles must have appeared incomprehensible. Even those who knew Schumann reasonably well appeared baffled. "If only I had a commentary to it!" noted his friend Carl Krägen.[11] "P.S.," wrote an admirer to Schumann, "Would you be so kind as to explain to me the four notes which constitute the enigma or sphinxes for *Carnaval*?"[12]

It says much about Schumann's naivete that he was convinced the sphinxes in themselves would create something of a sensation and help sales of the work—as if there were widespread interest in such musical games. But for much of his life Schumann was fascinated by puzzles and ciphers, particularly if they could be applied to music, and he seemed to believe that, as in the case of Jean Paul, many people shared his enthusiasm. His interest in ciphers was one that was common to not a few writers and artists associated with German Romanticism; Friedrich Schlegel, for example, described art itself as "an inner hieroglyphic writing."[13] Schumann would probably not have disagreed with the sentiment expressed by Blaise de Vigenère in his sixteenth-century treatise on ciphers: "All the things in the world constitute a cipher. All nature is merely a cipher and a secret writing."[14] "The Sphinxes," Schumann had written to Kistner on 3 July 1836, "are the cipher."

Schumann's interest in cipher, number symbolism, and musical/word puzzles is frequently encountered in his writings. There are a number

---

[10] A number of the remaining pieces later found their way into Schumann's piano miscellanies, the *Bünte Blätter* op. 99 (as the sixth) and the *Albumblätter* op. 124 (the fourth, eleventh, and seventeenth).

[11] Letter of March 1838 in Wolfgang Boetticher, ed., *Briefe und Gedichte aus dem Album Robert und Clara Schumanns* (Leipzig, 1981), p. 278.

[12] Letter of April 1848 of Jean-Joseph-Bonaventura Laurens in *Ibid.*, p. 107.

[13] Liselotte Dieckmann, "The Metaphor of Hieroglyphics in German Romanticism," *Comparative Literature* VII (1955), p. 311.

[14] From his *Traicté des chiffres* (1586) quoted in David Kahn, *The Codebreakers: The Story of Secret Writing* (New York, 1967), p. 146.

of instances of it: the probable creation of Raro from an amalgamation of his and Clara's names; a curiosity for palindromes (such as, Amor-Roma). While in Paris, Schumann advised Clara to make the acquaintance of the actress Rachel. "Her name," he wrote, "has always smiled at me. I see that your name is contained in hers" (15 January 1839). During their trip to Russia, he took obvious delight in the creation of an acrostic sonnet, using as a basis the words ROBERT UND CLARA.

Evidence of his interest in the playfulness and symbolism of number can be found in his diary (including an intriguing arrangement and sequence of the digits one to four), and, from later in life, a sketch of a letter to Brahms whose margins contain a series of four numbers, all beginning with 12, and placed for the most part in columns of five. Both seem to indicate an arrangement of numerical patterns, though of unknown meaning. At times Schumann seemed intuitively to think in number, as when, after the creation of pseudonyms for his acquaintances (the beginning of the *Davidsbund*), he noted with delight that he now had six friends with names one syllable in length and five with names of two syllables.

It is not surprising, then, that Schumann took pleasure in creating compositions based on words such as ABEGG or ASCH. Such an approach permitted him to add both mystery and an extramusical significance to his works—an aspect, incidentally, that would have had strong appeal to Jean Paul. An entire section of his *Aesthetics* is devoted to the creation of secrets and hidden identities, all for the delight of the "unraveling of little knots" for the reader.[15] It seems only natural that at one point Schumann revealed to Clara that the German word for marriage, "Ehe," created a perfect fifth (E to B [H]), or that he never seemed to tire of the musicality of the last name of his friend the Danish composer, Niels Gade.

Among musicians, Schumann's interests were not unique, and he probably examined with attention the curiosity published in the *Allgemeine musikalische Zeitung* in 1833 (Ex. 8.4). What set him apart was the intensity of his interest. For that reason, there has been speculation that Schumann actually devised a series of ciphers for use in his music—

---

[15] Jean Paul Richter, *Horn of Oberon: Jean Paul Richter's School for Aesthetics*, trans. Margaret R. Hale (Detroit, 1973), p. 195.

154 • SCHUMANN

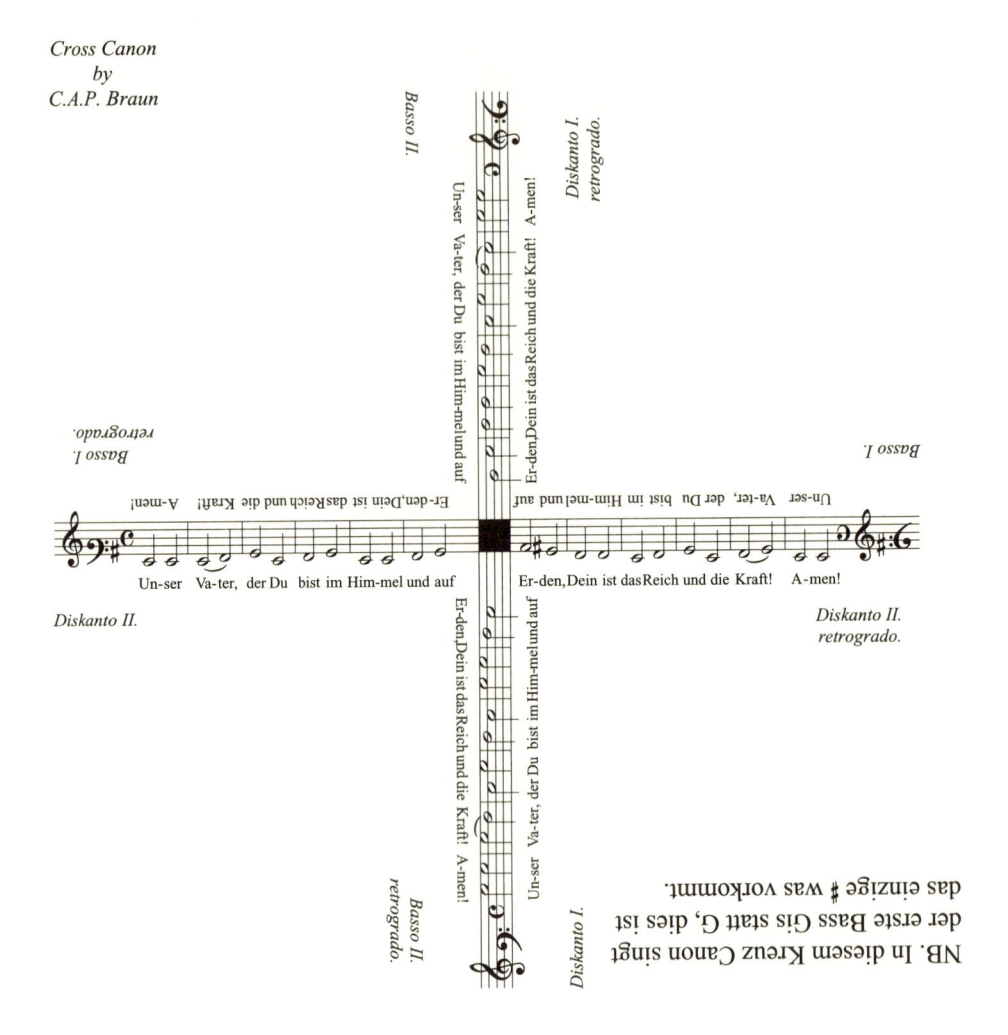

Cross Canon
by
C.A.P. Braun

that is, specific pitches were substituted for letters. Words and messages were supposedly created, often about or intended for Clara. Music is not an uncommon medium for encipherment. The standard practice had been to create a musical alphabet, using as a basis an ascending and descending diatonic scale (with the inclusion of B flat). No doubt such an approach would have had some appeal to Schumann. But was he aware of it? During the more than thirty years since the theory of Schumann's use of cipher was first presented, no substantial evidence has been presented to support its appearance. What seemed to interest him far more than an intricate (and possibly unmusical sounding) cipher was the use of brief musical/letter motives, such as those in *Carnaval*.

Yet another way in which Schumann added mystery to his music (and a code of sorts) was by the unacknowledged quotation within his own compositions of another composer's music. Frequently, this was intended to have special meaning. In the Fantasie op. 17, Schumann quoted from Beethoven's song-cycle, *An die ferne Geliebte* (To the Distant Beloved), a means of expressing his own love for Clara by alluding to that expressed by Beethoven in his songs. But of even greater significance during the 1830s was Schumann's secret reference in his own music to the compositions of Clara. Nearly every major composition created by Schumann during his courtship of Clara contains references to her work. He was thus able musically to join himself and Clara in a marriage of sorts. In *Carnaval*, the "Valse Allemande" is indebted to Clara's *Valses romantiques* op. 4.

The Piano Sonatas

While working on *Carnaval* and the *Etudes Symphoniques*, Schumann had already begun the composition of a piano sonata, published in 1836 as the First Piano Sonata op. 11 and dedicated to Clara. It indicated a marked change of direction for him. His previous attempt at a piano sonata, originally intended to impress Moscheles, remained incomplete. Schumann's lack of experience in creating movements of the length necessary for a sonata must have been a challenge. He must also have been apprehensive of contributing to a genre with such a distinguished past. There had been no true precedent for compositions such as the *Intermezzi* or *Carnaval*, and no basis for a direct comparison to the work of other composers. By composing a sonata, Schumann was entering an arena in which comparison and criticism would be expected.

Because of its eloquent tradition, Schumann's perception of the piano sonata was an exalted one (he characterized it as belonging to a "higher genre").[16] He was eager to become part of that tradition, but in writing sonatas he occasionally seemed preoccupied with the grand gesture, as if his usual style and approach would be inadequate. During the 1830s,

---

[16] Review in 1838 of "Etuden für das Pianoforte" in *GS I*, p. 389.

the sonata itself no longer had a broad base of popularity—Schumann noted that few were being composed and that the genre was in a period of stagnation. Composing sonatas could only have been perceived by him as a means of rejuvenating the genre, in the process gaining recognition among his colleagues as a "serious" composer.

During the 1830s, Schumann composed, if not in name then in format, four piano sonatas: the First op. 11, the Second op. 22, the Third op. 14 (so called in the second edition, 1853, but originally entitled *Concert sans orchestre*), and the *Faschingsschwank aus Wien* (*Carnival Jest From Vienna*) op. 26. Two others, a Sonata in F minor (worked on in late 1836) and what Schumann described as a "sonata or fantasie or etude or nothing" in C minor (December 1838), remained unfinished.[17]

The sonatas share several stylistic traits, most notably a concern with motivic structure, particularly for those movements in sonata form, such as the first and third movements in op. 14 and the first in op. 22, and virtuoso display (the first movement of op. 14 is a notable instance). With the exception of op. 11, there appears to be less reliance on the improvisatory elements that Schumann had introduced so successfully in his earlier compositions. The sonatas are clearly works that he strove to differentiate from those he had previously composed. But animated by what he seemed to perceive as their grandiose nature, he was at times unable to avoid creating an impression of undue ostentation and pretension.

Privately, Schumann referred to the *Faschingsschwank* as a "grand, Romantic sonata" (15 March 1839), an apt description. One notable feature distinguishing it from the usual sonata is the number of movements: five. But the second movement (a brief Romanze) and the fourth (entitled Intermezzo) can be perceived as providing balance and contrast to the other three movements, particularly since the first (Allegro) resembles a scherzo-rondo. The *Faschingsschwank* was composed during the spring and summer of 1839, a final testament to his stay in Vienna. It contains a brief quotation from the "Marseillaise," a tune banned by the reactionary Austrian regime and no doubt placed by Schumann in his work as a sardonic reflection on Austrian censorship.

[17] *Tgb II*, p. 85.

The *Concert sans orchestre*, dedicated to Moscheles, was composed in 1836. Like the *Faschingsschwank*, it was originally intended to have five movements (two of them scherzos). But the scherzos were deleted when the title *Concert* was decided on (probably at the suggestion of his publisher), and another finale was then created. As originally published, the work contained three movements, as would a concerto. But there is little concertolike about the piece—no attempt to reproduce the interplay between piano and orchestra nor to imitate orchestral timbres on the instrument. The title appears to have been adopted more as a publishing ploy. The second movement is a theme and variations, the theme being provided by an unpublished "Andantino" by Clara. A motive from this theme also begins the first movement, an instance of Schumann's growing concern with creating a sense of thematic unity within his compositions.

Schumann's first two piano sonatas were the work of several years. Both were started in 1833, but the first (completed in 1835) can be seen as having an even earlier beginning: its opening movement is based on the *Fandango* he composed in August and September 1832. The second occupied his attention well beyond the completion of the first. He continued to tinker with it for some time, intermittently working on it in 1835 and 1837, finally completing a new finale in 1838. Clara had expressed dissatisfaction with the original finale in the spring of that year, pronouncing it too demanding technically. Schumann agreed, and created a movement that he described to her as "very simple" (29 December 1838). The sonata appeared in print the following year, dedicated to Henriette Voigt.

Of Schumann's four piano sonatas, the first is the most unconventional and the most intriguing. Its title page gives some indication of its unusual nature (see illustration no. 9). Schumann took a strong interest in the visual impression created by the publication of his works. Because of the additional expense involved in the production of elaborate title pages, he was usually obliged to rely on standard title pages of the day—elegant and graceful, employing the numerous, contrasting fonts beloved in the nineteenth century. But for op. 11 Schumann used a title page created by Bonaventura Genelli (1798–1868), a gifted and eccentric artist known as a master of the imaginative and the erotic. He had been living in Leipzig since 1832 (returning to Germany after a ten-year stay in Rome), and was at work on frescoes for Dr. Hermann Härtel's extensive villa, an association that might have led to his meeting Schumann and the commission for the title page. To Kistner, who published the work, Schumann wrote of his desire for "something unusual" with "several emblems" (19 March 1836). Genelli's creation followed Schumann's general guidelines, but it is not known, unfortunately, to what extent Schumann may have influenced the final design.

The title page is striking, and bears witness to Genelli's fascination with antiquity and the occult. Two winged gryphons peer upwards at a somber angel who bears on a plaque the title of the piece. Genelli created an arabesque laden with symbolism and intended ambiguity. Gryphons can represent the sun or the dawn, as well as vigilance. The significance of the three disembodied heads in the engraving is equally perplexing. Schumann wanted "something unusual" for the title page, and in that Genelli succeeded admirably.

The sonata was also intended as a musical counterpart to Schumann's *Davidsbund*. The title page lists the composers as "Florestan and Eusebius"; the work is dedicated to "Clara."[18] Clara's presence is further emphasized by the use of material from her *Quatre Pièces caractéristiques* op. 5. The descending fifth bass motive of the introduction to the first movement, as well as the repeated rhythm of an eighth-note followed by two sixteenths, is derived from the fourth of Clara's pieces (entitled "Scène fantastique").

Schumann took considerable efforts to gain publicity for the sonata. Because it had not appeared under his own name, he felt no hesitation in publicizing it in the *Neue Zeitschrift für Musik*. A poetic effusion by Schumann's friend J. F. E. Sobolewski ("Reflections and Dreams Inspired by the F sharp Minor Sonata by Florestan and Eusebius") appeared in the 4 October 1836 issue. Later that month, a detailed review by Moscheles of the sonata appeared as a lead article. Despite Moscheles's age (he was forty-two at the time, and his most notable successes were behind him), Schumann viewed him as the progressive representative of an older school and, eager for his support, had requested the

---

[18] A new edition with a conventional title page, listing Schumann as the composer, appeared in 1844.

review. But had Schumann known of Moscheles's initial reaction to the sonata, it is unlikely he would have approached him.

In the fall of 1835, Moscheles had heard Clara play the sonata at Wieck's. Privately, he had found it to be "interesting," but had also described it as "very affected, difficult, and somewhat muddled."[19] After being asked by Schumann to write the review, Moscheles must have found himself in an unpleasant situation. He could hardly decline without offending Schumann, whom he sincerely liked. Yet, the novelty of some of the work both disturbed and perplexed him. He resolved his predicament wisely. Nearly one-half of the review does not discuss the sonata at all but focuses on the work of Beethoven and members of Schumann's generation (including Liszt and Chopin) with whom Moscheles found similarities. In his analysis of the sonata Moscheles was supportive but overall was unable to avoid pointing out several aspects that bothered him, such as an abrupt modulation from C major to E flat major in the finale (probably the passage thirty-four measures before the end).

The Sonata op. 11 consists of four movements: Introduzione/Allegro vivace, Aria, Scherzo ed Intermezzo, and Finale. The Introduzione sets out the thematic material that serves as the basis of the movement (recalled in the third and fourth movements). The most conventional movement, the second, is based on a song composed in 1828 "An Anna" (in a similar manner, the Andantino of op. 22 is based on the early song "Im Herbste"). The Scherzo, with lively, disjunct rhythm, is contrasted with the brief Intermezzo which serves as a trio and brings to mind the lyrical dances in *Carnaval*.

Of all of his compositions, Schumann could not have selected a more challenging one for Moscheles to analyze. In his piano sonatas, Schumann's handling of sonata structure is unquestionably distinctive (op. 22 is perhaps the most conventional). Sonata form relies greatly on balance and gradual contrast, in basis melodic, tonal, or both. In general, one or two melodies provide the thematic material for a movement of perhaps ten to twelve pages in length. Schumann was more used to composing short movements several pages in length. And he was often

---

[19] Quoted in *W*, p. 156.

profuse in his use of melodic material. Contrast was an essential aspect of his music, but contrast created suddenly, abruptly, and unexpectedly. His musical style was not compatible with traditional sonata structures, and his recognition of that necessitated the creation of distinctive musical forms.

It is the structure of the final movement of op. 11, much of which at first glance appears strongly improvisatory, which has generated the most controversy. Moritz Hauptmann's shallow criticism of musical Romanticism—that its "main characteristic" is a supposed "absence of form"—could well be applied here.[20] (Similar criticism, incidentally, was directed toward German literary Romanticism, particularly the novels of Jean Paul.) Hauptmann lamented the unwillingness (and what he felt was the ignorance) of young composers to follow traditional, late eighteenth- and early nineteenth-century models—a lapse that he felt resulted in formlessness. It seems odd to criticize Schumann for not using as a model the sonata structures of Mozart or early Beethoven. Yet that is precisely what Hauptmann intended, and his narrow stance prevailed well into the twentieth century. Schumann's "gifts were not those of a clear-sighted architect," wrote Kathleen Dale in 1952, "and his sonatas consequently convey little sensation of being compact structures whose ground-plan was determined from the very beginning."[21] In a similar manner, Schumann was criticized for his supposed inability to create "themes capable of development and further growth"—that is, themes in the manner of Beethoven.[22]

Schumann believed that one of the most significant characteristics of his music was its innovative approach to form. To his friend Hermann Hirschbach, he recommended an examination of his larger works such as the Sonata, where he would find "new forms" (7 September 1838). In an 1839 review, he noted the emptiness of simply "repeating" old structures, and advised devising "new ones" instead.[23] In the finale to the First Piano Sonata, Schumann put his theories to the test, and

---

[20] Letter of 13 August 1844 in Hauptmann, *Letters*, II, p. 16.
[21] Kathleen Dale, "The Piano Music," in *Schumann: A Symposium*, ed. Gerald Abraham (Oxford, 1952), p. 46.
[22] Mosco Carner, "The Orchestral Music," in *Ibid.*, p. 178.
[23] "Sonaten für Klavier" in *GS I*, p. 395.

adopted a new structural approach that bewildered and frustrated critics intent on perceiving it as a continuation of the classical style. The structure is bipartite. The first section (mm. 1–189) includes three major theme groups, with tonal centers of F sharp minor/A major, E flat major, and A major. The second section (mm. 190–396) is a reflection of the first, with the same thematic material, but with different tonal centers (C major, C minor, E flat major, and F sharp major). A coda in F sharp major (mm. 397–462) concludes the work. Its structure is distinctive but may disclose Schumann's adaptation of Bach, a transformation perhaps of the binary form often used by Bach in the preludes of the *Well-Tempered Clavier*.[24]

The Fantasie op. 17

A similar approach was followed with the Fantasie op. 17, begun not long after completion of the First Piano Sonata. It contains three movements, the second being a grandiose march (in lieu of a scherzo and trio). Instead of the exuberant finale to the work that many would have expected, the last movement is slow and lyrical, providing a conclusion of serenity and radiance. But it is the opening movement that is perhaps the most unusual. About two-thirds of the way into it, a new section enters—identified by Schumann as "Im Legenden Ton"("In the Manner of a Legend"). Its lyrical nature is emphasized by his original title for it: "Romanza."

The effect of Schumann's digression is to disrupt the flow of what had been perceived as a sonata form, in the process disorienting the listener. It can be perceived in a number of ways: as a development section of sorts, as a digression, or as an interlude. The inspiration for it Schumann probably found in literature—particularly the novels of Jean Paul, Brentano, and Eichendorff, which are composite in structure with frequent digressions, presenting a mixture of prose and poetry.

Like op. 11, the Fantasie was a work closely connected in Schumann's mind with Clara. He later described the first movement as "excessively melancholy" and wrote to Clara that it was his "most

---

[24] This movement is an example of what has been described as Schumann's use of "parallel form." See Linda Correll Roesner, "Schumann's 'Parallel' Forms," *19th-Century Music* XIV (1990–91), pp. 265–78.

passionate—a deep lament for you" (25 January 1839 and 19 March 1838). This first movement was sketched in June 1836. It was intended at that time to publish it as a single-movement work, entitled "Ruines. Fantasie"—a reflection of his despair at what he perceived as quite possibly the end of his relationship with Clara.

That autumn, Schumann decided to enlarge the work, and also to associate it with a memorial to Beethoven in Bonn. One hundred copies of the completed work were to be given to the Bonn committee, and the proceeds from their sale were to help defray the cost of the monument. By the beginning of December, all three movements were done. As was often the case, Schumann considered a number of possible titles, including "Dichtungen" ("Poetry"), as well as individual titles of "Ruins, Triumphal Arch, Constellation," and "Ruins, Trophies, Palms." The entire work was to be published as a "Grand Sonata" by Florestan and Eusebius in a grandiose edition with a black cover and prominent gold lettering. But no publisher expressed interest in the project.

When retitled "Fantasie" and published in 1839, the work was dedicated to Liszt—appropriately both because of the virtuoso nature of much of the piece and because of the prominent role Liszt had taken in raising funds for the Beethoven monument. Associations with Beethoven still remain, such as the persistent use of trills in the first and second movements: a hallmark of Beethoven's late style. But, more pointedly, in the first movement (and in an earlier version of the Fantasie, at the conclusion of the third movement as well) Schumann quoted from the opening of the sixth song of Beethoven's song-cycle *An die ferne Geliebte* op. 98 (1816) (Ex. 8.5, 8.6). It was not a quotation that he acknowledged in the score. Rather, it was intended as a private

Ex. 8.5

Andante con moto, cantabile

Nimm sie— hin denn, die - se Lie - der,
Accept, then, these songs

Ex. 8.6

and secret statement, and as a reference to Clara, Schumann's own "Distant Beloved."

The association of the Fantasie with Clara was strong in Schumann's mind. Its key, C major, was an unusual choice for Schumann, and probably intended as a connection to Clara's name. The work is prefaced by a quotation from a poem by Friedrich Schlegel, "Abendröte" ("Sunset"), published in 1801 in his novel, *Lucinde*:

Durch all Töne tönet
Im bunten Erdentraum
Ein leiser Ton gezogen
Für den, der heimlich lauschet.

("Through all the sounds in Earth's many-colored dream, sounds one soft, long-drawn tone for whomever listens in secret.")

Clara was particularly taken with the second movement in which she heard "an entire orchestra" (23 May 1839). But Schumann directed her elsewhere. Quoting the first phrase of the initial theme from the first movement, he asked: "Does it also suggest many ideas to you? The 'tone' in the motto is *you*? I nearly believe it" (9 June 1839). Clara replied a week later, now noting that this passage also was her favorite in the movement. Perhaps her change was in recognition of the resemblance between this theme and that of the "Notturno" in her *Soirées musicales* op. 6, a work of which Schumann confessed he was particularly fond (Ex.8.7, 8.8).

Ex. 8.7

Andante con moto

Ex. 8.8

Durchaus fantastisch und leidenschaftlich vorzutragen (♩ = 80)
Sempre fantasticamente ed appassionatamente

The Compositions from 1837 and 1838: *Davidsbündlertänze* op. 6; *Fantasiestücke* op. 12; *Novelletten* op. 21; *Kinderszenen* op. 15; *Kreisleriana* op. 16

After completing work on the Fantasie, Schumann returned to works of shorter length, similar both in structure and mood to the *Intermezzi*. In 1837, the *Fantasiestücke* op. 12 and the *Davidsbündlertänze* op. 6 were composed. Once again, in Schumann's mind both were tied to Clara. The *Davidsbündlertänze*, he wrote to her, were filled with "thoughts of marriage" and resembled a "Polterabend" (a wedding-eve party) (5 January and 6 February 1838). Their connection to Clara was emphasized by the quotation (indicated in the score as "Motto by C. W.") of a motive from a mazurka in Clara's *Soirées musicales* op. 6—a way of binding both their opus sixes. The brooding melancholy of the Fantasie is absent, perhaps a reflection of the optimism Schumann felt at the renewal of his relationship with Clara. To a friend he emphasized their whimsical nature, describing them as "dances of death, St. Vitus's dances, graceful dances, and goblins' dances" (20 October 1837).

As with op. 11, the *Davidsbündlertänze* appeared as the work of Florestan and Eusebius (and, consequently, was reviewed by Sobolewski in the 13 July 1838 issue of the *Zeitschrift*). The title page, too, was distinctive, heavily ornamented in the pseudo-Gothic style popular at the time (see illustration no. 8). All was intended to create an aura of mystery about the work. There are eighteen pieces in the set, many in the first half being simple, unpretentious dances. From No. 10 on, however, they become longer and more complex in structure. The work concludes in a mood of poignant simplicity with a Schubertian waltz. There are no titles, but each dance is attributed to either Florestan, Eusebius, or both (and signed "F" and/or "E"). Immediately preceding the ninth and eighteenth pieces, text is introduced (emphasizing the emotional reactions of Florestan and Eusebius, respectively)—an unexpected, extramusical element that Schumann deleted (along with the signatives "F" and "E") when the set was reissued in 1850 under his own name.

Schumann composed the last of the *Davidsbündlertänze* in August. As was often the case, at the same time he was working on several compositions: the previous month he had started the *Fantasiestücke*. There are eight pieces in the set, most in ternary form and linked by tonality

(D flat major, F major/minor, C major). Each has a title reflective of the fantastical and visionary implications of the general title for the set, a title that Schumann probably borrowed from E. T. A. Hoffmann. But there are programmatic elements in the work beyond the titles supplied for the pieces. For the fifth piece in the set, "In der Nacht," Schumann discovered after its completion that it contained in detail the story of Hero and Leander; he wrote to Clara sharing his excitement with her and asked if she too detected its presence. For the last piece, "Ende vom Lied," Schumann informed Clara of the thoughts of marriage that had animated him while composing it, although in this instance he remarked that in the end his hopes had been overshadowed by his pain. It is one of the most distinctive in the set, and may have had a more specific meaning that Schumann was hesitant to reveal in writing. Clara wrote to Schumann that portions of it reminded her of the music of Johann Rudolf Zumsteeg, a song composer popular at the turn of the century. Schumann praised her for her discernment. Perhaps a quotation from Zumsteeg is present in the work, providing yet another link to Schumann's extramusical intentions.

In January 1838, Schumann put the *Fantasiestücke* in order, readying them for publication. At the same time, he began work on another set of piano pieces, published as the *Novelletten* op. 21. The title, of his own creation for a musical work, has a literary connotation: "Novellen" are short stories. To Fischhof he described them as "grand, interconnected, adventurous tales" (3 April 1838). He took the opportunity to tease Clara by explaining the unusual title as a reference to the popular soprano Clara Novello, claiming that the unpleasant sounding "Wiecketten" simply did not work. Once again Schumann stated that this most recent musical work was merely a reflection of his life. The pieces included, he told her, "amusing tales, Egmont tales, family scenes with fathers, a marriage ... my bride—in the *Novelletten* you appear in all possible situations and settings" (6 February 1838; 30 June 1839).

The *Novelletten* are Schumann's largest piano work. He worked on them intermittently during the spring and summer, putting them in order in August. There are eight pieces (all untitled) in the set, each averaging six to seven pages in length. Many are dances: the fourth is a waltz, the fifth is polonaise like, the first trio of the eighth is a mixture of mazurka and galop. But the improvisatory elements of Schumann's music—still noticeable, for example, in the *Davidsbündlertänze*—is less in evidence here. Much of the music bears witness to what at the time must have been perceived as Schumann's unrepentant eccentricity. For example, the melody of the fifth is comprised of three separate motives, each of a distinctive, contrasting character, unified with total disregard for the barline (Ex. 8.9). The last piece is distinguished from the others both by its size (it is the longest in the set) and by the inclusion in it of what Schumann termed a "Stimme aus der Ferne" ("A Voice from the Distance"). On the surface, there would appear to be no particular reason for him to have drawn attention to the melody in the right hand in so striking a manner. But it was intended as a means of binding his compositions to Clara's: the "voice" appears to be derived from the "Notturno" in Clara's *Soirées musicales* (the same melody associated with the first movement of the Fantasie; see Ex. 8.7). Clara was delighted with Schumann's inclusion of the "Stimme" in the *Novelletten*. She wrote to him noting the presence of Eusebius in it and, in a rare show of humor, signed her letter "Eusebiana" (1 September 1838).

As had been the case with the *Fantasiestücke*, there are programmatic associations with several of the *Novelletten*, which were not indicated in the first edition. The second piece of the set was originally entitled "Sarrasin and Suleika" (a reference to Goethe's *Westöstlichen Divan*) and sent to Liszt for his perusal. And, prior to the publication of the *Novelletten* in 1839, the intermezzo from the third *Novellette* appeared separately as part of a musical supplement to the *Zeitschrift* (May 1838) As

Ex. 8.9

his diary confirms, it was associated in Schumann's mind with *Macbeth*, and when published in the *Zeitschrift* supplement was preceded by a quotation of the opening couplet from it.

Closely connected with the *Novelletten* were the *Kinderszenen* ("Scenes From Childhood") op. 15. It was Schumann's original intention to publish the two together (at this stage the *Kinderszenen* were referred to as *Kindergeschichten*, "Children's Tales," so a literary element bound them to the *Novelletten*). Schumann reported to Clara that the idea for the *Kinderszenen* originated in her remark that at times he seemed "like a child," resulting in February in "thirty small, droll things" (19 March 1838). Schumann loved children. He was charmed by the freshness, grace, and innocence of childhood, and eager to transmit those traits to his music. He selected thirteen of the pieces, and gave each a separate title, such as "Catch Me," and "By the Fireside." To an associate he described them as being "more cheerful, gentler, more melodic" than his previous compositions (28 September 1840).

The *Kinderszenen* are simple, unpretentious pieces. But they were not intended for children. Schumann's purpose was to create a loving and insightful representation of childhood for adults. Most are less than a page in length, and in content and structure are a world apart from the *Novelletten*. It is surprising that he originally coupled them with the *Novelletten*. But perhaps he perceived the *Kinderszenen* as creating a distinct impression for the more visionary *Novelletten*, at the same time taking pleasure in the startling contrast between the two sets. Clara was delighted with the *Kinderszenen* and wrote telling him that they "belonged only to us" (21 March 1839). Because of their personal nature, a dedicatee was conspicuously omitted.

To Clara, Schumann described the *Kinderszenen* as "gentle and loving and happy—like our future" (3 August 1838)—and presented them as distinctly opposite in mood to the composition that next occupied his attention: *Kreisleriana*. He began work on *Kreisleriana* in early May, completing it in mid-September, several weeks after putting the *Novelletten* in order. It is one of his most fanciful and eccentric compositions. Subtitled "Fantasies," it consists of eight pieces (linked tonally by the keys of D minor, G minor, and B flat major). The title was taken from E. T. A. Hoffmann: Johannes Kreisler was Hoffmann's most memorable creation, and Schumann succinctly described him as an "eccentric, wild, gifted Kapellmeister" (15 March 1839).

Seven years earlier, Schumann had recorded in his diary the "new worlds" opened up to him by his reading of Hoffmann. He now reacted similarly, noting the "completely new worlds" produced by his latest composition.[25] Despite his assertion that the music preceded the title, it seems allied to the paradoxical temperament of Kreisler, whether as an attempt at musical representation of Kreisler's character, or a transformation of Kreisler as performing artist. Schumann yet again informed Clara of the close association of the piece to her, and wanted to dedicate it to her, but Wieck refused to grant permission to do so.

In 1839, Schumann confessed that, of his works from op. 15 to op. 20, *Kreisleriana* was his favorite. Yet, when preparing the piece for a second edition in 1849, he explained to his publisher that in the past he had "unfortunately often ruined" his compositions, "and quite wantonly" (20 November 1849). This statement has been perceived as an acknowledgment and criticism of the eccentricities in his compositions, traits that hindered their comprehension and limited their sales. But too much weight should not be given to Schumann's words. His remarks were intended more to quiet his publisher's apprehensions. For the new edition Schumann actually changed little. Today the eccentricity and the resulting unpredictability of *Kreisleriana* seems one of its greatest strengths. Much of it appears passionate, frenzied, neurotic—all traits characteristic of Kreisler himself.

The Compositions of 1839: *Arabesque* op. 18; *Blumenstück* op. 19; *Scherzo, Gigue, Romanze und Fughette* op. 32; Piano Concerto in D minor; *Drei Romanzen* op. 28; *Humoreske* op. 20; *Nachtstücke* op. 23

Because of the demands made on his time (and his increasing frustration in dealing with the censor), while in Vienna Schumann was unable to continue the hurried pace of composition he had maintained for much of 1838. After his return to Leipzig, despite the death of his brother and preoccupation over court proceedings to gain permission to marry Clara, he worked diligently. The *Faschingsschwank aus Wien* op. 26

---

[25] Entry of 3 May 1838 in *Tgb II*, p. 55.

(started in Vienna) was perhaps the most ambitious composition completed. At the opposite end of the spectrum were the *Arabesque* op. 18 and the *Blumenstück* op. 19. Both compositions, he wrote to Becker, were "feeble and intended for ladies"—a reference to the popular market (15 August 1839). The *Arabesque* he curiously described to Clara as "variations, but on *no* theme" (25 January 1839)—an intriguing concept, but the *Arabesque* is a rondo with a clearly identifiable theme. It is possible that the reference to *"no* theme" was intended not as an allusion to the musical structure, but to the quality of the thematic material, for it is slight and no doubt in Schumann's eyes was fairly inconsequential. Both the *Arabesque* and *Blumenstück* are precisely the kind of composition (including the conventional and sentimental titles) that Schumann would never have composed if he had not been concerned about his income. Yet another indication is that they were sold separately, although both are short enough—each is only about a half dozen pages in length—that they could easily have been sold as a set.

During the final weeks of his stay in Vienna, Schumann worked on a surprising number of compositions. In addition to the *Arabesque* and *Blumenstück*, he completed a scherzo, gigue, and romance, to which he later added a fughetta, publishing the set in 1841 as op. 32. And he began work on the previously mentioned "sonata or fantasie or etude or nothing in C minor"(now lost)—an indication of his growing frustration. Considerable effort was spent as well on a piano concerto, a genre that he had previously attempted without success. Twenty-six pages of incomplete orchestral score and an additional four pages of the piano part (also incomplete) exist for a Piano Concerto in D minor, dated 20 March 1839. Schumann began work on it in January, describing it to Clara as "something between a symphony, a concerto, and a large sonata. I see that I can not write a concerto for virtuosos" (24 January 1839). Yet such a concerto would have done a great deal to bring his name before a broader public.

It is clear from his correspondence with Clara that he felt discouraged by his work on the concerto, and there is no indication that he ever made an attempt to finish it. He was more successful with three compositions (two on a fairly large scale) completed later in the year: *Drei Romanzen* op. 28, the *Humoreske* op. 20, and the *Nachtstücke* op. 23.

Chronologically, the *Romanzen* are the last of the series; with the exception of the Four Fugues op. 72 (1845), Schumann was not to compose another extensive work for solo piano for nearly a decade. These are easily accessible pieces, extremely tuneful—perhaps one reason for his choice of title. But their texture is unusually dense, and their lyricism is not necessarily vocal in nature, as the title might imply. It would not be unexpected if there was an association between them and Clara's *Romances* op. 11 (composed in 1839 and dedicated to Schumann).

The *Humoreske* was composed in early March 1839, while Schumann was living in Vienna. He characterized it as perhaps his "most melancholy" composition (7 August 1839). To Clara he wrote that while creating it he was both "laughing and crying" (11 March 1839)—an indication of the startling and abrupt contrasts within it (and an instance of "humor" in the style of Jean Paul). The *Humoreske* can be seen as containing five pieces (not marked as such in the score), following one another without pause. The second introduces an additional melodic line, indicated by Schumann as an "innere Stimme" ("inner voice"). It is not intended to be played. In function, it recalls the "Voice From the Distance" in the *Novelletten*.[26]

The *Nachtstücke* were also composed during the final weeks of Schumann's stay in Vienna. The title was probably appropriated by Schumann from Hoffmann's *Nachtstücke*, a collection of short stories. But there were a number of other literary works that could have served as his source, including tales by Tieck, Arnim, Contessa, and Bonaventura. In the literary "Nightpiece," elements that were emphasized included the supernatural, the grotesque, and, in particular, the ominous "dark side" of nature. In that sense, the "Nachtstück" was clearly differentiated from another musical nightpiece, the "nocturne" (especially as popularized by Chopin). Both referred to the night, but the nocturne depicted the night as it might be perceived by lovers—gentle, delicate, and soothing, definitely not the nightmarish visions of the "Nachtstück."

By selecting "Nachtstücke" as a title, Schumann was deliberately

---

[26] It may in a similar manner be related to Clara's music. H. J. Köhler, in the Peters edition of the *Humoreske* (Leipzig, 1981), associates the "innere Stimme" with Clara's "Romance" op. 11 no. 2, but does not present a convincing case (pp. 40–43).

setting his music apart from the numerous nocturnes and notturnos of the day. While composing the piece, he confessed to Clara that he saw "funeral processions, coffins, unfortunate, despairing people" (7 April 1839)—this before he had decided on a title for the work. When he later learned of the death of his brother Eduard, Schumann interpreted the music as a premonition of it.[27] The *Nachtstücke* contain four pieces—as published, all untitled. But at first Schumann planned titles for each: "Funeral Procession," "Odd Company," "Nocturnal Revels," "Round with Solo Voices." The title for the set was one that he selected with care, after rejecting his original choice: "Leichenphantasie" ("Funeral Fantasy").

The *Nachtstücke* were composed during a time when financial concerns were of particular significance to Schumann. More than ever he was determined to establish his reputation as a composer in order to prove Wieck mistaken in his assertions. It remained essential for him to gain a hearing for his works, if not by means of favorable reviews (which were rare), then through performances. Liszt, who, both privately and in print, had come out strongly in support of Schumann's compositions, occasionally performed works by Schumann—a most unusual gesture for the time. In Vienna, he performed the *Fantasiestücke*, and in Leipzig, in March 1840, excerpts from *Carnaval*. In 1838, another virtuoso, Anna Robena Laidlaw (an English pianist with whom Schumann had carried on a brief flirtation), performed in Berlin several of Schumann's compositions, including the second and third movements of op. 14 and one of his Paganini *Etudes*. While in Paris, Clara was pleased to report to Schumann that Charles Hallé had performed *Carnaval* (apparently for a select audience). But these isolated performances, while welcome, were an inadequate means of bringing Schumann's music before the public.

The primary interpreter of Schumann's music remained Clara. She performed his compositions regularly, both publicly and privately—even playing his music for individuals or small groups. But her public performances were often hampered by the difficulty in finding works

---

[27] Schumann's superstitious nature was evident while returning home from Vienna. During the trip he heard trombones playing a chorale—at the precise time, he later believed, that his brother had died.

suitable for a typical audience. Invariably she consulted with Schumann on the matter, who had strong, but changing, opinions. The compositions that he considered possibilities included the Toccata, several of the *Fantasiestücke* (including "In der Nacht" and "Traumeswirren"), the last of the *Kreisleriana* (with the ending changed to include a crescendo and a series of chords), the second movement of the Second Piano Sonata, and the second and seventh of the *Novelletten. Carnaval,* because of the rapid change of mood, he did not consider appropriate (although Clara did perform it while in Vienna for a group of about twenty people).

Schumann told Clara that in selections such as these it was his general intention to present to the public compositions that he believed were capable of creating the "greatest *effect*," that is, works of technical display and some brilliance (13 October 1839). Yet, it was obvious that not only did few of his compositions meet those criteria, those that did tended to be disconcerting to audiences. Schumann's predicament was a serious one but, because of his quest for originality, of his own making. As he prepared for marriage to Clara, he was obliged to acknowledge that, despite his efforts, his compositions were little appreciated, and that his fame, while growing, remained insubstantial.

CHAPTER 9

Married Life in Leipzig

A lady meeting a girl who had lately left her service, inquired, "Well, Mary! where do you live now?"—"Please, ma'am," answered the girl, "I don't live now—I'm married."
—Leigh Hunt, *Table-Talk*

THE MARRIAGE OF ROBERT AND CLARA SCHUMANN HAS traditionally been portrayed as a perfect union: five years of trial and hardship, the brunt of insult and castigation, rewarded by a truly remarkable partnership founded in love, sympathy, and understanding for one another. The nineteenth century was fond of happy endings, and seemed to believe that, after all the tribulations they had endured, the Schumanns deserved nothing less. "Truly, our life will be one of poetry and flowers," Schumann had written to Clara during their engagement, "Like angels, we will play and create poems together and bring joy to mankind" (13 April 1838). But their diaries reveal that married life brought unexpected discord and conflict.

They began keeping a joint diary immediately after their marriage. To do so was in keeping not just with their personalities, but compatible with the desires of an era that reveled in the maintenance of diaries, journals, and private chronicles. Their intention was to alternate the entries, each taking a week in turn, the contents to be shared and discussed at the week's end. The diary was to provide a means not just of recording events in their lives—visitors, concerts attended, work accomplished—but their reaction to these events, and, most important of all, their thoughts about one another. It was hoped that, by presenting openly any differences between them, the diary would bring them closer together. But as composition occupied more of his effort, Schumann in time lost interest in it (his last regular entry is in November 1843). He turned instead to a series of household books, originally intended as financial records, but to which he also added brief comments on his health, daily events, and compositions. The diary eventually was kept by Clara alone.

The manner in which each contributed to the diary is in itself revealing. Clara tended to be wordy, usually writing two to three times as much as her husband. She was inclined to write about more mundane matters, was often chatty, and prone to gossip. Like her father, she was quick to criticize, too much so—faults of some sort seem to be discovered in virtually everyone mentioned by her. Schumann too could be critical, but sparingly. And his focus was more on their relationship and his work.

His quiet, more introspective nature is readily apparent, an aspect of his personality that impressed friends and companions. Franz Brendel, a good friend who eventually purchased the *Neue Zeitschrift für Musik* from Schumann, recalled a typical walk taken with Schumann. He had discovered some wine, Markebrunner, at an inn and invited Brendel to share it with him:

> In stifling heat we made the trip together through Rosenthal Park without speaking a word. On arriving, the Markebrunner was his main concern. He spoke not a single word, and it was the same on the way back, when we were both silent. He made only one comment, but it provided me with a glimpse into his inner nature. He spoke of the special beauty of such a summer afternoon, when all voices were silent, when nature itself was completely peaceful and quiet. He was deeply moved, and noted that the ancient Greeks had a particularly appropriate description for it: "Pan is sleeping." The two of us made similar trips together, each time completely silent. At

such moments Schumann only took notice of the world around him when it happened to correspond to his reveries. He sought the presence of others only as relief from solitude.[1]

In time, this reluctance, or perhaps disdain, for speech became paramount. Ferdinand Hiller told of a visit made in 1845 to Schumann with the French composer Félicien David. The prolonged silence became embarrassing. "After a while," related Hiller, "I was beginning to feel hot and uncomfortable, when Schumann turned and murmured to me: 'David doesn't seem to talk much.' 'No, not much,' I replied. 'I like that,' said Schumann with a gentle smile."[2] To Louis Ehlert, it seemed on those occasions when Schumann spoke "as though he were first compelled to come to terms with an inner vision; everything about him appeared to beam in a radiance from another world. His glance, his speech and motions seemed veiled."[3]

At times, it must have been difficult for Clara to deal with this exceptionally quiet and introverted man, so different from herself. But for Schumann, the blessings of their marriage were many. Clara's companionship became the foundation of his life; it provided stability and an environment in which his work could flourish. That is precisely what had been lacking during the 1830s, and had contributed greatly to his loneliness, depression, and occasional fits of despair. "Nothing is missing to make me content," Schumann wrote to Clara prior to their marriage, "except you and what you will bring: domestic order, peace, and security" (8 June 1839).

Married life brought into focus another side of Schumann. While reading his entries in the diary, one finds oneself in the presence of, to put it simply, a rare human spirit: gentle, sensitive, honest, forthright, noble in the finest sense of the word. All of these were traits that had long been part of him, but dominated more by his moodiness and egotism. The marriage provided the opportunity to share ideas with Clara and to grow and develop together. Schumann assumed the role

---

[1] Franz Brendel, "R. Schumann's Biographie von J. W. v. Wasielewski," *Neue Zeitschrift für Musik* XLVIII (1858), p. 159.

[2] Gustav Jansen, *Die Davidsbündler* (Leipzig, 1883), p. 50. Translation from Ronald Taylor, *Robert Schumann: His Life and Work* (New York, 1982), p. 94.

[3] Louis Ehlert, *From the Tone World* (New York, 1885), pp. 220–21.

1 Portrait of August Schumann, Schumann's father. A successful writer and publisher, he greatly influenced his son's choice of career.

2 Schumann's first piano teacher, Johann Gottfried Kuntsch. Kuntsch early recognized Schumann's gifts, and did much to support him.

3 Jean Paul, Schumann's favorite writer. The style and content of Jean Paul's novels strongly influenced Schumann's piano compositions of the 1830s.

4 Friedrich Wieck, Schumann's piano teacher in the early 1830s, and father of Clara. His vehement opposition to the marriage of his daughter to Schumann created a breach that was never fully mended.

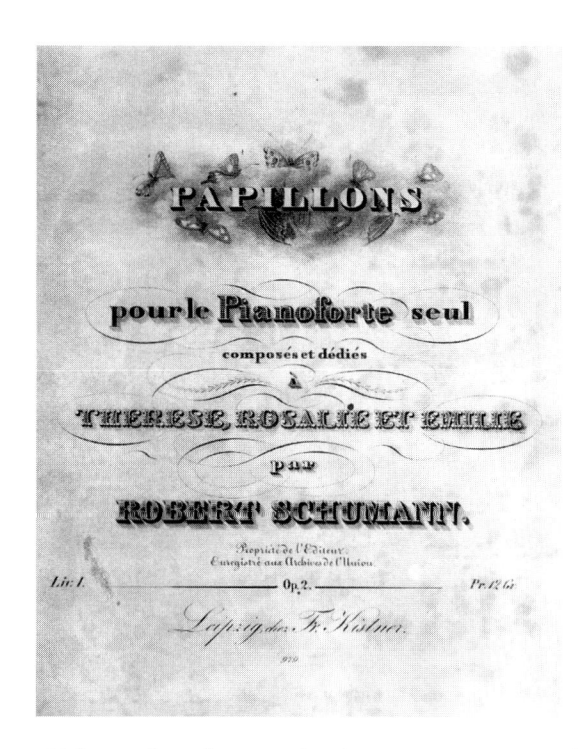

5   Title page of Schumann's *Papillons* op. 2 (1831). Its presentation is typical of the time.
The butterflies depicted on it likely misled many buyers who bought it
in the expectation of taking home a pastoral salon piece.

6   Ernestine von Fricken, a fellow student of Wieck, to whom Schumann was engaged
in 1834. She provided the inspiration for Schumann's *Carnaval* op. 9.

7 Clara Wieck in 1838 at the time of her triumphs in Vienna.

8 Title page of Schumann's *Davidsbündlertänze* op. 6 (1837).
It recalls the "Gothick" style popular at the time. Such designs were unusual
for music, and reveal Schumann's determination to distinguish his compositions
both by their musical content and visual impression.

9 Title page of Schumann's Piano Sonata No. 1 op. 11 (1836). Its unique musical qualities have been highlighted by enigmatic imagery (the work of Bonaventura Genelli).

10 Lithograph by Josef Kriehuber of Schumann made in 1839 during his stay in Vienna. It was regarded by contemporaries as a good likeness.

11   Engraving of a relief of the Schumanns made by their friend, Ernst Rietschel, in 1846.
It was a particular favorite of Schumann.

12   Schumann in 1847, not long after completing his Symphony No. 2 op. 61. The lithograph
(by Eduard Kaiser) was completed during the Schumanns' disappointing visit to Vienna.

9 Title page of Schumann's Piano Sonata No. 1 op. 11 (1836). Its unique musical qualities have been highlighted by enigmatic imagery (the work of Bonaventura Genelli).

10 Lithograph by Josef Kriehuber of Schumann made in 1839 during his stay in Vienna. It was regarded by contemporaries as a good likeness.

11   Engraving of a relief of the Schumanns made by their friend, Ernst Rietschel, in 1846.
It was a particular favorite of Schumann.

12   Schumann in 1847, not long after completing his Symphony No. 2 op. 61. The lithograph
(by Eduard Kaiser) was completed during the Schumanns' disappointing visit to Vienna.

13 Several months after their 1847 trip to Vienna, the Schumanns traveled to Berlin where Schumann conducted *Paradise and the Peri* op. 50. This portrait of Schumann by Auguste Hüssener was made during the Berlin visit.

14 Daguerrotype of Schumann taken in Hamburg in 1850, not long before assuming his new position in Düsseldorf.

15 Portrait of the Schumann children (without Julie) from about 1855. Schumann was deeply devoted to his children, and being separated from them while in the asylum at Endenich filled him at times with despair.

of teacher and mentor. They studied music together (especially the *Well-Tempered Clavier*), and read Shakespeare and Jean Paul.

What meant most to Schumann in marriage was raising a family. He loved children, and once expressed the opinion it was not possible to have too many. During the nearly fourteen years they spent together, he and Clara had eight children, two girls being born while they lived in Leipzig, Marie (born 1 September 1841) and Elise (born 25 April 1843). The children always seemed to delight Schumann, and he took great pleasure in observing their thoughts, growth, and development. "My two little girls are lovely, little angels," he chided Johann Verhulst, "my dear wife is wonderful. And you want to remain a bachelor?" (5 June 1844).

The conflict that was present in their marriage was a result of their ambition. At the time of their marriage, Clara's reputation as a musician far exceeded that of her husband. She had no intention of abandoning her career. Schumann, however, felt differently. During their engagement Clara had expressed her fear that she would be forgotten if she did not continue her career after marriage. Schumann had responded: "The first year of our marriage you *shall* forget the artist, and *shall* live only for yourself and your home and your husband, and only wait and see how I will make you forget the artist. A wife stands even higher than an artist. If I only achieve one thing—that you have nothing more to do with the public—then my deepest wish will have been achieved. Yet you will always remain the artist that you are" (13 June 1839).

Performing was Clara's life, and rather than retire from the stage after marriage, she wished to increase her reputation. In order to marry Schumann, she had been obliged to fight her father, in the process being torn by her love and devotion for him. With marriage, Clara had moved from one crisis to another, in both instances forced to confront men whom she hoped to please. It was the acknowledgement by Clara of Schumann's genius as a composer that served to dwarf her musical gifts. She felt it was her duty to serve and assist him. The role she gradually came to assume was one of subservience to her husband's genius—a martyrdom of sorts that earned her the encomium of the nineteenth century. Her own career would be sacrificed at the altar of Art.

To adopt such a role did not come easily to Clara. Nor was she able to find fulfillment as a mother. Her career meant too much to her, and from time to time the role of administering angel was dropped for that of performing artist. In the diary, Clara lamented that she was not permitted to practice when Schumann composed; it disturbed his concentration. Within a month of their marriage, Clara brought up the idea of a tour to Belgium and Holland, in its way the continuation of the plans she had had in 1839 while in Paris. Schumann was opposed. "Farewell, life of a virtuoso!" she wrote in the diary, and noted that it was "frightful" not to make use of her ability at a time when she felt at the height of her powers.[4] "Should I stay here for the entire winter, earning nothing, when I can easily earn more?"[5]

Clara did not return to the concert hall as a soloist until a Gewandhaus concert on 31 March 1841. Married life must have been a sobering experience for her. Little time for practice, motherhood, managing a home (there were servants, including wet-nurses for the babies)—all quite different from her life prior to marriage, and both more demanding and more monotonous in its routine than she had imagined it would be. Had there been sufficient income, Schumann probably would have been content for her to make a limited number of local appearances. "On the whole, I am content in my Inselstrasse [their place of residence]," he wrote in the diary in June 1842, "so that I have absolutely no desire to go elsewhere. But Clara wants very much to travel."[6] With a growing family and a limited income from the *Zeitschrift* and his compositions, it soon became clear that more money was needed. "We spend more than we earn," Schumann noted.[7]

Between 1840 and 1854, Clara gave nearly 150 concerts. This was far fewer than she desired, and most were local, occurring in the cities where the Schumanns were then living (Leipzig, Dresden, or Düsseldorf) or nearby. There were few tours, and those that were undertaken regularly met with Schumann's opposition. During their residence in Leipzig, a number were contemplated: St. Petersburg in 1840, Paris in

---

[4] 7 October 1840 in *Tgb II*, p. 110.
[5] 6 November 1840 in *Ibid.*, p. 121.
[6] End of June 1842 in *Ibid.*, p. 230.
[7] 17 February 1843 in *Ibid.*, p. 254.

1841, Holland and England in 1844 (Clara even began studying English). In February and March 1842, a trip to the United States was considered. The idea of traveling to America was grandiose, but not as far-fetched as it might seem. America was perceived as a land of plenty. Despite the rigors of the trip and the amount of time required for it, piano virtuosos such as Thalberg were to make the journey and find it extremely profitable.

During the first three-and-a-half years of their marriage there was but one concert tour: to northern Germany in February 1842. Despite several advantages to the trip for Schumann—including a performance of his First Symphony op. 38—he was clearly uncomfortable. In Oldenburg, only Clara was invited to perform at the court. She returned delighted by her success, but Schumann was angered at being snubbed. Her concerts were well received, and Clara wanted to continue the tour in Denmark, but Schumann wanted to return home.

There was some debate about their course of action. In a letter to Emilie List, Clara gave her reasons for continuing the trip without her husband: "I am a woman, I will not be neglecting anything at home, I earn nothing there—why should I not by means of my talent contribute my bit for Robert?"[8] It was a stance that Clara was frequently to adopt. There was never a question of her needing to perform because she wanted to, nor were her concerts presented as a means of furthering her career. It was simply a means of earning more money, of doing her "bit for Robert." At some point, she must have realized that her career was essential to her and that providing more income, while surely helpful, was merely a convenient justification for it.

On 10 March they parted; Clara traveled to Denmark and met a challenging itinerary and continued acclaim—including performing at the Danish court. She returned to Leipzig seven weeks later. Schumann went home and soon found himself lonely and disconsolate. "A miserable life," he wrote in the household books, "practiced counterpoint and fugue."[9] "Should I neglect my talent in order to serve as your

---

[8] Letter of 30 May 1842 in Clara Schumann, *"Das Band der ewigen Liebe": Briefwechsel mit Emilie und Elise List*, ed. Eugen Wendler (Stuttgart, 1996), p. 111.
[9] Entry of 20 March 1842 in *HSHLT*, p. 209.

travel-companion?" he wrote to Clara in the diary. "Should you waste your talent because I need to work on the journal and compose?"[10] It was a dilemma that was never satisfactorily resolved.

They had been married nine months when Clara wrote in the diary that the old adage, "Marriage kills the creative spirit," had not proven true in this instance.[11] The idea of an artist settling into a comfortable middle-class existence, and losing the desire and ability to create was a belief common at the time. If it was a fear also held by Schumann, it must have been overridden by his love for Clara and by the well-remembered advice given to him by the physician he had consulted during the crisis of October 1833: to find a wife. In the six months preceding his marriage, Schumann had been composing prolifically. Surprisingly, he had turned away from music for solo piano, and, after more than a decade of neglect, was writing songs. With marriage, writing music remained of paramount importance to him.

Less than a month after their marriage, he began work on a symphony in C minor, a work that remained incomplete. In the autumn, more songs were composed. Then, in January 1841, he completed the sketches for a symphony in B flat major (published as op. 38). It was orchestrated during the winter, and premiered on 31 March in Leipzig by Mendelssohn. Two months later Schumann completed another orchestral work, the *Overture, Scherzo, and Finale* op. 52, and began work on what eventually was to become the Piano Concerto op. 54. His feverish activity continued during the remainder of the year. Another symphony (later revised and published as his fourth, op. 120) was created, in addition to sketches for additional symphonic movements in C minor, and plans for opera. At the same time, he completed in all essentials the text for an oratorio, *Paradise and the Peri* (*Das Paradies und die Peri*); he would compose the music for it in 1843.

The brisk pace was maintained during 1842. The year began with three string quartets, completed during the summer and published as op. 41 (with a dedication to Mendelssohn). In addition to three other major chamber works completed during the year (the Piano Quintet op. 44, the Piano Quartet op. 47, and the *Fantasiestücke* for piano trio

[10] 14 March 1842 in *Tgb II*, p. 206.
[11] 1 June 1841 in *Ibid.*, p. 167.

op. 88), Schumann expended much effort—with considerable success—in interesting conductors in his First Symphony.

1843 was devoted to the completion of *Paradise and the Peri*, a work on a more impressive scale than any he had previously attempted, and one that, at the time of its completion, he regarded as his greatest accomplishment. That he was able during three years to compose so much music and at the same time maintain his duties as editor of the *Zeitschrift* testifies to his indefatigable industry. All of this was accomplished with little relief from work, and with little time away from home. A vacation trip from 6 to 22 August 1842 to Bohemia provided the major distraction, and both he and Clara delighted in it.

It has often been noted that Schumann tended to concentrate his efforts in one genre at a time. Music for solo piano was the focus of his attention from 1834 until 1839. Then, in the six months preceding his marriage, he abruptly turned to song, producing more than 120 in less than a year. In 1841 he composed three major orchestral works. The next year witnessed a move to chamber music. The explanation routinely offered for Schumann's approach—that he was systematically directed by his muse to explore specific genres—is naive. In reality, there were very practical reasons for his systematic approach: the desire to achieve a measure of popularity, earn money, and gain recognition as a composer.

Those were goals that Schumann himself acknowledged. "With a wife and children," he wrote to Carl Kossmaly, "it is a different matter. One must think of the future, to see the *fruits* of one's labors—not the artistic, but the prosaic" (5 May 1843). In 1838 he had made a half-hearted attempt to court popularity with the *Arabesque* op. 18 and the *Blümenstück* op. 19. Both works were less abstruse and more popular in style, but Schumann was disdainful of the results.

Also very much in demand were songs; they were a standard form of home entertainment, and the publishers' catalogues of the day bear witness to their popularity. In turning to song in 1840, Schumann was attempting to become part of that growing market. As the household books reveal, he was well paid for his efforts. In October 1840 for the *Drei Romanzen* op. 28, he had received 23 talers from Breitkopf & Härtel. He received more than twice that amount (54 talers) in April 1841 from Klemm for the *Lieder* op. 35, and 50 talers in December

1840 for a charming but inconsequential vocal work, the Four Duets op. 34. Financial considerations were foremost in Schumann's mind at the time. Here was a way in which his income could be dramatically increased, and at the same time provide an answer to Wieck's criticism of his earning capability.

In writing symphonies and chamber music, Schumann was attempting to gain popularity in a different manner. Success in those more challenging genres would lead to higher esteem and greater recognition by colleagues and connoisseurs. An established name and reputation—similar, for example, to that held by Mendelssohn—would lead not only to more performances of his music, but improve his association with publishers and hopefully increase sales of his work. Although more time was spent in the creation of these substantial works, he also earned more from their publication: 120 talers each for the First Symphony op. 38 and the String Quartets op. 41. As his fame and reputation increased, so did the amount he received. In 1851 he was paid 200 talers for the Third Symphony op. 97. To view this as an indication that as a composer Schumann was solely dominated by business concerns would do justice neither to his dedication to music nor to his determination not to compromise his convictions. But it is time to step away from fanciful idealism and to recognize that Schumann needed to earn money in order to live. There often were practical reasons for his ventures.

The early 1840s was a time of growing friendships with colleagues, a result now not just of his association with the *Zeitschrift*, but of his increasing reputation as a composer. In October 1843, the Danish composer Niels Gade arrived in Leipzig for a six-month stay. Seven years younger than Schumann and at the start of a promising career, he found in Schumann both a mentor and a friend. Schumann did much to promote Gade's music in the *Neue Zeitschrift für Musik*, and, as might be expected, reveled in the musicality (G-A-D-E) of his new friend's name. Over the years they remained close. "I have seldom met anyone," Schumann wrote in the diary in 1846, "with whom I am in such harmony as with Gade."[12]

Schumann also met Hector Berlioz. Berlioz arrived in Leipzig in late January 1843 as part of a concert tour intended to promote his music.

---

[12] April 1846 in *Ibid.*, p. 401.

Schumann had been among the first to support Berlioz. Eight years earlier he had published a lengthy review in the *Zeitschrift*—extended over three issues—of Berlioz's *Symphonie fantastique*. It showed keen discernment and appreciation of Berlioz's musical intentions, all the more notable because for the review Schumann had not had access to the orchestral score of the *Symphonie*, but had relied on Liszt's piano transcription. Berlioz wrote to Schumann in December 1836, thanking him for his kind words, and expressed a desire to know both him and his compositions.

Berlioz's visit to Leipzig provided an extended opportunity for the two if not to speak to one another at length—neither had proficiency in the other's language—then at least to experience one another's compositions. Schumann was able to hear a number of Berlioz's works, including the Overture to *King Lear*, and the offertory from the Requiem. To honor him, Schumann provided a reception, at which several of his own compositions (including the Piano Quintet and two of the string quartets) were performed. Although their relationship never became close, Berlioz and Schumann appear to have gotten along well together. Their temperaments were markedly different. Berlioz was excitable, talkative, and flamboyant—all traits that Schumann appears to have forgiven. But they shared a great love of literature, particularly for Shakespeare, Goethe, and Byron. After Berlioz's departure, Schumann wrote to Breitkopf & Härtel in an attempt to interest them in Berlioz's compositions and in his treatise on orchestration.[13]

Unfortunately, Clara did not share her husband's opinion of Berlioz, at least in part because of her dislike of Berlioz's conduct toward her in Paris in 1839. "He is cold, dispassionate, sullen," she wrote in the diary.[14] Schumann also had some reservations about Berlioz, but these were reservations that he seemed to retain for the French in general, and that included composers—regardless of nationality—exposed to the perils of residing in Paris. "Paris has clearly corrupted him," Schumann concluded, "also the dissolute life of young people there."[15]

---

[13] Härtel published the treatise. Contrary to what is reported in biographies of Berlioz and Schumann, this was not their only meeting. They met again in Berlin in February 1847, during Berlioz's trip to Russia.

[14] Entry of 27 February 1843 in *Tgb II*, p. 258.

[15] 17 February 1843 in *Ibid.*, p. 256.

Even Chopin was not exempt from this criticism. In time Schumann became critical of what he perceived as the repetitive nature of Chopin's oeuvre: "Always new and inventive in appearance—with the construction of his compositions, in certain pianistic effects, he remains the same—so that we fear he will go no higher than he has thus far."[16] Just as Schumann felt he himself had "progressed" by moving from compositions for solo piano to chamber works and symphonies, he felt failure to do so by others indicated apathy, lassitude, or a lack of ambition. For certain composers, Schumann seemed to feel that this lassitude stemmed from the Parisian way of life. He saw it as indulgent and decadent, mirrored not just in the music, but in the arts in general which he often found to be superficial, shallow, eager to astonish, shock, and please. He occasionally read the most famous novels of the leading French romanticists, such as Victor Hugo and George Sand, and his reaction was invariably one of displeasure and disgust.

Life after marriage included not only new friendships with composers such as Berlioz and Gade, but renewed association with old friends. Schumann's friendship with Mendelssohn remained constant. They frequently spent time together, not just discussing musical matters, but on purely social occasions as well, including playing billiards. Mendelssohn served as godfather to Schumann's first child, a clear mark of the esteem in which they held one another. On a professional level, Mendelssohn remained, in Schumann's eyes, a musician without peer. But, despite Schumann's admiration, Mendelssohn was unable to feel comfortable with some of Schumann's music. As their mutual friend Joseph Joachim recalled, Mendelssohn privately "often found faults" in it.[17] The oddities probably disturbed him, and he may have attributed them to what he perceived as Schumann's dilettantish background.

But whatever reservations he may have had, he continued to work on Schumann's behalf. In April 1843, as a result of Mendelssohn's strenuous efforts, a music conservatory was opened in Leipzig, the first in Germany. Mendelssohn became its director, and selected Schumann to teach composition, score reading, and piano. As a teacher, Schumann does not appear to have been inspired. His reticence and reserve were

---

[16] Review of 1841 of Chopin's opp. 37, 38, and 42 in *GS II*, p. 31.

[17] Frederick Niecks, *Robert Schumann* (London, 1925), p. 150.

major hindrances. On one occasion a student played Mendelssohn's *Capriccio brillant* op. 22 for him: at the conclusion of the performance, Schumann's only reaction was to remark that "sometime you will have to hear Clara play it."[18] But he was still popular with students. A number "worshipped Schumann with an almost fanatical idolatry"—an indication of his ability and accomplishments not as a teacher, but as a composer.[19] It was this growing reputation as a composer that led to him becoming dissatisfied with his work on the *Neue Zeitschrift für Musik*. He felt frustrated by his obligations—particularly the large amount of correspondence—and regretted time spent on such comparatively mundane matters and not devoted to composition.

Additional frustration was provided by Schumann's troubled relationship with Friedrich Wieck. After his previous treatment by Wieck, Schumann understandably wanted no further contact with him. Equally understandable were Clara's hopes for a reconciliation—if not between her husband and Wieck, then at least between father and daughter. Wieck now lived in Dresden, and remained embittered. Even the announcement of the birth of his granddaughter, Marie, failed to move him. In April 1842, while Clara was on tour in Denmark, Schumann wrote to her that her father was spreading rumors that they had separated. Then, on 12 January 1843, Wieck wrote to Clara, asking her to visit. She responded eagerly, and they began to visit one another the next month. It was not until December, however, that a rapprochement was effected between Schumann and Wieck. The success of Schumann's oratorio, *Paradise and the Peri*, provided the pretext for Wieck to write to him, suggesting that they forget the past. That was never achieved, but for a time they at least came to tolerate one another.

The continued friction with his father-in-law, the frustration concerning his duties with the *Zeitschrift*, the pressure to earn money to support his wife and growing family—all produced a time of unusual stress and tension during the first years of Schumann's marriage. The diary and household books record periods of depression and self-recrimination. "Always sick and melancholy" (30 January 1842); "A

---

[18] Carl Reinecke, "Mendelssohn und Schumann als Lehrer," *Neue Zeitschrift für Musik* LXXVIII (1911), p. 4.
[19] Ehlert, p. 56.

sinful life" (25 May 1842); "A damned life at present" (12 May 1843); "Frightful melancholy" (26 June 1843).[20] After completing three major chamber works within a short period of time, Schumann confessed that he had worked too much, resulting in a "nervous debility."[21] As in previous years, he also remained concerned about drinking to excess. While Clara was in Denmark, he offered this childlike reproach: "I drink too much. Robert!"[22]

It was not the best time for Schumann to deal with the turmoil of a strenuous and lengthy concert tour, but in order to relieve financial distress, it was decided late in 1843 to travel to Russia. It was an idea that they had had for several years, even before they had married. Piano virtuosos had found a concert tour to St. Petersburg and Moscow to be extremely profitable; most recently Liszt had successfully traveled there. As further incentive, Adolf Henselt had settled in St. Petersburg, and would be in a position to offer both advice and support. Schumann opposed the trip, however, giving as his reason the need to stay at home and compose. In particular, he was absorbed in the idea of writing an opera, and it was only after Clara spoke with Mendelssohn and asked him to try to change her husband's mind, that Schumann's objections were removed. They departed on 25 January, the children being left in the care of Schumann's brother, Carl.

It was a long and arduous trip, made all the more difficult by the notorious harshness of the Russian winter (they purchased a fur blanket on the way). Because of the snow, sleighs became their usual mode of transportation. They went first to Riga, and two weeks later to Dorpat. "You can not believe how much I am looking forward to traveling with you to St. Petersburg," Schumann had enthusiastically written to Clara prior to their marriage, "We'll sit side-by-side, cozy in thick furs, observing people, seeing foreign lands. Sometimes in the coach you will sing to me a melody from the Kinderszenen, softly, very softly so that I can scarcely hear it" (30 June 1839). But the trip began poorly. The diary relates the primitive conditions they encountered, and the

---

[20] *HSHLT*, pp. 206, 215, 251, 254.
[21] 17 February 1843 in *Tgb II*, p. 255.
[22] Entry of 12 April 1842 in *HSHLT*, p. 211.

malice and pettiness that often had to be overcome in order to arrange public performances.

They arrived in St. Petersburg on 4 March. Fascinating insights into the Schumanns' journey can be gleaned from the travel journal of their contemporary, the Marquis de Custine. The marquis traveled extensively through many of the same regions of Russia, and published an account of it in 1839. It is a discerning study, so perceptive that it has been compared to de Tocqueville's study of the United States. "At Petersburg everything has an air of opulence, grandeur, and magnificence," the marquis observed, "but if we should by this show of things judge of the reality we should find ourselves strangely deceived. Generally, the first effect of civilization is to render what may be called *material* life easy; but here everything is difficult."[23]

Custine found living conditions to be deplorable—Schumann makes no mention of the vermin that the marquis described as afflicting the homes of even the aristocracy. But Custine was especially disturbed by the state of the arts in Russia. "The Russians have not yet reached the point of civilization," he wrote, "at which there is real enjoyment of the arts."[24] There was little understanding of the arts, the prevailing fashion being unquestioned acceptance of current Western trends.

Custine's evaluation helps to explain reactions to Schumann's music and Clara's performances. The center of musical life was the salons of the noble and wealthy patrons of the arts, and Henselt was able to help the Schumanns gain entry to them. Particularly supportive was Count Michail Wielhorski, who, at his own expense, on 21 March provided a private performance of Schumann's First Symphony, with Schumann conducting. Three days later, Clara played for the imperial family. But the four public concerts Clara gave in St. Petersburg were only moderately successful, with mediocre attendance at the first two.

They left St. Petersburg on 2 April, and arrived in Moscow on the 10th, where they stayed for about a month. To Schumann, Moscow provided the highlight of the trip. He marveled at the beauty of the

---

[23] Marquis de Custine, *Empire of the Czar: A Journey Through Eternal Russia* (New York, 1989), p. 128.
[24] *Ibid.*, p. 206.

Kremlin, a point on which he and Custine were in agreement. "The Kremlin alone," the marquis had written, "is worth the journey to Moscow."[25] In Schumann's mind the city was filled with associations with Napoleon, and he noted with interest the residence where Napoleon had stayed in 1812. But for much of the time Schumann suffered from ill health, including bouts of dizziness, which severely limited his pleasure. He was also anxious to continue work on his compositions. He had left Leipzig with ideas of opera—in February he had worked on musical settings from Goethe's *Faust*—but he had become increasingly frustrated by the lack of time and quiet necessary for composition. There was also, to his mind, little memorable in Russian musical life. He had been deeply moved by the court choir—"the best I have ever heard"—but must have been disgusted by the prevailing passion in St. Petersburg for Italian opera.[26] Instead of music, Schumann turned to poetry and wrote a number of poems, including several about Napoleon in Russia, and the lengthy, historical ballad "The Bell of Ivan Veliky."

Throughout the trip, Clara was the focus of attention. Schumann had mistakenly believed that not only would the trip provide leisure for him to compose, but that it would be a dual tour, Clara as pianist and he as composer. But his works were completely unknown to the Russian public. Prior to the visit, none had been publicly performed in Russia. During the trip only two were performed in public: the *Andante and Variations* (in Moscow) and the Piano Quintet (in both Moscow and St. Petersburg).[27] Published reaction was neither kind nor perceptive. The *Biblioteka dlja čtenija* made reference to the "curious pieces by Herr Schumann," while the *Bibliothek für Lektüre* described

---

[25] *Ibid.*, p. 397.

[26] Letter of 27 June 1844 to Ignaz Moscheles in *Robert Schumann: Manuskripte. Briefe. Schumanniana. Katalog Nr. 188* (Tutzing, 1974), p. 146.

[27] Performances of Schumann's work during the trip included: in salons, *Kreisleriana* (St. Petersburg), several, perhaps all, of the string quartets (St. Petersburg; on two occasions), and the Symphony (in Wielhorski's salon in St. Petersburg); publicly, the *Andante and Variations* (Moscow; also privately in St. Petersburg), and the Piano Quintet (Moscow and St. Petersburg; also on two occasions privately in St. Petersburg). The listing in Daniel Wladimirowitsch Shitomirski, "Schumann in Russland," in *Sammelbände der Robert-Schumann-Gesellschaft* Vol. I (Leipzig, 1961), omits a private performance of the Quintet on 17 April; the string quartets were performed at Wielhorski's not on 14 May, but on the 15th. Also to be added is the date of the performance of op. 46 in St. Petersburg: 27 April.

the Piano Quintet as a "tormented, affected, unmusical work."[28] Schumann hardly helped matters by his behavior. He felt ill at ease in his role as traveling companion and little-known composer. During visits to salons, he generally remained silent, Clara even answering questions directed to him. Of one visit, a participant recalled: "The entire evening Schumann was as usual silent and aloof. He spoke very little, and to questions from Count Wielhorski and the host, A. F. Lvov, he mumbled unintelligibly . . . for the most part Schumann sat in a corner near the piano."[29] It would have been easy for some to have interpreted Schumann's conduct as arrogant, and few would have known that he was quiet by nature and, moreover, much of the time feeling poorly.

On 30 May, after an absence of more than four months, the Schumanns returned to their home in Leipzig. Financially (and artistically for Clara), the trip had been successful. But Schumann appeared to be eager to make up for lost time and, despite not feeling well, plunged into composition. Adding to his frustration were his responsibilities with the *Zeitschrift*, and he finally resolved to find a buyer for it in order to devote his time solely to composition. In July, he formally relinquished the editorship of the journal to Oswald Lorenz. Franz Brendel expressed interest in purchasing it, and it was arranged that he would become editor and proprietor on 1 January 1845.

Schumann continued to immerse himself in composition—particularly his settings from *Faust*. So engaged was he in his work that he failed to recognize how perilously close he was to exhaustion. Both physically and emotionally, the trip to Russia had been a severe strain. In the middle of August, his condition worsened. It precipitated a nervous breakdown later that month, one far exceeding in severity the breakdown of 1833.

A combination of circumstances contributed to Schumann's collapse, but all can be traced to dissatisfaction with his present state and concern for the future. His determination to be successful as a composer had, since his marriage, achieved a measure of urgency. In August 1842, during their vacation in Bohemia, familiar surroundings brought to mind his youth (he had previously visited the area with his mother) and

---

[28] Shitomirski, p. 24.
[29] J. K. Arnold quoted in *Eismann*, p. 144.

Schumann recalled: "Great expectations . . . were held of me; they have been only partially fulfilled . . . much more still remains to be accomplished."[30] The Russian trip had only seemed to emphasize how fruitless all his efforts over the past decade had been.

Adding to his frustration was the pressing need to earn more money, and his inability substantially to do so. Ironically, while his success as a composer seemed to be proceeding at a snail's pace, his fame as a critic and ability as an editor was substantial. In 1843 and again in 1846 Schumann declined the editorship of the *Allgemeine Musikalische Zeitung*. He explained his predicament with bluntness to Dorn: "I am basically very happy [working on the *Zeitschrift*]. But if I could only get away from the journal, live as an artist solely for music, not have to concern myself with so many of the little things which are part of an editor's responsibilities, then I would be completely content with myself and with the world" (14 April 1839). In his diary, Schumann asked: "Will I ever be able to live exclusively for my beloved Art? If only Heaven would one day grant me this favor—and while I am still young."[31] Schumann seemed to want nothing more than to be able to devote himself entirely to composing. But to do so, he was obliged to relinquish not just an important source of income but what had become an anchor for his life (and what he had described as his sole "regular sphere of activity," 5 June 1844). Would he be able to succeed as a composer now that he had firmly committed himself to that path? It can be no coincidence that less than two months after making what must have seemed to him an irrevocable decision, he suffered a nervous breakdown.

A trip to the Harz Mountains in September and an attempt at a cure in the baths at Carlsbad were ineffective. Thinking a change in scene might prove beneficial, early in October he and Clara visited Dresden. Schumann at the time was in the midst of what would be regarded today as a clinical depression, during which he felt it difficult, if not impossible, to accomplish even the simplest of tasks. He spent much of the day motionless, as if in a stupor. According to Clara, he "could scarcely cross the room without the greatest effort."[32] Wieck's idea for

---

[30] August 1842 in *Tgb II*, p. 235.
[31] 21 November 1843 in *Ibid.*, p. 270.
[32] *Litzmann II*, p. 76.

a cure was to attempt to "rouse [Schumann] by force,"[33] confirmation of Wieck's no-nonsense temperament, but hardly the best way to deal with his condition. Schumann was unable to sleep, and awoke in the morning in tears, drained of all energy.

Later that month he mistakenly felt the worst had passed, and wrote to a friend: "Now once again life has some luster to it. . . . I believe that I was too much involved with music, in the end became too occupied with my music for Goethe's *Faust*. . . . During this time I could hear no music at all—it cut through my nerves like a knife" (October 1844). But he still felt dejected, sought rest, and took walks for distraction. Unlike the nervous breakdown in 1833, its effects (and his depression) continued off and on for months. Writing to Mendelssohn in the autumn of 1845, he noted that he still had not recovered: "Every disruption of my simple, orderly life destroys my composure, and I feel sick and irritable" (22 October 1845).

By the time of Schumann's letter, Mendelssohn was no longer the full-time conductor of the Gewandhaus orchestra. In November 1842, he had accepted a position as music director in Berlin, and had moved from Leipzig one year later. For Schumann, the loss of interaction with Mendelssohn was a severe one. Ferdinand Hiller was chosen as conductor for the 1843–44 season, and Niels Gade for the next. Although it has become customary to note Schumann's anger over the selection—that he himself had not been chosen for the position or consulted about it—there appears to be no justification for this claim. Despite his fondness for Gade, however, Schumann was disturbed that a foreigner had been selected for the position.

It was decided to leave Leipzig, based in part on the premise that with Mendelssohn gone, musical life in the city would never attain a similar level. On a trial basis and on the recommendation of his physician, Dresden was selected for Schumann's new place of residence. On 13 December 1844, still in the midst of a severe depression, the move was made. Within a few months it became clear that Dresden was a far from ideal choice, and that his condition had not been improved by the change. But his continued ill health left little choice but to remain for the time being. In the end, they stayed for nearly six years.

[33] *Ibid.*

CHAPTER 10

The Compositions, 1840–44

We all strive after a wider field, and rush thither like the stream which at length loses itself in the ocean. The soul struggles for activity, and comprehends its individuality.
—Hans Christian Andersen, *O. T.*

"I WOULD OFTEN LIKE TO CRUSH MY PIANO," SCHUMANN confessed to Heinrich Dorn. "It has become too confining for my thoughts" (14 April 1839). After nearly a decade of writing almost exclusively for the instrument, Schumann appeared increasingly dissatisfied. "He who limits himself to the same forms and situations ultimately becomes a mannerist and a Philistine," he wrote in an 1839 review. "There is nothing more detrimental to an artist than to continue within a genre which has become convenient and comfortable."[1]

By 1840, Schumann may have felt that he himself was in danger of becoming "a mannerist and a Philistine." His music, while not losing its vitality, no longer presented with regularity new ideas or concepts. He had first expressed himself as a "serious" composer by writing lieder—a half dozen of which had been sent twelve years previously to Gottlob Wiedebein for his evaluation. Now Schumann turned once again to writing songs. He did so not just because he clearly needed a

---

[1] Review of Henselt's *Etudes de salon* op. 5 in *GS* I, pp. 389–90.

change from solo piano. There was a strong and growing demand for lieder in the marketplace. By entering the field, Schumann would be able not only to broaden his skills and reputation but increase his earnings.

Despite Schumann's attraction to poetry, during the 1830s he had shown little interest in setting any to music. On the contrary, he had expressed a marked preference for instrumental music, writing as late as June 1839 to Hermann Hirschbach that he did not regard vocal music as highly. But Schumann's attitude should not be interpreted as indicating any aversion toward vocal composition. Rather, it may express a confirmation of the belief he expressed in 1828, when he asserted that the composer was superior to the writer: "Every composer is a poet, only at a higher level." A composer, then, would not have any particular need to employ words in music; text could become an intrusion. But whatever debate Schumann may have inwardly conducted concerning the relative merits of instrumental or vocal music, his conviction that he was in danger of no longer developing as a composer helped to determine his course of action. In 1839 he began to fill a notebook with poetry suitable to set to music.[2]

The Songs

When Schumann started writing lieder in February 1840, he did so with enthusiasm. "Sometimes," he wrote to Clara, "it is as if I have discovered completely new paths in music."[3] "Above all else, also write songs," he later advised a young composer, "this is the quickest way to progress and to bring to blossom your inner musicality" (4 August 1842). More than 120 solo lieder resulted. Rather than flood the market, Schumann had a sufficient number to issue gradually over several years. With his compositions for solo piano, one of the major problems had been their limited appeal. But with lieder, the proposed audience was clearly defined. Not yet having attained the status of being suitable for concert performance, they were intended almost exclusively for performance at home. Schumann did his best to keep in mind for whom

---

[2] It was maintained until the early 1850s, and contained 169 poems by thirty-four poets. Of these, Schumann eventually set 101.

[3] Letter of 31 May 1840 in *JgBr*, p. 315.

he was now writing music. As a result, his songs are noticeably more melodic in a conventional manner—with melodies more singable and memorable.

Much of this change was the result of the different manner in which Schumann was now composing. Previously, he had composed at the piano. Now, as he told Clara, he wrote while standing or walking (obviously singing to himself the melody that he was creating). His new approach is documented by sketches for the songs, most of which consist of a single melodic line, with occasional but infrequent references to the piano accompaniment. Only after completing the melody did he compose the full piano part. The accompaniment, however, provides far more than harmonic support for the voice—and in this, as well as in the technique required, Schumann set himself apart from many lieder composers of his day.

Of the lieder composed in 1840, Schumann focused on writing for solo voice; fewer than two dozen were intended for vocal ensemble (and of these, most were duets). It is not surprising that he seemed to prefer to assemble the works of a poet in a single opus. By doing so, he was able to direct attention to each poet's individuality. The poets most closely associated today with Schumann—Eichendorff and Heine—are represented in the *Liederkreis* op. 39 (Eichendorff), and, for Heine, the *Liederkreis* op. 24, *Dichterliebe* op. 48, and *Belsatzar* op. 57. But he also devoted sets to poetry of Justinus Kerner, Emanuel Geibel, Rückert, Goethe, Robert Reinick, and Chamisso. These settings are not song-cycles in the conventional manner—that is, there is not a detailed story or plot related in them. But several are unified by mood, such as the somber melancholy of op. 39 or the drama of unrequited love and despair in op. 48. In selecting texts to set to music, Schumann seemed drawn not merely to sentiment (as had been the case in his juvenile settings), but to opportunities for character development and psychological representation. He seemed especially attracted to gloomy and melancholy themes—hopeless love, death, intransigence, despondency. Some of his interest can be traced to current fashion. But the number and intensity of his settings convincingly demonstrate that this was not merely an attempt to court contemporary taste.

The poetry selected by Schumann often pays tribute to his discerning taste. Much of his success as a songwriter has been attributed to his ability to enter into the spirit of the poem, and convincingly communicate it in music. His sensitivity to the text was remarkable. But what set Schumann apart from others was not simply his poetic sensibilities. He seemed driven to express in music not merely the text of the poem, but *his* reading of the poem. For that reason, Schumann did not hesitate to alter a text to suit his needs. Most frequently, words were changed or deleted in order to fit a melodic line (or simply to satisfy his fancy). Even titles were altered, such as Heine's "Die Grenadiere" to "Die beiden Grenadiere." A successful song was one that created "an impression similar to that awakened by its subject"—words used by Schumann to describe what he felt constituted effective music criticism—but an equally appropriate description of his approach to song-writing.

Such an approach was a deeply personal one that resulted in a correspondingly broad array of interpretation. For ballads, such as Chamisso's "Die rote Hanne" (op. 31 no. 3, a translation from Béranger; Ex. 10.1) Schumann used a modest, folklike melody, with unobtrusive piano accompaniment. More artful poetry demanded greater subtlety. In Heine's "Ich wandelte unter den Bäumen" (op. 24 no. 3), the dramatic final line, "Ich aber niemand trau" ("But I trust no one"), is accentuated by repetition and separation from the rest of the poem (using a quarter-note rest and harmonic contrast). A solo piano postlude demonstrates as well the prominence of the piano.

Schumann set nearly forty of Heine's poems to music. Irony and sarcasm—often placed as a jarring note in the concluding couplet—play an important role in much of Heine's poetry. But, while Schumann often plays Heine's irony for all of its worth (the disarming, artless tune in op. 24 no. 4 is a good instance), there are several instances (for example, "Das ist ein Flöten und Geigen" from *Dichterliebe*) where it passes without comment. At these times it seems that musical content—most notably tunefulness—took precedence.

Despite the striking originality of many of Schumann's lieder, they remained considerably more accessible and more comprehensible than his piano compositions of the 1830s. The public did not have to concern itself with arcane titles or word/music games. And the music was overwhelmingly tuneful, with a sense of natural spontaneity. Vocal lines

EX. 10.1

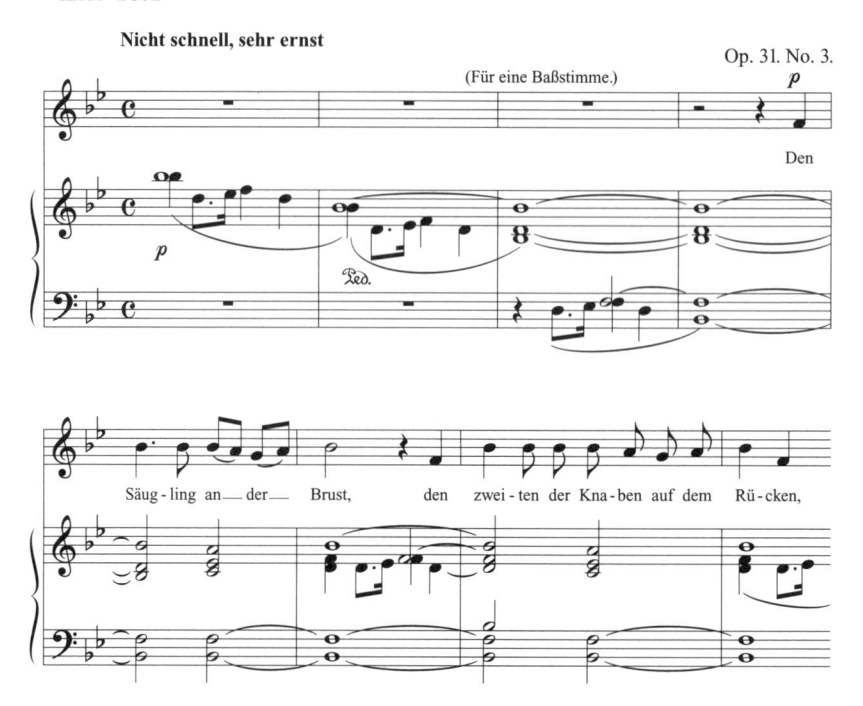

Nicht schnell, sehr ernst

Op. 31. No. 3.

(Für eine Baßstimme.)

Säug-ling an— der— Brust, den zwei-ten der Kna-ben auf dem Rü-cken,

are smooth with a modest range. Harmony is primarily diatonic in basis, with chromaticism presented to enhance the text. Unlike the piano works, the songs do not seem to create a decided break with musical tradition. Not surprisingly, the influence of Schubert is most noticeable. With its tuneful simplicity and vacillation between major/minor tonality, Schumann's setting of Kerner's "Erstes Grün" (op. 35 no. 4) could easily have found a place within Schubert's *Die schöne Müllerin*. More unusual, and less recognizable, are instances of Schumann's continued fascination with Bach. The melodic interplay in "Zwielicht" (from the Eichendorff cycle) resembles that of a two-part Invention.

Among Schumann's most successful songs are his settings from Adelbert von Chamisso's *Frauenliebe und Leben* (1831; "A Woman's Love and Life"). Chamisso's poems are the expressions of love of a dutiful, humble, and devoted wife. These are not poems of high quality—few would regard Chamisso as a great poet—and they are often marred by a maudlin sentimentality. But they are very much a product of their day, both in sentiment and in the servile attitude toward her husband adopted by the female narrator of the poems ("I want to serve him, to live for him,/To belong totally to him"). Schumann selected eight of Chamisso's poems, omitting the last in the set (its omission enhances the cyclic nature intended by Schumann). He worked rapidly, as was often the case when he was creating songs. The eight were composed in only two days, 11 and 12 July 1840, less than a week after learning that Wieck would no longer be able to prevent his marriage with Clara. Chamisso intended the poems as a tribute to his wife; Schumann probably thought of them in a similar manner, and regarded the settings as representative of Clara and her feelings toward him. They were revised in early May 1843 prior to publication.

Of Chamisso's poetry, much of which was occasional in nature, *Frauenliebe und Leben* was the most popular. Prior to Schumann's version, seven of the group (the same as the first seven selected by Schumann) were set in 1836 by Carl Loewe and published as his op. 60 that same year. Loewe's settings (entitled *Frauenliebe*) are a world apart from Schumann's. They are quite simplistic; many are in 6/8, an indication of their light, almost dancelike nature. Little attention is directed toward what attracted Schumann to Chamisso's *Frauenliebe und Leben*: the psychological basis of the poems. Schumann created an idealistic character portrait: woman as pure, noble, and altruistic. His success in doing so was largely overlooked in the twentieth century, primarily because of the subservient nature of the texts. But a contemporary review noted the "deep inwardness" of the songs and the glimpses provided into "the depths of the soul."[4]

Schumann's initial melodic sketches for the songs were hardly altered at all during the course of composition. But he made the usual comparatively modest deletions and additions to the text. The conclusion of the second song was altered by repetition of the second line; in the sixth poem, Chamisso's third stanza was deleted; in the third stanza of the seventh poem there is slight word substitution: "überschwenglich" is replaced by "überglücklich" (Schumann appears to have been

---

[4] Franz Brendel, "Robert Schumann mit Rücksicht auf Mendelssohn-Bartholdy und die Entwicklung der modernen Tonkunst überhaupt," *Neue Zeitschrift für Musik* XXII (1845), p. 122.

disturbed by the appearance of the same word in consecutive lines of the poem). A particularly interesting change illustrates his willingness to adapt and modify poetry to suit his musical ideas. For the fourth song of the set, "Du Ring an meinem Finger," he originally supplied the melody for a portion of the text shown in Ex. 10.2. Dissatisfied with the static, stultified effect, he decided to add movement to the melodic line, and a word ("schönen") to the poem (Ex. 10.3). This same song provides further indication of the significance Schumann attached to the symbolic value of rings. It relates the bride's delight in her own ("You, ring on my finger,/My little golden ring,/With devotion I press you to my lips,/And to my heart"). Schumann's setting uses a simple, descending melodic pattern (in thirds), which recalls the concluding movement of the Fantasie op. 17. The sixth song reveals yet another connection to the Fantasie: a quotation from Beethoven's *An die ferne Geliebte* (Ex. 10.4). Both the Fantasie and *Frauenliebe und Leben* were closely connected in Schumann's mind with Clara.

In contrast to his piano compositions, many of Schumann's songs were an unqualified success. "My lieder," Schumann wrote with pride to Ernst Becker, "are much spoken of" (28 June 1840). After years of comparative obscurity, he probably read with pleasure the review in the *Blätter für Musik und Literatur* describing him as "the new herald of new German Song."[5]

Ex. 10.2

Innig

[musical notation]

der Kind-heit fried-li-chen Traum

Ex. 10.3

Innig

[musical notation]

der Kind-heit fried - lich schön-en Traum

[5] *Eismann*, p. 126.

Ex. 10.4

Langsam, mit innigem Ausdruck

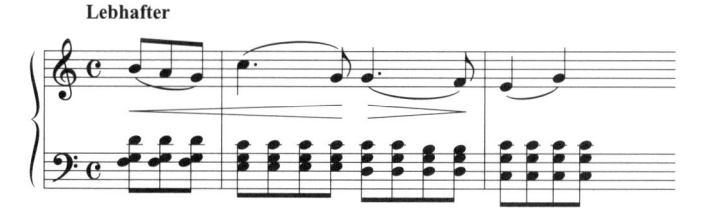

Lebhafter

The Orchestral Works of 1840

Despite his success, in Schumann's mind there was a greater reputation to be made in chamber and orchestral compositions. He consistently expressed his discontent with composers (such as Chopin and Bennett) who he felt repeated themselves and limited themselves to compositions within a particular genre or style. To younger composers seeking his advice, he invariably recommended a more challenging course. Compose songs, he advised, chamber music, orchestral compositions—a direction that he himself selected and, in his mind, the only true path for a composer.

In October 1840, the household books laconically noted: "Symphonic endeavors."[6] But this attempt ("Un poco Andante") remained unfinished. During the remainder of the year, Schumann returned to composing songs. Then, late in January 1841, for two days (the 21st and 22nd) the household books referred to work on a symphony in C minor. This work, too, was not completed. In September he returned to it, finishing the scherzo, but only publishing it in a version for solo piano as the thirteenth of the *Bünte Blätter* op. 99.

The problems Schumann was encountering in writing a symphony were probably a result of his own apprehension. Beethoven had died only thirteen years earlier, and Schumann not only venerated his symphonies but was concerned about comparisons of his own work with Beethoven's. Among contemporaries, it was a different matter. While there were a number of composers—including Wagner—who had written symphonies, many by Schumann's standards would have been

---

[6] 14 October 1840 in *HSHLT*, p. 164.

perceived as conservative, owing more to eighteenth-century ideals than to those of the *Davidsbund*. The descriptive term current at the time was "Neu-Romantisch" ("Neo-Romantic"), the earlier Romanticism being associated with composers of Beethoven's generation. Only a handful of composers of symphonies were representative of this more "progressive" style, most notably, Schubert, Mendelssohn, Norbert Burgmüller, and Franz Berwald. Both Schubert and Burgmüller were dead. Berwald was not to enter the field until 1842. In addition, Berwald's and Burgmüller's symphonies remained little known (Schumann was an admirer of Burgmüller's music, but there is no indication that he knew any of Berwald's).

At the time of Schumann's interest in writing a symphony, Mendelssohn's reputation as a symphonist rested primarily on his second, the symphony-cantata, *Lobgesang* ("Hymn of Praise") op. 52. The "Scottish" Symphony op. 56 was not composed until 1842; the "Italian" Symphony op. 90 and "Reformation" Symphony op. 107 were published posthumously. Without question, the composer regarded at the time as the greatest living symphonist was Ludwig Spohr. In 1841, Spohr was fifty-seven, and his greatest successes were past. He published nine symphonies (composed between 1811 and 1849) but, despite their merits, he was an innately conservative musician, drawing on Mozart rather than Beethoven as his model. In Schumann's eyes, since Schubert's death no one had stepped forth to create an instrumental symphony expressive of the new musical Romanticism.

After working with little success on the C minor symphony on 21 and 22 January, the very next day Schumann abruptly began work on another symphony, described in the household books as a "Spring Symphony."[7] In four days the entire four movements of the symphony were complete in a piano score. Orchestration was begun on the 27th, and finished (in its first version) on 20 February. It was an astonishing achievement; an entire symphony created in four days, and completed in all essentials within a month. Perhaps one reason for the facility with which it was produced can be found in the stimulus provided for the work. As was often the case with Schumann, there was a literary inspiration: a poem by Adolph Böttger, probably given to Schumann by

---

[7] 23 January 1841 in *Ibid.*, p. 172.

the poet in the hope that he would set it to music. At a time when, as Schumann admitted, he was "longing for spring" (10 January 1843), he took inspiration from the concluding couplet ("O turn, turn from your course,—/In the valleys spring is blossoming!"). Originally there were titles for each of the four movements: "Spring's Arrival," "Evening," "Merry Playmates," and "Spring in Full Bloom." But for the final movement Schumann later stated that he also had in mind spring's departure.

Mendelssohn was extremely supportive of the symphony, and conducted the premiere on 31 March. Schumann then put a great deal of effort into attempting to gain additional performances of the work. In time, he wrote to conductors in Berlin, Frankfurt, and Kassel (among others) to interest them in it. Eager to promote his work he described it to Spohr as "not all that difficult" to perform (23 November 1842). But despite its pleasing exterior there were aspects of Schumann's symphony that set it apart from those of his contemporaries. Much of it was grandiose. The ensemble required was larger than the usual symphony orchestra, and included three trombones, four horns, and, most unusual of all, a triangle. The structure of much of the symphony was equally distinctive.

The first movement opens with a majestic introduction, similar to the beginning of Schubert's Symphony No. 9. The Schubert symphony—discovered by Schumann two years earlier—had met with considerable acclaim in Leipzig, and in both performance and rehearsal Schumann had heard it no fewer than six times. What strongly ties the opening of Schumann's symphony to Schubert's is the reliance in both on the interval of a rising third—a similarity that caught the attention of at least one contemporary reviewer. This motive serves as the basis of much of the movement. Schumann wrote of the passage (Ex. 10.5) that he wanted the trumpets to sound as if "from on high, a call of awakening" (10 January 1843).

Ex. 10.5

This opening created some difficulty for Schumann. He considered notating it a major third lower, and it was in that version that the symphony originally was rehearsed. But there were no valves on French horns at the time, and the pitch had to be created by hand, producing a muted, muffled sound. It was not at all the vibrant effect intended, and he was embarrassed by the incident—a result of his unfamiliarity with instrumentation. Now that Schumann's original passage can be played with the effect he intended, should it be restored in the score? He never expressed a preference for the version performed at rehearsal—and both variants of the passage appear in sketches for the work. By the time the orchestral score was published in 1853, the valve horn had been developed and, if he had chosen to, Schumann could have altered the symphony to restore the rehearsal version.

Schumann's lack of experience in writing for an orchestra posed serious problems for him, and was probably a major source of frustration. Since his death, it has become commonplace to criticize his abilities as an orchestrator—Mahler even went so far as to reorchestrate Schumann's symphonies. In general, the criticism of Schumann's orchestration has focused on a supposed insensitivity to orchestral color, and a murky, often thick texture that can obscure thematic content. Mahler (who altered Beethoven's orchestration as well) decided to lighten the texture, and suggested cuts for performance.

Much of the lack of clarity in Schumann's instrumentation may be traced to his perception of the orchestra during these years. He did not think naturally—as did Berlioz or Wagner—in terms of the orchestra. A pianist by training, he seemed to think of the piano when orchestrating. While virtuosos such as Liszt often thought of the piano as an orchestra, and attempted to create orchestral effects on it, Schumann at times thought of the orchestra as a piano, and tried to transfer pianistic effects to it. The beginning of the second movement of the First Symphony provides a good example. The melody is played by the first violins (divisi). But the syncopation in the second violins and violas offers a rhythmic subtlety that—while effective on a piano—with an orchestra can easily sound muddled and blurred (Ex. 10.6).

As it stands, Schumann's orchestration, while ineffectual in places, hardly presents obstacles to its comprehension. In time he became more

Ex. 10.6

adept. Orchestration is handled with conspicuous sensitivity, for example, in the works of the latter 1840s and 1850s. What needs to be remembered is that the orchestra Schumann wrote for was about half the size of the orchestra of today. With a comparable reduction greater clarity might result, and complaints about his orchestral bumblings might diminish in their ferocity.

Of Schumann's four symphonies, the First is the brightest. That may have been a reason for its popularity. Between 1841 and 1855, there were at least fifty-three performances of it, including ones in Hamburg, Berlin, Düsseldorf, Dresden, and Vienna. Spohr, who performed the work on 18 January 1843 in Kassel, pronounced it "excellent," and told Schumann that it had been an "extraordinary" success.[8] But Moritz Hauptmann was more critical, describing it as "somewhat curious, but always musical."[9] There were a number of distinctive characteristics in the work that probably contributed to Hauptmann's opinion. In the first movement, the triangle—at the time regarded as inappropriate for a symphonic work—appears prominently. In the second movement, the intense lyricism (recalling that of the slow movements of Schumann's piano sonatas) is surprising—and rather than closing in a conventional manner, it moves to establish the tonality of the third movement. The third movement contains not one but two trios. And, in the fourth movement, a singular adagio cadenza appears in the development. Within the movement an alteration in mood is prominent, from light and graceful to a grandiose conclusion, an effective, but startling change. Schumann was to follow a similar but more marked approach in the finale of his Second Symphony.

Less than two weeks after the successful premiere of the symphony, Schumann began work on another major orchestral work, described in the household books as a "Suite."[10] It was completed on 8 May. Four days earlier he had begun to compose a single-movement concerto ("Phantasie") for piano. That, too, was completed—including orchestration—in a short period of time: only sixteen days. Nine days after

---

[8] Letter to Schumann of 20 January 1843 in Wolfgang Boetticher, ed., *Briefe und Gedichte aus dem Album Robert und Clara Schumanns* (Leipzig, 1981), p. 182.

[9] Letter to Spohr of 3 November 1843, in Moritz Hauptmann, *Briefe an Ludwig Spohr und Andere* (Leipzig, 1876), p. 17.

[10] Entry of 8 May 1841 in *HSHLT*, p. 182.

completing the concerto, the household books record: "thoughts spring up for a symphony," the first indication that Schumann was creating yet another substantial orchestral work.[11] Interrupted by revisions of the First Symphony and *Phantasie*, in all essentials this symphony (in D minor) was complete by October. It was an astonishing record of accomplishment. Most composers would have been content to rest after completion of a work of such dimensions as the First Symphony. Schumann appeared driven.

The "Suite," after extensive revision, was published as the *Overture, Scherzo, and Finale* op. 52. By composing a slow movement for it, Schumann could easily have converted it to a symphony. But that was precisely what he did not want to do. He preferred to emphasize its unique nature. To Hofmeister, he stressed the "light, friendly character" of the work, and suggested, despite thematic links between the movements, that they could be performed separately (5 November 1842). To Clara he described the *Overture* as "tender, merry . . . siren-like."[12] All of this was in contrast to the rather earnest and serious nature of a symphony, and Schumann evidently hoped that the work would appeal to those who welcomed a change from the standard fare.

Both the D minor Symphony and the *Overture, Scherzo, and Finale* were performed on 6 December 1841 at the Gewandhaus, under the direction of Ferdinand David, concertmaster of the orchestra. It was not the triumphant success for which Schumann had hoped. Public reaction was cool. At least some believed that he was attempting to accomplish too much too quickly. His own reaction was that it had been "too much at one time" for the audience to grasp, and he lamented as well that Mendelssohn had been unable to direct the performance (8 January 1842). Both works were revised, but Schumann did not find it a simple matter to find publishers for them. Op. 52 did not appear in print until 1846 (and in orchestral parts only). The D minor Symphony waited until 1853, when, after revision, it was published as the Fourth Symphony op. 120. There was difficulty as well in locating a publisher for the piano *Phantasie*, a performance of which had occurred privately on 13 August 1841. Only after two additional movements were composed

---

[11] Entry of 29 May 1841 in *Ibid.*, p. 184.
[12] Diary entry by Clara of 5–11 April 1841 in *Tgb II*, p. 158.

for it in 1845 (making it a traditional concerto in appearance) was a publisher found.

The Chamber Works

Schumann could hardly have been encouraged by the reception accorded his recent compositions. For the next six months he composed little. Then, in June 1842, he began work on a project that had been at the back of his mind for years: writing string quartets. During the next eight months he composed chamber music exclusively, writing for various ensembles but, with the exception of the string quartets, invariably including a piano. After finishing the string quartets in July (a set of three), he composed the Piano Quintet op. 44 (September and October), the Piano Quartet op. 47 (October and November), the *Fantasiestücke* for piano trio op. 88 (December), and the *Andante and Variations* for two pianos, French horn, and two cellos op. 46 (January and February).

Schumann's efforts in this new genre led to gradual change in his musical style, a key to which can be found in his correspondence. Writing in 1846 to Robert Franz, he offered an impromptu evaluation of the composer Julius Schäffer. Although he praised Schäffer's originality, he complained of the absence of a *"technician."*[13] What he found lacking in particular were "steadiness and clarity"—a criticism that recalls Hummel's, made fourteen years earlier, of Schumann's first two published works.[14] These had never been matters of concern to Schumann earlier in his career. On the contrary, he seemed to take pride in the obscure and unpredictable nature of his compositions. But Schumann's letter to Franz indicates a shift in musical values. Craftsmanship as well as clarity became of increasing importance to him, not just in the work of other composers but in his own. This change first becomes prominent in the chamber music created in 1842 and 1843. Schumann no longer seems interested in adapting literary models. Rather, reliance is shifted to the work of Haydn, Mozart, and, especially, Beethoven.

Clarity and independence of line were notable characteristics of

---

[13] Letter of 5 July 1846 in F. Gustav Jansen, "Briefwechsel zwischen Robert Franz und Robert Schumann," *Die Musik* VIII (1908/09), p. 354.

[14] *Ibid.*

much eighteenth-century chamber music. And, like Haydn in his op. 20 string quartets, Schumann used imitation and fugue as a means of achieving this independence. There are contrapuntal finales to both the Piano Quartet and the Piano Quintet. That for the quintet is particularly ingenious. It combines in a fugue the primary theme from the opening movement (now in augmentation) with that from the finale. The *Fantasiestücke* op. 88 and the Andante op. 46, while also indebted to eighteenth-century models, are more indicative of Schumann's fondness for experimentation. The *Fantasiestücke* actually form a four-movement piano trio. Although they do not recall the piano compositions of the 1830s as the title might imply, they are whimsical, and the length is shorter than that expected for a piano trio. Unlike the quintet and quartet, they are not showy and grandiose; to Verhulst, Schumann wrote of their "completely gentle nature" (19 June 1843).

The Andante op. 46 is an experiment in timbre. Schumann may have received his inspiration for it from his study of the music of Prince Louis Ferdinand, who explored unusual instrumental combinations in a chamber setting (such as the *Notturno* op. 8 for piano, flute, violin, cello, and two French horns). In the Andante, however, the two pianos dominate with their almost constant presence (a criticism that could be made with equal justice of the quintet, quartet, and *Fantasiestücke*).

Mendelssohn became closely associated with several of the chamber compositions. He played the piano at the first performance of the quintet (at the Voigts' on 6 December 1842). And it was his criticism of the Andante—whose instrumentation he found cumbersome—that led to Schumann preparing another version of the work for two pianos. It is in that version that the work is usually heard today, but Schumann's original conception possesses great charm. He described the work as "very elegiac. I was, I believe, feeling somewhat melancholy when I composed it" (19 June 1843).

During the 1840s, Schumann continued the practice of quotation he had demonstrated in his piano compositions. The Andante quotes (without acknowledgement) one of the most memorable passages from *Frauenliebe und Leben* (found in both the opening and conclusion of the set; Exx. 10.7, 10.8). The First Symphony includes a passage from *Kreisleriana* (Exx. 10.9, 10.10). No references to these quotations are found in Schumann's correspondence or diaries. That there is no mention of

Ex. 10.7

Ex. 10.8

them in nineteenth-century criticism—or privately from those, such as Brahms, who knew his work intimately—is surprising. It is as if a code of silence had been agreed to by those aware of their presence. Perhaps this silence stemmed from the often private and personal associations of the quotations. For these—and others that will be discussed later—seem to have been intended as autobiographical references.

Ex. 10.9

[Musical example: Allegro animato e grazioso, scored for Violin I, Violin II, Viola, Cello, and Bass, all pizzicato and *p*.]

Ex. 10.10

[Musical example: Schnell und spielend (♩. = 100), *Vivace e scherzando*, for piano, *pp*.]

Of all the compositions created during 1842, Schumann spent the most time and expended the greatest effort on the three String Quartets op. 41 (in A minor, F major, and A major). During the previous four years, he had sporadically expressed interest in composing string quartets. In February 1838, he had announced to Clara his intention of composing three of them. But she responded with considerable skepticism, and requested that they be "*completely understandable*" (17 March 1838)—a comment that did little to spur Schumann on. During that time, he was regularly attending performances by Ferdinand David's string quartet, as well as writing a series of string quartet criticism for the *Zeitschrift*. But more direct stimulus may have been provided by Liszt, who wrote to Schumann in May, suggesting that he turn to chamber music.

The following year, Schumann continued to think about string quartets. He wrote to Hermann Hirschbach, himself a composer of quartets, expressing the hope that, should his duties for the *Zeitschrift* permit, that summer he would begin work on them. In June, he informed Clara that he was composing several (the diary notes that he began work on one on the 8th; sketches for the opening of two, in E flat and D major, have survived). But once again she seemed to throw cold water on the project, suggesting in her reply that he write for orchestra.

Although little progress was made on their composition, time was found to study Beethoven's late quartets. Of Beethoven's sixteen string quartets, it was the five composed during the last three years of his life that held the greatest attraction to Schumann. "Along with some choral and original works of Sebastian Bach," Schumann wrote, "they [the late string quartets] seem to me to be on the extreme boundaries of human art and imagination thus far attained."[15] Schumann's desire to write string quartets resurfaced early in 1842. But composition of them was delayed, in part because of the concert trip to northern Germany. On returning, Schumann felt depressed and lonely, but by April he was immersed in a study of Mozart's string quartets. They were followed by an examination of Beethoven's and, finally, Haydn's (the household books do not specify which), as well as separate studies in counterpoint—all spread out over a period of two months. On 2 June, the household books announced: "Attempts at a quartet."[16]

It was a great deal of thought and preparation for a genre that was little appreciated at the time. "The quartet does not harmonize with the tendency of our age," wrote Louis Ehlert, "for [our time] rather inclines to orchestral music and massed choruses, and also to the stage, striving to express grand passions and moods by means of grand resources. The quartet, this classic, primal form of pure music, in our day

---

[15] "Rückblick auf das Leipziger Musikleben im Winter 1837–1838," in *GS I*, p. 380.
[16] *HSHLT*, p. 216.

is only touched upon from motives of traditional habit or devotion."[17] There was no question that the string quartet had become neglected, providing in Schumann's eyes an ideal opportunity to display his "devotion" for it.

Composition of his string quartets was, in contrast to the speed with which Schumann seemed usually to compose, a slow and laborious process. He spent two months (June and July) on them. The sketches are in piano score, often the melody alone being notated or melody and bass—an approach that recalls that adopted for his lieder. The effects of his study of the quartets of Haydn, Mozart, and Beethoven are evident. Several movements in the string quartets are monothematic, a favorite device of Haydn, but Schumann's monothematicism is often more lyrical in basis (as in the first movement of the Second Quartet).

It is the influence of Beethoven that is most noticeable, especially that of the late quartets: unusual and unexpected tonal relationships (the introduction to the first movement of the First Quartet is in A minor, the remainder of the movement in F major); extreme chromaticism (the third movement of the Third Quartet); disruptive rhythmic configurations (the second movement of the Third, the finale of the Second); emphasis on fugato and imitation (the first movement of the First Quartet); and adaptations of conventional structures (an unusual theme and variations replacing the scherzo in the Third; the introduction of a triolike section in the finale of the same quartet). But in addition to these general similarities, there is a specific association with Beethoven's String Quartet op. 132. It served as a model for Schumann's First Quartet, with strong structural and thematic similarities binding both the slow movements.

The string quartets always remained works that Schumann held in particular esteem (an opinion shared by their dedicatee, Mendelssohn). Reaction was broadly favorable, particularly among those who previously had had their doubts about Schumann's ability. Hauptmann praised their "artistic moderation with fresh, exuberant fancy."[18] Spohr, who privately had discovered "sheer revelings in strangeness" in

---

[17] Louis Ehlert, *From the Tone World* (New York, 1885), p. 242.
[18] Frederick Niecks, *Robert Schumann* (London, 1925), p. 222.

Schumann's earlier work, found "no lack of the unusual" in the quartets, but pronounced them "cleverly conceived."[19] Schumann's greater dependence on traditional models led those with more conservative taste to gain greater comprehension of his work. At the same time, he was being perceived as less of a fiery, musical hothead. The danger to Schumann lay in the degree to which he became dependent on musical tradition, with academicism replacing originality.

Paradise and the Peri

In February 1843, Schumann completed revisions of the Piano Quartet and Piano Quintet prior to publication. He then turned to a project that had first attracted his attention eighteen months earlier. The idea for it appears to have come from his boyhood friend Emil Flechsig—at least so Flechsig believed. Flechsig gave to Schumann his translation of a tale, "Paradise and the Peri," from Thomas Moore's *Lalla Rookh: An Oriental Romance* (1817). But Moore's poem (which consists of four tales, all in verse, interspersed with a prose narrative) had enjoyed considerable popularity not just in England but also in Germany, where several translations were available. One had even been published in 1822 by the Schumann firm, so there is a good possibility that, despite Flechsig's assertions, he was mistaken. Still, if Schumann had previously read the work, it had had no noticeable effect on him. When he read it in August 1841, he was enchanted by it. "Perhaps there is something of beauty in it which can be used in a musical way," he wrote in the diary.[20]

"At the moment," he informed Carl Kossmaly, "I am involved in a major project, the greatest that I have ever undertaken—it is not an opera—I nearly think of it as a new genre for the concert hall" (5 May 1843). Schumann later described it as an oratorio, "but not for the chapel—rather, for cheerful people" (3 June 1843). Unlike the usual oratorio, there were no religious themes or weighty biblical basis for his new work. Taking advantage of the popularity of oratorio in Germany, it was his hope that, by creating one markedly different in plot,

---

[19] *Ibid.*

[20] Entry of 18 July–8 August 1841 in *Tgb II*, p. 179.

his work would be judged both more entertaining and distinctive. As he wrote in the diary: "With the exception of some oratorios by Loewe—which lean towards the didactic—I know of nothing like it."[21]

To Schumann, Moore's tale seemed "made for music. The idea for it is so poetic, so pure, that I am completely inspired by it" (19 June 1843). There were several reasons for his enthusiasm. The four stories in *Lalla Rookh* are presented in a manner recalling the *Arabian Nights*: they are related by the Sovereign of Bucharia (disguised as the minstrel, Feramorz) to his betrothed. The entire work is imbued with the romantic allure of the Middle East, an exoticism much in vogue at the time. Schumann, too, was charmed by this exoticism, and hoped that the public's interest in it would increase popularity of his work. But he was also drawn by the plot of "Paradise and the Peri." In Persian mythology, a peri is a fairy descended from angels who have committed evil deeds. In order to gain admittance to paradise, the peri must submit to penance. In Moore's tale, the peri is asked to "*bring to this Eternal Gate/The Gift that is most dear to Heaven!/*Go, seek it, and redeem thy sin;—/'Tis sweet to let the Pardon'd in!'"[22] The peri makes three attempts to locate this precious "gift." Her first two gifts—the last drop of blood from one who has sacrificed his life in the cause of freedom and the final sigh of a maiden who sacrificed her life for love—are deemed noble but insufficient. When she brings the tear from a repentant sinner, the peri is welcomed into paradise. Moore's poem revels in sentimentality. And, despite Schumann's statement to the contrary, it is overwhelmingly didactic and moralistic. But what seemed to draw him to it was the concept of sin, guilt, and redemption. These were topics that greatly interested Schumann, and he returned to them in other major compositions, including *Faust, Genoveva, The Pilgrimage of the Rose (Der Rose Pilgerfahrt)*, the *Requiem for Mignon*, and *Manfred*.

Schumann began to adapt the text of *Peri* within days of reading it. Work continued intermittently during August 1841—interrupted by revisions of the First Symphony and *Phantasie* for piano. On 22 August,

---

[21] Entry of 28 June 1843 in *Ibid.*, p. 266. Schumann probably had Loewe's *Gutenberg* (1836) and *Palestrina* (1841) in mind.

[22] *The Poetical Works of Thomas Moore* (New York, n.d.), p. 414.

he noted in the household books: "Working on the text for "Peri"—nearly finished."[23] But he was overly optimistic. He turned to the poet who had supplied the inspiration for his First Symphony, Adolph Böttger, for assistance. According to the household books, work with Böttger occurred in August and December, after which Schumann continued for several weeks on the text himself, finishing it on 6 January 1842 (with some additional touches that autumn).

Paradise and the Peri was divided into three parts, each based on one of the peri's attempts to gain entry into paradise. It is an effective approach dramatically, for the angel's response to the first two of the peri's efforts is delayed until the succeeding part, heightening audience curiosity in the process. But, overall, Moore's poem posed a serious problem of which Schumann seemed unaware. The most exciting part of the narrative is that associated with the peri's initial attempt to enter paradise. It is filled with pomp and melodrama, and Schumann made good use of the battle scenes. But the remaining episodes—the maiden's self-sacrifice and the repentant sinner—are in essence contemplative, and offer little opportunity for contrast. Schumann created some much-needed variety with additions to the text, including the lively chorus (No. 18) that opens Part III—but it is not enough. "Paradise and the Peri" occupies less than a dozen pages in *Lalla Rookh*, and, for the reader, the lack of contrast creates little difficulty. But for an oratorio that lasts an hour and a half, contrast is essential. A more experienced composer might have realized from the start that Moore's poem was, from a musical point of view, flawed for purely practical reasons.

The composition of *Paradise and the Peri* was the most substantial work Schumann had undertaken: nearly 250 pages of full score, comprising twenty-six pieces for orchestra, solo voices, and chorus. He spent nearly four months on its composition, from 23 February until 17 June 1843. Additional time was spent revising the score in July; as late as 20 September he was reworking the concluding chorus for Part I (No. 9).

There were more new elements in *Paradise and the Peri* than its exotic

---

[23] *HSHLT*, p. 191.

subject matter. Schumann was attempting a new approach in the music for it as well. To Franz Brendel, he described the two most significant aspects: "the absence of recitative and the manner in which the musical pieces continuously move from one to another" (20 February 1847). Although the oratorio follows conventional practice in assigning numbers to the individual segments that comprise it, Schumann's goal was to create a composition without seams. In place of recitative, he created a distinctive arioso, one that often blurred the distinction between it and the more lyrical, arialike sections.

Yet another indication of Schumann's progressive spirit is the recurrent use of thematic motives both to unify and to offer a musical commentary on the text. Two themes—both initially presented within the first few pages of the score—are associated with the peri and recur with regularity (Ex. 10.11).

The *Peri* was first performed on 4 December 1843 in Leipzig under Schumann's direction, and repeated a week later, in both instances to acclaim. Between 1843 and 1855 it was performed approximately fifty times, a clear indication of its popularity. The innovations introduced by Schumann in *Peri* did not hamper its success, but neither did they noticeably contribute to it. The public seemed to be charmed not by Schumann's originality but by the work's tunefulness. Not unexpectedly, there was debate in the press over whether it was an oratorio or an opera (though the piece was not staged as an opera would have been)—clearly, some were confused by the original subject selected by Schumann. To those who had still held reservations about his ability, *Paradise and the Peri* seemed to resolve them. "[The composer] has found his

Ex. 10.11

way out of the fog," wrote Hauptmann, "and learnt how to enjoy loveliness and simplicity."[24]

All was part of Schumann's growing fame. The number of his followers was now steadily increasing, and formed the basis of what could easily be perceived as a Schumann school of composition. Works with distinctly Schumannian titles began to appear, such as Robert Volkmann's *Phantasiebilder* op. 1. The *Leipziger Zeitung* described *Paradise and the Peri* as Schumann's "first *great* composition."[25] The praise undoubtedly was welcome, but Schumann may well have asked himself what he would need next to accomplish both to substantiate and maintain his growing reputation.

---

[24] Letter of 18 December 1843 in Moritz Hauptmann, *Letters of a Leipzig Cantor*, 2 vols. (New York, 1972), II, p. 11.

[25] Gerd Nauhaus, "Schumanns *Das Paradies und die Peri*," in Akio Mayeda and Klaus Wolfgang Niemöller, eds., *Schumanns Werke: Text und Interpretationen* (Mainz, 1987), p. 144.

CHAPTER 11

The Years in Dresden

A poet, as he is to others of the highest wisdom, pleasure, virtue, and glory, so he ought personally to be the happiest, the best, the wisest, and the most illustrious of men . . . the greatest poets have been of the most spotless virtue, of the most consummate prudence, and, if we could look into the interior of their lives, the most fortunate of men.

—Shelley, *A Defence of Poetry*

EVEN PRIOR TO THEIR MARRIAGE, SCHUMANN HAD BRIEFLY considered settling with Clara in Dresden (primarily as a means of avoiding Wieck). It was only about sixty miles southeast of Leipzig and since 1839 connected by train—a three-hour journey that Schumann had felt was convenient enough for him to continue his work with the *Zeitschrift*. But it was a city markedly different in character from Leipzig: not a bustling commercial center, but residence of the King of Saxony and his court. As might be expected, it was far more stratified socially. Its artistic climate differed as well. Dresden did not possess the stimulating and variegated musical life of Leipzig. Rather, it was renowned for its academy of art and the distinguished painters associated with it. If, in selecting a new residence for Schumann, the intention had been to choose one that bore little resemblance to any other place in which he had lived, then Dresden was an ideal choice. But if—and this would have made greater sense—the goal had been to achieve some measure of continuity, the selection could hardly have been more unfortunate.

In the weeks and months following the Schumanns' move to Dresden, the primary concern remained his health. In the household books, Schumann continued to note the lack of improvement: "Once again great nervous debility" (7 February 1845); "Ill in the evening—sleepless night—the day on which Beethoven died" (27 March 1845); "Nervous complaint" (2 May 1845); "Very ill" (20 August 1845); "In the evening, problems with nerves" (19 November 1845). In June, he complained of weakness in his eyes and dizziness.[1]

Within a short time of arriving in Dresden, Schumann met Dr. Carl Gustav Carus, physician to the court. He soon became Schumann's physician as well. Carus was a remarkable man, in many ways possessing ideal credentials to help Schumann regain his health. At the time of their meeting, Carus was fifty-five, and had served as physician at the court since 1827. He was a man of wide interests and accomplishments. Like Schumann, he had studied at the University of Leipzig, where he had earned degrees both as a doctor of philosophy and doctor of medicine. His scientific expertise was broad, and in medical circles he possessed a formidable reputation for his studies in gynecology, anatomy, and physiology. What distinguished Carus from more conventional physicians was his fascination with the human spirit, and, in particular, the significance of dreams. He published several books associated with the subject, most notably *Psyche* (1846; 2nd edition in 1850) and *Mnemosyne* (1848). Mental illness was a related area of interest.

Carus had an extraordinary curiosity about the arts and the creative process. Music was one of his great passions (Mozart and Bach were his favorite composers). His home was always open to gifted musicians. In the winter of 1829–30, accompanied by her father, Clara Wieck had performed at Carus's home and astounded him with her ability. Among modern composers, his tastes were broad and discerning, and included Berlioz, Paganini, Wagner, Mendelssohn (a particular favorite), and Liszt (whom he described as a "volcano").[2]

---

[1] *HSHLT*, pp. 380, 383, 387, 391, 397, 406.
[2] Carl Gustav Carus, *Lebenserinnerungen und Denkwürdigkeiten*, ed. Elmar Jansen. 2 vols. (Weimar, 1966), II, p. 107.

It would be difficult to conceive of someone with greater understanding and sensitivity to the music and literature of his day. Yet, this was by no means the extent of his fascination with the arts. He was also a gifted landscape artist. As a painter, he was naturally very much at home in Dresden, and he associated regularly with the artists at the Academy. Carus had been a close friend as well of the greatest German landscape painter of his time, Caspar David Friedrich. His friendship with Friedrich led to the publication of *Nine Letters on Landscape Painting* (1831; 2nd edition 1835), a valuable aesthetic treatise on the art of the time.

Physician, painter, aesthetician, lover of music—Carus's unique personality and remarkable gifts could have helped him gain unusual insight into the nature of Schumann's illness. The first indication of a professional relationship between Carus and Schumann is found in a reference in the household books for 27 August 1845: "Early in the day consultation with Hofrath Carus."[3] On 25 October, Schumann noted: "Bad reaction to Carus's pills—evil day."[4] References to Carus in the household books continue until the Schumanns' departure from Dresden in 1850, but no further particulars of the treatment are offered. Additional notices are brief, and most refer to social engagements. The only further information concerning Carus's treatment of Schumann is found in a letter to Mendelssohn, in which Schumann wrote that Carus had advised early morning walks, "which suit me very well" (20 September 1845).

The absence of details concerning the treatment is both frustrating and perplexing. There can be little doubt that Schumann's illness would have been of interest to Carus. He was especially familiar with the effects of melancholia—aspects of which he had witnessed for years in the behavior of Caspar David Friedrich (and that he had discussed in a biography he had written of Friedrich in 1841). It is puzzling why absolutely no mention of Schumann or his condition occurs in Carus's writings and, in particular, his autobiography. Anecdotes and evaluations of other musicians (including Clara) are frequently present, so much so that Schumann is conspicuous by his absence. Carus published his

---

[3] *HSHLT*, p. 398. "Hofrath" was Carus's court title.
[4] *Ibid.*, p. 404.

autobiography in two parts in 1865 and 1866, three years before his own death. At that time, Clara was still active as a concert artist. Given his attachment to the family and the scandal often associated in the nineteenth century with mental illness of any type, it appears likely that Carus exercised discretion and eliminated all references to Schumann from his text.[5]

In addition to Carus, while in Dresden Schumann was under the care of another physician, Dr. Carl G. Helbig. Schumann's association with Helbig had begun in October 1844, and lasted the entire time of his stay in Dresden. Other than the use of cold plunge baths and undetermined medication (which Schumann often found a pretext for not taking), details of Helbig's treatment are not known—although there was an attempt at mesmerism (hypnosis) in January 1845. Helbig later provided Wasielewski with details of the most disturbing aspects of Schumann's general condition:

> As soon as [Schumann] concerned himself with anything of a mental nature, he trembled, felt faint, and cold in his feet. He was in an anxious state with a particular fear of dying. This expressed itself with a fear of high mountains and buildings, of all metal objects (even keys), of medicines and of being poisoned. He suffered from insomnia, and felt worst in the morning.[6]

Helbig was of little help to Schumann; Carus's early morning walks were probably more efficacious. But he did suggest to Schumann that he spend less time on music and find distraction in other subjects. Unfortunately, it was advice that Schumann did not follow.

During his illness, Schumann was never reluctant to discuss the matter with friends and associates, at least in part because he wished to explain why he was composing so little. But he was truly unaware of the seriousness of his condition. He was eager to attribute his collapse to overwork—"too much involved with music," as he put it—particularly the work on *Faust*. "I lost every melody just as I thought of it," he later told August Kahlert.[7] To Robert Franz, Schumann noted that

---

[5] A number of Carus's writings, including portions of his autobiography, remain in manuscript. There is a good possibility that an examination of these sources may provide further information about Schumann's mental health during the 1840s.

[6] *W*, pp. 351–52. Helbig also noted the presence of "auricular delusions" (p. 352).

[7] *Ibid.*, p. 356.

he had to be careful because all music "often made me very melancholy."[8]

That Schumann tended to underestimate the severity of his illness—and to believe that it was a result of nerves and too much contact with music—is not surprising. Moritz Hauptmann had suffered symptoms superficially similar to Schumann's in 1827, and had simply attributed them to an attack of nerves. Hauptmann wrote: "The very first note or chord gives me such a jar (whether physical or mental I cannot say), that I am only too glad to stop at once. I feel the note and the vibration of the metal string in my eyes and in my teeth (as a galvanized frog might) . . . Long walks, quiet mornings spent in the calm of open-air nature, where everything is so *natural*—these are the antidotes."[9]

While Hauptmann bounced back from his attack with little difficulty, Schumann's return to health was a slow process with frequent setbacks. In his attempt to cure himself and return stability to his life, he turned to literature, more specifically the *Davidsbund*, conceiving the idea of writing the biography of a member of the *Bund* with himself as model. And he returned to an old pastime, one that he had used before in times of boredom and depression: the study of counterpoint. The game—the playful quality of counterpoint—seemed to serve as a beneficial source of relaxation for him. It also provided him with a continued sense of accomplishment. Late in January 1845, he noted in the household books: "Studies in counterpoint begun with Clara."[10] February and March were spent on fugue, resulting in what Schumann described as a "passion for fugues."[11] At the same time Schumann's interest in Bach grew more lively. Late in January 1845, he wrote to Breitkopf & Härtel, offering to assemble a new edition of the *Well-Tempered Clavier* using available manuscript and early editions as his primary sources—an edition very much needed at the time (unfortunately, nothing came of the proposal).

Schumann's study resulted in a series of compositions created in 1845,

---

[8] Letter of 21 November 1844 in F. Gustav Jansen, "Briefwechsel zwischen Robert Franz und Robert Schumann," *Die Musik* VIII (1908/09), p. 347.

[9] Letter of 15 June 1827 in Moritz Hauptmann, *Letters of a Leipzig Cantor*, 2 vols. (New York, 1972), I, pp. 7–8.

[10] 23 January 1845 in *HSHLT*, p. 379.

[11] 21 February 1845 in *Ibid.*, p. 381.

primarily contrapuntal in nature, including the Studies for Pedal Piano op. 56, the Sketches for Pedal Piano op. 58, the Four Fugues op. 72, and his monumental tribute to Bach, Six Fugues on the Name, "Bach" op. 60. In no way do these works give an indication of Schumann's mental turmoil. But in a fragile mental state, he must have thought it helpful as a composer to be obliged to follow the numerous rules of counterpoint required by the style he had selected; in that sense, it was as if self-imposed boundaries had been erected, and some of the freedom of thought that appeared to frighten him at the time had been removed. During the summer—an interlude from his contrapuntal obsessions—Schumann completed the final two movements of the Piano Concerto op. 54 (the first movement, the "Phantasie," had been composed in 1841), a work that was to become a staple of Clara's concert tours.

Some distraction was provided during the year by reading, including Goethe, Schiller, and Shelley. But invariably his reading served less as distraction than as thoughts for compositions. Opera was still on his mind. It remained the one significant genre that he had not yet attempted, and it was as well an assured though difficult means of building on his growing fame. He had during these years a great number of ideas for possible libretti, including legends (King Arthur, Tristan), and plots from the works of Byron, Hoffmann, and Goethe, among others—but none completely satisfied him.

On 11 March 1845, the Schumanns' third daughter, Julie, was born. During the years in Dresden, the family grew considerably. Emil, their first son, was born on 8 February 1846, and was followed by two others, Ludwig on 20 January 1848 and Ferdinand on 16 July 1849. Clara was pregnant much of the time, and had, as might be expected with six children all under the age of eight, little time for music.

By December 1845, Schumann's condition had improved to such an extent that he was able in an exceptionally short period of time to sketch a symphony in C major, published in 1847 as the Second Symphony op. 61. He came to view the work as representative both of the difficulties of the past year, and of his return to health. But he must have known that there was little chance of the symphony being performed in Dresden. Even prior to the move Schumann had written to Ferdinand David, noting that in the city "there is so little music to

he had to be careful because all music "often made me very melancholy."[8]

That Schumann tended to underestimate the severity of his illness—and to believe that it was a result of nerves and too much contact with music—is not surprising. Moritz Hauptmann had suffered symptoms superficially similar to Schumann's in 1827, and had simply attributed them to an attack of nerves. Hauptmann wrote: "The very first note or chord gives me such a jar (whether physical or mental I cannot say), that I am only too glad to stop at once. I feel the note and the vibration of the metal string in my eyes and in my teeth (as a galvanized frog might) ... Long walks, quiet mornings spent in the calm of open-air nature, where everything is so *natural*—these are the antidotes."[9]

While Hauptmann bounced back from his attack with little difficulty, Schumann's return to health was a slow process with frequent setbacks. In his attempt to cure himself and return stability to his life, he turned to literature, more specifically the *Davidsbund*, conceiving the idea of writing the biography of a member of the *Bund* with himself as model. And he returned to an old pastime, one that he had used before in times of boredom and depression: the study of counterpoint. The game—the playful quality of counterpoint—seemed to serve as a beneficial source of relaxation for him. It also provided him with a continued sense of accomplishment. Late in January 1845, he noted in the household books: "Studies in counterpoint begun with Clara."[10] February and March were spent on fugue, resulting in what Schumann described as a "passion for fugues."[11] At the same time Schumann's interest in Bach grew more lively. Late in January 1845, he wrote to Breitkopf & Härtel, offering to assemble a new edition of the *Well-Tempered Clavier* using available manuscript and early editions as his primary sources—an edition very much needed at the time (unfortunately, nothing came of the proposal).

Schumann's study resulted in a series of compositions created in 1845,

---

[8] Letter of 21 November 1844 in F. Gustav Jansen, "Briefwechsel zwischen Robert Franz und Robert Schumann," *Die Musik* VIII (1908/09), p. 347.

[9] Letter of 15 June 1827 in Moritz Hauptmann, *Letters of a Leipzig Cantor*, 2 vols. (New York, 1972), I, pp. 7–8.

[10] 23 January 1845 in *HSHLT*, p. 379.

[11] 21 February 1845 in *Ibid.*, p. 381.

primarily contrapuntal in nature, including the Studies for Pedal Piano op. 56, the Sketches for Pedal Piano op. 58, the Four Fugues op. 72, and his monumental tribute to Bach, Six Fugues on the Name, "Bach" op. 60. In no way do these works give an indication of Schumann's mental turmoil. But in a fragile mental state, he must have thought it helpful as a composer to be obliged to follow the numerous rules of counterpoint required by the style he had selected; in that sense, it was as if self-imposed boundaries had been erected, and some of the freedom of thought that appeared to frighten him at the time had been removed. During the summer—an interlude from his contrapuntal obsessions—Schumann completed the final two movements of the Piano Concerto op. 54 (the first movement, the "Phantasie," had been composed in 1841), a work that was to become a staple of Clara's concert tours.

Some distraction was provided during the year by reading, including Goethe, Schiller, and Shelley. But invariably his reading served less as distraction than as thoughts for compositions. Opera was still on his mind. It remained the one significant genre that he had not yet attempted, and it was as well an assured though difficult means of building on his growing fame. He had during these years a great number of ideas for possible libretti, including legends (King Arthur, Tristan), and plots from the works of Byron, Hoffmann, and Goethe, among others—but none completely satisfied him.

On 11 March 1845, the Schumanns' third daughter, Julie, was born. During the years in Dresden, the family grew considerably. Emil, their first son, was born on 8 February 1846, and was followed by two others, Ludwig on 20 January 1848 and Ferdinand on 16 July 1849. Clara was pregnant much of the time, and had, as might be expected with six children all under the age of eight, little time for music.

By December 1845, Schumann's condition had improved to such an extent that he was able in an exceptionally short period of time to sketch a symphony in C major, published in 1847 as the Second Symphony op. 61. He came to view the work as representative both of the difficulties of the past year, and of his return to health. But he must have known that there was little chance of the symphony being performed in Dresden. Even prior to the move Schumann had written to Ferdinand David, noting that in the city "there is so little music to hear" (25 November 1844). This was a complaint that continued over the years. To Mendelssohn, he remarked on how much he missed the musical life in Leipzig, "so dead is it here in comparison" (27 October 1846).

Two weeks after arriving in Dresden, Schumann had made a solitary pilgrimage to the grave of Carl Maria von Weber. For nine years, Weber had been Kapellmeister of the German opera in Dresden; in Schumann's eyes he represented both the musical potential of the city and its subsequent decay. Weber's successor was Carl Reissiger (1798–1859) who, Schumann wrote, "understands only his own music and that of Philistines" (2 January 1849). Schumann was never able to become part of official musical circles in Dresden. "Always, a solitary life," he wrote in the household books.[12]

There were few musicians with whom Schumann enjoyed associating while in Dresden. He admired the artistry of the soprano, Wilhelmine Schröder-Devrient, at the time approaching the close of a remarkable career (his *Dichterliebe* op. 48 was dedicated to her). But he had little in common with her extravagant lifestyle and temperament. Probably his closest friend in Dresden was Ferdinand Hiller. Hiller, one year younger than Schumann, was a gifted pianist and composer whom Schumann had first met in Leipzig in December 1839. From the start, Schumann had liked him. Hiller was also a good friend of Mendelssohn and, as a result of a seven-year residence in Paris, knew Chopin, Liszt, and Berlioz. He and Schumann got along well, but Hiller's friendship was small recompense for the numerous friends and musical associates Schumann had had while living in Leipzig.

While in Dresden, Schumann also came into fairly frequent contact with Richard Wagner (they had probably first met in 1830). It would be difficult to conceive two more different temperaments. Wagner was self centered and, although possessed of great charm, dominated his relationships. He was, as well, extremely talkative, which Schumann found annoying—just as Wagner was vexed by Schumann's imperturbable silence during conversations. "He has an enormous gift of gab," Schumann observed of Wagner "stuffed full of overwhelming ideas.

---

[12] 2 March 1845 in *Ibid*.

One can not listen to him for long."[13] In Dresden, Wagner held the position of court Kapellmeister, second in seniority to Reissiger.

Schumann's opinion of Wagner's music was mixed. He studied the score of *Tannhäuser* and wrote to Mendelssohn finding nothing of merit in it: "[Wagner] is unable to write four measures in succession well" (22 October 1845). But after seeing the work performed, he wrote again the next month, taking back his earlier comments. To Dorn he described the work as "deep, original, in general 100 times *better* than [Wagner's] earlier operas," although containing some "musical trivialities" (7 January 1846). Still, Schumann retained serious reservations about Wagner. "He is . . . not a good musician," Schumann concluded, "he lacks a sense of form and euphony" (8 May 1853).

In the absence of a core of professional musicians with whom Schumann could associate, he found himself spending more time with dilettantes. There were a number of passionate music lovers in Dresden, many of them artists associated with the Academy. A devoted circle, including Eduard Bendemann, Ernst Rietschel, Rudolf Hübner, and Ludwig Richter (Carus was also a member of the group), met frequently. Social evenings often occurred in the Bendemann home, and performances of chamber music were a standard feature.

During the years in Dresden, Schumann's life gradually took on a daily routine: work in the mornings, ideally a walk after lunch (his preferred form of recreation, often taken with Clara), work resumed in the afternoon until six, then to a favorite restaurant to read the paper and have a glass of beer, returning at eight to dine (Clara's practice time was from six until eight). Such routine—which all his life Schumann seemed partial to—no doubt helped to stabilize his life in Dresden, and had a beneficial effect on him. Nonetheless, there were recurrences of nervous depression and disturbing physical complications. In February 1846, he began orchestrating the Second Symphony (premiered in Leipzig nine months later). In March he noted singing and noises in his ears, and in the household books described himself as *"very ill."*[14] The condition persisted until the autumn.

Dissatisfaction with their status and life in Dresden remained con-

---

[13] 17 March 1846 in *Tgb II*, p. 398.
[14] 5 March 1846 in *HSHLT*, p. 415.

stant, and led to thoughts of moving elsewhere. Despite Schumann's unpleasant experience eight years earlier, it was decided to give a series of concerts in Vienna, with the possibility of settling there. They left on 23 November, taking Marie and Elise with them. The Schumanns gave four concerts in Vienna: 10 December, 15 December (at which the Quintet and the Andante op. 46 were performed), 1 January (Schumann conducted the First Symphony op. 38 and the Piano Concerto op. 54), and 10 January. Attendance at the concerts was poor. What salvaged the trip for them was the presence in Vienna of the singer Jenny Lind, then at the height of her fame. She graciously offered to appear with Clara at her final concert, and as a result the concert was sold out.

They returned to Dresden on 4 February, but stayed less than a week. A performance of Schumann's *Paradise and the Peri* was scheduled later in the month in Berlin, and it was decided to combine that performance (which Schumann would conduct) with several recitals by Clara. They left on the 10th. The presentation of the *Peri* by the prestigious Singakademie was to occur on the 20th, but Schumann found the rehearsal time to be inadequate and the singers testy. Two soloists—the tenor and soprano—suddenly withdrew shortly before the concert (Schumann described their conduct as "perfidious," 20 February 1847) and replacements for them had to be found hurriedly. The work was performed, without the benefit of a full rehearsal, to only moderate acclaim. Clara's recitals on 1 and 17 March were better received. Still, despite their less than spectacular success, dissatisfaction with Dresden now led them to contemplate the possibility of moving to Berlin, where, they felt, there at least existed a more active musical life.

During 1847, Schumann remained busy as a composer, most notably completing two piano trios (of contrasting character, in D minor op. 63 and F major op. 80). But much of his effort was devoted to opera. Since settling in Dresden, he had been searching diligently for a suitable text. On 1 April he read Friedrich Hebbel's drama *Genoveva*, and was immediately taken with it. Converting it to a libretto occupied him for much of the remainder of the year, the music being created during the first eight months of 1848.

Schumann's slow progress with *Genoveva* was interrupted by tragedy. On 22 June 1847 Emil—at that time the Schumanns' only son—died.

Sixteen months old, he had not been well for weeks and his death was not unexpected. At an earlier time, it probably would have plunged Schumann into despair, but he had recovered sufficiently from his depression to respond with fortitude and resignation—in the nineteenth century it was not uncommon for parents to have to deal with the grief of losing an infant. Plans had been under way in Zwickau for a small music festival devoted to Schumann's most recent compositions. Because of Emil's death, it was postponed until mid-July. The intention of the festival was to pay homage to Zwickau's successful, native son, and for two days (10 and 11 July) his music was performed, including the Second Symphony and the Piano Concerto. Schumann was welcomed by Kuntsch, and there was a torchlight procession and serenade in his honor.

Yet the autumn brought additional discouragement. In September, Schumann learned that Ferdinand Hiller would soon be leaving Dresden in order to assume the position of music director in Düsseldorf. The loss of frequent contact with Hiller was truly unfortunate. But of even greater effect on Schumann was the death of Mendelssohn on 4 November. Schumann was devastated. Mendelssohn died as the result of a series of strokes, and according to Dr. Helbig, Schumann now feared he would die in a similar manner. During the previous year, the relationship between Mendelssohn and Schumann had (on Mendelssohn's part) become somewhat strained. He had been convinced that Schumann had "stirred up a very ugly story about me."[15] The nature of the "story" is not known, but Mendelssohn's accusation makes little sense. Pettiness and malice were far removed from Schumann's character. Mendelssohn was by nature extremely sensitive and quick to take offense. More than likely, the basis for his anger was a misunderstanding.

After Mendelssohn's death, Schumann organized his personal recollections of him. They were probably intended to serve as the basis for an extensive tribute, similar in nature to the eulogy Schumann had written for Ludwig Schuncke in 1834. But the essay was never written. Notes for it have survived, and they continue to show the high regard in which Schumann held Mendelssohn. In December, Schumann wrote

---

[15] Letter to Karl Klingemann of 31 January 1847 quoted in Frederick Niecks, *Robert Schumann* (London, 1925), p. 153.

to Breitkopf & Härtel, publishers of the string quartets op. 41. Because the quartets were dedicated to Mendelssohn, the work had taken on particular significance to Schumann, and he wrote expressing the wish that the full score (and not just the parts) would finally appear in print. As time passed, his reverence for Mendelssohn did not diminish. In 1850, he made a point of visiting Mendelssohn's grave in Berlin.

Perhaps the most damaging aspect of Schumann's stay in Dresden was the infrequent opportunity for social interaction, particularly involving music. Ironically, Hiller's departure for Düsseldorf provided Schumann with the occasion to become more actively engaged in the musical life of the city. Since 1845, Hiller had been director of an amateur men's choral group, the Liedertafel (Wagner had been Hiller's predecessor). Schumann now took over the group. Choral societies—for men, women, and mixed—flourished in Biedermeier Germany. Male choral groups were particularly popular, and Dresden, with nearly a half dozen, was a center of their activity. Schumann had had some experience conducting choral ensembles (most notably, as part of *Peri*) and in 1846, inspired by a choral group that Mendelssohn had founded in Leipzig, he had composed several choral works, including the Five Songs by Robert Burns op. 55. On 20 November, he assumed direction of the Liedertafel, and within a short period of time had created several pieces for it, including the three songs of op. 62 and the *Ritornelle* op. 65.

Schumann's association with the group was beneficial. It provided him with an opportunity to refine and develop his skills as a conductor but, more important, could serve as a center of activity replacing his work for the *Zeitschrift*. Schumann recognized the significance of the work to his well-being, and wrote to Hiller that it had "restored in me the conviction of my ability to direct, which, in my nervous hypochondria, I thought was completely gone" (10 April 1849). As a result of his relationship with the group, he decided to create a larger, mixed choral ensemble, later named the Verein für Chorgesang (Choral Society). The idea came to him only nine days after the first rehearsal of the men's chorus, and he moved quickly to form the group, its meetings beginning early in January. At its largest, there were thirty to forty sopranos, twenty altos, fifteen tenors, and thirty basses. Schumann clearly enjoyed his work with the Chorverein, and decided to concentrate on it; in October 1848, he gave up his association with the men's chorus. "I found too little true musical aspiration," he wrote to Hiller of the Liedertafel, "and did not feel suited to it, although they were fine people" (10 April 1849).

Schumann took his duties seriously, at times seeming to forget that he was dealing with amateurs who preferred their musical experience to be both amusing and entertaining. There were challenging goals for the group, Schumann selecting for study only works he felt to be of particular merit. Taking advantage of the opportunity available to him, over the next several years he composed a number of choral compositions, most notably the romances and ballads opp. 67 and 75 (comprising ten pieces), and the romances for female voices opp. 69 and 91 (twelve pieces). Although disturbed at times by the irregular attendance of members in the group (particularly the men), in all Schumann found his connection stimulating. But he still remained disheartened by the musical life in Dresden. "Here unfortunately there is no prospect for the performance of new works," he wrote to Hiller, "You know the situation well. The laziness is greater than ever" (10 April 1849).

About a month after the successful first concert of the Chorverein on 30 March, Liszt was a guest at the Schumann house. For the occasion, Schumann arranged a performance of the Piano Quintet. It was a hurried visit by Liszt, and he seems to have behaved in his most cavalier manner. He arrived several hours late, described the quintet as "leipziger-isch," and criticized Mendelssohn by comparison with Meyerbeer. By "leipziger-isch," Liszt was referring to those composers (most notably, Mendelssohn and Schumann) whom Liszt now saw as being conservative and academic—in contrast to his own music and that of Wagner. Liszt's comments were tactless. He knew of Schumann's reverence for Mendelssohn, and he knew as well of Schumann's aversion to Meyerbeer's music. Not surprisingly, Schumann took Liszt's remarks as a personal affront and, according to Clara, grabbed Liszt by the shoulders saying, "Who are you to speak in such a manner about Mendelssohn!" He then abruptly left the room.[16]

---

[16] This is the version of the incident given by Clara Schumann to Jansen in 1879. The entry in the diary (made by Clara) makes no reference to Schumann grabbing Liszt, and summarizes additional statements made by Schumann when speaking angrily to Liszt, statements that

Liszt took the incident well, realizing that his behavior had been rude and intolerant. But the breach that had been created was never fully closed. Privately, Schumann became critical of Liszt's music ("pepper and seasoning à la Liszt"; 30 June 1848), and in the spring of 1849, when Liszt wrote to Schumann requesting the score of his recently completed *Faust* music hoping to perform it at Weimar, Schumann's response showed that he was still hurt by Liszt's comments. Perhaps, he wrote, Liszt would find the music *"too Leipziger-isch."* But, he continued, "Seriously—from you, who know so many of my compositions—I had expected something more than such a broad pronouncement on an entire artistic life. If you look at my compositions more closely, you would surely find diversity, for I have always endeavored to bring something new to light in each of my compositions, and not only concerning form. And truly those of us who were together in Leipzig—Mendelssohn, Hiller, Bennett, and others—did not do so badly—we could hold our own against those in Paris, Vienna, and Berlin. . . . So much for your remarks, which were unfair and insulting. For the rest, let us forget the evening—words are not arrows—and the main thing is to strive ever onwards" (31 May 1849).

Financial worries continued to be a concern for Schumann during these years. On 19 June 1848, he wrote to his brother, Carl, requesting a loan, giving as a reason that as a result of his continued work on *Genoveva* he had been able to earn little. It must have been particularly difficult for Schumann, since Carl himself was frequently short of funds. Much in his life seemed only to remind Schumann of the stability and financial independence that continued to elude him. The success of *Genoveva*, he hoped, would change that. The opera was completed in August. He then began work on two compositions, vastly different in character. From his youth he had been a great admirer of Byron, particularly Byron's somber drama *Manfred*. In August, he read it to Clara and began sketching incidental music for it. Then, in striking contrast, he began work at the end of the month on a collection of simple, piano pieces for children, later published as the *Album for the Young (Album für die Jugend)* op. 68. They had been conceived with Marie in mind, and

---

were supportive of Mendelssohn's work (see *Litzmann II*, pp. 121–22). In the household books, Schumann tersely referred to his "rage" (p. 462).

in two weeks he completed more than three dozen short pieces. He had great expectations for them, knowing that there was an unquestioned need for well-written and entertaining piano pieces for children, those currently available generally being dull and simplistic. He enthusiastically sent the set to Breitkopf & Härtel for publication.

Over the years, Schumann had frequently expressed concern with the visual presentation of his published compositions. This became particularly important for him with the *Album*. Among his friends in Dresden was the artist Ludwig Richter. Richter, in addition to being a painter, was known as an illustrator for books, particularly children's books. On 25 October, Schumann met with Richter in an attempt to interest him in providing a title-page vignette for the *Album*. Richter's charming illustration (based on the titles of a number of the individual pieces from the *Album*) formed an admirable complement to the music, and helped increase sales of the work.

Schumann's efforts on behalf of the *Album* had been given some urgency by Breitkopf & Härtel's response. They had declined to publish the work. Raymond Härtel wrote to Schumann explaining why: "The fact is that sale of your compositions has in general shrunk considerably, more so than you can believe. Sometime we must frankly discuss the matter. Eleven years have now passed since we published your first work, and since that date we have published 16 others. . . . With considerable regret I share with you the results of this venture: the firm has lost a significant amount in the publication of your works and as yet there is no prospect of compensation."[17]

Over the years, Breitkopf & Härtel had published some of Schumann's finest music, including *Carnaval*, the Fantasie, the First Symphony, the string quartets, and *Paradise and the Peri*. It would not have been unexpected for Schumann to have reacted to Härtel's letter with dejection and dismay. That was not the case. In the household books, he curtly referred to Härtel's "stupid letter."[18] And he convinced Julius Schuberth in Hamburg to undertake the publication of the *Album*.

---

[17] Letter of 30 September 1848 quoted in Wolfgang Boetticher, "Robert Schumann und seine Verleger," in *Musik und Verlag. Karl Vötterle zum 65. Geburtstag*, ed. R. Baum and W. Rehm (Kassel, 1968), p. 172.

[18] 2 October 1848 in *HSHLT*, p. 472.

Rather than being discouraged, in the succeeding year Schumann composed more music than he ever had before, leading to what he referred to as "my most fruitful year" (10 April 1849). Fruitful it was, but in many ways it may have been a forced harvest.

During 1849, Schumann produced forty works, many falling into the category of Hausmusik, that is, unpretentious, utilitarian works intended for home consumption. It was a way both to earn more money, and to bring his name before the public. Works such as the *Fantasiestücke* op. 73 (for clarinet, or violin, or cello with piano accompaniment), the *Adagio and Allegro* op. 70 (for horn, or cello, or violin, with piano accompaniment), and the *Spanisches Liederspiel* op. 74 (for one, two, and four voices with piano accompaniment) all fall into that category. That is not to say that compositions of this type were in some way "inferior" in quality to Schumann's more "artistic" works. They invariably succeed in their intentions, but were simply intended for a different audience than the string quartets or symphonies. Income was often a major motivation for their creation.

The *Album for the Young* appeared in January 1849. Within months, it became immensely popular. His payment for it (226 talers) nearly equaled that which he had been paid for the *Peri*. In April, Schumann composed as a companion to it twenty-nine songs for children, the *Song Album for the Young* (*Lieder-Album für die Jugend* op. 79), now published without any reluctance by Breitkopf & Härtel. He received a bountiful payment for it as well, 220 talers. That year he earned 1,275 talers for his compositions, more than four times the amount he had earned in 1848. It was by far the most he had ever received, the previous highest amount having been 575 talers in 1844. In each succeeding year of his creative life he would exceed, sometimes substantially, the record amount he had earned in 1849.[19] For once, Schumann began to express satisfaction with his position: "I am completely content with the recognition which has come my way in ever greater measure" (18 September 1849); "I have never been busier or happier with my work" (29 November 1849).

Now that *Genoveva* was completed, it was necessary to locate an opera house willing to stage it. As it turned out, finding a suitable

---

[19] 1850: 1,584 talers; 1851: 1,439 talers; 1852: 1,717 talers; 1853: 1,925 talers (*Ibid.*, p. 669).

location did not prove particularly difficult. It was decided that Schumann's new opera would be performed in Leipzig, but no firm date was decided upon. He was delighted, but in his inexperience did not realize that complications would invariably arise, in this instance delaying the premiere for over a year. The good news concerning *Genoveva*, however, was tempered by news received early in April. Schumann's brother Carl died on the 9th. Schumann took the loss well but was probably also sobered by the thought that he was now the only surviving member of his family.

1848 and 1849 were years of political turmoil and revolution in Europe, as attempts were made to remove the oppressive and often reactionary governments that had been in place since the fall of Napoleon in 1815. In Saxony, the king guaranteed reform (including removal of censorship and abolition of feudal rights), but then returned to a more conservative stance. Discontent and unrest led to open revolt in Dresden on 3 May 1849. Streets were torn up and barricades erected. On the 4th, the king fled the city, and a provisional government was installed. Prussian and Saxon troops began to close in on the city to restore the monarchy. In response, a civic guard was created. When, on the 5th, the civic guard was presented with a demand of unconditional surrender, they hurriedly attempted to bolster their force, rounding up all able-bodied men. Patrols were sent to assemble "recruits," but when they arrived at the Schumann residence, he was in hiding. After the patrol left, Schumann, Clara, and Marie hurriedly fled out the back door, and found shelter in the suburbs. The remaining Schumann children were left with servants.

The attack on the city began on the 6th and lasted for three days. It was a one-sided struggle, and on the 9th those active in the revolt (including Richard Wagner) fled the city as best they could. Official totals listed nearly two hundred dead, thirty-one of whom were soldiers, but fatalities were probably much higher among civilians. It was not until the 7th, at three in the morning and seven months pregnant, that Clara, accompanied by a female friend, had been able to return to their home to get the rest of the children (it was still feared that if Schumann accompanied them, he would be drafted into the revolutionary forces). On the 11th, the family settled in Kreischa, on the outskirts of Dresden, and remained there in comparative safety for about a month.

Despite his flight, Schumann sympathized with the revolt, particularly after viewing firsthand the gory aftermath of the attack. There had been indiscriminate killing, and considerable damage to the city. Schumann quickly wrote a series of four marches for piano, patriotic in nature and stirring in their fervor. They were hurriedly published as his op. 76. "The revolutionary spirit of this year," he wrote to Julius Rietz, "has done me good. I have never been so industrious."[20]

Schumann continued to remain interested in locating a suitable musical position. With Wagner in exile, his post was now vacant, and Schumann expressed interest in it, speaking with Carus to ask him to use his influence with the king. Then, in November 1849, Schumann received a letter from Ferdinand Hiller, asking him if he would be interested in Hiller's position as music director in Düsseldorf. Hiller intended to give up the post in 1850 in order to accept one in Cologne, and, if Schumann wanted it, Hiller would recommend him as his successor.

Schumann was surprisingly cool in his reaction. To leave Dresden and find employment in Düsseldorf would have been welcome several years earlier. But perhaps now that his music was enjoying more popularity, he felt he could be more selective. Schumann had heard criticism of Düsseldorf from Mendelssohn and Rietz, both of whom had served as music directors there prior to Hiller. In his usual mixture of frankness and naivete, Schumann confessed to Hiller: "When you went from here to Düsseldorf, [Rietz said] 'that he could not understand why you took the position.' I did not tell you at the time in order not to upset you" (19 November 1849). In his response to Hiller, Schumann raised a number of points, including the cost of living, salary, and the need for suitable musical activities for Clara as well. He was obviously far from enthusiastic. "Could the contract be worded," he wrote, "so that if I were offered another position I could renounce it?"

On 10 December, Schumann received what he described as an official letter from Düsseldorf, presumably one inquiring whether he was interested in the position. A week earlier, Schumann had written again to Hiller with additional questions, including one that was quite odd.

---

[20] Letter of 6 July 1849 in Hermann Erler, *Robert Schumann's Leben Aus seinen Briefen geschildert*. 2 vols. (Berlin, 1887), II, p. 93.

234 • SCHUMANN

He had noted in an old atlas that there was an insane asylum in Düsseldorf, and was bothered by it; he hoped the atlas was in error. In a similar manner, during the revolt in Dresden (while living in the suburbs) Schumann had been disturbed by the proximity of the insane asylum at Sonnenstein, which he could see out of the window in his room. "I am obliged," Schumann wrote to Hiller, "to avoid carefully all melancholy impressions of the kind. And if we musicians live so often, as you know we do, on sunny heights, the sadness of reality cuts all the deeper when it lies naked before our eyes."[21] One can sympathize with Schumann's view. In appearance and often in management the insane asylums of the nineteenth century resembled prisons—hardly conducive to pleasant thought. Yet, Schumann's reaction in 1849 is quite different from that of twenty years earlier when, during his Rhine journey, he had found lodgings in Frankfurt near a church and a madhouse. "I am uncertain," he had joked to his mother, "whether to become a Catholic or a madman."[22]

Schumann delayed a decision on Düsseldorf until the spring of 1850, still wishing in the meantime for something else—hopefully, the position in Dresden. Much of his attention was now focused on the performance in Leipzig of *Genoveva*. But the premiere continued to be delayed by what appeared to be intrigues. The situation became so serious that early in 1850 Schumann wrote to Härtel, asking if in his opinion legal action might be necessary. When the opera was finally scheduled for performance in February, Schumann traveled to Leipzig to be present for the rehearsals. Once again, however, the premiere was postponed, and, adding insult to injury, Meyerbeer's *Le prophète* was put on in its stead.

Since the Schumanns had planned to be away from Dresden for six weeks for the rehearsals and performances of *Genoveva*, they decided to make use of the remaining time by undertaking a concert tour to Bremen and Hamburg, where they had been invited earlier in the year. It was a successful trip; both the *Genoveva* overture and the Piano Concerto were performed, and they were delighted once again to spend time with Jenny Lind (who kindly performed at two of their concerts,

[21] Letter to Hiller of 3 December 1849 in *Br*, p. 323. Translation in Niecks, p. 253.
[22] Letter of 24 May 1829 in *JS*, p. 147.

assuring a sizable profit for the trip). On 29 March, they returned to Dresden. Two days later, Schumann wrote to Düsseldorf formally accepting the position. Despite the efforts of Carus and others (including a testimonial on his behalf signed by eighty members of the Choral Society), Schumann had not been offered the conducting position in Dresden.

The premiere of *Genoveva* had been rescheduled for June, late in the season and hardly an advantageous time for Schumann's work to be heard. There were three performances; the first on 25 June, was conducted by Schumann before a distinguished audience that included Liszt, Hiller, and Kuntsch. But *Genoveva* was not the success that Schumann had hoped for. Probably at fault was its distinctive style, not tuneful and simplistic enough for the majority, not "progressive" enough for the Wagnerians.

Schumann returned to Dresden on 10 July, in a rather somber frame of mind. He went to work setting to music six poems of Nikolaus Lenau. While engaged in the project, he learned of Lenau's death, and he decided to create the work as a tribute to him, publishing it with a funereal cover. Much work remained, too, for the move to Düsseldorf. Schumann was scheduled to assume duties there at the beginning of September, and there was packing to be completed, and farewells to be made to their few close friends. They left on 30 August, and arrived in Düsseldorf three days later, stopping briefly in Leipzig on the way.

"You will never be the wife of a Kapellmeister," Schumann had written to Clara prior to their marriage, "but in spirit we are a match for any of them. You know what I mean."[23] At that time, to Schumann the position of Kapellmeister had resembled that of crowned, musical mediocrity. Now, ten years later, he was about to undertake in Düsseldorf duties very much like those of a Kapellmeister. Until the end, he had remained hesitant about accepting the post. The impression given to Hiller was that his hesitancy was the result of the less than ideal musical climate in Düsseldorf. But, privately, Schumann may also have feared that he lacked the experience, temperament, and expertise to succeed in the position.

---

[23] Letter of 31 May 1840 in *JgBr*, p. 315.

CHAPTER 12

Schumann's Dramatic Works

> *For centuries it was as if music and literature were divided by a wall.... When they came into contact, they resembled Pyramus and Thisbe, peering at and touching one another in secret through the cracks and crevices of the stones piled up between them. Schumann was at home in both lands...*
> —Franz Liszt, "Robert Schumann" (1855)

SCHUMANN'S INTEREST IN AND LOVE OF LITERATURE SEEMED naturally to lead to thoughts of opera. For much of his adult life, he was involved with one. Not long after beginning study with Wieck in 1830, he considered the possibility of *Hamlet* as an opera, but got no farther than creating sketches for an overture. The next year found him reading E. T. A. Hoffmann, and he was enthusiastic about the operatic possibilities of two tales—"The Mines at Falun" and "Doge and Dogaressa." But, for the remainder of the decade, as Schumann focused first on his career as a piano virtuoso and then as a composer of music for piano, little attention was devoted to opera. Then, in February 1840—at a time when he had turned away from the piano and was beginning to write songs—once again opera began to interest him. He returned to the subject of Hoffmann's "Doge and Dogaressa." To Clara, he described Hoffmann's story as "noble and natural," and, with the aid of the writer Julius Becker, for the next few months he worked on producing a libretto in verse.¹ The music for it, however, was not written.

Hoffmann's tale was the first of a large number of concepts Schumann would consider for opera. It was the only significant musical genre he had not attempted, and in his eyes, both the ultimate manner in which firmly to establish his reputation as a composer and at the same time to build on the reputation he had created with *Paradise and the Peri*. In his quest, Schumann considered a truly astonishing array of possibilities. From Hoffmann, he moved to Calderón, a dramatist enjoying renewed interest at the time. In July 1841, he was enthusiastic about the prospect of several of Calderón's plays, and produced a brief scenario for "The Bridge of Mantible." During the next six years he considered, among others, the Nibelung myths (1842–47), Thomas Moore's "The Veiled Prophet" (1843; from *Lalla Rookh*), the legend of King Arthur (1845), Christopher Columbus and Shakespeare's *The Tempest* (1846), and Mazeppa (1847—he was familiar with the versions of Byron and Julius Slowacki). Scenarios have survived for "The Veiled Prophet" and "Mazeppa," but no music was composed.

Although the ideas considered by Schumann vary greatly, there seem to have been distinct characteristics that attracted his attention: elements of mystery and the fantastic, and the heroic (often with a conspicuously moral message). In both of the tales by Hoffmann that interested him, there are strong elements of the supernatural. "The Mines of Falun" relates the obsession and resulting madness of the miner Elis Fröbom. In its emphasis on fantasy and in its somber, inexorable representation of Fröbom's doom, it recalls in mood *Hans Heiling* (1833), a popular opera by Heinrich Marschner. But in a purely practical manner, it would have been nearly impossible to represent the visionary side of the "Mines of Falun"—an essential aspect of the story—on the stage. "Doge and Dogaressa" contains as a central character a witch who can cure illness and predict the future. But the story itself is primarily a tale of love. While it is not difficult to detect in the two lovers' characters the "noble" elements mentioned by Schumann, it is more of a challenge to discover the "natural" aspects that attracted him to the tale. Reunited after years of separation, the lovers ultimately perish in rapture during

¹ Letter to Clara of 13 March 1840 in *JgBr*, p. 310.

a storm at sea—a conclusion Schumann felt obliged to alter in his scenario by providing a happier ending.

Of the many operatic possibilities contemplated by Schumann during these years, music was created for only one: *The Corsair*. Byron's poem served as the basis for Schumann's libretto. There is little plot; rather, the focus is on the personality of a typical Byronic hero: the pirate Conrad. The sketchy dramatic outline—Conrad is captured by the Pacha Seyd, and rescued by a Leonore-like heroine—would have required much filling-in by Schumann. He worked on the project in June and July 1844 (approaching the dramatist Oswald Marbach for assistance), but there exist only twenty pages of score, comprising a chorus and the beginning of an aria. While working on "Doge and Dogaressa" Schumann had noted to Clara the difficulties he was having with it, and complained of the absence of "a deep, German element" in the story.[2] That may have been a reason for his abandonment of *The Corsair*. The exotic locales of each story—Venice and the Middle East, respectively—contributed not a little to their popularity among readers, but Schumann seemed more interested in creating an opera nationalistic in basis. "Do you know my daily prayer as an artist?" he confided to Carl Kossmaly. "It is *German opera*" (1 September 1842).

Schumann's idea was not a novel one. There was at the time in Germany a deliberate effort being made to establish in the arts a truly distinctive artistic style, one that could be identified as uniquely German. The initial summons for the movement had been made at the turn of the century by the writer Heinrich Wackenroder who, using the work of Albrecht Dürer as an example, called on German artists to resist foreign influences and to turn inward for motivation. To many, the writings of Wackenroder proved inspiring, but while in literature and the visual arts the idea of a German Art took hold and expanded, in opera, foreign products seemed to rule the stage. What undoubtedly provided impetus to Schumann's desire was the overwhelming popularity in Germany of Italian opera and the operas of Meyerbeer, both of which he strongly disliked.

There had been some effort made to advance German opera. Among German composers then living, Spohr had been the most successful.

---

[2] Letter of 4 May 1840 in *Ibid.*, p. 312.

But his two most popular works—*Faust* and *Jessonda*—were more than twenty years old and hardly in the musical style admired by Schumann. Most other composers of German opera relied heavily on foreign models (especially opéra-comique). During the 1840s, Wagner's reputation was growing, but Schumann did not hold him in high regard. In 1843, he briefly studied the score of *The Flying Dutchman*, and two years later attended a performance of *Rienzi*, but without pleasure. Of contemporary German composers of opera, Schumann most admired Marschner, particularly his *Templar und die Jüden* (1829). But Marschner's *Templar* had as its basis not a German story but Scott's *Ivanhoe*. Since the untimely death of Weber in 1826, in Schumann's eyes the field had lain comparatively free. "Compose truly original, simple, deep, German operas," Schumann wrote in the *Neue Zeitschrift für Musik* in 1842, advice intended as much for himself as for other composers.[3]

It was Schumann's determination to create not just opera but German opera that probably led him to serious consideration of other texts. At the time of working on *The Corsair*, he was also involved in an adaptation of Immermann's *Till Eulenspiegel*. Two years later, Immermann's *Tristan* spurred further effort. But both projects resulted in scenarios only. Given Schumann's inclination, it seemed inevitable for him to turn his attention to Goethe. *Wilhelm Meister* and *Hermann and Dorothea* attracted his notice in 1844 and 1845–47, respectively (at one point Schumann noted that he was reading *Meister* for the third time). But it was *Faust* that held the greatest promise to him.

"I would now like soon to get to work on an opera," Schumann noted on 23 January 1844. Two days later he left with Clara on their concert tour of Russia. During the journey he read *Faust, Part II*, and began to think of possible musical settings. While in Dorpat, he began musical sketches for it. It is quite possible that initially Schumann thought of *Faust (Parts I and II)* in operatic terms. But it seems that he soon determined that the expansiveness of the subject was unsuitable for opera. In addition, his admiration for Goethe's text was so great that there was no possibility in his mind of patching together a libretto from it. Instead, he began work that summer on setting to music excerpts from *Faust*, creating an oratorio of sorts. It was the beginning of a

---

[3] Review of Reissiger's *Adele de Foix* in *GS II*, p. 94.

project that would occupy him intermittently for nearly a decade. Eventually, he divided his settings into three sections, preceded by an overture.

In June and July—while still working on *Till* and *The Corsair*—Schumann composed more of *Faust*. His breakdown and continued ill health that autumn precluded concentrated effort, but at the end of December he noted completion of the project. What was actually finished was a large part of what was to be the third section, "Faust's Transfiguration." Of the seven numbers comprising it, five had been composed. The concluding piece (the "Chorus Mysticus" in two different settings) was composed from May to July 1847, and the fourth (the chorus "Gerettet ist das edle Glied" ["Saved is the noble part"]) was completed in May and June of the following year. In July and August 1849, Schumann returned to his work on *Faust* creating all of the first section (the "Garden Scene," "Gretchen before the Image of the Mater Dolorosa," and the "Scene in the Cathedral"), as well as the first scene of the second section ("Ariel: Sunrise"). The remaining two scenes of the second section ("Midnight" and "Faust's Death") were created in April and May 1850. The last part of the work to be composed was the overture (August 1853).

Schumann's *Scenes from Goethe's Faust* is not an opera: there is no recognizable dramatic flow, and a staging of the work would make little sense. But neither is it an oratorio in the conventional manner. What Schumann produced were musical settings of excerpts from *Faust*, settings that assume the listener's familiarity with Goethe's two *Faust* dramas. The bulk of Schumann's selections were from *Faust, Part II* (only the first section uses material from *Faust, Part I*). That in itself was a curious approach. The first part of Goethe's *Faust* is better known, relating in general terms Faust's pact with the devil and love for Gretchen. The second part is far more unconventional with little distinct plot, presenting instead an often deeply symbolic and mystical representation of Faust's death and redemption. *Faust, Part II* was by no means broadly admired in Schumann's time, and, like Beethoven's late string quartets, there were many who found it to be disappointing and incomprehensible.

Schumann's selections from *Faust* make clear both his intentions for the work and his deeply personal understanding of the drama. He refrained from setting in both parts songs or ballads, and avoided all scenes that seemed naturally to call for musical accompaniment—such as, in *Part I*, the invocation of spirits. Schumann seemed determined to make clear that he was not attempting to compose incidental music for the play. From *Part I* he selected an episode depicting the avowal of love between Faust and Gretchen (the "Garden Scene"), and two representations of Gretchen's remorse and guilt over her affair with Faust. As a transition to his other settings, he began his second section with the opening scene of *Part II*, presenting a renewed and refreshed Faust. He then skipped to the conclusion of Goethe's drama: the fifth, sixth, and seventh scenes (with numerous cuts). The fifth scene recounts Faust's demise. The final two scenes are more spiritual and serene, representing the preservation of Faust's soul. Schumann's selections emphasize neither the dramatic intensity nor melodrama in Goethe's play, but are psychological in basis and focus on the inner natures of Faust and Gretchen, culminating in their redemption.

Schumann's admiration for Goethe was extraordinary. He owned the forty-volume edition of Goethe's works issued from 1827 to 1830, as well as the twenty-volume set of the *Nachgelassenen Werke* (1832–33, 1842). "Above all, he is a poet," Schumann wrote to Clara—a simple statement, but perhaps the highest compliment he could have made (11 February 1838). Yet the esteem that Schumann felt for Goethe led to some trepidation. "I often feared the reproach: 'Why music for such perfect poetry?'," he confessed to Brendel ([5] July 1848). His apprehension continued even after most of the music for the project had been completed. Prior to creating the overture, he remained hesitant, and told Wasielewski of the "gigantic elements" that would need to be part of it.[4]

The first complete performance of Schumann's *Faust* was presented in 1862 in Cologne under the direction of Ferdinand Hiller, six years after Schumann's death. But performances of the third section were given in August 1849 in Dresden, Leipzig, and Weimar as part of the centenary of Goethe's birth, and were well received. That they were is somewhat surprising, for Schumann's work made no concessions to public taste. The music is not particularly tuneful, but then the public

---

[4] *W*, p. 440.

may not have expected such an approach with the at times austere drama created by Goethe. Much of the work uses the declamatory melodic style employed in *Paradise and the Peri*. There are no arias for Faust or Gretchen in the grand manner.

Schumann's *Faust* is a Faust for connoisseurs. There are subtle touches generally focusing on psychological representation, such as the disjunct, pulsating violas used to represent the gnawing remorse and pain experienced by Gretchen in the Mater Dolorosa scene. An eerie solo trumpet with rhythmic contrast in the woodwinds complements the grotesque appearance of the lemurs (it was Schumann's preference that the part be sung by boys), culminating in Faust's death. Instances such as these should help to put to rest perceptions of Schumann's supposedly awkward handling of the orchestra. Because of the lack of contrast—particularly in the third section, where there is a reliance on the chorus—Schumann's work requires an unusual amount of concentration from the listener. Had he selected passages from Goethe's text less abstruse and more popular in style, greater variety would have been possible. But it is clear that Schumann's intention was to create a work in which the music attempts to accompany and, ultimately, elucidate the most spiritual elements of Goethe's text.

The long-drawn-out work on *Faust* took its toll. "I thought I would never be finished," he told Carl Reinecke after finishing what would become the third section (30 June 1848). Yet, while engaged on *Faust*, the desire to create an opera was ever present, and Schumann still continued to consider possible librettos. The very summer when he first started work on *Faust* was the time of his most intense activity with *The Corsair*.

It was Schumann's policy when attempting to create a libretto to seek the assistance of a collaborator. He was eager to gain the expertise of writers who had experience, if not in writing opera libretti, then in creating works for the stage. The writer most often associated with Schumann's opera projects was Robert Reinick. Reinick, who was five years older than Schumann, was both a writer and an artist. In 1840, Schumann had set six of his poems to music, published in 1842 as *Aus dem Liederbuch eines Malers* (From A Painter's Songbook) op. 36. Reinick had collaborated recently with Ferdinand Hiller on his opera *Conradin*.

By the spring of 1847, it appears that an opera based on Mazeppa was foremost in Schumann's mind. But there had also been discussions with Reinick about the possibility of creating an opera with the legend of Genoveva as its basis. Genoveva, the wife of Count Palatine Siegfried of Brabant, lived during the eighth century. Falsely accused of marital infidelity by a trusted friend of the count (whose advances she had rebuffed), she was sentenced to death. But those chosen to take her life spared her, and left her deep in the forests of the Ardennes. She lived there for six years, forgotten. During this time she gave birth to Siegfried's son, the child being nourished by the milk of a doe that she had befriended. Siegfried eventually learns of his wife's innocence. All concludes happily when during a hunt he accidentally comes upon her and his son, and restores them both to their rightful positions.

The Genoveva legend was well known in nineteenth century Germany. There was a fascination at the time with the Middle Ages in general, and the combination of pious simplicity and the miraculous contained in the tale seemed to many to make it an ideal and charming representation of the age. The most famous nineteenth-century setting of the legend was the drama by Ludwig Tieck, *Leben und Tod der heiligen Genoveva* (1800; an unsuccessful ballet with Tieck as its source had been produced with music by Louis Huth in 1838). Reinick produced two sketches for Schumann based on Tieck's work. He made no use of another interesting setting (although it might have proved useful): Maler Müller's *Golo und Genovefa* (1808). Then, on 1 April 1847, Schumann read Friedrich Hebbel's play *Genoveva*. It had been published four years earlier but had yet to be staged. The next day Schumann wrote to Reinick, bringing the work to his attention. Inspired by Hebbel's drama, within a week Schumann had sketched an overture and, after consultation with Reinick, had completed a draft scenario for an opera. After years of searching, he had come across a work that he felt was ideally suited for opera, and he lost no time in plunging into work on it.

Throughout April and May, the adaptation of the drama into a libretto continued. But disappointed by Reinick's contributions—Schumann later characterized him as "a good fellow, but terribly sentimental" ([beginning of July 1847])—Schumann soon decided that he would make better progress on his own. Although he continued sporadically to consult with Reinick, within a short period of time frustration set in and on 14 May he wrote directly to Hebbel, whom he did not know, asking if he would help arrange his drama for the musical stage. At that point Schumann had completed two acts, but felt that the libretto lacked "strength"; Hebbel was asked to provide assistance, but nothing extensive, "merely here and there" (14 May 1847). Schumann's confidence in Hebbel's ability was misguided, for he had no experience in creating operas. But he responded to Schumann's request with interest.

They met at Schumann's home on 27 July, their only meeting. Despite Schumann's high hopes, Hebbel was put off by what he perceived as Schumann's unpleasantly quiet and reserved nature. Progress on the libretto proceeded at a tedious pace. By November, Reinick's good nature had been exhausted. He informed Hiller that he had gone through the text twice, but it had been reworked so often that his own work was now unrecognizable. When completed, the libretto was almost entirely Schumann's; by his reckoning, only about two hundred lines of Reinick's work remained.

That Schumann was frustrated by the slow progress on the text is not surprising. The legend itself posed a significant obstacle. It is essentially in two parts. The first part tells of the accusation made against Genoveva, the basis for it, and her punishment. The second part represents the many years spent by her in the forest, her miraculous survival, the birth of her son, and fortuitous discovery by Siegfried. Both parts are lengthy and would need to be abridged for the stage. But, because of the passage of time, both are also independent of one another. Schumann needed to adapt each part in order to create a whole, one in which the dramatic flow appeared natural and unimpeded. But there was yet another complication: despite his clear preference for Hebbel's *Genoveva*, while creating the libretto Schumann used Tieck's version as well. This created an additional problem, for Schumann was attempting an amalgamation of what were in effect two strongly contrasting versions of the legend.

Tieck's drama is panoramic in scope. His intention was to create a pseudomedieval epic, and for that reason there is more emphasis on images and action, and less on character development. Much of the dialogue appears artificial and somewhat stilted. Hebbel's *Genoveva* was written, as the author frankly admitted, in opposition to Tieck's setting. It is far more of a psychological drama, his primary concern being not the re-creation of the Middle Ages, but to bring to life both the characters in the play and their motivations. The central figure of Hebbel's drama is not Genoveva, but Golo, the trusted confidante of Genoveva's husband, Siegfried. It is Golo's passion for her, and Genoveva's determined rejection of it, that leads Golo to plot her downfall. Golo has an identical role in Tieck's version, but is far less prominent.

The legend of Genoveva had served as inspiration for a number of paintings and engravings—perhaps most notably by Schumann's friend Ludwig Richter. While composing the music for *Genoveva*, Schumann placed in his workroom images of her, the better, so he believed, to create the proper mood for the work. A special sketchbook 188 pages in length was used, consisting for the most part of a piano/vocal arrangement, although there are instances of voice alone. Each of the four acts was finished in order during 1848, the dates of completion (fully orchestrated) being 23 January, 30 March, 13 June, and 21 July. Schumann then devoted his attention to securing a performance. Dresden was the nearest location, and known for its production of opera. But the most likely possibility remained Leipzig, where Schumann was more highly esteemed and where there were friends who could work on his behalf. There appears to have been little difficulty in having the work accepted for performance there, and he was hopeful of having it performed early in 1849.

The premiere was eventually scheduled for February 1850, but when Schumann arrived in Leipzig to attend rehearsals he learned that *Genoveva* had been postponed in favor of performances of Meyerbeer's *Le prophète*. The director of the theater told Schumann of the necessity at that time of staging a popular spectacle. Although an effort was made to appease Schumann with "better terms" (presumably, financial), he was angered, irritated, and no doubt insulted by the preference given to a composer whose works he disliked.[5] The premiere of *Genoveva* was rescheduled for June. Not only was Schumann exasperated by the delay, he was concerned about the choice of date. The regular musical season was over, and to many the performance of *Genoveva* must have seemed an appendix to it, certainly not a highlight of it. The premiere

---

[5] Letter of Clara to Emilie List of 6 May 1850 in Clara Schumann, *"Das Band der ewigen Liebe." Briefwechsel mit Emile und Elise List*, ed. Eugen Wendler (Stuttgart, 1996), p. 162.

occurred on the 25th (conducted by Schumann), with additional performances on the 28th and 30th (the final performance was conducted by Julius Rietz). Despite Schumann's high expectations, *Genoveva* was not warmly received. At best, it was a *succès d'estime*, a point that in time Schumann himself was obliged to acknowledge. Although the work was performed more than thirty times during the last quarter of the century, it never established itself as part of the repertory.

The reasons for the failure of *Genoveva* are complex. Traditionally, the blame has been placed on the libretto. But the problem lay more in the goals that Schumann had set for himself while creating the work. He thought of his *Genoveva* as not at all like the "old sentimental" versions (6 November 1849), best represented in Schumann's eyes by that of Tieck. Rather, it was strongly dramatic, with characters of flesh and blood. "To approach closely nature and truth: that was always my aim," Schumann wrote to Spohr on 27 August 1850. It was for that reason that Schumann had felt strongly attracted to Hebbel's version. This was not the "old sentimental" Genoveva, but one completely new, and one represented in modern garb—Hebbel's setting is not the Middle Ages, but a fictional and subjective one ("The Poetic Age").

Yet, despite the differences between the versions of Hebbel and Tieck, Schumann persisted in drawing upon both sources for his libretto. As a result, many of the characters in Schumann's text lack the vibrancy and spirit found in Hebbel. Siegfried awakens little understanding or sympathy; his actions seem hasty and confused. Golo no longer is the central figure intended by Hebbel. Rather, as in Tieck, it is Genoveva, and Schumann seemed determined to represent her nobility and virtue at the expense of whatever human frailty she may have possessed. She appears strong and determined, but stiff and one-dimensional. In addition, Schumann was unable to resolve successfully the dichotomy created by the two distinct episodes comprising the legend. The second portion of the legend—Genoveva's lengthy stay in the woods and birth of her child—has been largely eliminated. Instead, in a melodramatic touch, Siegfried soon learns of Genoveva's innocence and is led to her—resulting in precisely the sentimental effect that Schumann was anxious to avoid.

Given his admitted goals of depicting "nature and truth," perhaps the most disconcerting element in the libretto is the introduction of the supernatural. In order to convince Siegfried of his wife's infidelity, a witch in league with Golo produces a magic mirror that enables Siegfried to view Genoveva's supposed infidelity. Schumann's witch (Margaretha) appears in both Tieck's and Hebbel's versions, although in his adaptation Schumann has combined several characters into one by making her Golo's wetnurse (Golo is of unknown parentage) and ardent supporter. In what is intended to be a predominantly realistic drama of passion, virtue, and justice, her elaborate magical arts appear incongruous. Yet this fantastical element is undoubtedly one that had particular appeal to Schumann—a similar character appears in Hoffmann's "Doge and Dogaressa." Still, rather than faulting Schumann, the episode seems more a confirmation of the nineteenth century's love for such devices. In Tieck's drama, it seems more at home, but even Hebbel was unable to resist including it in his predominantly naturalistic setting.

Despite Schumann's mixture of elements from Tieck and Hebbel, his libretto remains one concerned with character development. The wickedness of Margaretha, the battle between good and evil within Golo, the nobility and sense of outrage of Genoveva—all are present in the text to a varying degree. What is often lacking is an effective counterpart in the music. That is not to say that drama within the music is lacking. Perhaps the most startling moment in the opera occurs during the sexual confrontation between Golo and Genoveva when, losing all control of himself, Golo ignores Genoveva's remonstrances and advances threateningly toward her. Genoveva hurls his illegitimate parentage at him—"Back, back, dishonorable bastard!"—a scene that has lost none of its ability to shock. Schumann set the text with stark orchestral accompaniment. With great effect, Golo's response to Genoveva's insult is not the violent outburst of anger that might be expected, but a curse uttered pianissimo with unison strings, tortuously chromatic (Ex. 12.1). But while Schumann does show himself more than able to create music that ably complements moments of dramatic intensity—a characteristic present, after all, in his lieder as well—he is unsuccessful in creating music that sustains character development. Margaretha, the most unredeemingly evil character in the tale, never appears dark or menacing. The music Schumann created for her more often seems lively and sprightly, never wicked or diabolical—an effect created at least in part by the bright woodwind instrumentation associated with her.

Ex. 12.1

Ex. 12.1 continued

The inability consistently to infuse life into his characters is obviously a flaw of great import in an opera intended to be predominantly psychological in nature. But Schumann was far more successful in meeting other goals he had set for himself. As intended, *Genoveva* is a German opera, both in text and music. Genoveva is, as Siegfried at one point reminds her, "a German woman"—and it is her German nature that is presented as the source of her strength and much of her nobility. This was not an element that Schumann needed to add to his libretto. It is found in both Tieck and Hebbel, though interestingly, in Hebbel's version it is Genoveva herself who makes a point of noting her German heritage with pride. In his music Schumann instilled what he no doubt perceived as a distinctly German character by his use of a chorale-like melody (Ex.12.2), both at the very beginning and near the conclusion of the opera.[6]

But what is perhaps most striking about Schumann's music for *Genoveva* is not its "German-ness," but its progressive tendencies. To Schumann it remained essential that the dramatic action in the libretto move naturally. If it were to do so, that necessitated in Schu-

Ex. 12.2

[6] The chorale is not "Ermuntre dich mein schwacher Geist"—a claim that seems to have been first put forth by Hermann Abert in 1910—although the opening of Schumann's "chorale" does bear a resemblance to it.

mann's eyes a break with tradition, for it would not be possible to have the drama interrupted by unnecessary occasions for vocal display or fragmented into sections of aria and recitative. Schumann had followed a similar approach in *Paradise and the Peri* and in those scenes thus far completed from *Faust*. *Genoveva* contains twenty-one set numbers, but they are individual musical sections in name only. For the most part, the opera exhibits few seams. As had been the case in the past, Schumann relies on a distinctive form of arioso in lieu of conventional operatic melody. Even those parts of *Genoveva* referred to in the score as arias disdain operatic display, avoid tunefulness, and depart from four-bar symmetrical phrasing (with their expected cadential structure). Genoveva's "aria" (No. 11; Act 2) is a representative example. It commences with two symmetrical and tuneful four-bar phrases—an opening that audiences easily could have followed—but then the declamatory, ariosolike style preferred by Schumann enters. It is a musical style that ideally complements the text, but that many could only have found disconcerting.

Because less emphasis has been placed on traditional vocal melody, the orchestra has been increased in prominence. Frequently it supplies the tunefulness, in contrast to the strictly declamatory vocal lines. Schumann employs as well a musical device that has come to be associated with Wagner—the leitmotive. This was, of course, not an invention on Wagner's part. It is used with considerable effect, for example, by Weber in *Euryanthe* (1823), a work greatly admired by Schumann.[7] Schumann's use of the leitmotive is subtle. Most recognizable is the motive associated with Margaretha (at least in part because of its distinctive orchestration). It is based on a motive previously heard in the opera, and identified with Golo—a means by which Schumann emphasizes the association between the pair. But even more subtle is the psychological association created by Schumann with it, for the theme itself is a transformation of the chorale that appears at the beginning of the opera (Exx. 12.3, 12.4).

Schumann did make several concessions to public taste, such as the

---

[7] In Schumann's diary, he notes hearing the overture and excerpts from *Euryanthe* in January and February 1829 (*Tgb I*, pp. 168, 172). He saw the work on 23 September 1847, and expressed his admiration for it (*HSHLT*, p. 440). In addition to musical similarities, there are strong resemblances in plot between *Euryanthe* and *Genoveva*.

Ex. 12.3

Margaretha: Sieh' da, welch' fei-ner Rit-ters-mann!

Ex. 12.4

Chor: Lan-de ist der Knap-pe Herr im Haus!

lively choral march "Auf, auf in das Feld" (No. 5) and the lied "Bald blick' ich dich wieder" (No. 14), but there are few attempts to introduce the type of tunefulness welcomed by listeners of Schumann's day. Contemporary audiences found a great deal of the music austere and demanding, and critical reaction revealed that much of Schumann's efforts had been misunderstood. "The aria and recitative," noted one review, "blend into one another, only increasing the dreary monotony

Ex. 12.4 continued

of this ostensibly new operatic style."[8] On the other hand, the *Deutsche allgemeine Zeitung* in Leipzig wrote that, with *Genoveva*, Schumann "along with Mendelssohn stood on the edge of a new musical classicism."[9] How can these two criticisms be reconciled? Schumann had displayed in *Genoveva* not an "ostensibly new operatic style"—it *truly was* a new operatic style, having much in common with that being developed by Wagner. But it is difficult to imagine Mendelssohn being in sympathy with the approach adopted by Schumann. In fact, Mendelssohn had even considered and ruled out the subject of Genoveva as suitable for opera noting, with perhaps more discernment than Schumann, that it was flawed as a result of the "passiveness" of the

---

[8] From the *Düsseldorfer Journal* (14 July 1850) quoted in Reinhold Sietz, "Zur Textgestaltung von Robert Schumanns 'Genoveva'," *Die Musikforschung* XXIII (1970), p. 410.
[9] *Eismann*, p. 167.

heroine.[10] Schumann could have avoided the confusion over *Genoveva* if he had from the start made a point of making clear how different the music was. That in itself might have ensured a warmer reception for it. But Schumann lacked the gift for publicity possessed by Wagner, and as a result *Genoveva* perplexed not just his contemporaries but has continued to perplex audiences to this day.

Schumann lost no time after the completion of *Genoveva* in beginning a new dramatic project. Several weeks after finishing the score, he began work on a setting of excerpts from Byron's *Manfred*, adopting an approach recalling the one taken with *Faust*. Schumann had been familiar with *Manfred* since his youth—the diary notes that he had read it, perhaps for the first time, on 26 March 1829. Nearly twenty years later, he returned to it: "Manfred—Inspiration—Sketches."[11] He worked on *Manfred* in October and November, creating first an overture for the drama, then composing incidental music for selected portions. Orchestration was not finished until 23 November but, in fact, much of the work had been done quickly. Schumann noted with pride that the music for Act 1 had been sketched in only a day.

The reason for Schumann's rapid pace can be found in the intense interest he felt for the drama itself. More than one contemporary noted that in his passionate readings of the drama to family and friends Schumann appeared to identify with Manfred. Wasielewski was present on one occasion when Schumann was so deeply moved that tears came to his eyes, and he was unable to continue. Byron's play was published in 1817, one of several he intended more to be read than performed. It has similarities to the Faust legend, although Byron had not read Marlowe's version and was only slightly familiar with Goethe's (*Part I* only had thus far appeared in print).

Faust and Manfred represent much of what is most noble and most debased in the human spirit. But, unlike Faust, Manfred is burdened by guilt, satiated with life, and seeks death in the hope of blotting out an unnamed sin in his past. The cause of his guilt is never stated, but Byron does make clear that it concerns Manfred's deceased love, Astarte.

---

[10] Letter to Charlotte (not Charles) Birch-Pfeiffer of 10 December 1841 quoted in Sietz, p. 410. Birch-Pfeiffer supplied Mendelssohn with a scenario for the project, intended for Jenny Lind.

[11] Entry of 29 July 1848 in *HSHLT*, p. 466.

Manfred summons her spirit and tells her that "it were the deadliest sin to have loved as we have loved" (II, iv)—a line, incidentally, set with emphasis by Schumann in his version. Later a servant remarks: "The only thing [Manfred] seemed to love,—As he, indeed, by blood was bound to do, [was] the Lady Astarte, his—," at which point the servant is interrupted, leaving the sentence incomplete. It is commonly believed that Byron through the character of Manfred portrayed himself and his sexual liaison with his half-sister, Augusta Leigh. The "deadliest sin," then, would have been incest, and it is for that reason that Manfred, overwhelmed by remorse, is eager to die.

Schumann's music for *Manfred* is little known, yet among his most successful. It is a pity that Byron's drama does not lend itself well to performance. The overture Schumann created for it remains the best known of the *Manfred* music, but there are fifteen other pieces, including music for the entr'acte. Much of it is keenly evocative, and provides an effective counterpart to Byron's text. Schumann described his work to Liszt as new and different—a comment that seems to refer both to the extensive amount of music created for the project and the intimate liaison between text and music. There is, however, a clear distinction between these settings and those made for Goethe's *Faust*. For *Manfred*, Schumann made use of all possible means of musical accompaniment for the drama; the musical selections for *Manfred* provide incidental music in the strictest sense and were intended to be performed as accompaniment for presentations of the drama in its entirety.

In his *Manfred* settings, Schumann frequently made use of melodrama—that is, spoken word with musical accompaniment. It was an unusual musical device. Weber's use of it in *Der Freischütz* (1821) was probably the most celebrated instance. But despite the criticism of it as a bastardized genre, a number of Schumann's contemporaries (including Marschner and Liszt) displayed interest in it. Schumann's use of melodrama in *Manfred* often creates a particularly convincing complement to the dramatic action, and an unobtrusive and natural enhancement to the spoken word.

In Byron's drama, Manfred dies fearless and unrepentant, defiantly spurning the opportunity to die as a Christian—a scene in many ways recalling the death of Mozart's Don Giovanni. It was an ending that Schumann was incapable of retaining. As Manfred dies, Schumann added a chorus chanting a requiem for him, providing hope for redemption. Schumann's alteration to Byron's play is a sentimental touch Byron would have abhorred. But it emphasized Schumann's own hopes and sense of compassion.

Related to *Manfred* is Schumann's *Requiem für Mignon* op. 98b. It is a setting of an extended excerpt from Goethe's novel *Wilhelm Meister's Apprenticeship*. Schumann composed it in July 1849, and included with it, when published, nine solo songs from the novel (published as op. 98a). The requiem is a short work (about a quarter of an hour in length) for orchestra, chorus, and soloists. The text selected by Schumann—in itself an unusual choice—depicts the elaborate ceremony associated with the burial of perhaps the most remarkable character in Goethe's novel. Mignon, a child traveling against her will with a group of carnival-like entertainers, is rescued by Wilhelm Meister when he sees the manager of the troupe abusing her. She devotes herself blindly to him, and becomes jealous when any other female displays interest in him. She eventually dies, overwhelmed by despair, when a woman confesses her love to Meister in Mignon's presence. Throughout the novel, Mignon behaves in a mysterious and often inexplicable manner. The greatest mystery about her, however, concerns her origin. Only near the end of the work is it revealed that she is the result of an incestuous union.

Schumann was profoundly taken with the character of Mignon. He was attracted by her childlike innocence, but he was also moved by the sorrow of her existence. As had been the case with Manfred, Schumann seemed eager to represent by means of the requiem a tortured soul finding peace—once again, with incest as the basis. His setting is poignant and bittersweet (an interesting change in performance would be to replace the soprano soloists with boy sopranos, as called for in Goethe's text). Related in mood is the guilt-laden song of the Harper, Mignon's father: "Wer nie sein Brot mit Tränen ass" ("Who never ate his bread with tears"). Schumann's setting, chromatic and deeply expressive, is included in op. 98a.

After the rather cool reception accorded *Genoveva*, Schumann seemed to become less enthusiastic about writing opera. In May 1850— prior to the performances of *Genoveva*—he had contemplated an opera based on *Romeo and Juliet*. But no music for it was created, and after 1850 surprisingly few references to possible operas are found in his correspondence or household books.[12] Rather than working on opera, Schumann directed his efforts toward oratorio and choral music of a dramatic nature.

Early in 1851, Schumann entered into correspondence with the writer Richard Pohl concerning the possibility of creating an oratorio based on the life of Martin Luther, broad in its appeal, and suitable for performance in both church and concert hall. Pohl's concept of the project became increasingly grandiose: he envisioned it as a Reformation trilogy, an approach that Schumann did not support. They met in September to discuss the work, but, except for a draft scenario, nothing came of it. Although he continued to mention the idea as late as December 1852, Schumann's duties in Düsseldorf and the erratic state of his health precluded work on it.[13]

Instead, Schumann's dramatic instincts during these years primarily found their expression in a series of ballads for chorus and orchestra: *The King's Son* op. 116 (1851), *The Minstrel's Curse* op. 139 (1852), *The Princess and the Page* op. 140 (1852), and *The Luck of Edenhall* op. 143 (1853). The idea of creating a series of short choral ballads with orchestral accompaniment—their average length is less than a half hour—was new. Probably the closest in concept had been Niels Gade's *Comala* (1846)—a work (based on Ossian) that Schumann knew well and that was a mixture of oratorio and opera approximately an hour in length. In Schumann's choral ballads, soloists were involved, so it permitted him to write a kind of opera in miniature, but without having to deal with the expense and complications of a large-scale dramatic work. There would be more of a demand as well for these comparatively modest works, both by choral societies and by the numerous choral festivals. Schumann's approach was to select as the basis for the work a well-known and popular ballad, which then was adapted into sections appropriate for a musical setting.

The major weakness of the choral ballads is the lack of variety in them. To a certain extent, that may have been a result of the texts

---

[12] A two-page scenario for *Romeo and Juliet* exists. Schumann also expressed interest in Kleist's *Michael Kohlhaas* (27 August 1852), and a fairy opera (*Der Rittermond*; spring of 1853).

[13] Schumann provided three sketches for the project (seven pages long); Pohl provided two (a total of ten pages).

themselves—all are fairly gloomy in subject matter; only *The King's Son* has what might be termed a "happy ending." In that sense, they seem to reflect Schumann's own feelings during these years. Still, there is nothing about these works to merit the neglect they have suffered over the years, other than the fact that they fall into a genre for which today there is little demand. Of the four, *The Princess and the Page* is comparatively light, and the most popular in style. The others continue the manner of *Genoveva*, relying heavily on a declamatory arioso. The emphasis is clearly on the dramatic structure of the narrative—a notable exception being *The King's Son*, where the episodic nature of the tale requires a more fragmented representation. As in *Genoveva*, Schumann was particularly attracted to the psychological aspects of the characters in the ballads—and in that respect (especially in *The Minstrel's Curse*) he is now more successful. Perhaps Schumann thought of these in their way as operatic studies. But even if that were not the case, they provided him with the opportunity further to refine his musical dramatic skills.

CHAPTER 13

The Years in Düsseldorf

> *You know what musical life is like in a small German city—God help us!*
>
> —Mendelssohn on Düsseldorf

THE ARRIVAL OF THE SCHUMANNS IN DÜSSELDORF ON THE evening of 2 September 1850 could not have been more auspicious. They were greeted by Ferdinand Hiller and a committee from the city, and escorted to the Hotel Breidenbach—the city's finest hotel—where they found rooms awaiting them decorated with flowers. Later in the evening they were serenaded by Düsseldorf's Choralverein. It was the start of festivities in their honor. On the 7th, as he attended a concert consisting solely of his own works, Schumann was greeted by a flourish of trumpets when he entered the hall. Every effort was made not just to make the Schumanns feel welcome, but to make clear to them they were honored and distinguished guests.

Schumann's employer was the city, represented by the Burgomeister and a music committee. The duties associated with his new position were numerous. He was to direct both the choral society and the orchestra, producing ten concerts as part of an annual series. In addition, he was required each year to direct four programs of music for the Maximilian and Lambertus churches. It was also expected that he would assume an active role in the annual Nieder-Rheinische Music Festival, a large festival that combined the resources of several Rhenish cities.

Rehearsals of both the vocal and instrumental ensembles were held weekly. Initially, Schumann was apprehensive and concerned about the level of musical ability. He determined it was essential to have a strong leader within the orchestra, and hired as concertmaster a young violinist and former student at the Leipzig Conservatory, his future biographer Wilhelm von Wasielewski. Schumann had similar concerns with the choral group, comprised mostly of amateurs. It appears that from the beginning Clara went with her husband to the vocal rehearsals, where she served as piano accompanist and provided moral support. Schumann had done the same with the choral groups he had directed in Dresden, and decided to continue the practice.

The first concert on 24 September was an unqualified success. The audience was appreciative and enthusiastic, and Schumann expressed his satisfaction both with the concert and the musical life in Düsseldorf in general. He had entered into his duties expecting the worst, but now felt "extremely pleased and surprised," both by the musical ability of the groups and by the public "which only desires good music and loves it" (20 September 1850). He was in an expansive frame of mind, and in January wrote to Sterndale Bennett expressing interest in traveling to England. Clara had for years longed to perform there, and Schumann hoped his *Paradise and the Peri* would be well received. Now that he was living considerably closer to England and established in his new position, the trip seemed more of a possibility than it ever had, and the idea persisted until the summer. Clara, too, was finding benefits to the musical life in Düsseldorf, both in performing and in an increasing number of private students. It seemed that after years of struggle, they had found happiness and stability. On 1 December 1851, their seventh child, Eugenie, was born.

Schumann's primary professional associate in Düsseldorf was Julius Tausch. He directed several choral ensembles (including the men's), and served as Schumann's assistant. Tausch was twenty-three at the time of Schumann's arrival, and had studied from 1844 to 1846 at the Leipzig Conservatory, where Schumann had been one of his teachers. On Mendelssohn's recommendation, Tausch had come to Düsseldorf in 1846 to conduct the men's chorus. He was a composer as well as a skilled pianist and accompanist. Schumann was supportive of his young colleague, writing on his behalf to Breitkopf & Härtel recommending Tausch's *Fantasiestücke* for publication and describing him as a "gifted musician" (24 February 1851).

Despite the hectic schedule and difficulty in finding a suitable place to live, the move to Düsseldorf in no way hampered Schumann's creativity. Within several months of his arrival, he had completed a new symphony, the Third op. 97. In the following year, eighteen works were composed, including a revision of the D minor symphony of 1841, eventually published as the Fourth Symphony op. 120. Among works completed were three concert overtures (for Schiller's *Bride of Messina* op. 100, Shakespeare's *Julius Caesar* op. 128, and Goethe's *Hermann and Dorothea* op. 136), lieder (including poems by Elisabeth Kulmann for op. 103 and op. 104, and Lenau for op. 117), a Third Piano Trio op. 110, two violin sonatas (op. 105 and op. 121), a return to solo piano music (*Drei Fantasiestücke* op. 111), *The King's Son* op. 116 (the first of his four ballads for chorus and orchestra), and what perhaps might best be described as a chamber oratorio, *The Pilgrimage of the Rose* op. 112. In all, this was an astonishing amount of music, especially when account is made for his settlement in Düsseldorf. In 1850, prior to the move, Schumann had composed comparatively little, being preoccupied with the production of *Genoveva*. After settling in Düsseldorf, it was as if he were eager to return to the pace of 1849. But instead of focusing primarily on Hausmusik, he returned to music of greater dimension— such as the third and fourth symphonies and the overtures—perhaps viewed by him as more in keeping with the prestige of his new position.

At the same time, he worked diligently to promote his compositions. Publishers were contacted, and with the Düsseldorf orchestra at his disposal, there was ample opportunity to program his new works, the Third Symphony first being performed on 6 February 1851. Schumann seemed full of hope and eager to branch out as a composer. With *The King's Son*, he had created a new genre, a mixture of opera and oratorio in miniature. It was a genre that had the practical benefit of taking advantage of the need for music for the numerous choral societies in Germany and Britain. On a larger scale, in 1851 Schumann became absorbed in the idea of a grandiose oratorio that he hoped would have broad appeal based on the life of Martin Luther. It was a fascinating idea, and one that he would return to in 1852, but the project (a proposed collaboration with the writer Richard Pohl) never progressed beyond the preliminary stages.

Schumann's health bore the strain of the move to Düsseldorf well. Except for a complication with his eyes ("weakness"; 5 October 1850), and a reference to Wasielewski that he was still "sometimes affected by the nervous complaint" (11 June 1852), there seem to have been few problems. His good health and spirits are all the more remarkable given the complications that soon developed in the performance of his duties as a conductor.

Schumann appeared to enjoy conducting (he felt that he had ability for it), but at first had always limited himself to conducting his own compositions. Since making his debut as a conductor with a performance of *Peri* on 4 December 1843, he had conducted on numerous occasions and in major cities, most notably Berlin and Vienna. His association with the choral groups in Dresden had been helpful both in broadening his repertory and in giving him an opportunity for more consistent practice of his craft. But having to conduct an orchestra on a regular basis and in works other than his own was new to Schumann and must have presented a challenge.

Discontent with Schumann's ability as a conductor first manifested itself in a less than flattering anonymous review in the *Düsseldorfer Zeitung* of a concert on 13 March 1851. Schumann took particular offense, because he suspected the author was a member of the music committee. The first season ended splendidly with a well-received performance of Beethoven's "Pastoral" Symphony on 18 May. But the sign of discord was an indication of troubles to follow. This was not the first occasion on which there had been criticism of Schumann as a conductor. Privately, in Dresden it had been said that he had expected too much of the chorus, and that he had failed at times to assert himself and exercise decisive control of the group.

The absence of close friends and the increasingly less rewarding duties as conductor led Schumann to consider the wisdom of remaining in Düsseldorf. "Loneliness. Thoughts about staying long in D[üsseldorf]," Schumann wrote in the household books.[1] In the fall of 1851, he wrote

---

[1] Entry of 17 March 1851 in *HSHLT*, p. 556.

to the conductor Julius Stern in Berlin, laconically noting that he had no intention of remaining in Düsseldorf forever. Clara was of the same opinion. In April, she had written to her sister-in-law, commenting that Schumann was "unappreciated" and that they intended to leave.[2]

From 18 July until 5 August, they were absent from Düsseldorf, traveling in Switzerland, a refreshing trip that Clara in particular long remembered fondly. They traveled down the Rhine, stopping at Heidelberg, which Schumann found little changed after twenty-two years. They continued to Basel and Geneva, enjoying themselves immensely. Returning to Düsseldorf, they did not remain long. On the 16th, they made a journey of about a week to Antwerp and Brussels. In Antwerp Schumann was one of the judges at a men's choral competition, tedious work that he did not like. With the contest completed, however, they enjoyed the artistic attractions of the city, especially paintings by Rubens.

In the autumn, when work with the chorus resumed, attendance was poor. After rehearsals of Bach's Mass, Clara was indignant. The members, she felt, only wanted to amuse themselves and had "respect neither for art nor their conductor!"[3] Despite his contractual commitment, for a time Schumann considered giving up his association with the chorus. As the 1851–52 concert season unfolded, the diary revealed Clara's continued exasperation with what she perceived as the coldness of the public and the frivolous behavior of the musicians. Her reaction only exacerbated the situation. She had always been quick to criticize, and as time passed grew increasingly intolerant. In her mind, it was never a question of herself or Schumann being in the wrong; others were always at fault. What made Clara's stance particularly dangerous was that Schumann relied on her perceptions almost exclusively. The result was a distorted and one-sided view of the situation, and an attitude that admitted no compromise.

Criticism of Schumann as a conductor in Düsseldorf invariably focused on his supposed lack of skill, but it is clear that at least equally unnerving to the ensembles he led was his personality. He appeared detached, uncommunicative, and to many he probably appeared

---

[2] Nancy B. Reich, *Clara Schumann. The Artist and the Woman* (Ithaca, NY, 1985), p. 134.
[3] Diary entry for 23 September 1851 in *Litzmann II*, p. 240.

supercilious. He was not physically imposing, and by his presence and actions did little to inspire obedience from those he directed. At the same time he did not know how to please them. He was totally lacking in social graces and in the ability to charm; neither did he have a gift for small talk. To many in the choral society, their purpose in becoming members was both to sing and enjoy themselves socially. But it is clear that Schumann expected from those he led not only total dedication to music but unusual sensitivity to it as well. Rehearsals with Schumann appear to have been a serious if not a solemn affair.

There were times, too, while conducting, that Schumann appeared to be completely absorbed in the music and unaware of what was occurring around him—and it was those occasions that seem to have led to the open criticism of his ability. Tausch recalled one incident during a choral rehearsal when the sopranos were so ineffective in attempting to sing several high notes that laughter resulted. First the sopranos stopped singing, then the others, until the only performer left was Tausch, who was serving as accompanist at the piano: "Schumann noticed nothing and went on beating time, and Tausch, thinking it was no use going on by himself, stopped too. Schumann beckoned to him to come, and Tausch expected a reproof for having broken off. But no—Schumann showed him a passage in the score and said: "Look, this bar is beautiful."[4]

At times Schumann would let the most glaring mistakes pass without comment. At other times, when dissatisfied with a passage, he would repeat it frequently, but without pointing out what was wrong or how it could be improved. Wasielewski felt that Schumann was not accurate in giving the beat, and that the tempos were often too slow. In fact, it is nearly impossible to encounter a kind remark about Schumann's ability as a conductor. Ferdinand David in describing Schumann's conducting of *Paradise and the Peri* in 1843 noted that he had had "four orchestral rehearsals. Even if he had had ten, it wouldn't have gone better."[5] When conducting, he seemed on a purely subjective level to become so immersed in the music that his own vision of the score

---

[4] Quoted in Frederick Niecks, *Robert Schumann* (London, 1925), p. 270.

[5] Letter to Mendelssohn of 6 December 1843 quoted in Reinhard Kapp, "Das Orchester Schumanns," *Musik-Konzepte: Sonderband Robert Schumann II* (1982), p. 145.

blinded him to the reality of the performance. And he showed little inclination or ability to transmit that vision to the musicians around him. Criticism of Schumann as a conductor both by professional and amateur musicians is so widespread as to leave little doubt of his ineffectiveness.

Yet, it was criticism the validity of which Schumann vehemently denied. When he learned of it, he was not only offended but appeared outraged by its preposterous nature. To understand his reaction, it is necessary to take into account his home life and, in particular, the changing relationship with his wife. Clara increasingly assumed two primary functions: she became Schumann's intermediary to the world, and, at the same time, in Schumann's eyes she became the most significant representative of it. "She watched over him," wrote Frederick Niecks, who was able to speak with many who knew the Schumanns during these years. "She placed herself between the outside world and him, and prevented, as far as possible, those rubs which tortured his sensitive mind."[6] Her approach was unorthodox enough to be criticized privately by at least one member of the music committee (one of Schumann's physicians, incidentally), who felt that Clara's actions robbed her husband of his "manly decisiveness."[7] Her position was a powerful one and, whether she acknowledged it or not, did much to bolster her own ego. In the end, her actions only served to isolate Schumann and distort his perception. The "balance with the outside world," which Schumann had expressed concern about maintaining in 1832, remained a problem throughout his career. Her protective stance led to a change in his behavior. He became insensitive and, at times, dictatorial. Niecks revealed two episodes from the years in Dresden. On one occasion, at a party at the Bendemann's during which Clara had performed, Clara went to Schumann stating that she was unwell and suggested that they leave. He responded:

> "But why should we go? It is so nice here." And they remained. At last Bendemann said to Schumann: "Although it is very impolite for a host to say so to a guest, I cannot help saying that you should have taken your

---

[6] Niecks, p. 302.
[7] Letter of Dr. Wolfgang Müller von Königswinter to Reinecke of 10 October 1851, quoted in Paul Kast, ed., *Schumanns rheinische Jahre* (Düsseldorf, 1981), p. 96.

wife home by now." Schumann said nothing but was angry. Next day Bendemann received a letter in which Schumann said in an irritated way that he did not need to be told of his wife's excellences, that he was well aware of them. Bendemann apologized and the friendship was restored. On another occasion Bendemann called to take Schumann out and found him dressing. After fumbling with his tie for some time he called out, "Clara, my waistcoat." And she brought it, and afterwards his coat. Bendemann reproved him for this, but without convincing him.[8]

Schumann appeared increasingly closed-minded and disdainful of others' opinions. According to Tausch's recollections, Schumann "could not brook opposition, even in trifling matters of opinion; he even took offense if, when he asked a question, the answer was not to his taste. In such cases he usually rose and walked away without saying a word."[9]

Despite the increasingly tense situation, there was no open breach. But, perhaps in sympathy with more somber thoughts, as a composer Schumann turned to an area he had previously neglected: church music. In February and March 1852, he composed a Mass for chorus and orchestra (published as op. 147), and in April and May created the Requiem op. 148. Except for two more choral ballads, *The Minstrel's Curse* op. 139 and *The Princess and the Page* op. 140, little else was composed during the year. In number, it was a marked decline from the previous year, and an indication of the effect his stressful position was having on him. He may have taken some consolation from a Schumann Festival of sorts scheduled in Leipzig, including performances of his work both at the Gewandhaus and privately. There were three concerts (on 14, 18, and 21 March); included were performances of the Third Symphony, the *Pilgrimage of the Rose* (both conducted by Schumann), the overture to *Manfred*, the First Violin Sonata op. 105, and the Third Piano Trio op. 110.

---

[8] Niecks, pp. 290–91. The household books for 15 and 16 February 1849 refer to Bendemann's "rudeness" (p. 483)—probably a reference to the first episode. Schumann also could be harsh in his criticism of Clara's performances; on one occasion in Düsseldorf, his cold reaction to her playing reduced her to tears.

[9] *Ibid.*, p. 270.

In May, Schumann decided to organize and edit his music criticism for publication in book form. There had been no music critic more influential nor one whose criticism had withstood so well the test of time. Schumann wanted to preserve it in more permanent form. He wanted as well to present it to those who, he felt, now might solely be familiar with his work as a composer. It only took him about a week to complete the project, and he sent it to Breitkopf & Härtel for consideration, writing that he intended it both as a memento of the times and of himself. To undertake such a project when only forty-two—a summing up of a time admittedly past but to which he might very well make additional contributions—appears unusual. But during the next few years, it often seems as if Schumann was concerned about putting his house in order, as if the best years had passed and little remained to be done. In the fall of 1853, he wrote to Breitkopf about the possibility of issuing a complete catalogue of his compositions. At the same time he went through his unpublished piano works from the years 1832–45, many of which he now assembled in a collection later published as the *Albumblätter* op. 124.

Some of these activities may have been a reflection of the growing deterioration of his health and his concern over it. Writing on 27 December 1852 to his collaborator on the Luther project, Richard Pohl, Schumann revealed that he had been "very ill" for about six months— "a severe nervous disorder"—and only for the past five or six weeks had he felt somewhat better. His situation had been complicated by a serious problem with hemorrhoids, and for much of the summer and autumn he had been obliged to rest. The "nervous disorder" had begun in April with sleeplessness (the stressful conditions of his work had probably contributed). A brief trip nearby on the Rhine from 26 June until 7 July was intended to provide distraction but did not. On the 2nd, while walking along the river, he suffered a nervous attack with spasms that cut short the trip. The household books document the onset of the illness and its effect: "Nervous complaint" (8 July); "Wretched wearing down of my strength" (3 August); "Grievous time of suffering" (8 August).[10] Cold baths in the Rhine were attempted as a cure. And from 12 August until

---

[10] *HSHLT*, pp. 597, 601.

17 September, he stayed in Scheveningen, hoping the change of scene and sea baths would be beneficial.[11] Many of Schumann's symptoms, although less severe, recall those of 1844–45 at the time of his nervous breakdown.

Except for conducting his *Julius Caesar* Overture on 3 August, during this period Schumann was unable to conduct, and his duties were taken over by Tausch. The previous March, while Schumann had been in Leipzig, Tausch had also served as his replacement and been warmly received. What were perceived as Schumann's deficiencies as a conductor became all the more glaring in comparison with Tausch. Schumann's return to conducting on 3 December only served to increase the discord. As a result of growing dissatisfaction, three members of the committee responsible for the direction of the choral society pointedly asked him to resign. It was an independent action on their part—and apparently a hotheaded one—but indicative that for some the situation was growing intolerable. On 15 December, Schumann received a letter from twenty-two members of the chorus condemning the action of the three.

But Schumann's reputation as a conductor continued to deteriorate. In the spring of 1853, he shared duties with Hiller for the direction of the Nieder-Rheinische Music Festival. It was a prestigious event and Schumann's first appearance with it. The festival lasted three days (15–17 May), and contained lengthy programs. Schumann's role in the festival was extensive (several of his works, including the Fourth Symphony and Piano Concerto were performed). At the conclusion of the festival, Schumann was generally pleased with his performance in it. But he had been hurt by criticism that had compared his conducting unfavorably with that of Hiller (Hiller long remained a favorite with the Düsseldorf public).

Despite the continued difficulties Schumann was encountering as a conductor, his mood during much of 1853 was surprisingly bright. But the tension of his situation is revealed by his limited activity as a composer. During the first half of the year, he composed comparatively little: *Das Glück von Edenhall* (The Luck of Edenhall) op. 143, the *Faust*

---

[11] While there, Clara apparently suffered a miscarriage (as she may have in 1846 during a visit to Nordeney).

overture, and Seven Piano Pieces in the Form of Fughettas op. 126. In January and March, he composed piano accompaniments for Bach's violin partitas and sonatas, and cello suites—a sign that the creative spirit had not yet returned after the difficulties of the previous year, for although the work with Bach was a labor of love for Schumann, it was not the creation of original compositions. In its way, the association with Bach served as a prelude to the Fughettas op. 126 and are an indication yet again of Schumann's immersion in counterpoint as a basis of regaining stability. In addition, he devoted considerable time to work on the *Dichtergarten*, his collection of excerpts dealing with music from the works of writers whom he admired. In April, he completed a re-reading of Shakespeare for it.

That same month, Schumann became infatuated with a fad that was sweeping Europe at the time: table-rapping. Table-rapping consisted of a séance of sorts, and was conducted around a table in which spirits were contacted and asked questions. They responded by rapping on the table and moving it. In the household books, Schumann first made reference to table-rapping on 18 April. The numerous references that followed over the next month (and continued sporadically until mid-November) testify to his fascination. He wrote to Hiller about the phenomenon, describing one incident in which he had requested the table to tap out the opening of Beethoven's Fifth Symphony. It did so, "but at first somewhat slowly; I said: 'But the tempo is quicker, dear table' " (25 April 1853). To Schumann's satisfaction, the table picked up the pace.

Much has been made of Schumann's infatuation with table-rapping. In Wasielewski's biography, he related his own contact with Schumann and reported that Schumann not only expressed his fervid belief in the phenomenon, but showed astonishment that Wasielewski knew nothing of it. To Wasielewski, this was yet additional proof of Schumann's growing mental instability, a stance that has unquestioningly been adopted by succeeding biographers. But Schumann's interest in table-rapping is better seen as a manifestation of his naivete and often childlike nature. His fascination needs as well to be put in perspective. At about the time of Schumann's experiments with it, for years Victor Hugo was enthralled with table-rapping. In Hugo's case, his enthusiasm has prompted amusement, not concern for his mental health.

During 1853, far more disturbing signs of a decline in Schumann's health were evident than his delight in table-rapping. Recovery from his infirmities of the previous year was slow. "I do not yet feel in me," he confided to Moritz Horn, "the strength necessary to undertake a large, extensive work."[12] His physical actions, including the pace at which he walked, appeared slower, and his speech at times was slurred and difficult to comprehend. On 30 July while in Bonn Schumann collapsed, and was fearful he had suffered a stroke.[13] In October, the French artist Jean-Joseph-Bonaventure Laurens, an admirer of Schumann, traveled to Düsseldorf to make his acquaintance. The portrait he drew of Schumann during the visit clearly shows a sick man. Schumann's face appears unnatural: puffed, but haggard and dour.

Yet, Schumann's illness did not prevent him from planning an extravagant birthday for Clara in September, the last they were to celebrate together. He presented her with the scores of two recently completed compositions—the Fantasy for Violin op. 131 and the *Concert-Allegro* op. 134 for piano—both placed on a new grand piano that had been smuggled into the house without her knowledge. She was delighted by the instrument (but concerned over its cost). The *Concert-Allegro* had been written specifically for her, and was Schumann's first work for piano and orchestra in four years. Both compositions were an indication of renewed activity. In September, he composed a collection of piano duets for children, the *Kinderball* op. 130, a companion to three *Kindersonaten* op. 118 he had composed in June. The next month he produced a fascinating chamber work for piano, viola, and clarinet (the *Märchenerzählungen* op. 132), and a series of five pieces for solo piano entitled *Gesänge der Frühe* ("Songs of Dawn"), published as op. 133 in 1855. There was also a new interest in works for violin, including in addition to the Fantasy, a violin concerto.

The compositions for violin had been inspired by a friendship Schumann had established with the virtuoso, Joseph Joachim. Joachim (whom Schumann had first met as a child prodigy in 1843) was twenty-one years younger, and one of a number of young men who had be-

---

[12] Letter of 11 April 1853 in Hermann Erler, *Robert Schumann's Leben: Aus seinen Briefen geschildert*, 2 vols. (Berlin, 1887), II, p. 191.
[13] *HSHLT*, pp. 631, 806. Particulars of the illness are not known.

come admirers of Schumann's music. Schumann's friendship with Joachim blossomed when he came to Düsseldorf for the Nieder-Rheinische Music Festival in May 1853 in order to perform Beethoven's Violin Concerto. It had been a great success and Schumann had been deeply moved by Joachim's artistry. Rupert Becker, son of his old friend Ernst Becker, was another youthful admirer; he had arrived in Düsseldorf in the autumn of 1852 as replacement for Wasielewski who had accepted a position in Bonn. In addition there was Joachim's friend, the composer, Albert Dietrich. It was a sign of Schumann's growing popularity among a younger generation.

The most notable member of this youthful group arrived on Schumann's doorstep on 30 September 1853 with a recommendation from Joachim. "Herr Brahms from Hamburg," Schumann noted in the household books.[14] Johannes Brahms played several of his compositions for Schumann, including the F sharp minor Piano Sonata (later published as his op. 2). Schumann could not have been more impressed: "Visit from Brahms (a genius)."[15] On the 9th, after continued contact with him, Schumann began writing an article for the *Neue Zeitschrift für Musik*. It had been ten years since he had published any music criticism, and the article on Brahms was to be his last. Entitled "New Paths," it was filled with praise, compared Brahms to Beethoven, and—unintended by Schumann—in many ways placed an onerous burden upon him. Yet, while the aim of the article was to bring Brahms before the public's eye, much of it can be interpreted as Schumann's farewell, as if, his work completed, he was now paving the way for the arrival of another generation. It is appropriate that the *Bund* makes a final appearance in the concluding sentences: "There is at all times a secret league of kindred spirits. Close tightly the circle, you who belong to it, that the truth of art may shine ever brighter, spreading joy and blessings to all!"[16]

During Brahms's visit (he was to remain until 3 November), Joachim returned to Düsseldorf. His *Hamlet Overture* and a reprise of the Beethoven concerto were to be performed at the end of the month,

---

[14] *Ibid.*, p. 637.
[15] Entry of 1 October 1853 in *Ibid.*
[16] *GS II*, p. 302.

Schumann conducting. Rehearsals did not go smoothly. On the 27th, scandal was narrowly averted when a cellist walked out during rehearsal (he later gave ill-health as the reason). Once again, Schumann's lack of skill as a conductor became pointedly displayed. He had become particularly fond of one passage in Joachim's overture, a section in which the French horns made a striking effect with their entry. During rehearsal, the horns twice failed to enter. Schumann made no comment to the orchestra. Instead, he "turned sadly to Joachim and said, 'They don't come in.' "[17]

Dissatisfaction with Schumann as a conductor was finally coming to a head. A concert earlier in the month—a mass by Hauptmann, for which Tausch had prepared the chorus and that at the last moment Schumann had decided to direct—had nearly been a fiasco. As a result, on 19 October Schumann was asked by the music committee to permit Tausch to conduct "smaller works" (such as the mass)—a half-hearted attempt not to offend Schumann, but an act that he characterized in the household books as "shameless."[18] The difficulties with the performance of Joachim's *Hamlet* later that month exacerbated the situation. Joachim wrote to Dietrich on 6 November of a "crisis": "Schumann and his wife are completely unaware [of the situation], and I am afraid that, even if they are told in the kindest manner, it will be a severe blow for them."[19]

On 7 November, several members of the music committee visited the Schumann home to request that in the future he conduct only his own works, the remainder to be conducted by Tausch. The representatives of the committee did not deliver their news to Schumann personally, but to Clara, who, outraged and insulted, informed them (without consulting Schumann) that their action would necessitate his resignation. Schumann tersely noted in the household books: "Decisive day. Shameless behavior."[20] On the 9th, he wrote to the committee to inform them he would not comply with the changes demanded by

---

[17] Niecks, p. 293.
[18] Kast, p. 31 and *HSHLT*, p. 639.
[19] Letter to Albert Dietrich of 6 November [1853] in *Briefe von und an Joseph Joachim*, ed. Johannes Joachim and Andreas Moser, 3 vols. (Berlin, 1911), I, p. 102.
[20] Entry of 7 November in *HSHLT*, p. 641.

them and that he would resign his position at the earliest date permissible by contract: 1 October 1854.

Schumann refused to conduct the next concert, and wrote to Tausch on the 19th informing him that if he did so, he would not interpret his action in a friendly manner. Tausch found himself in a difficult position. Although he and Schumann had never become close, they were on friendly terms. As recently as the previous January, Schumann had written yet again on Tausch's behalf to Breitkopf recommending his work. At the same time it was evident that as Schumann's ability as a conductor had become unacceptable, Tausch's skill had been perceived as a more than adequate replacement. If he did not conduct the forthcoming concert, he would retain Schumann's support. But it must have been clear to him that the complaints made against Schumann were not unjustified, and by refusing to conduct he was alienating the influential music committee. He decided to conduct the concert.

By doing so, he became the villain in Clara's and Robert's eyes. Clara had disliked Tausch from the moment she had met him. "If only he were more pleasant. There is something . . . in his face which I can not become used to," she had written in the diary.[21] Now he became an intriguer who had curried favor with those in authority in order to undermine Schumann's position (later Schumann actually accused the committee of negotiating with Tausch behind his back). That had not been the case. Those who had known Tausch later testified that he was a competent musician and an honest one, far from Machiavellian and not at all malicious. The predicament that had developed had been brought about not by his machinations, but by Schumann's ineptness as a conductor and by Tausch simply being on hand.

Still, the blame for the confrontation between Schumann and the music committee should not be placed solely on Schumann. The attempt to remove him had been handled poorly, and with little regard for his reputation and self-esteem. If Schumann had consented to conduct only his own compositions, there can be little doubt that his reputation as a conductor would have been severely damaged. Word of his supposed incompetence would have spread rapidly in the musical world. Since his reaction to the committee's demand was to resign, in

---

[21] Diary entry of 7 September 1850 in *Litzmann II*, p. 225.

effect the predicament had been resolved: with further negotiation it might have been possible for Schumann to continue his duties as conductor until the summer, at which time his musical commitments to the city would have ceased. There is no indication that Schumann's competency as a conductor had deteriorated to such an extent that he would have been incapable of completing the musical season. It had been Joachim's opinion—prior to the committee's demand—that all might turn out well if the public reacted favorably to the next concert, an opportunity that Schumann was denied. In fact, the entire incident could have made him more fully aware of the breadth of the discontent, and might have led to a more determined effort on his part to conclude his duties in an honorable and professional manner. During the remaining months in Düsseldorf, Schumann would have had ample time to search for another position, and there would have been sufficient time as well to find a replacement for him. His reputation would not have emerged unsullied, but the public embarrassment implicit in the committee's original demand would have been avoided. In its handling of the situation, the committee made only a superficial attempt to understand Schumann's perspective of it and displayed little concern to treat him in the manner his stature in the musical world justified.

The remaining weeks in November became increasingly distasteful for Schumann. "Miserable people here," he noted on the 18th.[22] Discouragement had set in, too, over the publication of his music criticism. Despite the value of his work as a critic and his accomplishments as a musician, for the past year and a half Schumann had experienced the humiliation of having his book rejected in succession by several publishers, including Breitkopf, Wigand, and Kahnt. Now, late in the month he finally received some good news. Wigand had reconsidered and would publish it. But remaining in Düsseldorf was only a reminder of his unpleasant situation, and, as a change of scene, a concert tour in Holland was hastily put together. He and Clara left on the 24th, and did not return to Düsseldorf until 22 December. Concerts were given in Utrecht, The Hague, Rotterdam, and Amsterdam, and included performances of the Second and Third symphonies, the *Concert-Allegro* (with Clara at the piano), and *The Pilgrimage of the Rose*. Their warm

[22] *HSHLT*, p. 642.

reception was in stark contrast to their difficulties in Düsseldorf. When they returned home, they stayed for less than a month. Schumann worked on a revision of *Kreisleriana*, but mostly continued compiling his *Dichtergarten*.

It was at this point that Joachim's friendship became of inestimable value. For some time he had been attempting to arrange a performance of the *Peri* in Hanover, where he was concertmaster. Although the performance fell through, Schumann and Clara decided to travel to Hanover anyway, hoping for other concert opportunities and looking forward once again to contact with Joachim and Brahms, who was also in Hanover. They left on the 19th, and returned on 30 January. While there, Clara played with success at the court, and Joachim performed the Violin Fantasy. Schumann also made the acquaintance of Julius Otto Grimm, a composer and friend of Brahms, who soon became yet another member of Schumann's youthful circle.

Schumann had been in good spirits during the trip. He greatly enjoyed the company of Joachim and Brahms. There was a playfulness in his friendship with them—including frequent jokes—that was not present in his association with others. On his return from Hanover there was no attempt at composition. Schumann occupied himself with correspondence, continued work on the *Dichtergarten*, and on 3 February wrote the preface to the forthcoming edition of his collected criticism. It was a rather wistful, poetic, and romanticized look at his past:

> At the end of the year 1833 there met in Leipzig every evening and as if by chance a number of musicians, mostly young, in the first place for social intercourse, but also for exchange of ideas about the art that was the meat and drink of their life—music. . . . Then one day the thought flashed across the young hotheads: let us not look on idly . . . let us set about restoring the poetry of art to its place of honor. So there appeared the first pages of a new music periodical . . . one of them, the musical dreamer of the party, whose life had hitherto been dreamed away at the pianoforte rather than among books, resolved to take the editing in hand himself, and carried it on for about ten years until the year 1844. The result was a series of essays many of which are contained in this collection. Most of the opinions therein expressed he still holds today.[23]

[23] *GS I*, p. 1. Translated in Niecks, p. 131.

Schumann's attempt to maintain the illusion of life as usual was not successful. For both Mendelssohn and Rietz, Düsseldorf had been a kind of musical backwater, and had served as a stepping-stone to more prestigious positions. From the start, Schumann had portrayed the position as not a particularly good one, yet he had not been successful. After the debacle in Düsseldorf, where else could he go? A personal crisis of major proportions had developed, similar to that which Schumann had experienced in 1833 and 1844. In each instance, the basis for the crisis had been concern for his livelihood: in 1833, the abandonment of his career as a pianist, the failure of his symphony, and the lack of recognition for his compositions; in 1844, the abandonment of his association with the *Zeitschrift* and concern that he would be unable to be successful solely as a composer. In both 1833 and 1844, he had become severely depressed and suffered nervous breakdowns. Now, ten years later, Schumann once again found himself at a crossroads, anxious and fearful about his future. But this crisis was more perilous than those in the past. There were fewer options available to him and, ten years older, Schumann lacked the buoyancy of youth.

On 6 February, he wrote to Joachim, with fond remembrances of the recent visit. He complained that he had not yet received a word from him, and added, "but I have often written to you in invisible ink, and between these lines runs a cipher which will later become apparent." This could have been simple playfulness on Schumann's part—he often wrote silly, seemingly nonsensical comments to Joachim ("I am always in good humor when I write to you," Schumann had joked in a letter of 6 January)—but given the disturbing events that were to occur over the following weeks, it may have been an ominous foreshadowing of Schumann's mental state.

Several days after writing to Joachim, Schumann noted in the household books: "In the evening very strong and painful hearing disturbances."[24] There had been a similar occurrence during the trip to Holland, and as a result Schumann had spent a sleepless night in Emmerich. But that attack had subsided. This one continued for six days. Clara's diary entries provide some details:

---

[24] Entry of 10 February 1854 in *HSHLT*, p. 648.

Friday the 10th and during the night on Saturday the 11th, Robert had such severe hearing disturbances the entire night that he did not sleep at all. He kept hearing the same pitch, and in addition at times another interval [. . .] The night of Sunday the 12th was just as bad and the day also, for the suffering was absent for only two hours in the morning, and at 10 o'clock returned. My poor Robert suffers frightfully! All noises sound as music to him. He says it is magnificent music with wonderfully sounding instruments such as no one on earth has ever heard before! . . . The following nights were very bad—we hardly slept at all. . . . He tried to work during the day, but it required strenuous efforts on his part. He said many times that if it did not stop, he would lose his mind.[25]

On the 14th, Rupert Becker visited Schumann. He later recalled that Schumann had told him of hearing extremely beautiful music "in the form of complete compositions! The sound to him is as of wind instruments playing in the distance." At a restaurant that evening, Schumann commented that the music had started again: "This is how it must be in another life, when we have shed our mortal coil."[26]

On the evening of the 17th, his condition intensified:

In the night not long after we had gone to bed, Robert got up and wrote down a theme which, he said, angels had sung to him [Joachim wrote that Schumann felt the theme was sent " 'by an angel as a greeting from Mendelssohn and Schubert' "[27]]. When he had finished it, he lay down again and had fantastic visions the entire night, always staring with wide-open eyes at the heavens. He truly believed that angels hovered above him and made amazing revelations to him, all accompanied by wonderful music. They welcomed us, and told us we would be together with them before the year passed. . . . Morning came and with it a terrible change. The angels' voices were transformed into those of demons with monstrous music. They told him that he was a sinner and they wanted to hurl him into hell. His condition worsened until he became frenzied. He screamed in pain (he later told me that hyenas and tigers were attacking him).[28]

---

[25] *Litzmann II*, pp. 295–96.
[26] Excerpts from Becker's diary in *Eismann*, p. 190.
[27] Letter to Woldemar Bargiel of 6 March 1854 in Joachim, *Briefe*, I, p. 171.
[28] *Litzmann II*, p. 297.

The days that followed were similar, a nightmarish time for Schumann, and for Clara—five months pregnant—a time of growing helplessness and despair. Schumann became obsessed with his guilt, claimed he was an "evil person," and spoke "continually about being a criminal and that he should always be reading the Bible."[29] There were occasional periods of comparative calm and lucidity, and over several days, Schumann used the melody sent to him by angels as the basis for a theme and variations for piano. On the 21st, he was again visited by Rupert Becker. "It would never have occurred to me to believe that he was ill," Becker wrote in his diary. "I found him the same as usual."[30]

On Sunday the 26th, Schumann seemed much improved. He wrote a letter to Richard Noel in Amsterdam about the *Rose* that gives no indication of any mental problems. And in the evening he played through a piano sonata sent to him by a young musician, Martin Cohn, eager for his advice. He examined the work "with the greatest interest," but in "a state of such joyful exaltation that perspiration poured down from his brow."[31] Later that night, Schumann "suddenly got up and wanted to have his clothes. He said he had to go to an asylum because he was losing control of himself, and did not know what he might do during the night [. . .] When I said to him: 'Robert, do you want to abandon your wife and children?' he answered, 'It will not be for long. I will soon return cured!' "[32]

During his illness, Schumann was being attended to by a pair of physicians, Dr. Richard Hasenklever (who had arranged the text for the *Luck of Edenhall*) and a Dr. Böger, a physician for the military. Clara sent for Dr. Böger, who managed to convince Schumann to return to bed. The next morning Schumann was "so profoundly melancholy that it can not be described. When I simply touched him, he said, "Ah, Clara, I am not worthy of your love."[33] During the day he made a fair

---

[29] Letter to Emilie List of 15 March 1854 in Clara Schumann, *"Das Band der ewigen Liebe." Briefwechsel mit Emilie und Elise List*, ed. Eugen Wendler (Stuttgart, 1996), p. 179; entry in Clara's diary of 21 February in *Litzmann II*, p. 298.

[30] *Eismann*, pp. 190–91.

[31] Clara's diary entry of 26 February in *Litzmann II*, p. 299.

[32] *Ibid.*

[33] *Ibid.*, p. 300.

copy of the piano variations. Clara consulted with Dr. Hasenklever and asked their daughter Marie, twelve years old, to keep an eye on her father:

> I was supposed to sit in my mother's little room and let them know if my father, who was in his room close by, needed anything. I sat at my mother's desk for a while when the door of the room alongside opened. My father stood there in his long dressing gown with the green flowers on it. His face was extremely pale. As he caught sight of me, he clasped both of his hands in front of his face and said, "Oh, God." And then he disappeared again.[34]

When Marie went into her father's room a short while later, she found it empty. Schumann had left the house, walking toward the Rhine. It was Carnival season at the time, so his unusual attire attracted less attention than it normally would have. He came to a toll bridge over the river and, having no money, offered his handkerchief to the tollkeeper before continuing on his way. When over the river, it appears that Schumann removed his wedding ring and threw it into the water (Clara later found among Schumann's papers a note that read: "Dear Clara, I am throwing my wedding ring into the Rhine. You do the same. Then both rings will be united").[35] Schumann then jumped over the side of the bridge into the river. Two fishermen saw him and went out in their boat to rescue him. When they drew him on board, he is said to have attempted to leap out yet again.

At Schumann's home, his absence had been noted, but all attempts to locate him were unsuccessful. And then about an hour later, he was brought back. "When I went into the street," Marie recalled, "I saw from afar a large and very noisy group of people heading towards me. As I came closer I recognized my father who, supported by two men under his arms, held his hands in front of his face. I was terrified."[36] Schumann's suicide attempt was concealed from Clara. He was kept in isolation at home under observation by his physicians. On the 28th, he

---

[34] Eugenie Schumann, *Ein Lebensbild meines Vaters* (Leipzig, 1931), p. 391.

[35] *Litzmann* II, p. 301. Clara attached no significance to Schumann's message until she later realized that his wedding ring was missing.

[36] Eugenie Schumann, p. 392.

sent to her the fair copy of his piano variations, but was reported at times to be "violently agitated."[37]

To his doctors he invariably said that "they should send him to an asylum, because only there would he recover."[38] It was decided to transfer him to a private asylum of good reputation in Endenich near Bonn. His children were allowed to observe his departure. "We stood upstairs at a window and saw him," Marie remembered. "The carriage was driven into the courtyard so that it could not be noticed from the street. . . . We were told that our father would soon return to us completely cured, but the servant girls standing near us were crying."[39]

---

[37] Diary entry by Clara in *Litzmann II*, p. 302.
[38] *Ibid.*
[39] Eugenie Schumann, p. 392.

CHAPTER 14

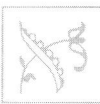

The Compositions, 1845–54

The difference, so far then, between sleeping and waking seems to be, that in the latter we have a greater range of conscious recollections, a larger discourse of reason, and associate ideas in longer trains and more as they are connected one with another in the order of nature; whereas in the former, any two impressions, that meet or are alike, join company, and then are parted again, without notice, like the froth from the wave. So in madness, there is, I should apprehend, the same tyranny of the imagination over the judgment; that is, the mind has slipped its cable, and single images meet, and jostle, and unite suddenly together, without any power to arrange or compare them with others with which they are connected in the world of reality. There is a continual phantasmagoria: whatever shapes and colours come together are by the heat and violence of the brain referred to external nature, without regard to the order of time, place, or circumstance.
—Hazlitt, "On Dreams"

DURING THE FINAL EIGHT YEARS OF SCHUMANN'S CREATIVE life, he produced ninety-three works, nearly two-thirds of his oeuvre. Among them—in addition to *Genoveva, Manfred,* and the *Scenes from Goethe's Faust*—are two symphonies, three piano trios, concertos for piano, violin, and cello, three violin sonatas, an oratorio, and three concert overtures, as well as numerous songs, choral compositions, and pieces for piano. In the eyes of Schumann and many of his contemporaries, included in the number are a substantial portion of his most popular and most significant compositions. Yet, no works by Schumann have generated more controversy than these. To many, if Schumann had died in 1844, his stature as a composer would have been greater, and his contributions more broadly acknowledged.

Criticism of Schumann's work created during the latter years of his life gained momentum after his death. Invariably, the basis for it was his mental collapse and confinement in Endenich. It was felt that because Schumann was insane, no doubt his mental deterioration had affected his compositions. The music was perceived as uninspired, illogical, at times incomprehensible—to use Hazlitt's expression, "a continual phantasmagoria." The opinion expressed by Felix Clément in his popular text, *Les musiciens célèbres* (1887) was typical: "The 'Rhenish' Symphony [the Third], the overtures of *Julius Caesar, Hermann and Dorothea*, and *The Bride of Messina*, the choral ballads: *The King's Son, The Minstrel's Curse*, etc.—all were clearly conceived and created under the influence of his diseased mind."[1] Those who wrote about Schumann in the decades after his death agreed that there was a clear decline in his creative powers. Wasielewski shared this view. Another early biographer, August Reissmann, in 1865 described Schumann's later compositions as "formless and chaotic," traits that he attributed to Schumann's illness.[2] Reissmann went so far as to trace this supposed decline in Schumann's powers as far back as his Four Marches op. 76 (composed in June 1849).

It is curious that a similar critical approach did not find a broad following with other nineteenth-century composers who were mentally ill—Hugo Wolf, for instance. Nor can comparable examples be found among artists (Carl Blechen, Alfred Rethel) or writers (such as Hölderlin or Lenau)—to limit oneself roughly to Schumann's German contemporaries. Schumann's case was special, and probably was due both to the change in musical style adopted by him around 1845, and to the rather fearful and apprehensive attitude assumed by his wife and close

---

[1] Felix Clément, *Les musiciens célèbres* (Paris, 1887), p. 545.
[2] August Reissmann, *Robert Schumann: Sein Leben und seine Werke* (Berlin, 1865), p. 174.

friends. Rather than attempting to combat the often harsh criticism directed toward Schumann's later works, they seemed to share it.

To a considerable extent, these views persisted well into the twentieth century. Writing in 1928, Henry MacMaster concluded: "Between 1850 and 1853 only a single work—the D minor Violin Sonata [op. 121]—is worthy of mention. . . . The remaining works consist of nothing more than automatism."[3] Frederick Niecks, in his biography of Schumann written at about the same time, emphasized that the deterioration in Schumann's creative powers was by no means limited to the last few years of his life, but began during his residence in Dresden: "It has to be admitted that his creative powers were already on the wane—the occasional successes cannot blind us to the frequent dimnesses."[4] Ronald Taylor's 1982 biography of Schumann continues to make note of the "uneven" quality of the late works: "so little of it is truly original and memorable."[5]

The unacknowledged basis for much of this criticism is a deep-seated misunderstanding of and aversion to mental illness, an approach characteristic of the nineteenth century. But as the twentieth century drew to a close, there was an attempt to reevaluate the compositions of Schumann's final years, and to view them in a less biased and more objective manner. No longer is it possible to accept unquestioningly those evaluations of Schumann that seemed only too eager to dismiss a substantial portion of his work.

The Dresden Compositions

To a certain extent, the music Schumann created after 1844 seems different because starting in 1845 he composed in a different manner. After his marriage, he had turned away from literary models (specifically Jean Paul) as a source of inspiration, and developed instead a more faithful representation from musical models (notably the compositions of Haydn, Mozart, and Beethoven)—composers who were a part of a distinguished and recognizable musical tradition. As a result, his compositions became more traditional in basis and more comprehensible to

---

[3] Henry MacMaster, *La folie de Robert Schumann* (Paris, 1928), p. 46.
[4] Frederick Niecks, *Robert Schumann* (London, 1925), p. 4.
[5] Ronald Taylor, *Robert Schumann: His Life and Work* (New York, 1982), p. 275.

many. In 1845, Schumann rejected the piano as a tool for composition. He began instead to compose without use of it (or any other musical instrument), as he put it, "inventing and working out everything in my head."[6] This naturally led to a more intellectual and more reflective approach. It was a means of overcoming what Schumann perceived as an unwonted dependency. By relying on the piano for the expression of musical ideas, he felt he was placing an obstacle between himself and his musical nature (inspiration). He later advised composers to act in a similar manner and to do away with working at the piano. "The most important thing," he wrote, "is for the musician to purify his inner ear" (10 May 1852).

The first works to exhibit this new approach were a series of essentially contrapuntal compositions: the Four Fugues op. 72, the Studies for Pedal Piano op. 56, the Sketches for Pedal Piano op. 58, and the Six Fugues on the Name, "Bach" op. 60. In 1845, Schumann was still recovering from his nervous breakdown of the previous year. Most of the first half of the year was devoted to the composition of these contrapuntal works, with a return in September and November to the "Bach" fugues. Immersion in counterpoint had become a standard means for Schumann to achieve equilibrium and to begin once again to write music. It also was an ideal way to begin composing away from the piano; contrapuntal complexity demanded a more cerebral approach, one better achieved away from the keyboard.

It is appropriate that Schumann's homage to Bach was written for the instrument most readily associated with Bach: the organ. Schumann worked on the Six Fugues with dedication. "This is a composition," he wrote, "on which I have labored for an entire year in order to make it worthy of the distinguished name it bears" (15 March 1846). The challenge was to create six compositions, each based on the same four notes, yet to retain a measure of variety. The subject itself is chromatic in nature, and resulted in some of the most sustained, chromatic music he had yet composed (Ex. 14.1, 14.2). Schumann later described the Four Fugues op. 72—whose models are those of Bach's *Well-Tempered Clavier*—as "character pieces, only in strict form" (19 November 1849). Much the same could be said of the "Bach" fugues. While writing

---

[6] Entry of 1846 in *Tgb II*, p. 402.

Ex. 14.1

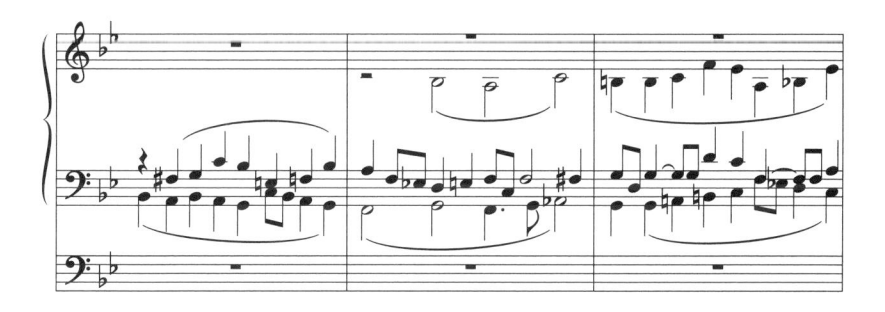

Fuga I

Langsam

them, Schumann rented a pedal piano—a piano fitted with pedals for the feet like an organ—in order to become familiar with the technique involved. He became fascinated by the instrument, and produced the Studies op. 56 and Sketches op. 58 for it. The four Sketches are primarily studies in homophonic texture, but the six Studies are all canonic

Ex. 14.2

Fuga II

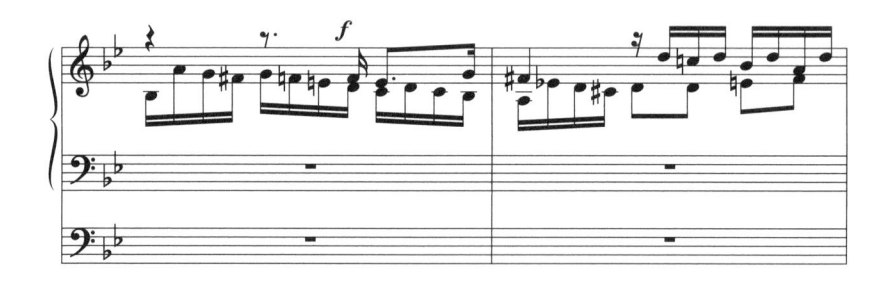

Lebhaft

in basis. These Studies, however, bear their contrapuntal essence lightly. "The best fugue," Schumann had written in a review of Mendelssohn's *Preludes and Fugues* op. 35, "is always that which the public takes for a Strauss waltz"—that is, one easy to listen to and in which artifice is subdued.[7] With op. 56, the listener is so captivated by the melodic charm that the canonic inventiveness becomes almost imperceptible. Pleased with his efforts, Schumann sent a copy of the Studies to Dorn. "Perhaps," he wrote, "you will find them to be not entirely unworthy of your earlier instruction" (7 January 1846).

After months of contrapuntal interests, in the summer of 1845 Schumann returned to the piano concerto whose single movement he had completed in 1841. Attempts to sell it as a fantasie for piano and orchestra had been unsuccessful. From 21 June to 12 July, Schumann composed a finale for it. Later that month, he revised the first movement, and completed the second movement (finding it a particular challenge to create a smooth transition from the second to the third movement). It was first performed in Dresden on 4 December 1845 to laudatory reviews, and soon became one of his most popular works.

While working on the abortive Piano Concerto in D minor in Vienna in 1839, Schumann had confessed to Clara that he was incapable of writing a concerto in the style of a virtuoso. The same holds true of the Piano Concerto op. 54; it exhibits none of the flamboyant and showy traits characteristic of the concertos of, for example, Liszt or Henselt. Except for some clearly improvisatory elements in the development section and the cadenza, there is little remaining in the first movement that would bring to mind a fantasie. At first glance, there seems to be a profusion of melodic ideas present (a major reason for its charm). But this variety is deceptive. Much of the thematic material is based on the opening theme (particularly the outline of a descending minor or major third). This theme appears in various guises in all three movements, and serves as the basis of the transition to the finale. Given Schumann's contrapuntal studies in the first half of the year, his interest in making the most of his thematic material is not surprising.

The most substantial composition created by Schumann during his recovery to health was the Second Symphony op. 61. The idea for it

---

[7] Review of 1837 in *GS I*, p. 253.

first came to him that autumn; he wrote to Mendelssohn on 20 September 1845 that for several days he had been hearing drums and trumpets in C major ("I do not know what will come of it")—a reference to what would become the opening motive of the symphony. On 28 December, Schumann wrote that he was "completely finished" with the symphony, but the project would occupy him intermittently until October 1846.[8] Orchestration commenced in February and April, followed by a more concentrated effort in September and October, the entire work being completed on the 19th.

As Schumann so readily admitted, much of his music reflected events in his life (or, more accurately, his reaction to them). The Second Symphony was intended to portray his depression and return to health. It was begun when he was still ill—an aspect that he felt the sensitive listener would hear in the first movement. To Wasielewski, he spoke of the "struggle" depicted in the first movement and of its "very moody and unruly" character.[9] But it was Schumann's intention to represent in the broadest possible sense struggle and conflict, culminating in the finale with triumph. The Symphony was performed at the Gewandhaus on 5 November 1846, and the score published the following year. It was well received. His general programmatic intentions were perceived, critics noting similarities in mood with Beethoven's Fifth Symphony and Mozart's Symphony No. 40. But, in time, critical reaction turned against it. Its attempt at thematic unity has been described as simplistic and the distinctive structure of the finale has been misunderstood. Once again, the basis for this misperception has been an attempt to interpret Schumann by means of the classical style, an approach (as with the piano compositions of the 1830s) of little value.

The Second Symphony consists of four movements, with the typical order of the second and third movements reversed: Sostenuto assai/ Allegro ma non troppo; Allegro vivace (the Scherzo); Adagio espressivo; Allegro molto vivace. The work begins with a distinctive motive for brass that is restated near the conclusion of the second movement and—most dramatically—the fourth movement. It is by the use of this motto

[8] *HSHLT*, p. 410.
[9] *W*, p. 366.

that Schumann openly unifies the movements of the symphony (Ex. 14.3). But, as contemporary critics noted, there is more to the thematic unity of the symphony than the motto. At the initial appearance of the motto, it is accompanied in the strings by a distinctive quarter-note passage that begins with a chromatic descent and then outlines the C major triad (Ex. 14.4). Both the motto and its accompaniment serve as a "motivic embryo," and much of the thematic material from the remainder of the Symphony can be seen as being derived from it.[10]

The following movement, the Scherzo, contains two trios. The second bears witness to Schumann's continued interest in counterpoint, and the lingering influence of the "Bach" Fugues. B-A-C-H appears as a theme in it, as a tribute to the composer to whom Schumann credited, at least in part, his recovery. The influence of Bach continues in the Adagio, with a stark fugato section. Near the beginning of the movement, there is a duet for oboe and bassoon. Schumann responded warmly to a friend's fondness for this passage, and noted his own partiality for the "melancholy bassoon" (2 April 1849).

It is the structure of the finale of the symphony that has generated the most criticism. Schumann was convinced that it was essential for a finale to reflect the nature of the work as a whole. Yet, the primary theme for

Ex. 14.3

[10] Anthony Newcomb, "'Once More Between Absolute and Program Music'": Schumann's Second Symphony," *Nineteenth-Century Music* VII (1983–84), p. 242.

Ex. 14.4

Ex. 14.5

Allegro molto vivace

this finale (Ex. 14.5) lacks the vigor and gravity of the preceding movements ("its coarse, rustic character" has been noted).[11] The finale gives the impression that the movement will be a rondo, and that this italianate melody will serve as its basis. But with more than half of the movement concluded, it is discarded and another takes its place: the theme from Beethoven's *An die ferne Geliebte* (Ex. 14.6). It would seem, then, that the initial theme for the finale was chosen by Schumann both to cozen the listener, and to produce a startling and dramatic contrast for the conclusion of the symphony.

The use of the *An die ferne Geliebte* theme by Schumann directly associated the symphony in his eyes with Clara. To those unfamiliar with the origin of the tune, it simply served to create an effective finale, one in strong contrast to the "dark time" represented in the opening movement. But identification of the theme—including its appearance in the Fantasie and *Frauenliebe und Leben*—connects the work to Clara. So does the key, C major, selected by Schumann for all four movements of the symphony. If, as he intended, the finale represented recovery, then he seemed to be crediting Clara with a major role in it. In the broadest sense, the Second Symphony provided Schumann with the opportunity of paying tribute to the nurturing role of women, and he continued the tribute in the work composed immediately after completion of the symphony. Schumann returned to the *Scenes from Goethe's Faust*. And he began by setting the celebrated "Chorus mysticus," with its concluding line: "Das ewig weibliche zieht uns hinan" ("Eternal womanhood leads us upward").

Was Clara aware of the theme and its association with her? In her Second Scherzo op. 14 (published in 1845), she quotes the theme (emphasizing its presence by abrupt change in register and dynamics) as if acknowledging the bond between herself and her husband (Ex. 14.7).

[11] *Ibid.* p. 244.

Ex. 14.6

Ex. 14.7

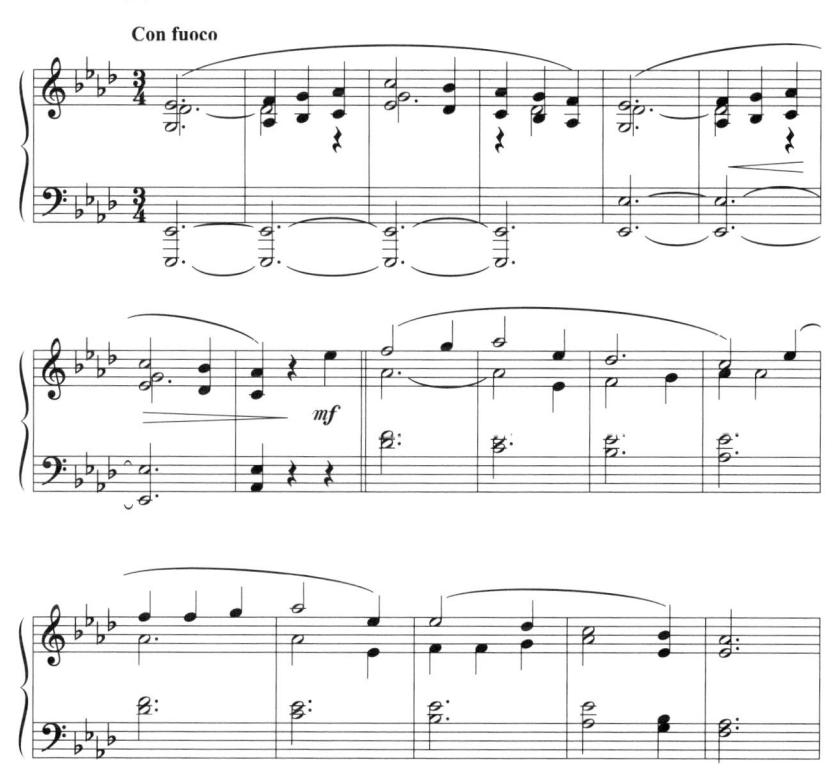

Schumann viewed the creation of the Second Symphony as providing him with a beneficial catharsis. After its completion, he resumed composition with renewed vigor. He returned to chamber music, with two piano trios, published in 1848 and 1849 as his op. 63 and op. 80. They are in their way counterparts to the first and second symphonies. The Second Piano Trio resembles the First Symphony, bright in mood and buoyant. Schumann characterized this trio as being "friendlier" than the first (1 May 1849). The first movement quotes the melodic opening from "Intermezzo"—the second song from Schumann's *Liederkreis* op. 39. The text—"Dein Bildnis wunderselig" ("Your blessed image") could be another reference to Clara and her role in his recovery. The First Piano Trio op. 63 mirrors the mood of the Second Symphony. It too relates a program of struggle and melancholy to triumph. The first movement ("Mit Energie und Leidenschaft") sets the stage. As in the symphony, the third movement is the slow movement. It contains a duet between violin and cello that is a counterpart to the duet between oboe and bassoon in the symphony, and flows without pause into the finale, one of heroic character.

Much of the following year, 1848, was devoted to the composition of *Genoveva*, resulting in a decline in income. As a result, Schumann turned with determination to the creation of numerous works intended for performance at home and with amateur ensembles. Of these, the *Album for the Young* op. 68 was the most successful, becoming his most popular work and providing momentum for much of his output over the next two years. The *Album* consists of forty-three piano pieces for children. Schumann had high hopes for the work after completing it in September 1848, but could not have anticipated the immense popularity it would enjoy. He had created the work for his own children, only too aware of the need for simple music of superior quality for children to study.

Most of the music composed over the next few years was similarly utilitarian in nature. It covered a broad range of genres: music for children, such as the *Song Album for the Young* op. 79; a cappella choral compositions (the *Romanzen und Balladen* op. 67 and op. 75); vocal duets (for soprano and tenor op. 78); four-hand piano compositions (*Bilder aus dem Osten* op. 66; and miscellaneous chamber works at times comparatively modest in technique for instruments generally neglected in the repertory, such as the *Fantasiestücke* (for clarinet, or violin, or cello, and piano) op. 73, the *Drei Romanzen* (for oboe, or violin, or clarinet, and piano) op. 94, and the charming *Fünf Stücke im Volkston* op. 102 (for cello, or violin, and piano). With the exception of op. 66 (which was composed in 1848), all the other works are from what Schumann referred to as his "most fruitful year": 1849.

Composing mixed choral music seemed a priority, not surprisingly given his duties as a choral conductor while in Dresden. Schumann had first entered the field in 1846 with two a cappella compositions (*Fünf Lieder von Robert Burns* op. 55 and *Vier Gesänge* op. 59). But he was not content to create choral pieces in the usual format. The *Spanisches Liederspiel* op. 74 (1849), based on texts by Geibel, contains, in addition to choral settings, several for solo voice and pairs of voices, with duet piano accompaniment. In creating it, Schumann was convinced he had assembled a distinctly original work, and one that would have broad appeal. A similar approach was followed in the *Minnespiel* op. 101 (1849; based on texts from Rückert's *Liebesfrühling*), and *Spanische Liebeslieder* op. 138 (1849; also using poems by Geibel). The *Jagdlieder* op. 137 (1849; texts by Heinrich Laube) for male chorus with accompaniment ad libitum for four French horns draw more on Schubert and the male choral tradition.

The uprisings in Europe during these years found expression as well in Schumann's music. The *Drei Gesänge* for men's chorus op. 62 (1847) are patriotic in nature. And the revolution in Dresden and its aftermath inspired the Four Marches op. 76 for solo piano. Schumann was pleased with them—he referred to them as "republican" in nature (17 June 1849)—and Whistling hurriedly published them with an eye-catching cover.

Much of the music Schumann composed during these years remains little known. To a great extent, it has been dismissed as academic, stiff, conservative, or uninspired. Schumann would have perceived a substantial amount of the music created during the latter 1840s as being primarily pragmatic—intended to be pleasurable to listen to and pleasurable to perform. In those goals it often admirably succeeds. The emphasis is on a lyrical simplicity. As Schumann frequently mentioned to prospective publishers, much of it is fairly easy to perform. And there is often a clear attempt to amuse, as in the humorous setting "Zahnweh" ("Toothache") in op. 55 or the droll "Lager-Scene" in op. 76. He never intended these compositions to be those on which his reputation as a composer would be based, but rather as an adjunct to his other work and as a much-needed means to earn additional income. But while the bulk of the music he created in the late 1840s may have been Hausmusik, there was still time devoted to compositions of greater scope. *Manfred* and portions of the *Scenes from Goethe's Faust* were composed in 1848–9. And, in 1849, he set to music a large-scale choral work with orchestral accompaniment: Hebbel's *Nachtlied*. The *Nachtlied* op. 108 has a kinship with *Manfred*, and, like it, deserves to be better known. It is somber and reflective, with dark, distinctive use of the orchestra.

That same year, Schumann completed two concertos: the Concerto for Four Horns op. 86 and the Introduction and Allegro op. 92. The

Concerto for Four Horns is an unusual work that draws not on the concerto grosso (as the title might imply) but on the concertante concept. Schumann seemed to take pride in what he described as its "curious" nature (27 February 1849), a reference not to the multiple solo instruments of the concerto but to the fact that four horns were used. In fact, distinctive combinations of instruments in a concerto were not all that unusual for the time: there are concertos for two and four violins, two horns—even one, by Rietz, for wind quintet. The Introduction and Allegro op. 92 is a single-movement piano concerto, linked thematically (the theme from the introduction reappears in the development and coda of the Allegro). Its length (only about fifteen minutes) has made it difficult to schedule in standard orchestral concerts, and it remains little known. But it is a worthy, although somewhat stolid, companion to the Piano Concerto op. 54.

The Düsseldorf Compositions

After the sale of the *Zeitschrift* in 1845, although Schumann no longer wrote about music, his reputation as critic became enhanced by his growing fame as a composer. He continued actively to examine new music, and frequently was sent compositions by young composers, eager for his advice and hopeful of his support. His reaction to a set of compositions sent to him in August 1848 by Carl Wettig reveals a great deal—both about Schumann's musical ideals and about his own compositions. In general, his response to the numerous (and usually unsolicited) compositions sent to him was generous. He always seemed to have in mind the kind letter he had received in 1828 from Gottlob Wiedebein, and was eager to be encouraging. But Schumann's reaction to Wettig's compositions was exceptional. Wettig, who was only twenty-one, quickly received a letter from Schumann, which praised the "clarity and beauty" of Wettig's work. "It was such a great joy," Schumann wrote, "to discover at one time what I so long have looked for in vain"(5 August 1848). Schumann did have reservations. Some piano pieces sent by Wettig Schumann compared favorably to Mendelssohn's *Songs without Words*, but, he told him, "for all that, I believe we must come up with something else, something new" (27 November 1848).

Schumann's attraction to Wettig's compositions is not hard to discover. His music is dynamic, and quite distinctive (and deserves to be better known). But the basis for Schumann's interest becomes clearer when placed in perspective. At about the same time as his discovery of Wettig, Schumann was sent—via a mutual friend (Gustav Nottebohm)—the Piano Sonata op. 3 by Johann Rufinatscha. Rufinatscha was Austrian, two years younger than Schumann, and a student of the distinguished theorist Simon Sechter. Schumann was appalled by what he found in the work. "Can it be that you actually like such music?" Schumann wrote to Nottebohm. "I do not. It seems completely foolish to me" (4 December 1847). What Schumann found "foolish" in the sonata was its conservative style. Here was a composer so beholden to tradition that all individuality was stifled. Everything about the work seems predictable, including the textbook sonata structures and square melodic lines.[12]

Rufinatscha's sonata provides an exemplary instance of the academic "classicism" that Schumann deplored, and that he has been accused of adopting. Wettig's music, on the other hand, used tradition as a point of departure—an approach Schumann had adopted during much of his career. It was the progressive nature of Wettig's compositions—as well as their "clarity and beauty"—that appealed to Schumann. As he approached his fortieth year, he continued to advocate change in music—as he had put it to Wettig, "something else, something new"—an approach reflected in his own compositions during the last years of his life.

In his lieder, Schumann increasingly adopted the more declamatory vocal style used in larger-scale works such as *Genoveva*. The songs of op. 89 (1850) and op. 107 (1851–52) are notable instances. They emphasize, too, the transition the lied was making from the home to the concert hall. But Schumann did not disdain more tuneful, popular elements. The Six Songs of op. 90 (on poetry of Lenau) begin with a folklike "Blacksmith's Song," with the piano imitating the syncopated rhythmic clang of the blacksmith's hammer. The fifth song of the set ("Loneliness") and the second ("My Rose") require greater sensitivity from both singer and pianist. There is a wonderful interplay between piano and voice recalling that found in the lieder from 1840, but no

---

[12] In later years, Rufinatscha wrote music more original in style. His *Grand Caprice* op. 5 was dedicated to Schumann, and was favorably reviewed in 1851 in the *Zeitschrift*.

Ex. 14.8

Langsam, mit innigem Ausdruck (♪ = 108)

Mit Pedal

Dem hol- den Lenz- ge-schmei-de, der Ro-se, mei-ner Freu-de, die schon ge-beugt und blas-ser vom hei- ssen Strahl der Son-nen,

longer is there a reliance on more conventional melodic patterns or on symmetrical four-bar phrasing (Ex. 14.8). Schumann felt that a number of the compositions he was now creating—those that he described as "the best and deepest"—a substantial proportion of the public would be unable to comprehend at "first hearing" (17 December 1851). Although he still composed works that he felt would be more readily accessible—such as the *Vier Husarenlieder* op. 117 (to texts by Lenau; 1851), the *Fantasiestücke* op. 111 (for solo piano; 1851), and the charming *Ballszenen* op. 109 (for piano, four-hands; 1851)—he felt it was essential to create works challenging both to himself and to his audience.

The idea of creating "something new" led to exploration and creation of other musical genres, as well as different approaches to the genres he had already attempted. In 1849, while still in Dresden, Schumann set to music Hebbel's ballad, "Schön Hedwig," but did so in a manner that he believed to be completely original. His idea—setting a poem not as a song but as a recitation with piano accompaniment—had first occurred to him four years earlier. It was a form of melodrama, a device he used so effectively with orchestral accompaniment in *Manfred*. But what Schumann did not realize was that the idea of adapting it for piano was not original; other nineteenth-century composers, including Schubert, had used it. Schumann was enthusiastic, noting that the work could even be performed without recitation as a solo piano piece. Hebbel's ballad was published as his op. 106, and Schumann wrote two additional pieces in similar format (on texts by Hebbel and Shelley), the *Zwei Balladen* op. 122. These are exceptionally dramatic settings, and it is not difficult to imagine the thrills they produced in the parlor or music room.

In contrast to Schumann's declamatory pieces are his efforts in another genre, one that truly was new and original. He composed several chamber works inspired by the "Märchen" (the German fairy-tale, often intended for adults): the *Märchenbilder* op. 113 (1851) and the *Märchenerzählungen* op. 132 (1853). The titles for these two works are usually translated as "Pictures from Fairy-Tale Land" and "Fairy-Tales" respectively, but the translations do not capture the essence of Schumann's intentions. While some reference to the simple fairy-tales ("Volksmärchen") of, for example, Andersen or the Grimm brothers may be intended, there is also an association with the more complex and elaborate conceptions ("Kunstmärchen") of Hoffmann, Tieck, and others. Schumann made no claims, as in the case of the declamatory pieces, for having created a new type of musical composition, but he could have.

Other compositions by Schumann from these final years were more traditional in genre. The Third Symphony was completed in November and December 1850, and first performed on 6 February of the following year to acclaim. What seemed to contribute to its success was its tunefulness and genial nature. It has received the nickname "The Rhenish," but the title was not Schumann's. The general programmatic associations of the work appear justified. At its premiere, the concert program included the title "Intermezzo" for the third movement and "In the Character of the Accompaniment to a Solemn Ceremony" for the fourth movement—an annotation also present on the autograph but one that was not included in the score when published in 1851. The "Solemn Ceremony" has long been thought to refer to one that Schumann witnessed in Cologne on 11 December 1850: the elevation of an archbishop to a cardinal. But although he probably read accounts of the ceremony in local papers (and admired the Cologne cathedral), the household books reveal that he was not in Cologne at the time.

Although its supposed program may be open to conjecture, Schumann's intentions with the symphony are not. As he told Wasielewski, he wanted "popular elements" to predominate.[13] On the surface, the most unconventional aspect of the Third Symphony is its number of movements: five, arranged in the order "Lebhaft," "Scherzo" ("Sehr mässig"), "Nicht schnell," "Feierlich," and "Lebhaft." But as Schumann hastened to assure his publisher, the additional movement did not make the symphony bulky. In fact, both the third and fourth movements are fairly short—in effect, creating one large "slow" movement. They provide variety and contrast that seemed to be welcomed by contemporary audiences. The "popular elements" alluded to by Schumann refer to the tunefulness of much of the work. There is a folklike character present, seen as well in the ländlerlike scherzo.

Not surprising is the thematic unity among the movements, characterized by themes that emphasize a descending and ascending fourth. Less noticeable is the unusual structure of the melodies themselves. There are folklike tunes, such as that for the scherzo, in symmetrical four-bar phrases. But others reveal much ingenuity in their construction. The symphony opens with a melody seventeen measures long. The syncopation of the first six measures creates a disruptive effect, and

[13] *W*, p. 456.

sets these measures off from the remaining eleven, arranged in units of three and four. The contrasting theme of the movement is actually based upon two seven-measure sections with a pair of additional repetitive measures added to give the impression of symmetrical eight-bar phrases.

The fourth movement—that associated with the "solemn ceremony"—is the most distinctive. It is a ricercare, in which Schumann employs a brief two-measure motive, and, as counterpoint to it, the motive in diminution. It is an unsettling piece of music, somber and deliberate. This movement, incidentally, was one that Clara confessed she had considerable difficulty understanding. Its archaic style must have perplexed not a few. But the confusion was likely outweighed by its grandeur and the power of the orchestration, in which the brass have a preponderant role.

Late in the autumn of 1851, Schumann was approached by friends and family of Norbert Burgmüller (a Düsseldorf native). At his death, Burgmüller left unfinished the final two movements of his Second Symphony, and Schumann was asked to complete it for publication. He declined to finish the finale, for which only some sketches survived. But for the scherzo it was primarily a matter of orchestration, and he completed it on 2 December. It was an unusual gesture on Schumann's part, and an indication of the esteem in which he held Burgmüller's work. It can be no coincidence that ten days later he began work on the "reinstrumentation" of his own symphony, the symphony that he had completed in 1841 and that had been performed along with the *Overture, Scherzo, and Finale* to little acclaim that December.

It was this revised symphony that Schumann was to publish as his fourth (first performed on 3 March 1853). He spent a week on it. Much of his efforts reorchestrating it were devoted to making the thematic material more recognizable—that is, his goal was increased clarity. But he did not limit himself to instrumentation: he altered the transition from the introduction to the Allegro of the first movement, and in the third movement he deleted a brass fanfare opening and changed the transition to the finale. Not everyone felt that the symphony had been necessarily improved by his changes. Brahms was fond of the first version, and promoted it in the 1880s. But although there are attractive elements in Schumann's initial version—including a guitar (not notated) to accompany pizzicato strings in the Romanze—the revision has its strengths. As Schumann intended, greater lucidity resulted from the instrumentation. And the transitions altered by him now appear more refined.

Perhaps the most revealing change made by Schumann occurred in the transition to the finale, where he restated the theme from the Allegro of the first movement. It was intended to emphasize both the thematic unity in the symphony and the unusual structure of it. Schumann's Fourth Symphony is not a symphony in the traditional sense; at first he wanted to refer to it as a "Symphonic Fantasy."[14] The four movements are to be performed with brief pauses between them. Overall, the symphony attempts to create the effect of a single-movement work in a broad, generalized sonata form. There is no recapitulation in the first movement—a new theme is introduced in its stead. Rather, the finale of the symphony serves as a varied recapitulation for the entire work. Themes within the symphony (outlining a minor third and minor second) are clearly related (Ex. 14.9).

Ex. 14.9

Introduction to Movement I

[14] *HSHLT*, pp. 580, 795.

Ex. 14.9 continued

Movement I

Finale

Because of its structure, in many ways the fourth is the most difficult of Schumann's symphonies to comprehend. That it was not understood in 1841 is not surprising. The idea of having each of the movements proceed with little pause from one to another was not new: Mendelssohn followed a similar approach in his symphonic cantata *Lobgesang* "Hymn of Praise" op. 52 (1840), and Schumann had noted this innovation in his review of the work. What was new was the idea of creating a symphony that in effect was a single movement, with all sections united by similar thematic material. Liszt later pursued a similar technique in his tone poems, and in his Piano Sonata—a work that was dedicated to Schumann.

In addition to the two symphonies, Schumann composed three concert overtures during the years in Düsseldorf, each inspired by a literary work: Schiller's *Bride of Messina* op. 100, Shakespeare's *Julius Caesar* op. 128, and Goethe's *Hermann and Dorothea* op. 136. All were composed in 1851. The overtures seemed to answer Schumann's need to compose dramatic music, if not as opera, then as orchestral compositions imbued with the spirit of the stage. Schiller's drama provided him with yet another tale of incest. Schumann described his overture for it as not so much a concert but a "theater overture" easily comprehensible in a single hearing (17 December 1852). The *Hermann and Dorothea* Overture was the sole result of Schumann's interest in composing an opera based on Goethe's idyllic love poem. Schumann was particularly fond of the poem. In 1845, he noted that he had read it "at least 10 times."[15] In 1851 he briefly considered arranging it as a Singspiel (an idea that had also occurred to him five years earlier) and then as an oratorio.

None of these three overtures is particularly successful. They are conventional and filled with bombast. *Hermann and Dorothea* relies heavily on the "Marseillaise" (a reference to the role of French revolutionary forces in Goethe's drama) and is Schumann's most Meyerbeerian work. His obvious intention was to court public favor, and the model was Beethoven, particularly the overtures to *Coriolanus* and *Egmont*. But at times the overtures seem to owe more to Beethoven's symphonic spectacle, *Wellington's Victory, or The Battle of Vittoria*.

---

[15] Gerd Nauhaus, "Schumanns 'Lektürebüchlein'," in *Robert Schumann und die Dichter: Ein Musiker als Leser*, ed. Joseph A. Kruse (Düsseldorf, 1991), p. 59.

During the first years of Schumann's residence in Düsseldorf, he composed a substantial amount of chamber music, including another piano trio (October 1851), and two violin sonatas (the first, op. 105, in September and the second, op. 121, two months later). The Third Piano Trio op. 110 echoes the program for the First Piano Trio: struggle to triumph. But it is unusually melancholy in mood, an aspect of which Schumann was aware and which he attempted to lighten in the finale. That same melancholy permeates the First Violin Sonata but in this instance without a triumphant finale. The initial theme from the first movement returns in the finale (still in minor mode), as if to emphasize the continuing gloom. The works were created during a time of growing disillusionment with life in Düsseldorf.

These chamber works confirm the new direction in Schumann's music. There is more use of asymmetrical melodies, and shorter melodic lines emphasizing distinctive motives. Within individual movements—the opening movements of op. 110 and op. 105 are good examples—Schumann is often monothematic. Motivic development becomes a dominant structural principle. At its most successful, Schumann's music appears more compact and terse. This approach served as an ideal means of avoiding what he felt was the excessive pathos in the music of many of his contemporaries. "Here and there I was struck by a considerable amount of sentimentality in your compositions," he wrote to one colleague. "Don't let it get the upper hand! Bach and Beethoven are good antidotes for it" (10 April 1848). Contemporary critics took note of the change in Schumann's music, but frequently unfavorably. A review of the *Requiem für Mignon* and accompanying lieder from Goethe's *Wilhelm Meister's Apprenticeship* pointed out their "new manner" and described the style as "original, but all in all unpleasant."[16]

Schumann composed little in 1852. For much of the time he was ill and depressed. The two choral ballads, *The Minstrel's Curse* op. 139 and *The Princess and the Page* op. 140, were composed in January and June/July, respectively. The only other substantial compositions from the year were the Mass op. 147 (February and March) and the Requiem op.

---

[16] Review of 1851 quoted in Friedhelm Krummacher, "Requiem für Mignon: Goethes Worte in Schumanns Musik," in Klaus Hortschansky and Konstanze Musketa, eds., *Georg Friedrich Händel—Ein Lebensinhalt: Gedenkschrift für Bernd Baselt (1934–1993)* (Halle, 1995), p. 271.

148 (April and May). In the previous year, Schumann had advised a young composer that the creation of religious music was the "highest goal of the artist" (13 January 1851). Yet, he was not religious in a conventional manner (regular attendance at church, for example). References to church and religious matters are uncommon in his correspondence and diaries.

At the time of Schumann's move to Düsseldorf, he had only composed two pieces that might be construed as church music. The *Adventlied* op. 71 (for soprano, chorus, and orchestra, to a text by Rückert) had been written in 1848. Schumann did not like the title, however, which he considered too seasonal, and privately referred to it as a "church piece."[17] The motet *Verzweifle nicht* op. 93 (1849; for double male chorus and organ ad libitum, also to a text by Rückert) would be a work suitable for performance in church. But the Mass and Requiem were the only compositions created by Schumann with a liturgical basis. He may have been inspired by his duties as a conductor of church music in Düsseldorf, but that he would now direct his attention to religious music seems a confirmation of his reflective and at times gloomy state of mind. "[A requiem] is written for oneself," he told Wasielewski.[18] It all seemed to be part of Schumann's growing conviction that he was nearing the end of his career. The Mass is an austere work. There are inspired moments—such as the passage for soprano and cello accompanied by muted strings in the Offertorium—but the work suffers from little variety in texture and melody. The Requiem, an elegiac work of calm resignation, is less static with more contrast. Both works were published posthumously.

Schumann's ill health continued sporadically during the first half of 1853, and he showed little interest in writing music. Instead, he studied Bach's partitas and sonatas for solo violin and the suites for solo cello, and prepared piano accompaniments for them. This was not as unusual a venture as it might seem today; similar revisions had been attempted by several composers, including Mendelssohn, all in an attempt to adapt Bach to nineteenth-century taste. As a result of his work on Bach, in April Schumann started writing contrapuntal pieces of his own: the

[17] *W*, p. 405.
[18] *Ibid.* p. 404.

Seven Piano Pieces in the Form of Fughettas op. 126. As he confessed to the publisher Arnold, these were "mostly of a melancholy character."[19] The contrapuntal exercise seemed to have its usual stimulating effect. In August, he returned to compositions of greater dimensions, beginning with the *Faust* Overture.

After completing the overture, Schumann turned his attention to a single-movement concerto for piano, a work that he described in the household books as a "Phantasiestück."[20] Published in 1855 as the *Konzert-Allegro mit Introduction* op. 134, the "Phantasiestück" reaffirms Schumann's interest in writing a single-movement concerto for piano. As had been the case with the Introduction op. 92 (and initially with the Piano Concerto op. 54), he seemed intrigued with the concept of one movement embodying in principle the effect of a three-movement concerto. As the title implies, the Concert-Allegro is more virtuoso in nature, an aspect that was probably gratifying to Clara, to whom the work was given as a birthday gift.

In the autumn of 1853, Schumann wrote two additional concertos, both for violin. These were his final large-scale compositions and resulted from his friendship with Joachim. The Violin Fantasy op. 131 was composed in September 1853. Schumann had in 1850 written a cello concerto (op. 129) for the Frankfurt cellist Robert Bockmühl—a work that, after decades of neglect, has become a vital part of the repertory. Schumann was enthused by the possibilities of writing a similar piece for the violin, but was somewhat anxious about the results, and he shared the initial version with Joachim, asking him to point out anything that did not seem "practical" (14 September 1853). To Kistner, he described the Fantasy as "brilliant," and "very cheerful in character" (17 November 1853)—terms nearly identical to those that he had used in reference to the Cello Concerto.

At about that time, Schumann prepared a version for violin of the Cello Concerto for Joachim. Then, in the opening days of October— during the initial visit of Brahms—he completed a violin concerto in

[19] Letter of 24 February 1853 in Wolfgang Boetticher, "Robert Schumann und seine Verleger," in *Musik und Verlag: Karl Vötterle zum 65. Geburtstag*, ed. R. Baum and W. Rehm (Kassel, 1968), p. 174.
[20] Entry of 23 August 1853 in *HSHLT*, p. 633.

three movements. To Joachim, Schumann described the work as "lighter" in nature than the Fantasy—that is, not as showy—and with an increased role for the orchestra (13 October 1853). Joachim tried it out in rehearsal on 25 January 1854 during Schumann's visit to Hanover. But, although he did not admit it to Schumann, he did not like the piece. A month later Schumann's suicide attempt occurred, and that seemed to confirm Joachim in his dissatisfaction with the concerto. He became convinced that it showed a decline in Schumann's creative powers. In particular, Joachim criticized the third movement, which he described as monotonous and repetitive, a criticism shared by Clara. It was decided not to publish the work. Joachim, to whom Schumann had given the autograph score, retained the manuscript. After his death it was sold by Joachim's son to the Preussischer Staatsbibliothek in Berlin, with the stipulation that it not be published until at least one hundred years after Schumann's death.

At that point, the fate of the concerto took a strange twist. In 1933, the violinist Jelly d'Aranyi received, via the aid of a spiritualist, a message from Schumann informing her of the existence of the concerto, and asking that she perform it. The manuscript was traced to Berlin, and soon performances and publication of the score were scheduled. Schumann's Violin Concerto, however, had not been forgotten prior to d'Aranyi's interest in it. Its existence was known to readers of Jansen's edition of Schumann's letters, and to anyone familiar with Moser's standard biography of Joachim. Attempts to bring the work to light were vehemently opposed by Schumann's daughter, Eugenie, who agreed that the work was unworthy of her father. A controversy of major proportions developed. "Our mother gave us children to understand in the tenderest way that the concerto bore distinct traces of his last illness," Eugenie wrote in a letter to the editor of the *The Times* in London. And she reiterated Clara's conviction that "the concerto is not to be published, not now nor at any time."[21]

Despite Eugenie's opposition, publication and performance of the work went forward. But only in the past few decades have more tempered evaluations of the concerto prevailed. As had become typical in Schumann's later works, the themes of the three movements are linked

---

[21] Letter to *The Times*, London, 15 January 1938.

motivically. And, as in both the piano and cello concertos, the second and third movements are joined by a transition (the finale in this instance being a polonaise). Much of the writing for the violin recalls Bach, with baroquelike figuration. While it would be foolish to dismiss the work as shoddy or "unworthy" of Schumann, few would deny that it is uneven.

If, as Hazlitt put it in the quotation at the beginning of this chapter, during madness the mind has "slipped its cable" producing jarring and incongruous juxtapositions, its counterpart in Schumann's music often affects structural design. Sections appear to terminate abruptly, as in the passages prior to the codas of the first and third movements of the concerto. Transitions appear ungainly and gaps in the musical flow are created, as if several measures have inexplicably disappeared. What seems to be missing is the craftsmanship—how to move smoothly from one place to another. Similar criticism can be made of all of Schumann's larger-scale compositions created during the late summer and autumn of 1853, including the *Faust* Overture, and opp. 131 and 134. His recovery to health after the illness of 1852 had been gradual. The active return to conducting in the autumn and the growing criticism of his abilities created a situation of immense stress, reflected in his compositions.

Schumann completed the concerto on 3 October 1853. During the next five weeks, he composed four additional works: the *Märchenerzählungen* op. 132, the *Gesänge der Frühe* op. 133, the Third Violin Sonata (WoO 27), and the *Romances* for cello. The *Romances* were later destroyed by Clara, who felt the work to be inferior in quality. The Third Violin Sonata, although not destroyed, has in its way suffered a similar fate. It was not published until 1956, and few are aware of its existence. It came into being under unusual circumstances. It was decided by Schumann, Brahms, and Albert Dietrich jointly to surprise Joachim with a sonata, using as its basis a motive (F-A-E) derived from Joachim's personal motto "Frei aber einsam" ("Free but alone"—Joachim was a bachelor, and preferred not to be). Dietrich composed the first movement, Brahms the scherzo, and Schumann the slow movement and finale. After the work had been completed, in late October Schumann decided to make use of the two movements he had already composed by creating his own violin sonata. He replaced the two movements of

Brahms and Dietrich with newly composed ones (these two movements do not use the F-A-E motto).

The *Gesänge der Frühe* is a collection of five short pieces for solo piano, first referred to by Schumann rather cryptically as "*Diotima*."[22] Diotima was an Arcadian priestess and supposed teacher of Socrates. But it seems more likely that Schumann's allusion was to Hölderlin's Susette Gontard—referred to as Diotima in some of his most famous poems. The title, given Schumann's precarious mental state, reveals both a sense of hope and resignation. "Songs of Dawn" is an appropriate translation, although the usual one is "Morning Songs". Three days before his suicide attempt, Schumann described the work to a prospective publisher as an attempt not to represent the dawn itself but to portray the feelings awakened by the approach and gradual arrival of daybreak.

It is surprising that the *Gesänge* did not suffer the same fate as the *Romances* for cello. Perhaps what saved the Songs was Schumann's continued interest in them. He wrote to Clara from Endenich on 10 October 1854 asking to examine the manuscript, and was clearly anxious that they appear in print (they were published the following year). Much of the criticism made of the Violin Concerto is applicable to them as well. They often appear fragmented and unpolished. They are also distinctly unpianistic, that is, the music does not lie at all comfortably under the fingers. Much of this is the result of the unusually thick texture. The first piece is in many ways the most effective, a majestic hymnlike tune stated at first pianissimo in unison.

Hymns may have offered Schumann a measure of consolation. A setting of a chorale is the only work that has survived from his years in Endenich. And the last composition he completed before his mental breakdown in February 1854 was a set of five variations for solo piano in which the theme resembles a hymn (Ex. 14.10). This is the melody that Schumann believed had been sent to him by angels. It is similar to the primary theme of the second movement of the Violin Concerto. But it bears a strong resemblance as well to the opening theme of Norbert Burgmüller's Second Symphony, revised by Schumann in 1851.

---

[22] Entry of 15 October 1853 in *HSHLT*, p. 639.

Ex. 14.10

This final composition was not published during Schumann's lifetime. The theme alone was included as an appendix to his complete works (edited by Brahms), which appeared near the close of the century. It has much in common with the *Gesänge der Frühe*, although the overall texture is by no means as ponderous. The variations themselves are fairly straightforward, with distinct and clearly recognizable appearances of the theme in all but the final, free variation. Schumann worked assiduously on the pieces in the days preceding his attempted suicide. The manuscript has survived, a clean copy in Schumann's own hand. It is not dated, but Schumann's signature, unusually distinct and legible, appears at the end. The title page bears the simple dedication: "To Clara."

CHAPTER 15

Endenich

> *The prison became a veritable tomb, but one in which all peace was denied us. One by one all human consolations were taken away; our sufferings became ever greater. I resigned myself to the will of God, but in sorrow.*
> —Silvio Pellico, *My Prisons*

IT WAS AN EIGHT-HOUR JOURNEY TO ENDENICH. UNTIL THEY reached Cologne (about two-thirds of the distance), Schumann had appeared restful, but from that point on he continually asked if they would arrive soon. On 6 March, Dr. Hasenklever (who had accompanied Schumann) returned to Düsseldorf and portrayed Endenich as pleasantly as possible, noting that from his room Schumann had a beautiful view of nearby mountains, and that he had been received "with affection."[1] For the first week, Clara received no news of his condition. She was in a distraught state, often unable to sleep. Friends and family came to her support. Her mother arrived from Berlin, and the day before Schumann's departure for Endenich, Brahms arrived. Joachim appeared two days later. Wasielewski, who now lived in Bonn not far from Endenich, eventually was able to send sporadic news of Schumann's condition. But it was not until 10 March that Clara finally re-

---

[1] *Litzmann II*, p. 304.

ceived official word from Endenich that Schumann was "pretty much the same," though "overall somewhat quieter."[2]

The asylum in Endenich had been the first facility of its type built in the area. Its reputation was good, and by all accounts it was well maintained. It was, fortunately, a private institution, for conditions in public facilities were often horrific. For much of the nineteenth century, little attempt was made to comprehend mental illness. Enlightened facilities only began to appear on the continent (at first in France and then in Germany) in the 1840s. Complicating treatment was the shame associated by many with mental illness. It was not uncommon for the family to attempt to ignore what had happened, institutionalizing the mentally ill until death, as if attempting to create the illusion that the person had never existed. Because of Schumann's stature, it was impossible to pretend that nothing had occurred to him. But it is significant that, for the final years of his life, notice of Schumann in the music world dropped sharply, as did his reputation as a composer—this despite the fact that in 1854 and 1855 alone, nine new compositions (all composed prior to his breakdown) appeared in print.

Endenich was a seven-acre estate, originally built in 1790 as a summer residence. It still retained some of its original character, and contained extensive gardens. The director, Dr. Franz Richarz, was two years younger than Schumann. In 1844, he had purchased the estate, and converted it into an asylum. For its time, policies there appeared strongly progressive. Patients, although under constant supervision, were allowed some freedom, and walks both on and off the grounds were permitted (always attended, in Schumann's case). Treatment at the asylum was costly, in time a major concern for Clara. But she remained strongly independent and determined to provide as much as possible herself. On the 22nd, she received a letter from Härtel offering to arrange a benefit concert for her and the children in Leipzig, but quickly refused. "I will [give concerts] myself, if necessary," she wrote in her diary.[3]

Communication with Endenich was primarily conducted through Dr. Peters, Richarz's assistant. It was he who supplied reports on

---

[2] *Ibid.*, p. 306.
[3] *Ibid.*, p. 309.

Schumann's state. Direct communication with Schumann was not permitted, apparently in the belief that he would return quicker to health if "everything which might bring to mind his accident" was kept from him."[4] Such an approach was an unusual one for Richarz, who in general viewed "as very beneficial communication between those who were ill and their family."[5] The weekly reports from Peters at first offered Clara little consolation or hope for a quick return to health. On 20 March, he described Schumann as being "better than at first," but still susceptible to relapses when he would become restless and "kneel and wring his hands."[6] He seemed burdened by guilt. While in Endenich, he noted he would "burn in hell" for his "evil" conduct.[7] The guilt that troubled Schumann had a moral basis and seemed to be associated with an act of his that occurred prior to marriage. In his correspondence with Clara in the 1830s, despite his apparent frankness, Schumann was never completely open. When he wrote to her about his association with Ernestine von Fricken, there was an attempt to minimize it, and he never mentioned his sexual liaison with Christel. In Ernestine's case, he later felt guilt over his conduct, and acknowledged that he had been unfair. How could he not have felt similar guilt in his relationship with Christel, and in his concealment of it from Clara?

Yet another possibility might be his relationship with his sister-in-law, Rosalie, whose death in 1833 precipitated his breakdown. His relationship with her was extraordinarily close—but he assured Clara that it had been platonic. If that were not true, that, too, could have been a source of anguish for him, and provided an overwhelming burden of guilt in his relationship with Clara. Whatever the source may have been, it was this profound sense of guilt coupled with despair over his future that seem to have been at the core of his breakdown.

---

[4] Letter of 6 March 1854 of Joseph Joachim to Woldemar Bargiel (Clara's stepbrother) in *Briefe von und an Joseph Joachim*, ed. Johannes Joachim and Andreas Moser, 3 vols. (Berlin, 1911), I, p. 171.

[5] This concept is expressed in Richarz's *Ueber öffentliche Irrenpflege* (1844). See Eva Weissweiler, *Clara Schumann* (Hamburg, 1990), p. 312.

[6] *Litzmann II*, p. 309.

[7] Entry in Richarz's diary of 11 April 1854 in Aribert Reimann and Franz Hermann Franken, eds., *Robert Schumanns letzte Lebensjahre: Protokoll einer Krankheit* (Berlin, 1994), p. 17.

As time passed, Schumann decidedly improved in Endenich. The report Clara received at the beginning of April noted that he often went into the gardens. To Peters, this indicated that Schumann was beginning to take an interest in the world around him. In many ways, he appeared in better spirits, and even made an April Fool's Day joke. But Peters noted that Schumann did not appear interested in carrying on a conversation—obviously he did not realize that Schumann was never inclined to talk at length.

During the summer, Schumann had three "visitors." They were allowed only to observe him, and not permitted either to speak with or be seen by him. In July, Mathilde Hartmann, a singer and friend of the family, saw Schumann and later reported that he "looked very well," in fact better than she had ever seen him.[8] During the first half of August, Julius Otto Grimm visited Endenich, and spent two hours there:

> In no way did Herr Schumann express himself confusedly. The sound of his voice was, as usual, somewhat soft. . . . When he was not speaking, he continuously held his white handkerchief with his right hand to his lips. In his eyes I detected no indication of insanity—his eye contact was steady, directed towards Dr. Peters, and as friendly, gentle, and mild as in the past. . . . Overall, Herr Schumann looked well and vigorous—only he appears to have gained some weight. . . . His auditory delusions and agitated states have, as you know, for a long time not been present. Dr. Peters mostly complained about Herr Schumann's taciturnity which makes it difficult if not impossible to investigate his inner life.[9]

But there were obvious indications that Schumann was far from recovered:

> Herr Schumann told Dr. Peters that the city which he saw was not Bonn. Dr. Peters replied: "What is that? Aren't those the towers of the Bonn cathedral?"—Herr Schumann: Obviously. He knows very well that Beethoven's monument is near the Bonn cathedral. . . . Yesterday evening he drank his wine, but towards the end suddenly stopped and said his wine was poisoned. He poured the remainder on the floor. He does some

---

[8] Letter of 27 July 1854 to Joachim from Brahms in Andreas Moser, ed., *Johannes Brahms im Briefwechsel mit Joseph Joachim*, 2 vols. (Tutzing, 1974), I, p. 54.

[9] Letter to Clara of 13 August 1854 in *Litzmann II*, p. 327.

writing, but so illegibly that Dr. Richarz and Dr. Peters can only decipher occasional words. . . . He has done no composing during this time.[10]

It is important to note that the disturbing incident concerning the wine and, apparently, the confused perception of Bonn were not witnessed by Grimm; he was told of them. What Grimm saw was in many ways Schumann as he always was, that is, "normal"—including typical gestures (such as the hand before the mouth), the usual taciturnity, and his illegible handwriting. But these typical characteristics of Schumann were being perceived as abnormalities and continued evidence of his mental illness. Unfortunately, Grimm did not know Schumann well enough to be able to explain these idiosyncrasies to Peters.

Brahms saw Schumann on 19 August, and related his observations to Clara in a letter two days later. He was told that Schumann, after seeing a collection of portraits of famous men ("Schiller, Goethe, Copernicus, etc."), identified those whom he recognized, including several whom he had met. But he also wrote that Schumann still had delusions of hearing. And Brahms advised Clara in her correspondence with Endenich to write with more caution, lest the doctors consider her excessively optimistic. It is clear from Brahms's letter that he handled himself well in what must have been trying circumstances. But his youth and inexperience (Brahms was only twenty-one at the time) is apparent. "My head was filled with what I wanted to tell and ask the doctor [presumably, Peters]," he wrote, "but when I looked into his cold face, not a word came to me."[11]

Late in May, Clara received a letter from Liszt accompanied by a copy of his recently published Piano Sonata, dedicated to Schumann. Unfortunately, Clara was finding both Liszt and his music more and more distasteful, and described the sonata as "ghastly."[12] Schumann did not share her reaction. He was later able to examine the work at Endenich, and was "extremely pleased" by the dedication.[13] Liszt contin-

[10] Ibid., p. 328.
[11] Letter to Clara of 21 August 1854 in Berthold Litzmann, ed., *Clara Schumann, Johannes Brahms: Briefe aus den Jahren 1853–1896*, 2 vols. (Wiesbaden, 1970), I, p. 13.
[12] Diary entry of 25 May 1854 in *Litzmann II*, p. 317.
[13] According to Brahms's recollections. See Richard Heuberger, *Erinnerungen an Johannes Brahms*, ed. Kurt Hofmann (Tutzing, 1971), p. 73.

ued his support of Schumann in a number of ways. He performed *Genoveva* in Weimar in April 1855, and wrote an emotional and laudatory article about Schumann for the *Neue Zeitschrift für Musik*.

On their fourteenth wedding anniversary, Clara received a letter (probably from Dr. Peters), and noted: "Robert doubts the existence of myself and the children, because it has been so long since he has received a letter from us. I cannot say how much this shocked me! The doctor now asked me to write a few lines to him."[14] To try to return some balance into his life by removing all associations of his suicide attempt appeared sensible for a time. But six months after his entry into Endenich, Schumann must have been as perplexed as Clara by the absence of communication, and might easily have felt abandoned. She wrote to him, and Schumann quickly responded. His letter shows no signs of illness, and is filled with reminiscences of their life together, and questions about her, the children, and their present way of life: "Oh! if only I could see and speak to you again.... There is so much I would like to know—what your life is like in general, where you are living, and if you play as splendidly as in the past?" (14 September 1854).

This first letter led to four more over the next month. There is no record of any additional letters to Clara for the year except for one of 27 November (published in fragmentary form and referring to Brahms and his works), and one she received on 30 December (contents unknown), which Clara described in her diary as giving her both "joy and grief at the same time."[15] But the few extant letters to Clara after 12 October are not necessarily an indication that he did not write to her more often. All correspondence was subject to the approval of the staff at Endenich. Schumann's contact with the world outside of Endenich was assiduously monitored.

For much of the autumn of 1854, Clara was on tour, including concerts in Hanover, Leipzig, Weimar, Frankfurt, Hamburg, and Berlin. In 1855, she was on tour intermittently from January until July, and from October until December. The following year included tours from January until March (Vienna, Prague, and Budapest); from April until July

---

[14] Diary entry of 12 September 1854 in *Litzmann II*, p. 329.
[15] *Ibid*, p. 361.

1856 she fulfilled her long-held wish of performing in England. The total is revealing: of the twenty-two-month period from October 1854—when she decided to return to performing in public—until Schumann's death in July 1856, Clara spent about 90 percent of it performing or preparing for tours. After Schumann's death, she noted for her children's benefit that during his illness and confinement not only had Schumann's capital remained untouched but she had been able to add 5,000 talers to it—nearly three times what Schumann would have earned in his position at Düsseldorf during that period.

"I do it for him," Clara wrote on 17 October in her diary.[16] But there was no pressing financial need for her to perform. Yet, while not calling into question what Clara represented as her selfless and noble motivations, it is impossible not to take notice of her delight in returning full time to the career of concert artist. "Only now am I fully aware of how splendid it is to be an artist," Clara wrote to Joachim, "as my suffering and joy becomes expressed in divine music."[17] Despite the grief Clara felt for her husband's condition, there is no denying that his confinement provided her with the opportunity to do what she had always wanted to do. She now appeared in a new light: "a consecrated, faithful, and austere priestess," as Liszt extravagantly described her in the *Neue Zeitschrift für Musik*, "the gentle, suffering prophetess who, breathing the air of heaven, remains bound to the earth only by her tears."[18]

During the autumn of 1854, Schumann was on the road to recovery. Although he may not have written to Clara, during November and December he broadened the number of his correspondents by writing to Joachim (25 November) and Brahms (27 November and 15 December). The contents of these letters betray some nervousness—most notably, Schumann at times jumps from one thought to another. To Joachim, he confessed that he wished he had more strength, and complained of sleeplessness. The letters to Brahms display remarkable clarity,

---

[16] *Ibid.*, p. 349.

[17] Written in reference to her piano-playing in general, before her return to giving concerts. Letter of 21 September 1854 to Joachim in Joachim, *Briefe*, I, p. 211.

[18] Quoted in *Litzmann II*, p. 351.

and, at times, a wistfulness. "We have not seen one other since Hanover," he wrote on the 15th. "Those were happy times."[19]

Perhaps because of growing skepticism about Schumann's treatment, on 22 December Joachim went alone to Endenich and met with him. It had been nearly ten months since Schumann had met with any of his friends, or, for that matter, with anyone outside of the staff at Endenich. It is not known what details of the visit Joachim supplied to Clara. He later recalled Schumann's "friendly glance" and that "he spoke a great deal and in a hurried manner, asking about friends and events in the musical world."[20] There was much that recalled the Schumann of old. But one incident in particular disturbed Joachim. "When I wanted to leave, [Schumann] mysteriously led me into a corner (although we were not being watched) and said that he wanted to leave the place. He had to leave Endenich, because the people there completely misunderstood him."[21]

As the new year began, Clara made preparations for a concert tour in Holland. Prior to her departure for Rotterdam, she received on 8 January "a splendid letter from Robert. . . . He writes so beautifully; in the best of health he could not have written better. It is as if he were completely recovered."[22] Joachim may have not told Clara of Schumann's desire to leave Endenich, wishing to spare her additional anxiety. But, given their intimacy, it is unlikely that he would not have mentioned the matter to Brahms. Perhaps for that reason, Brahms visited Schumann on the 11th. He described him to Clara as "well and cheerful," and played several of his compositions for him.[23] As Clara left Düsseldorf on the 15th, the outlook for Schumann seemed much improved.

But Schumann's perception of his own situation must have appeared less hopeful. Although there is no record of it, perhaps he mentioned to Brahms as well his desire to leave Endenich. On the 26th, while in

---

[19] Letter to Brahms of 15 December 1854 in *Clara/Brahms Briefe*, I, p. 53.
[20] *Eismann*, pp. 192–93.
[21] *Ibid.*, p. 193.
[22] *Litzmann II*, p. 362.
[23] *Ibid.*

Utrecht, Clara received a letter from Schumann, "which so disturbed me, that I spent the entire night in tears."[24] What seems to have bothered Clara was not that Schumann's letter was disjointed or gave indication of mental stress but rather his anxiety about the future and his desire to see his family again. His situation was beginning to frighten him. "My Clara," he wrote, "I feel as if something dreadful lies before me. What sorrow—if I never see you and the children again!"[25] The physicians at Endenich as well as Schumann's wife and friends interpreted his remarks as hinting at another attempt at suicide. But they seem instead to refer to his dissatisfaction with Endenich and concern over his treatment there.

Clara was perceptive, strong-willed, and independent. Capable of managing both a household and her own successful concert career, it would appear that Schumann could not have had a more potent ally. Yet, she merely continued with her tour. It was Brahms who was Schumann's next visitor. He arrived on 24 February—more than a month after Schumann's letter to Clara—and spent four hours with him. Schumann was delighted with the present of some cigars, and noted that he had not had any since Joachim's visit. Then he told Brahms that he did not like "to ask the doctors for anything. . . . 'Clara has certainly often sent me some, but I do not receive them.' "[26] Brahms suggested that Schumann write more often to her. "I would love to—daily, always," Schumann replied, "if only I had paper."[27] And Brahms confirmed that Schumann truly had none. Brahms noted that Schumann said he was composing fugues. In fact, Schumann had turned to writing music during the winter of 1854–55. His primary project appears to have been a set of piano accompaniments for Paganini's *Caprices*—a return to his youthful interests (and a project begun in October 1853). That he was writing contrapuntal music is revealing. So often in the past, contrapuntal studies had provided a sense of stability.

If Clara had been unaware of Schumann's wish to leave Endenich, she now learned of it from Brahms. "I have nothing sad to tell you,"

---

[24] *Ibid.*, p. 364.
[25] *Ibid.*
[26] Letter to Clara of 23 and 24 February 1855 in *Clara/Brahms Briefe*, I, p. 79.
[27] *Ibid.* p. 80.

Brahms informed her, "except that at times he expressed very forcefully his desire to be out of there. He spoke quietly, because he is frightened of the doctors."[28] Schumann wrote to Brahms on 11 March, and once again brought up his wish to leave Endenich, emphatically noting that he needed to get "completely away from here! For over a year—since 4 March 1854—exactly the same kind of life." He even mentioned two clinics as possibilities. It was perhaps this letter that finally prompted Brahms and Clara to take action. Gradually there was an acknowledgement—not of the gravity of the situation, but at least of Schumann's wishes. In the spring, Brahms began to examine the possibility of Schumann being transferred to another asylum.

Schumann wrote again to Brahms on 20 March, quite lucidly, discussing in some detail Brahms's Second Piano Sonata. In his previous letter, Schumann had requested more music paper, as well as a copy of Paganini's *Caprices*. Now he was making good progress on his work: "I have already harmonized several of them (five). But it is more difficult work than my earlier free arrangements [op. 10]. So often the bass is present in such a distinctive manner in the violin." Schumann also prepared an arrangement for piano four-hands of Joachim's Overture to *Henry IV* op. 7. After Schumann's death, Joachim saw a portion of this arrangement, as well as "many complicated musical studies," and noted that Schumann had written them "*correctly.*"[29] Schumann asked as well for an atlas—quite possibly to aid in his search for another clinic. Joachim—who had seen Schumann's recent letters to Clara—now felt that the reports Clara had been receiving from Endenich were, at best, pessimistic. "I can not accept the doctor's words as those of an absolute oracle," he wrote to Clara on 18 March.[30]

On 2 April, Brahms met again with Schumann. Once more, Schumann spoke of his wish to leave Endenich. What would have proved invaluable at this point was an evaluation of Schumann by physicians not associated with Endenich. That was not to occur, but—perhaps because of the quandary she was in—Clara did welcome the offer of Bettina von Arnim to visit Schumann. Bettina (she was generally

---

[28] *Ibid.*, p. 84.
[29] Letter of 8 August 1856 to Gisela von Arnim in Joachim, *Briefe*, I, p. 364.
[30] Letter of 18 March 1855 in *Ibid.*, I, p. 270.

referred to by her first name) was in many ways the *grande dame* of German letters. Born in 1785, she had been closely associated with the Heidelberg phase of German Romanticism. Her brother was Clemens Brentano; in 1811 she married his best friend (and collaborator on *The Youth's Magic Horn*) Ludwig Achim von Arnim. By means of her great beauty, enthusiasm, and unconventional intellect, she had fervently attached herself to a number of the leading figures of her day, most notably Beethoven and Goethe. They had been charmed by her, and she had published adoring and highly embroidered portraits of them.

For decades, Schumann had been fascinated by Bettina. But they did not meet until October 1853, when she visited Düsseldorf with her daughter, Gisela. During her visit she heard with pleasure several of Schumann's most recent works. Clara, however, was not an admirer of Bettina—who, in the 1830s, had broadly criticized Clara's musicianship. After Bettina's visit, Clara noted in the diary: "I appear not to have displeased her—at least so she told me—after which she gazed upon me for a long time and held my hand in hers."[31] At some point—probably in early April 1855—Bettina offered to visit Schumann at Endenich. On 13 April, Clara wrote to Bettina thanking her, and telling her that she had written to Schumann to let him know of the coming visit.

Schumann wrote to Clara on 5 May—it was to be his last letter to her—with no mention of Bettina's visit, but with kind words about Brahms's forthcoming birthday on the 7th. On the 8th, Clara received word from Endenich that Schumann was having "restless days, lacked sufficient sleep, and speaks once again of voices," symptoms which Clara attributed to overwork.[32] It is not known at what point Bettina visited Schumann. But it must have been prior to the "restless days" (or perhaps they lasted but a short length of time), for he appeared quite healthy to Bettina during her visit. In fact, on the basis of what she had seen, she wrote to Clara, recommending that Schumann return home.

Bettina had been deeply disturbed by her visit to Endenich. Schumann was the "only rational human being" in Endenich, she concluded,

---

[31] Entry of 29 October 1853 in *Litzmann II*, p. 284.
[32] *Ibid.*, p. 374.

and she expressed her determination to do all she could "to free poor Schumann as soon as possible from his imprisonment."[33] The asylum, she wrote to Clara, was a "desolate building without signs of life," but Schumann's face had "lit up with joy" as she walked to meet him.[34] They discussed "everything which was of interest to him," and to Bettina it seemed clear that "his surprising illness was only an attack of nerves which would have ended sooner if he had been better understood or if there had been any insight into his inner nature."[35] She went on to attack the director of the clinic, describing Richarz as a "hypochondriac, himself ill in body and spirit."[36] In Bettina's eyes, Richarz completely misunderstood Schumann, and perceived what she described as Schumann's "nobility of soul" more as an indication of his illness.[37] She wrote as well that she was delighted to know that Clara was awaiting Schumann's return to his family "very soon," and suggested that to avert the possible shock of the abrupt change, some initial contact with his children might prove beneficial.[38] Although not mentioned by Bettina, it seems likely that Schumann revealed to her his apprehensions and concerns. The similarity of her evaluation of Schumann's situation to Schumann's own perception of it are too striking to be coincidental.

Bettina's letter hardly brought welcome news to Clara. Despite Schumann's letters and favorable reports from friends who had seen him, for months there had been no discussion of the possibility of Schumann returning home. Had his health been restored? Despite the doctors' assertions to the contrary, Bettina believed so. It would seem that now, of all times, a visit by Clara to Schumann would resolve the issue. But it is clear that by this stage of his confinement she had little desire to see him, even if she refused to admit it to herself. Since his removal to Endenich, Clara had established a new life for herself, one

---

[33] Wilhelm Joseph von Wasielewski, *Aus siebzig Jahren* (Stuttgart, 1897), pp. 152–3.
[34] *Litzmann II*, p. 375.
[35] *Ibid.*, pp. 375–76.
[36] Weissweiler, *Clara Schumann*, p. 333.
[37] *Litzmann II*, p. 376.
[38] *Ibid.*

of independence as a concert artist. It was what she had always wanted. Schumann's return, particularly in a state of only partial recovery, would have brought it all to an end.

As Clara's concert career had grown, so had her friendship and familiarity with Joachim and Brahms. She performed regularly with Joachim, both publicly and privately, often including works by Schumann on the program. But it was her friendship with Brahms that truly grew in intimacy. They spent much time together, traveling, taking walks, as well as performing music. There can be no doubt that Brahms fell in love with her despite their difference in age (Clara was fourteen years older). "I love her and am under her spell," he confessed to Joachim, "I often have to restrain myself forcibly from just quietly putting my arms around her."[39] It is not known whether Clara returned that love with the same intensity, but it is clear that her attachment to him was profound and distinctive. There is no indication of sexual intimacy. But Brahms, who never married, always remained deeply devoted to her.

In order to evaluate Bettina's assessment, it was decided that Joachim would visit Schumann. But even before seeing him, Joachim admitted to Brahms that he was opposed to moving Schumann, primarily because Richarz had not diagnosed Schumann as *"incurable,"* and because Schumann had decidedly improved during the months he had been at Endenich.[40] "Early this morning I saw the dear master," Joachim wrote to Clara, "and he was in good spirits and obviously delighted by my visit. . . . We often laughed heartily—and he is glad that I will be returning with Johannes to play him the Paganini Etudes [Schumann's accompaniments for the *Caprices*]."[41] There can be no doubt of Joa-

---

[39] Letter of 19 June 1854 in Artur Holde, "Suppressed Passages in the Brahms-Joachim Correspondence Published for the First Time," *The Musical Quarterly* XLV (1959), p. 314.

[40] Letter to Brahms of [about 17 May 1855] in *Brahms Briefwechsel*, I, p. 109.

[41] Letter of [May 1855] in Joachim, *Briefe*, I, p. 287. But Joachim's cheerful letter is contradicted by what he later told the music critic Eduard Hanslick. He informed Hanslick that he had visited Schumann three times during his years in Endenich, and that the last two times he saw him (which would include the recent visit at Clara's request) Schumann had deteriorated both in mind and body. Perhaps Joachim was attempting to place Schumann in the most favorable light possible to Clara. According to Litzmann, after returning from his visit, Joachim described Schumann as being "very agitated," and told Clara that the doctors were opposed to him being moved elsewhere (p. 376).

chim's good intentions. Apparently he also spoke with a Dr. Wolf in Bonn to gain further insight into Schumann's condition. But even prior to seeing Schumann, Joachim was in favor of Clara meeting privately with Richarz.

In order to resolve the matter, a few days later Clara finally met with Dr. Richarz in Brühl, a city about fifteen miles from Endenich. It was their first meeting. Richarz assured her of his firm belief that Schumann would be restored to health but not for some time. For that reason, he needed to remain in Endenich at least until the winter. Clara was satisfied. On 26 July, she wrote to Joachim, telling him "God willing, Robert and I will visit you [later this year, when a cure has been affected]."[42]

Schumann eventually wrote to Bettina, thanking her for her visit, noting that he had been unable to write to her sooner, because he had been "not well for some time."[43] She replied (via Joachim), warmly thanking him. And there the incident ended. Schumann remained in Endenich, Bettina's advice being dismissed as perhaps well intentioned, but that of an amateur, misinformed and misguided. Clara wrote to her on 25 May, thanking her coldly, and informing her that her perception of the situation had not been accurate. Her visit only stirred up ill will. After Schumann's death, Brahms made a point of noting the "malicious rumors" that had circulated around Clara—"from Bettina, for example."[44]

Although no one realized it at the time, Bettina von Arnim's intervention had been Schumann's last hope. The rejection of her advice would ultimately lead to tragedy. And to dismiss it as well intentioned but amateurish was to disregard her enlightened perception of the mentally ill. The suicide in 1806 of her friend, the writer Caroline von Günderode, had first awakened her concern. She took an interest as well in the madness of Hölderlin and the painter Carl Blechen, in Blechen's case attempting to raise money to assist him. "How can it be possible that the spirit which once animated this great artist will totally

---

[42] Letter of 26 July [1855] in Ibid., I, p. 290.

[43] Letter (undated) in Anonymous, "Robert Schumann and Bettina von Arnim," *Monthly Musical Record* LIII (1928), p. 230.

[44] Letter to J. O. Grimm of [September 1856] in Johannes Brahms, *Johannes Brahms im Briefwechsel mit J. O. Grimm*, ed. Richard Barth (Tutzing, 1974), p. 45.

vanish?" she wrote in one of her letters of solicitation.[45] When she learned of Schumann's plight, it probably seemed only natural to her to attempt to be of assistance.

Over the summer, Schumann's condition appeared to worsen. On 4 September, Clara wrote to him but received no reply. Then, on the 10th, she received a letter from Richarz, removing "all hope of a complete recovery."[46] "I no longer know what to think," Clara wrote in the diary.[47] Now that Richarz had concluded that a full recovery was not possible, it would seem that there was no longer any reason for Schumann to remain in Endenich. It was Richarz's policy to release those inmates who he felt could not be cured. Such had been the case with Alfred Rethel. Rethel, an artist whom Schumann had met in 1849, had suffered a nervous breakdown, and from 24 May 1853 until 2 May 1854 had been a patient at Endenich. He had been released (with the diagnosis: "Dementia, general paralysis") when it had been determined that recovery would be impossible. But perhaps Richarz felt that in Schumann's case, although it was no longer a question of full recovery, some progress still could be made. It now appeared that the only possibility of granting Schumann's wish of leaving Endenich would be as a result of an attempt to save money. In September and again in the spring of 1856, Clara considered transferring Schumann to another institution because of what was felt to be the excessive cost of Endenich—this despite the repeated offer from friends in Leipzig to establish a fund to bear the expense of Schumann's confinement.

What had happened to Schumann during the summer of 1855? Why were there no visitors? What had led to Richarz's determination that there was no longer any possibility of curing Schumann when, only four months earlier, he had spoken to Clara of a full recovery? Richarz's autopsy reports provide some clues. One report was supplied at Wasielewski's request for his biography of Schumann. The other was published as a brief article by Richarz in 1873.[48] The autopsy was

---

[45] Paul O. Rave, *Karl Blechen* (Berlin, 1940), p. 49.
[46] Apparently Richarz's words. *Litzmann II*, p. 387.
[47] *Ibid.*
[48] Richarz's full autopsy report (discovered in 1973) is discussed in Franz Hermann Franken, *Die Krankheiten grosser Komponisten*, 3 vols. (Wilhelmshaven, 1991).

considered crucial by Richarz in determining a diagnosis, and he does produce a diagnosis, of sorts, for Schumann. Unfortunately, the autopsy report itself is of little value. "There are many vague and contradictory statements [in it]," a recent, expert evaluation concluded, "and no one today would accept these findings as being reliable."[49]

After Schumann's death, Richarz concluded that his illness had been present for "many years," and diagnosed Schumann as having "incomplete general paralysis," the result of a "slow, but irreversible and progressive deterioration in organisation and strength of the entire nervous system."[50] Richarz attributed this deterioration to "overexertion"—that is, " 'immoderate mental, especially artistic productivity' had 'exhausted the substance of psychically active central components of the nervous system.' "[51] Richarz traced Schumann's hallucinations to "issues of the artistic value of his own work. He would grow indignant. The voices apparently criticized his capabilities as a musician."[52] Always present was what Richarz referred to as Schumann's "melancholic depression."[53] "As a result of frequently refusing all nourishment," Richarz concluded, "[Schumann's] condition worsened, and consequently he died in a state of extreme emaciation."[54]

Richarz's diagnosis—combined with other details of Schumann's condition—has led to numerous attempts to determine a more precise diagnosis of Schumann's illness. Two psychiatric diagnoses have garnered the most support: schizophrenia and bipolar depression. Schizophrenia does not refer here, as has been commonly believed, to multiple personalities; it is not a question of Schumann having had more than one personality, his Eusebius and Florestan side, for example. Schizophrenia is a thinking disorder—both the thought process and content can be affected—characterized by difficulty with attention and in forming concepts. As a result, reality becomes severely distorted, and this distortion often is accompanied by delusions and hallucinations. As in

---

[49] Peter Ostwald, *Schumann: The Inner Voices of a Musical Genius* (Boston, 1985), p. 296.

[50] *W*, p. 507; Ostwald, pp. 298–9.

[51] Ostwald, p. 299.

[52] From Richarz's 1873 article, quoted in *Ibid.*, p. 287.

[53] *W*, p. 507.

[54] *Ibid.*, p. 509.

Schumann's case, auditory hallucinations can be encountered. Schizophrenic communications often appear unintelligible with wording that seems abruptly to jump from one idea to another, and ideas that often seem to appear unrelated.

Bipolar depression (also known as manic-depression) is an affective—that is, an emotional or mood—disorder. It produces alternations of depression with mania. Throughout his life, Schumann suffered from many of the symptoms of depression: extreme sadness, doubt, and pessimism about the future (probably a result of the helplessness he felt at achieving his goals), dulled response to the world around him, and sleep disturbances. Mania, on the other hand, is characterized by excessive elation. Manic periods in Schumann's life appear less noticeably, although instances might include periods of inspired composition (such as the creation of the First Symphony in four days). Today, mania is perceived not necessarily as a time of euphoria but as a defense against a deeply ingrained depression. Severe depression often leads to a sense of hopelessness and a strong and natural desire to escape from it. For that reason, depression and suicide are often closely related.

Neither the diagnoses of schizophrenia nor bipolar depression adequately explain Schumann's condition. If Schumann were schizophrenic, how can his power of communication and accurate perception of the world be explained? Richarz himself reported that Schumann's "self-awareness was beclouded, distorted, but not destroyed . . . he was not alienated from himself, not transformed."[55] If Schumann suffered from bipolar depression, what explanation can be offered for his hallucinations or vertigo? Such discrepancies led to what became perhaps the most commonly accepted interpretation of Schumann's illness—that he had syphilis.

The initial, overt symptoms of syphilis—sores on the genitals—disappear within a short period of time. But for much of the nineteenth century it was not known that, with the disappearance of the sores, the disease itself had not ended. A new stage had been entered, and the central nervous system was attacked. Over a considerable period of time—often several decades—nerve cells were affected, leading to mental deterioration, paralysis, and, ultimately, death. The entire process and

---

[55] From Richarz's 1873 article, quoted in Ostwald, p. 300.

the resulting disorder is referred to as tertiary syphilis (or general paresis). Schumann possessed a number of the symptoms associated with tertiary syphilis, including hallucinations, difficulty enunciating and moving, and, apparently, a gradual mental collapse. But again there are symptoms of Schumann's condition—his anxiety attacks, for example—that have no relation to tertiary syphilis.

Those who assume that Schumann did have syphilis believe confirmation has been supplied by published excerpts from a diary maintained by Richarz. On 12 September 1855, Richarz recorded that Schumann noted that in 1831 he had had syphilis and for treatment had taken arsenic. This occurred at the time of Schumann's affair with Christel. In the midst of the affair, Schumann's diary made several references to a "painful wound" he had suffered, and there is now speculation that the wound was an indication of the onset of the disease.[56] But whether this was a reference to a penile lesion, often an initial indication of syphilis, is uncertain. There are no references in the diary to the secondary stages of the disease. That Schumann thought he had syphilis is merely an indication of his belief, and not proof of his infection. Not until 1906 was a test developed to determine the presence of syphilis. In Richarz's diary, many of the overt symptoms associated with the advanced stages of syphilis are noted. But his autopsy report does not give any indication of an "infectious process," such as would be associated with the disease.

In the absence of conclusive evidence, all attempts to diagnose Schumann today must remain conjectural. The later symptoms, which have been used as a basis for asserting that he had syphilis, simply do not provide the proof necessary. Many can be associated with other illnesses, such as malnutrition (or the stroke Schumann believed he may have suffered on 30 July 1853). Schumann *may* have had syphilis—according to Richarz, he believed he did. And Richarz may himself have become convinced that Schumann was syphilitic, but concealed it in order to

---

[56] Entry of 24 May 1831 in *Tgb I*, p. 332. I should like to thank Dr. George T. Ho of Urological Associates (Columbus, OH) for kindly providing me with his evaluation of Schumann's symptoms. If Schumann had syphilis, Clara could have acted as a carrier (similar to "Typhoid Mary"), and not necessarily suffered from the disease herself. Transmission of syphilis to at least one of their children would not have been unexpected, but there is insufficient medical evidence.

spare Schumann's family the shame and humiliation associated with the disease. But that does not explain the crises of 1833 and 1844 (or the attempt at suicide in 1854). Schumann's mental illness appears more complex, and can not be resolved by the presence of syphilis alone, or by a single mental disorder, for symptoms of several were present. The diagnosis presented by Dr. Peter Ostwald seems most convincing: that Schumann suffered from a major affective disorder—"severe, recurring depressive episodes," with indications of mania (bipolar depression).[57] What is clear is that Schumann's mental disorder was exacerbated by the treatment he received at Endenich.

It now appears that Bettina von Arnim's assessment of Schumann's situation was in many ways accurate: Richarz totally misunderstood the nature of Schumann's illness. In general, Richarz associated mental illness with what he perceived as sinful behavior. This was in keeping with his diagnosis of "incomplete general paralysis"—French psychiatrists had attributed the condition to " 'moral' excesses such as alcoholism, 'violent passions,' or sexual overindulgence."[58] For a cure, Richarz's approach was to deal with the body (hence his concern with an autopsy). Mental problems would then heal of their own accord. Treatment included cold baths, copper- and opium-based medication, and strict regulation of diet. In an attempt to purify the patient's system, an increasing regimen of laxatives and diuretics preceded by substantial meals, heavy in calories, were prescribed. Reacting strongly to this barbaric treatment, several patients protested with hunger strikes. The staff responded with a number of tortuous devices intended to force them to eat.[59] In desperation, patients were restrained and force-fed (with a diet of port wine and meat extract) by means of enemas.

Schumann may have been among the patients who refused to eat. Richarz himself attributed Schumann's death "in a state of extreme emaciation" to his "frequently refusing all nourishment." It would also explain why shortly before his death Clara fed him wine and jellied consommé, the type of fare, according to Clara, he had been taking for

---

[57] Ostwald, p. 303.

[58] Ibid., p. 299.

[59] In an article written in 1871, Richarz revealed "very cautiously . . . an epidemic of suicides by self-starvation" (Ostwald, p. 278). Schumann was not mentioned.

weeks. The published extracts from Richarz's diary, unfortunately, give little information about Schumann's diet or eating habits. There is no mention of Schumann starving himself.

The diary is equally silent concerning the crude and often cruel methods of treatment advocated at Endenich. Only once, for example, is mention made of forcible restraint—the use of a straitjacket not long after Schumann's arrival (on 20 April 1854). But Schumann must soon have recognized Richarz's lack of understanding and sympathy. Several incidences of it are found in the diary. On one occasion, apparently as punishment for unacceptable behavior, all of Schumann's books, writings, and writing materials were confiscated without his knowledge. The next day, he was upset and disturbed by the loss of what he described as "his property"—a statement so preposterous in Richarz's eyes that he felt obliged to make note of it.[60] It is difficult to reconcile the portrait of Schumann found in Richarz's diary—Schumann's violence, sleeplessness, unintelligible mumbles, and hallucinations—with his correspondence and the reports of those who visited him. Immersed in the world of Endenich, Schumann seemed to become a different person.

Most notable is the aggressive turn in his behavior after the visits of Bettina von Arnim and Joachim—that is, probably after he had lost hope of leaving the institution. On 25 July, Richarz reported that he struck one of his attendants. On 8 September, all attempts to persuade him to write to his wife were fruitless. That autumn, Schumann complained about his food and drink, complaints that were to crop up intermittently in Richarz's diary. These seem to have been intended as acts of defiance by Schumann, an angry response to what he probably perceived as a hopeless situation. By the spring of 1856, the aggressiveness had been replaced by resignation and preparation for his end: on 16 and 17 April, he burned Clara's letters and other material.

In addition to detailing Schumann's decline, Richarz's jottings reveal much about himself. What is most striking is the absence of compassion and sensitivity. Not only was no attempt made to comprehend Schumann's temperament, little interest was shown in it. And, invariably, what Richarz saw in Schumann displeased him. After hearing Schumann play the piano early in May 1855, Richarz dismissed it as "very

---

[60] Entries of 10 and 11 October 1855 in Reimann and Franken, pp. 21–22.

wild and incoherent"—perhaps it was, but then hostile critics had been describing Schumann's music in similar terms for decades.[61]

Much has been made of the enlightened nature of Richarz's medical practice—and there can be little doubt that on the surface it was far more tolerant than that of many in his profession, particularly that found in state institutions. But, when compared to progressive physicians in his field, Richarz fares poorly. Dr. Emile Blanche, a French contemporary of Richarz, managed an asylum in Paris among whose inmates were the poets Gérard de Nerval and Antoni Deschamps. Blanche focused on the mental and spiritual basis of their illness, and encouraged creativity as a means for a cure. Such an approach would not have found favor with Richarz, who did not encourage the artistic endeavors of his patients but, rather, seemed convinced of their detrimental affect. "[Schumann] wrote yesterday a clear and coherent letter to the doctors," noted Richarz, "in which he asks permission to play the piano, enumerating in a somewhat feeble-minded manner the composers he wishes to play."[62] Such comments reveal more than a lack of sensitivity; they demonstrate the arrogance and narrow-mindedness that so angered Bettina von Arnim. As a result of his bias, Richarz's observation of Schumann tended to emphasize and, at times, distort those aspects of Schumann's behavior that confirmed his own diagnosis.

Based on his correspondence and the reports of those outside of Endenich, for a period of eight months—roughly from October 1854 until May 1855—Schumann returned sufficiently to health to justify his removal from Endenich. Even if he had been suffering from syphilis at the time and had not long to live, there can be no doubt that the treatment he received at Endenich was harmful to recovery from his depressive state. More than a year after he had first told Joachim of his wish to leave Endenich, Schumann probably felt abandoned. Because he was completely at the mercy of his physicians and unable to control his treatment, he may have realized that the only aspect of his existence still remaining under his control was whether to live or to die. If Schumann were among those inmates who starved themselves, by choosing

---

[61] Entry of 8 May 1855 in *Ibid.*, p. 20.
[62] Entry of 29 April 1856 in *Ibid.*, p. 23.

to die, he was not only escaping the horrors of his life but also exercising the only authority left to him.

Brahms visited Schumann twice in 1856. During a visit in April, he found him with an atlas, arranging names of cities and rivers in alphabetical order: "We sat down, it became increasingly painful for me . . . he spoke continually, but I understood nothing . . . often he only babbled, something like bababa—dadada. . . . He understood me with difficulty, and only partially."[63] He returned on Schumann's birthday in June, bringing with him a larger atlas that Schumann had requested. To Clara, Brahms wrote that Schumann took "little notice of him, but rather constantly studied the atlas."[64] Later that month, while on tour in England, Clara received a telegram from Endenich, informing her that Schumann was "totally debilitated," but "still conscious."[65]

She arrived in Düsseldorf on 6 July, aware of the seriousness of Schumann's condition but still not realizing how close he was to death. On the 14th, she traveled to Bonn and spoke with Richarz, who informed her that "he could not promise [Schumann] an additional year of life."[66] Richarz's statement is so extraordinary, given what is known of Schumann's state at the time, that there has been speculation that it was intended to absolve him of any responsibility for Schumann's condition. Nine days later, Clara received a telegram informing her that Schumann was dying.

She saw Schumann on the evening of the 27th, only after disregarding the objections of Brahms and the physicians (who wanted to spare her the shock). "He smiled at me and, with great exertion (he no longer has full control of his limbs), placed his arm around me. I will never forget it. . . . He spoke with spirits, so it seemed, and would not permit anyone around him for long, or he would become restless. It was nearly impossible to understand him any longer."[67] Schumann's disorientation and torment continued the next day, much of which Clara and Brahms

---

[63] Letter of [25 April 1856] in *Brahms Briefwechsel*, I, pp. 134–35.

[64] Diary entry of 11 June 1856 in *Litzmann II*, p. 413.

[65] Nancy B. Reich, *Clara Schumann: The Artist and the Woman* (Ithaca, NY, 1985), p. 150.

[66] Clara's words, apparently quoting Richarz, in *Litzmann II*, p. 413.

[67] *Ibid.*, p. 414.

spent with him, either in his room or observing him. "He suffered terribly, although the doctor said differently. His limbs were in continual convulsions. His speaking was often very vehement. Ah! I prayed to God to release him, because I loved him so. . . . His sole nourishment for weeks had been some wine and jellied consommé. Today I gave it to him, and he took it with the happiest expression. He licked the wine from my fingers."[68] Schumann died in his sleep on the 29th at four in the afternoon. Clara saw him a half hour later: "I stood by the corpse of my dearly beloved husband and was at peace; all my feelings went in thanks to God that he was finally free."[69] The funeral followed quickly, four days later. Brahms and Joachim were present, as was Ferdinand Hiller who arrived from Cologne.

To many, Schumann's passing provided a sense of relief and resolution. For nearly two and a half years, to those outside of Endenich it had seemed as if he were already dead. There was now, wrote Stephen Heller, "no more reason to hope for improvement to what had become a miserable existence."[70] But while death released Schumann from his suffering, that of the Schumann family continued. In 1871, Clara and Robert's son, Ludwig (he was twenty-three at the time), was diagnosed insane. He entered the state asylum in Colditz two years later. Clara first visited him at his request in 1875, and again the following year—visits that "left her feeling miserable for weeks."[71] There are no records of any visits after 1876. Ludwig died twenty-three years later, on 9 January 1899. "The shadows closed more and more around him," recalled his sister Eugenie, "and at last he became, as my mother often said in deep distress, 'buried alive.' "[72]

---

[68] *Ibid.*, pp. 414–15.

[69] *Ibid.*

[70] Letter to Ferdinand Hiller of 30 August 1856 in *Aus Ferdinand Hillers Briefwechsel (1826–1861)*, ed. Reinhold Sietz (Cologne, 1958), p. 118.

[71] Reich, p. 166.

[72] Eugenie Schumann, *The Memoirs of Eugenie Schumann* (New York, 1927), p. 65.

EPILOGUE

"The Poet Speaks": Schumann and Childhood

Come, let us live with our children, that all things may be better here on earth.
—Friedrich Froebel

"WRITE TO ME IN DETAIL ABOUT THE CHILDREN," Schumann asked Clara in his first letter to her after being admitted to Endenich (14 September 1854). In succeeding letters he inquired about them regularly, and was particularly interested in their continued musical development—whether they were playing Beethoven, Mozart, and his own *Album for the Young*. He mentioned writing letters to them as well, although these do not appear to have survived. Schumann deeply loved his children, and certainly one of the greatest sacrifices he had to endure while at Endenich was being separated from them. "I always tell my wife that it is not possible to have too many children," he once wrote to Mendelssohn. "It is the greatest blessing that can happen to us on earth" ([November 1845]). It was his hope that after his death his work as a composer would ensure a "loving remembrance" for them.[1]

Schumann delighted in being with his children. He read to them, went on walks with them, picked flowers with them, and accompanied them on sledding expeditions. While this may not seem all that unusual

---
[1] Diary entry of June 1843 in *Tgb II*, p. 266.

by modern standards, it would not have been common for fathers in the Germany of Schumann's day to participate so actively in their children's lives. His interest in them went well beyond play and recreational activities. He taught their eldest child, Marie, how to count. He compiled a list of authors whom they should read as they grew up, including Jean Paul, Goethe, Shakespeare, Byron, Sophocles, and Homer. He noted with pleasure the children's efforts at writing poetry, and worked with them on rhyming words. Not surprisingly, music was also an important part of their lives. When Marie was four, he began to teach her the keys on the piano—the children later studied the piano with their mother and with other instructors. And there were collaborative artistic projects. For Clara's birthday in 1852, Schumann wrote a little song with Marie, using as a basis a poem she had written.

Not long after Marie's birth, Schumann noted with interest the effect of music on her: when she was restless, Clara's piano-playing would soothe her. He decided to maintain as a memorial a record of her first year of life—addressing it to her, and including in it melodies that had often been played to her. Four years later, he decided to create a booklet in a similar manner for all the children. He entitled it "A Little Book of Memories For Our Children," and made the first entry in it on 23 February 1846. The book contains a record of their births, a listing of their godparents, and incidents that he wanted them to remember. He discussed the death of their brother Emil, the death of Mendelssohn ("an irreparable loss"), their flight from Dresden during the insurrection in 1849, and their stay in nearby Kreischa, with its "beautiful trees and fields, springs and fountains, the cuckoo, the lilies of the valley."[2] But also included were everyday occurrences, including statements of theirs that struck his fancy—such as Marie's request that God "throw down a few stars" for her.[3] The entry for 7 June 1846 reads: "Papa found (for the first time in his life) a bird's nest. Therefore, patience dear children. What one has not accomplished in thirty-six years, one may yet accomplish on the last day before entering upon the thirty-seventh, as to my great pleasure I did today."[4]

---

[2] Eugenie Schumann, *The Memoirs of Eugenie Schumann* (London, 1927), pp. 214, 216.
[3] Ibid., p. 207.
[4] Ibid., p. 209.

Although the booklet is entirely about his children, it is Schumann's personality that animates it. It would be a mistake to regard his efforts simply as those of a doting father or to perceive what he has written as a display of *bürgerlich* contentment. Rather, the booklet documents Schumann's periodic immersion into the world of his children. While observing them, he was able to observe himself. "Happy childhood— one lives it anew in one's children," he noted in 1846 in the diary.[5] It was not just the joys that were relived: "Grief when a good child tells a lie for the first time."[6]

In observing his children and, by recollection, reliving aspects of his own childhood, Schumann was attempting to recapture and retain for himself the essence of an idealized childhood, one that could serve as a source of inspiration for his work. Similar ideas were current in painting (such as those of Philipp Otto Runge) and literature (Jean Paul, Novalis, and Wackenroder). "In every child is found a wondrous depth," Schumann wrote in 1833.[7] During his courtship of Clara, he occasionally called her a child, at which Clara took offense, determined to assert her maturity. But it had been intended by Schumann as perhaps the ultimate compliment—as he explained, "the most beautiful word" he could have chosen to address her (11 May 1838).

Schumann's interest in childhood first found musical expression in the *Kinderszenen* op. 15. Despite its simplicity, it was a work revolutionary in concept. Liszt played the pieces for his daughter (three years old at the time) with delight. Henriette Voigt was charmed by them and wrote poems to accompany each one. But critical reaction at first was not favorable. In an 1839 review, Ludwig Rellstab castigated the work, writing that the pieces were too demanding technically for children, and wondering whether Schumann intended the *Kinderszenen* as a joke. Schumann was deeply offended by Rellstab's review, and disturbed that he missed the entire point of the pieces. They had been created not for children, but as a re-creation of childhood for adults. The titles, as always, Schumann claimed to have added after the music had been composed and as a guide to its interpretation. Rellstab found

---

[5] Entry of 13 April 1846 in *Tgb II*, p. 400.

[6] *Memoirs*, p. 212.

[7] In "Aus Meister Raros, Florestans und Eusebius' Denk- und Dichtbüchlein" in *JS*, p. 30.

them nonsensical and inappropriate. But they provide the key to Schumann's intentions: they represent not just the world of childhood with its fun and games, but also Schumann's perception of childhood. The next-to-last piece in the set is entitled "Child Falling Asleep." It leads directly into the final piece, "The Poet Speaks." In Schumann's mind, the child and the poet are the same person—the poet representing the child in its natural and unconscious state.

Contemporaries invariably noted the childlike side of Schumann. But there could be perils associated with it. During his visit to Vienna in 1846–47, Marie (who was five) and Elise (who was not yet four) went along. Marie recalled that:

> Mama was out and Papa asked us whether we could remember the way to Dr. Fischhof's house. We confidently answered, "Yes!," and he gave us a letter to take to this gentleman, whose quarters were in the same block of houses as ours, in the Grundlhof, but not quite easy to find. We became suddenly aware of having gone too far and arrived in St. Stephen's Square; we looked about in consternation. We did not know how to get home, did not even remember the name of our street. We began to be frightened, for we had been told of the Bohemian rat-catchers who were on the lookout for little children. When our apprehension had reached its climax, we suddenly saw Mama coming towards us like an angel from heaven. She was horrified to find us in the centre of the large town, took us home, and remonstrated with Papa. But he took it quite calmly, and said the children had assured him they knew the way.[8]

Part of the growing interest in children in the first half of the nineteenth century focused on their education. It was an age of reform. Even Jean Paul had written a book on the subject, *Levana; or, The Doctrine of Education* (1807). One of the most prominent reformers was Heinrich Pestalozzi (1746–1827). He emphasized the importance of a broad and challenging curriculum (in contrast to the rote memorization then current). Classes were often conducted out-of-doors, and opportunity for physical exercise was also provided. Many of Pestalozzi's ideas were used as a point of departure by Friedrich Froebel (1782–1852). But Froebel was especially concerned with a child's spiritual develop-

---

[8] *Memoirs*, pp. 210–11.

ment. "The child's soul is more tender and vulnerable," Froebel wrote, "than the finest or tenderest plant"—a statement that echoes Schumann's own description of his daughter Julie (about a year old at the time) as a "delicate, sensitive little plant."⁹ It was Froebel's likening of children to plants that led to the establishment of the first kindergartens. He believed that educating a child was similar to nurturing a garden.

Schumann enrolled his two eldest children, Marie and Elise, in one of the first kindergartens established, that directed by Adolph Frankenberg in Dresden. At first they were "very happy" there, but after about eight months Marie complained that she was " 'doing no work,' " and Schumann felt that perhaps she had outgrown it.¹⁰ For a time, she was sent to another school, and returned home so enthused that she offered to attend school the entire day. "I told her," Schumann wrote, "I would remind her of this in four weeks' time."¹¹ In the summer of 1849, it was Julie's turn to attend kindergarten. Schumann's support of kindergarten reveals not only his strong interest in education but his progressive nature. Kindergartens were regarded by many as experimental, and of dubious value. It was maintained that education of children so young was a wasted effort. Liszt, for example, was critical of the concept, and remarked that "one could not help genius yet in its swaddling-clothes."¹²

Music had a significant role in Froebel's concept of education. It was introduced to the child in its early years as an instance of "beauty."¹³ Music was published to accompany kindergarten activities, most notably Robert Kohl's *44 Mutter-, Kose- und Spiellieder*, which received the distinction of a lead review in the 18 March 1844 issue of the *Neue Zeitschrift für Musik*. But the review (not by Schumann), while favorable toward the idea, was critical of the product. Schumann found much of the music for children to be dry and pedantic, simplistic, and uninspired. It was because he could find nothing suitable to use with his

---

⁹Bertha von Marenholz-Bülow, *Reminiscences of Friedrich Froebel*, trans. Mrs. Horace Mann (Boston, 1882), p. 155; *Memoirs*, p. 208.
¹⁰ *Memoirs*, p. 209.
¹¹ Ibid., p. 214.
¹² Liszt later changed his mind and "then he promised he would compose songs for the kindergarten, a promise which yet awaits its fulfillment." Marenholz-Bülow, p. 27.
¹³ Ibid., p. 99.

own children that the *Album for the Young* op. 68 came into being. The first pieces were originally written for Marie as a birthday gift in 1848. During their composition, Schumann felt as if he "were composing for the first time" (6 October 1848). He gave titles to all but two of the forty pieces in the set (expanded to forty-three pieces in later editions). A number of them took their inspiration from the activities of his children. "When he saw you children at play," Clara told Eugenie, "little pieces of music grew out of your games."[14] Schumann's example has been followed by so many other composers that it is difficult today to put his achievement into perspective. For the first time, music of quality had been created specifically for children to study and enjoy. There is great diversity in the *Album*: imaginative entertainment ("The Wild Rider"), glimpses into the technique of composition ("Little Canonic Song"), and, a typical Schumann touch, "Northern Song (Greeting to G.)", in which the theme G-A-D-E is noted. He wrote a collection of *Maxims for Young Musicians* (1850) for inclusion in subsequent editions. The *Album* filled a void that had existed in music and, at the same time, created a new genre.

During the next five years, Schumann composed four additional works for children. The first, composed in April and May 1849, was a counterpart to the *Album for the Young*: the *Song Album for the Young* op. 79. The album contained twenty-nine songs and, at Schumann's request, was published with a cover by Ludwig Richter (similar to the one he had created for the *Album for the Young*). Schumann took particular care in his choice of poems, and included in the collection poetry by Hoffmann von Fallersleben, Geibel, Uhland, Goethe, and Schiller, among others. Mignon's poignant "Kennst du das Land" concludes the set. Many of the songs are folklike in their simplicity; others are at a more demanding technical level (for both voice and piano) and were intended for a more advanced student. Still others are more suitable for parents to sing to their children.

Four months after completing the *Song Album*, Schumann directed his attention toward four-hand piano music for children. Its origin was a "Birthday March" created with Marie for Clara's birthday. A dozen pieces, each with a title, were assembled and published in 1850 as *Zwölf*

---

[14] *Memoirs*, p. 98.

vierhändige Klavierstücke für kleine und grosse Kinder (Twelve Four-Hand Piano Pieces for Children, Big and Small) op. 85. It was followed by a set of a half dozen four-hand dances, the *Kinderball* op. 130, composed in September 1853. Both sets were intended as playful Hausmusik for children, a way for them to socialize and at the same time learn how to play music with others. Most of the pieces make few technical demands on the performers—the dances are especially simple—and are light, tuneful, and often humorous in nature.

The *Kinderball* had been preceded in June 1853 by *Drei Klaviersonaten für die Jugend* (Three Piano Sonatas for Children) op. 118. These are sonatas in miniature, each consisting of four movements, most with a title. Schumann made a point of not calling them "sonatinas;" he must have wanted to emphasize the distinction between them and the typical, dry sonatina. They were originally conceived for his own children. Although they can be studied individually, Schumann thought of them as a set: the last movement of the third sonata (entitled "A Child's Dream") restates thematic material from both of the other sonatas.

Schumann lived during a time when the *Märchen* (fairy tale) developed and flourished in Germany, both the simple, folklike tales of Andersen and the more elaborate ones of Tieck, Novalis, Hoffmann, and Arnim. He read them for his own enjoyment and to his children, and, inspired by them, created several musical counterparts. His *Waldszenen* (Forest Scenes) op. 82 (1850) is a collection of nine, short piano pieces, each with a distinctive title: "Entrance," "Hunter in Ambush," "Lonely Flowers," "Cursed Place," "Friendly Landscape," "Country Inn," "Prophet Bird," "Hunting Song," and "Farewell." The forest represented is one of mystery and imagination—a musical counterpart to the forests portrayed in *Märchen* such as Tieck's "The Runenberg" (1802). For "Prophet Bird," a sinister connotation was intended. Although deleted when published, it originally was prefaced by the concluding line from Eichendorff's "Zwielicht" (set by Schumann in 1840 in the *Liederkreis* op. 39): "Take care, be alert and on guard." The entire set attempts to re-create the mood of the *Märchen* by programmatic depiction of an enchanted forest.

Writers of *Märchen* were quick to note its musical association. *Märchen*, wrote Ludwig Tieck, need to possess "a quietly progressive tone, a certain innocence of representation . . . which hypnotizes the soul like quiet musical improvisations without noise and clamor."[15] Novalis described the *Märchen* as resembling "a vision in a dream—incoherent—an ensemble of wonderful things and events, for example, a musical fantasy—the harmonic sequences of an Aoelian harp—nature itself."[16] As Schumann thought about the *Märchen*, it must have struck him that it would be possible to create a *Märchen* without a text, that is, a strictly musical *Märchen*. Two compositions were created by him in this new musical genre: the *Märchenbilder* op. 113 and the *Märchenerzählungen* op. 132 ("bilder" is best translated as "pictures," "erzählungen" as "tales").

Each was created for an unusual and distinctive combination of instruments. The *Märchenbilder* were composed in March 1851 for viola and piano. In the household books, there was deliberation over the title, Schumann referring to the work as "Violageschichten" ("Viola Tales"), "Märchengeschichten," and then "Märchenlieder."[17] The *Märchenerzählungen* were composed in October 1853 for clarinet, viola, and piano. In both works, Schumann seemed to be in search of a darker and richer sound, but one that could also, in contrast, become bright. With its lower range, the viola could accomplish this in a way in which the violin could not, and Schumann used to advantage its rich, warm tone. In a similar manner, of all the woodwind instruments the clarinet best offers the timbre Schumann was seeking, and it also complements the viola exceedingly well. Each of the *Märchen* compositions consists of four movements, untitled. There is no mistaking that these are works from Schumann's final years. Half of the movements are monothematic, creating a sense of restraint and terseness. And, although there is considerable contrast among the movements, they are intimate in nature, disdaining all ostentation. Their lyricism is one of profound simplicity.

Schumann's most extensive *Märchen* is the oratorio, *The Pilgrimage of the Rose* op. 112. He composed it in April and May 1851, and described it as a "very charming and idyllic märchen" (27 December 1851). The text for it was based on a poem sent to Schumann by Moritz Horn. Schumann expressed interest in setting it if it were considerably short-

---

[15] Quoted in Marianne Thalmann, *The Romantic Fairy Tale* (Ann Arbor, MI, 1964), p. 34.
[16] *Ibid.*, p. 13.
[17] Entries of 1, 2, and 15 March 1851 in *HSHLT*, pp. 554, 556.

ened, and for several months he took an unusually active role in revising the text with Horn. Originally, the *Rose* was composed for soloists and chorus with piano accompaniment. But the performance (on 6 July 1851) was so successful that friends persuaded Schumann to orchestrate it in order to broaden its audience.

The Pilgrimage of the Rose tells the story of an elfin rose who eagerly wishes to experience life as a person. Her wish is granted by the princess of the elves, and she is given a rose to take with her in order to enable her to enjoy happiness on earth. Rose is adopted by a miller's family, falls in love, and marries. She gives the rose to her firstborn child, but in doing so, she dies and becomes an angel (Schumann's suggestion). There are resemblances in the plot—as Schumann acknowledged—to *Paradise and the Peri*. But the tale is related in a much more direct and simple manner, befitting a *Märchen*, and, as Schumann put it, is "more German and rustic in nature."[18]

This "rustic" nature is expressed in music more folklike in basis, such as the chorus of elves (No. 3), or the lively female duet (No. 20). In comparison to his other dramatic works, much of the *Rose* is more tuneful in a conventional manner, with dissonance employed sparingly. But in this miniature oratorio (the work is only about an hour in length), Schumann continued to apply the dramatic principles displayed in *Peri*, *Faust*, and *Genoveva*. There is a consistent dramatic flow with many of the musical sections leading without break from one to another. And there is no use of recitative; once again Schumann's distinctive arioso is employed.

As with earlier works, a brief, recurring motive is associated with the main character (the rose). But, in general, Schumann's guiding principle seemed to be to avoid complexity. Artifice is concealed beneath a pleasant exterior, as in the tuneful canon that opens the work. The result is the canonic equivalent of what Schumann had once described as the "best fugue"—one that the public could mistake for a dance tune. Far more successfully than in *Genoveva*, Schumann succeeded in creating music that ably complements the text and brings it to life. Here, it

---

[18] Letter to Klitzsch of 9 August 1851 in Hermann Erler, *Robert Schumann's Leben. Aus seinen Breifen geschildert*, 2 vols. (Berlin, 1887), II, p. 61.

seems, lay his strength as a dramatic composer—not in psychological representation but in depicting the miraculous and improbable world of the *Märchen*.

During the final years of his life, Schumann seemed to become more interested in children than ever. One notable instance is his fascination with the poetry of Elisabeth Kulmann, a literary prodigy who died at the age of seventeen in 1825. Schumann discovered her work in 1851, and set eleven of her poems to music—four as duets in the *Mädchenlieder* op. 103 and the remainder as solo songs in *Sieben Lieder* op. 104 (the latter work dedicated to her memory and bound together in the first edition by brief introductory texts written by Schumann). A portrait of her was placed in his workroom. Friends and associates were informed of his discovery, and he was anxious that his settings appear in print as quickly as possible. This was no passing fancy on Schumann's part. While in Endenich, he wrote to Brahms requesting her poetry.

Acting on the assumption that Kulmann was a little-known second-rate poet, it has become fashionable to see in Schumann's interest confirmation of his growing mental instability. But Kulmann was not an obscure discovery by Schumann. She was an extremely popular poet. The first publication in German of her poetry appeared in 1835; by 1857 there had been eight editions. Popularity may not assure quality, but, for a child, Kulmann's poetry is noteworthy. That is how Schumann perceived it—beauty and wisdom "from the mouth of a child."[19] And that explains to a great extent his enthusiasm. Schumann had discovered in Elisabeth Kulmann the ideal poet: the child as poet.

---

[19] From Schumann's dedication of op. 104.

APPENDIX A

Calendar

Year	Age	Life	Contemporary musicians and events
1810		Robert Schumann born on 8 June in Zwickau, Saxony, son of August Schumann and Christiane (née Schnabel).	Chopin born, 1 March. Burgmüller born, 7 May. Nicolai born, 9 June. Schuncke born 21 Dec. Arriaga aged 4; Beethoven 40; Bellini 9; Berlioz 7; Berwald 14; Cherubini 50; Clementi 58; Donizetti 13; Field 28; Hérold 19; Hoffmann, 34; Hummel 32; Lortzing, 9; Marschner, 15; Mendelssohn 1; Meyerbeer 19; Moscheles 16; Paganini 28; Rossini 18; Schubert 13; Spohr 26; Spontini 36; Weber 24.
1811	1		Liszt born, 22 Oct.; Hiller born, 24 Oct.
1813	3		Wagner born, 22 May; Verdi born, 10 Oct.; Alkan born, 30 Nov.
1814	4		Henselt born, 12 May.

1815	5		Battle of Waterloo.
1816	6		Rossini: *Barber of Seville*
			Hoffmann: *Undine*
1817	7	Begins piano lessons. First compositions (dances).	Gade born, 22 Feb.
			Byron: *Manfred*
1818	8		Spohr: *Faust*
			Beethoven: "Hammerklavier" Sonata.
1819	9		Clara Wieck born, 13 Sept.
			Schubert: "Trout" Quintet
1820	10	Enters Zwickau Lyceum.	
1821	11		Weber: *Der Freischütz*.
			Napoleon dies, 5 May.
1822	12	Composes *Psalm 150*. Active in performances at home and with Kuntsch.	Franck born, 10 Dec.
			Hoffmann dies, 25 June.
			Schubert: "Unfinished" Symphony.
1823	13	Passion for poetry and the theater.	Beethoven: Symphony No. 9.
			Weber: *Euryanthe*.
			Schubert: *Die schöne Müllerin*.
1824	14		Bruckner born, 4 Sept.
			Cornelius born, 24 Dec.
1825	15	Death of sister, Emilie. Creates student literary group.	Smetana born, 2 March.
			Boïeldieu: *La dame blanche*.
1826	16	August Schumann dies, 10 Aug.	Arriaga dies, 17 Jan.
			Weber dies, 5 June.
			Mendelssohn: *A Midsummer Night's Dream* Overture.
1827	17	Intense interest in Schubert and Jean Paul.	Beethoven dies, 26 March.
			Schubert: *Die Winterreise*.
			Chopin: Variations op. 2.
1828	18	April, May: travels in Bavaria. May: enrolls as student of law at University of Leipzig. Meets Friedrich and Clara Wieck. Neglects studies. Dec.: starts student chamber ensemble. Early lieder: WoO 10, 19, 21.	Schubert dies, 19 Nov.
			Marschner: *Der Vampyr*.

1829	19	May: Rhine journey. Transfers to University of Heidelberg and meets Thibaut. Aug.-Oct.: visits Switzerland and Italy. Piano Quartet WoO 32.	Rossini: *Guillaume Tell.* Mendelssohn revives Bach's *St Matthew Passion.*
1830	20	Apr.: hears Paganini. July: informs family of desire to switch to music. Oct.: begins study with Wieck. *Abegg Variations* op. 1. Toccata op. 7.	Berlioz: *Symphonie fantastique.* Hugo: *Ernani.* July Revolution in Paris.
1831	21	Affair with Christel. Studies theory with Dorn. July: creates *Davidsbund.* Dissatisfaction with Wieck grows. Beginning of hand injury. Dec.: publishes review of Chopin in *AMZ* *Papillons* op. 2. Allegro op. 8.	Bellini: *Norma.* Meyerbeer: *Robert le diable.* Goethe: *Faust II.*
1832	22	Growing interest in Clara. May: severe hand problems. 18 Nov.: G minor Symphony performed in Zwickau. Paganini Etudes op. 3. *Intermezzi* op. 4	Donizetti: *L'elisir d'amore.*
1833	23	17–18 Oct.: suffers nervous breakdown. Gradual recovery. *Impromptus* op. 5. Symphony WoO 29.	Brahms born, 7 May. Burgmüller: Symphony No. 1. Marschner: *Hans Heiling.*
1834	24	3 Apr.: first issue of *NZfM*. Fall: engagement with Ernestine von Fricken. *Etudes symphoniques* op. 13.	Schuncke dies, 7 Dec. Borodin born, 12 Nov. Berlioz: *Harold in Italy.*
1835	25	Summer: meets Mendelssohn. Growing intimacy with Clara. *Carnaval* op. 9. Piano Sonata No. 1 op. 11.	Bellini dies, 24 Sept. Donizetti: *Lucia di Lammermoor.*
1836	26	Jan.: ends engagement with Ernestine. Feb.: death of his mother. Wieck prohibits relationship with Clara. Sept.: meets Chopin. *Concert sans orchestre* op. 14. Fantasie op. 17.	Burgmüller dies, 7 May. Meyerbeer: *Les Huguenots.*
1837	27	Aug.: S. and Clara become secretly engaged. Sept.: Wieck formally refuses permission and pursues a strategy of delay and separation. *Davidsbündlertänze* op. 6.	Hummel dies, 17 Oct. Berlioz: Requiem. Lortzing: *Zar und Zimmermann.*

1838	28	Sept.: leaves for Vienna. Increased sense of isolation. *Kinderszenen* op. 15. *Kreisleriana* op. 16. *Novelletten* op. 21	Bizet born, 25 Oct. Berlioz: *Benvenuto Cellini*. Chopin: *Préludes* op. 28.
1839	29	Jan.: Clara leaves for Paris tour. Apr.: S. returns to Leipzig. June: begins legal steps to gain consent for marriage. Aug.: Clara returns to Germany. Dec.: Wieck defames S. in court. *Arabesque* op. 18. *Humoreske* op. 20. *Nachtstücke* op. 23.	Musorgsky born, 21 Mar. Berlioz: *Roméo et Juliette*. Chopin: Piano Sonata op. 35
1840	30	Mar.: meets Liszt. Aug.: court grants permission for marriage. 12 Sept.: married. *Liederkreis von Heine* op. 24. *Liederkreis von Eichendorff* op. 39. *Frauenliebe und Leben* op. 42. *Dichterliebe* op. 48.	Chaikovsky born, 7 May. Goetz born, 17 Dec. Paganini dies, 27 May. Chopin: *Ballade* op. 38
1841	31	31 Mar.: Mendelssohn conducts Symphony No. 1. 6 Dec.: unsuccessful premiere of op. 52 and first version of op. 120. Growing discontent with journalistic duties. Symphony No. 1 op. 38. *Overture, Scherzo, and Finale* op. 52.	Chabrier born, 18 Jan. Dvořák born, 8 Sept. Gade: *Ossian* Overture.
1842	32	Feb. and Mar.: tour in northern Germany. 6 Dec.: premiere of Piano Quintet with Mendelssohn. 3 String Quartets op. 41. Piano Quintet op. 44. Piano Quartet op. 47.	Cherubini dies, 15 Mar. Mendelssohn: "Scottish" Symphony. Lortzing: *Der Wildschütz*. Wagner: *Rienzi*.
1843	33	Growing financial worries. Jan.: meets Berlioz. Sells *NZfM*. *Paradise and the Peri* op. 50.	Grieg born, 15 June. Berwald: Symphony No. 1.
1844	34	25 Jan.: leaves for Russian tour (returns 30 Mar.). Summer: onset of nervous breakdown. 13 Dec.: moves to Dresden.	Rimsky-Korsakov born, 18 Mar. Henselt: Piano Concerto.
1845	35	Illness persists. Renewed study of counterpoint. 4 Dec.: premiere of Piano Concerto. Piano Concerto op. 54. Six Fugues on the Name, "Bach" op. 60.	Wagner: *Tannhäuser*. Mendelssohn: Violin Concerto.
1846	36	Still ill. Increased interest in opera. 23 Nov.: leaves for Vienna tour. Symphony No. 2 op. 61.	Berlioz: *La damnation de Faust*. Mendelssohn: *Elijah*.

1847	37	4 Feb.: returns to Dresden from unsuccessful tour. 20 Feb.: conducts *Peri* in Berlin. July: Zwickau festival in his honor. 20 Nov.: assumes direction of Liedertafel. Piano Trio. No. 1 op. 63. Piano Trio No. 2 op. 80.	Mendelssohn dies, 4 Nov. Alkan: Piano Sonata. Verdi: *Macbeth*
1848	38	26 Mar.: creates choral society. 9 June: breaks with Liszt. Eager for a more prestigious position. *Album for the Young* op. 68. *Genoveva* op. 81.	Donizetti dies, 8 Apr. Liszt: *Les préludes*. Revolution in Paris and Vienna.
1849	39	May: revolution in Dresden. Temporary move to Kreischa. Fall: informed of directorship opening in Düsseldorf. Composes prolifically. *Nachtlied von Hebbel* op. 108. *Manfred.* op. 115.	Nicolai dies, 11 May. Chopin dies, 17 Oct. Meyerbeer: *Le prophète*. Nicolai: *Die lustigen Weiber von Windsor.*
1850	40	Mar.: Bremen and Hamburg. 25 Jun.: premiere of *Genoveva*. 1 Sept.: assumes position in Düsseldorf. Symphony No. 3 op. 97. Cello Concerto op. 129.	Wagner: *Lohengrin.*
1851	41	Disillusionment with Düsseldorf. Criticism of his conducting. Piano Trio No. 3 op. 110. *Der Rose Pilgerfahrt* op. 112. Symphony No. 4 op. 120.	d'Indy born, 27 Mar. Spontini dies, 14 Jan. Lortzing dies, 21 Jan. Verdi: *Rigoletto.*
1852	42	5 Feb.: premiere of *Rose*. Spring: immersed in work on *Dichtergarten*. Problems with "nerves" in summer and fall. Criticism of his conducting continues. Mass op. 147. *Requiem* op. 148.	Berlioz: *Soirées de l'orchestre.*
1853	43	May: Nieder-Rheinische Festival. July: suffers stroke? Sept.: meets Brahms. Nov.: committee asks S. to limit conducting duties. S. resigns effective 1 Oct. 26 Nov.: visits Holland (returns 22 Dec.). *Gesänge der Frühe* op. 133. Violin Concerto WoO 23. *Scenes from Faust* WoO 3.	Verdi: *Il trovatore.* Liszt: Piano Sonata.
1854	44	19–30 Jan.: visits Joachim in Hanover. 10 Feb.: onset of breakdown. 27 Feb.: attempts suicide. 4 Mar.: taken to asylum in Endenich. Sept.: begins to correspond with Clara and others. Dec.: Joachim visits S. who asks to be moved to another asylum.	Janáček born, 4 July. Liszt: *Orpheus.* Berlioz: *L'enfance du Christ.*

1855	45	11 Jan. and 24 Feb.: Brahms visits S. who is anxious to leave. Spring: visit of Bettina von Arnim. July: Clara meets S.'s chief physician and agrees to his remaining in Endenich. S. abandons all correspondence.	Chausson born, 21 Jan. Verdi: *Les vêpres siciliennes*.
1856	46	S. becomes increasingly despondent. Apparently refuses to eat. Informed of his weak condition, on 27 July Clara visits S. In a weak and emaciated state, he dies on 29 July.	Liszt: *Dante Symphony*.

APPENDIX B

List of Works

	Date of Composition	Date of Publication

1. Compositions For Keyboard

a. Solo Piano

Papillons op. 2	1828–31	1831
Thème sur le nom Abegg varié op. 1	1829/1830	1831
Toccata op. 7	1829–33	1834
VI Etudes d'après des Caprices de Paganini op. 3	1832	1832
Intermezzi op. 4	1832	1833
Allegro op. 8	1832	1835
Canon "An Alexis" WoO 4	1832?	1858
Albumblätter op. 124 1. *Impromptu*. 2. *Leides Ahnung*. 3. *Scherzino*. 4. *Walzer*. 5. *Phantasietanz*. 6. *Wiegenliedchen*. 7. *Ländler*. 8. *Lied ohne Ende*. 9. *Impromptu*. 10. *Walzer*. 11. *Romanze*. 12. *Burla*. 13. *Larghetto*. 14. *Vision*. 15. *Walzer*. 16. *Schlummerlied*. 17. *Elfe*. 18. *Botschaft*. 19. *Phantasiestück*. 20. *Canon*.	1832–45	1854
Impromptus über ein Thema von Clara Wieck op. 5	1833	1833
VI Etudes de concert d'après des Caprices de Paganini op. 10	1833	1835
Etuden über ein Thema von Beethoven WoO 31	1833	1976
Grande Sonate op. 11	1833–35	1836
Sonate op. 22	1833–38	1839
Carnaval op. 9	1834–35	1837

Etudes symphoniques op. 13	1834–35	1837
Etudes symphoniques (five additional) WoO 6	1835?	1873
Variations on Chopin's Nocturne op. 15 no. 3	1835?	1992
Scherzo und Presto passionato WoO 5 (*Scherzo* originally intended for op. 14, the *Presto* for op. 22)	1835, 1836	1866
Concert sans orchestre op. 14 (revised and published as *Piano Sonata No. 3* in 1853)	1836	1836
Fantasie op. 17	1836	1839
Bunte Blätter op. 99 1.–3. *Drei Stücklein*. 4.–8. *Fünf Albumblätter*. 9. *Novellette*. 10. *Präludium*. 11. *Marsch*. 12. *Abendmusik*. 13. *Scherzo*. 14. *Geschwindmarsch*.	1836–49	1852
Davidsbündlertänze op. 6	1837	1837
Fantasiestücke op. 12	1837	1838
Fantasiestück (not included in publication of op. 12) WoO 28	1837	1958
Kinderszenen op. 15	1838	1839
Novelletten op. 21	1838	1839
Kreisleriana op. 16	1838	1838
Arabesque op. 18	1838/1839	1839
Blumenstück op. 19	1838/1839	1839
Vier Klavierstücke: Scherzo, Gigue, Romanze, und Fughette op. 32	1838/1839	1841
Humoreske op. 20	1839	1839
Nachtstücke op. 23	1839	1840
Faschingsschwank aus Wien op. 26	1839	1841
Drei Romanzen op. 28	1839	1840
Albumblatt für Gade WoO 8	1844	1887
Vier Fugen op. 72	1845	1850
Album für die Jugend op. 68	1848	1848
Album für die Jugend (four additional) WoO 16	1848	1924
Album für die Jugend (seventeen additional) WoO 30	1848	1973
Waldszenen op. 82	1848–49	1850
Vier Märsche op. 76	1849	1849
Drei Fantasiestücke op. 111	1851	1852
Drei Klaviersonaten für die Jugend op. 118	1853	1853
Sieben Klavierstücke in Fughettenform op. 126	1853	1854
Gesänge der Frühe op. 133	1853	1855
Theme in E Flat WoO 10e	1854	1893
Theme in E flat [WoO 10e] and Variations WoO 24	1854	1941

b. Pedal Piano

Studien op. 56	1845	1845
Skizzen op. 58	1845	1846

c. Organ

Sechs Fugen über den Namen, "Bach" op. 60	1845	1846

d. Piano Duet

Acht Polonaisen WoO 20	1828	1933
Bilder aus dem Osten op. 66	1848	1849
Zwölf vierhändige Klavierstücke für kleine und grosse Kinder op. 85	1849	1850
Ballszenen op. 109	1851	1853
Kinderball op. 130	1853	1854

2. Vocal Compositions

a. Solo Lieder

Early Lieder WoO 10b, c, d 　1. *An Anna* (Kerner). 2. *Im Herbste* (Kerner). 　3. *Hirtenknabe* (Schumann).	1827–28	1893
Der Fischer (Goethe) WoO 19	1827–28	1933
Sechs Frühe Lieder WoO 21 　1. *Sehnsucht* (Schumann). 2. *Die Weinende* (Byron). 3. *Erinnerung* (Jacobi). 4. *Kurzes Erwachen* (Kerner). 5. *Gesanges Erwachen* (Kerner). 6. *An Anna* (Kerner).	1827–28	1933
Liederkreis von Heine op. 24 　1. *Morgens steh' ich auf und frage*. 2. *Es treibt mich hin*. 3. *Ich wandelte unter den Bäumen*. 4. *Lieb' Liebchen*. 5. *Schöne Wiege meiner Leiden*. 6. *Warte, warte, wilder Schiffmann*. 7. *Berg' und Burgen schaun herunter*. 8. *Anfangs wollt ich fast verzagen*. 9. *Mit Myrten und Rosen*.	1840	1840
Myrthen op. 25 　1. *Widmung* (Rückert). 2. *Freisinn* (Goethe). 3. *Der Nussbaum* (Mosen). 4. *Jemand* (Burns). 5. *Sitz' ich allein* (Goethe). 6. *Setze mir nicht* (Goethe). 7. *Die Lotosblume* (Heine). 8. *Talismane* (Goethe). 9. *Lied der Suleika* (Goethe). 10. *Die Hochländer-Witwe* (Burns). 11. *Lied der Braut No. 1* (Rückert). 12. *Lied der Braut No. 2* (Rückert). 13. *Hochländers Abschied* (Burns).	1840	1840

14. *Hochländisches Wiegenlied* (Burns). 15. *Mein Herz ist schwer* (Byron). 16. *Rätsel* (Byron). 17. *Leis' rudern hier* (Moore). 18. *Wenn durch die Piazzetta* (Moore). 19. *Hauptmanns Weib* (Burns). 20. *Weit, weit* (Burns). 21 *Was will die einsame Träne* (Heine). 22. *Niemand* (Burns). 23. *Im Westen* (Burns). 24. *Du bist wie eine Blume* (Heine). 25. *Aus dem östlichen Rosen* (Rückert). 26. *Zum Schluss* (Rückert).

Lieder und Gesänge, Heft I op. 27 1. *Sag an, o lieber Vogel mein* (Hebbel). 2. *Dem roten Röslein gleicht mein Weib* (Burns). 3. *Was soll ich sagen?* (Chamisso). 4. *Jasminenstrauch* (Rückert). 5. *Nur ein lächelnder Blick* (Zimmermann).	1840	1849
Drei Gedichte von Geibel op. 30 1. *Der Knabe mit dem Wunderhorn*. 2. *Der Page*. 3. *Der Hidalgo*.	1840	1840
Drei Gesänge von Chamisso op. 31 1. *Die Löwenbraut*. 2. *Die Kartenlegerin*. 3. *Die rote Hanne*	1840	1841
Zwölf Gedichte von Kerner op. 35 1. *Lust der Sturmnacht*. 2. *Stirb, Lieb' und Freud*. 3. *Wanderlied*. 4. *Erstes Grün*. 5. *Sehnsucht nach der Waldgegend*. 6. *Auf das Trinkglas eines verstorbenen Freundes*. 7. *Wanderung*. 8. *Stille Liebe*. 9. *Frage*. 10. *Stille Tränen*. 11. *Wer machte dich so krank?* 12. *Alte Laute*.	1840	1841
Sechs Gedichte von Reinick op. 36 1. *Sonntags am Rhein*. 2. *Ständchen*. 3. *Nichts schöneres*. 4. *An den Sonnenschein*. 5. *Dichters Genesung*. 6. *Liebesbotschaft*.	1840	1842
Zwölf Gedichte von Rückert's 'Liebesfrühling' op. 37 1. *Der Himmel hat eine Träne geweint*. 2. *Er ist gekommen*. 3. *O ihr Herren*. 4. *Liebst du um Schönheit*. 5. *Ich hab in mich gesogen*. 6. *Liebste, was kann denn uns scheiden?* 7. *Schön ist das Fest des Lenzes*. 8. *Flügel! Flügel!* 9. *Rose, Meer und Sonne*. 10. *O Sonn, o Meer, o Rose!* 11. *Warum willst du andre fragen*. 12. *So wahr die Sonne scheinet*. (numbers 2, 4, and 11 are by Clara Schumann)	1840	1841
Liederkreis von Eichendorff op. 39 1. *In der Fremde*. 2. *Intermezzo*. 3. *Waldesgespräch*. 4. *Die Stille*. 5. *Mondnacht*. 6. *Schöne*	1840	1842

Fremde. 7. *Auf einer Burg.* 8. *In der Fremde.* 9. *Wehmut.* 10. *Zwielicht.* 11. *Im Walde.* 12. *Frühlingsnacht.*		
Fünf Lieder op. 40	1840	1842
1. *Märzveilchen* (Andersen). 2. *Muttertraum* (Andersen). 3. *Der Soldat* (Andersen). 4. *Der Spielmann* (Andersen). 5. *Verratene Liebe* (Chamisso).		
Frauenliebe und Leben (Chamisso) op. 42	1840	1843
1. *Seit ich ihn gesehen.* 2. *Er, der Herrlichste von allen.* 3. *Ich kann's nicht fassen.* 4. *Du Ring an meinem Finger.* 5. *Helft mir, ihr Schwestern.* 6. *Süsser Freund, du blickest.* 7. *An meinem Herzen.* 8. *Nun hast du mir den ersten Schmerz getan.*		
Romanzen und Balladen, Heft I op. 45	1840	1843
1. *Der Schatzgräber* (Eichendorff). 2. *Frühlingsfahrt* (Eichendorff). 3. *Abends am Strand* (Heine).		
Dichterliebe (Heine) op. 48	1840	1844
1. *Im wunderschönen Monat Mai.* 2. *Aus meinen Tränen spriessen.* 3. *Die Rose, die Lilie.* 4. *Wenn ich in deine Augen seh'.* 5. *Ich will meine Seele tauchen.* 6. *Im Rhein, im heiligen Strome.* 7. *Ich grolle nicht.* 8. *Und wüssten's die Blumen.* 9. *Das ist ein Flöten und Geigen.* 10. *Hör' ich das Liedchen klingen.* 11. *Ein Jüngling liebt ein Mädchen.* 12. *Am leuchtenden Sommermorgen.* 13. *Ich hab' im Traum geweinet.* 14. *Allnächtlich im Traume.* 15. *Aus alten Märchen.* 16. *Die alten, bösen Lieder.*		
Romanzen und Balladen, Heft II op. 49	1840	1844
1. *Die beiden Grenadiere* (Heine). 2. *Die feindlichen Brüder* (Heine). 3. *Die Nonne* (Fröhlich).		
Romanzen und Balladen, Heft III op. 53	1840	1845
1. *Blondels Lied* (Seidl). 2. *Lorelei* (Lorenz). 3. *Der arme Peter* (Heine).		
Belsatzar (Heine) op. 57	1840	1846
"*Der Deutsche Rhein*" (Becker) WoO 1	1840	1840
Zwei Balladen-Fragmente WoO 11	1840	1897
1. *Die Reiter* (Schwab). 2. *Die nächtliche Heerschau* (Zedlitz).		
Lieder und Gesänge, Heft III op. 77	1840, 1850	1851
1. *Der frohe Wandersmann* (Eichendorff). 2. *Mein Garten* (Hoffmann von Fallersleben). 3. *Geisternähe* (Halm).		

4. *Stiller Vorwurf* (Anon.). 5. *Aufträge* (L'Egru).

Romanzen und Balladen, Heft IV op. 64	1841, 1847	1847

1. *Die Soldatenbraut* (Mörike). 2. *Das verlassene Mägdelein* (Mörike). 3. *Tragödie* (Heine): a. *Entflieh mit mir*, b. *Es fiel ein Reif*, c. *Auf ihrem Grab* (S. & T. duet).

Lieder und Gesänge, Heft II op. 51	1842	1850

1. *Sehnsucht* (Geibel). 2. *Volksliedchen* (Rückert). 3. *Ich wand're nicht* (Christern). 4. *Auf dem Rhein* (Immermann). 5. *Liebeslied* (Goethe).

"Soldatenlied" (Hoffmann von Fallersleben) WoO 7	1845	1845
Lieder-Album für die Jugend op. 79	1849	1849

1. *Der Abendstern* (Hoffmann von Fallersleben)). 2. *Schmetterling* (Hoffmann von Fallersleben) 3. *Frühlingsbotschaft* (Hoffmann von Fallersleben). 4. *Frühlingsgruss* (Hoffmann von Fallersleben). 5. *Vom Schlaraffenland* (Hoffmann von Fallersleben). 6. *Sonntag* (Hoffmann von Fallersleben). 7. *Zigeunerliedchen No. 1* (Geibel). 8. *Zigeunerliedchen No. 2* (Geibel). 9. *Des Knaben Berglied* (Uhland). 10. *Mailied* (Overbeck) (Duet). 11. *Käuzlein* (from *Des Knaben Wunderhorn*). 12. *Hinaus ins Freie!* (Hoffmann von Fallersleben). 13. *Der Sandmann* (Kletke). 14. *Marienwürmchen* (from *Des Knaben Wunderhorn*). 15. *Die Waise* (Hoffmann von Fallersleben). 16. *Das Glück* (Hebbel) (Duet). 17. *Weihnachtsied* (Andersen). 18. *Die wandelnde Glocke* (Goethe). 19. *Frühlingslied* (Hoffmann von Fallersleben) (duet). 20. *Frühlings Ankunft* (Hoffmann von Fallersleben). 21. *Die Schwalben* (Anon.) (duet). 22. *Kinderwacht* (Anon.). 23. *Des Sennen Abschied* (Schiller). 24. *Er ist's* (Mörike). 25. *Spinnenlied* (Anon.) (trio). 26. *Des Buben Schützenlied* (Schiller). 27. *Schneeglöckchen* (Rückert). 28. *Lied Lynceus des Türmers* (Goethe). 29. *Mignon* (Goethe).

Drei Gesänge (Byron) op. 95	1849	1851

1. *Die Tochter Jephthas.* 2. *An den Mond.* 3. *Dem Helden.*

Lieder aus Goethe's Wilhelm Meister op. 98a	1849	1851

1. *Kennst du das Land.* 2. *Ballade des Harfners.* 3. *Nur wer die Sehnsucht kennt.* 4. *Wer nie sein*

Brot nit Tränen ass. 5. *Heiss mich nicht reden.*
6. *Wer sich der Einsamkeit ergibt.* 7. *Singet nicht in Trauertönen.* 8. *An die Türen will ich schleichen.* 9. *So lasst mich scheinen.*

Drei Gesänge op. 83	1850	1850

1. *Resignation* (J. B.). 2. *Die Blume der Ergebung* (Rückert). 3. *Der Einsiedler* (Eichendorff).

Sechs Gesänge (von der Neun) op. 89	1850	1850

1. *Es stürmet.* 2. *Heimliches Verschwinden.* 3. *Herbstlied.* 4. *Abschied vom Walde.* 5. *Ins Freie.* 6. *Röselein.*

Sechs Gedichte von Lenau und Requiem op. 90	1850	1851

1. *Lied eines Schmiedes.* 2. *Meine Rose.* 3. *Kommen und Scheiden.* 4. *Die Sennin.* 5. *Einsamkeit.* 6. *Der schwere Abend.*

Lieder und Gesänge, Heft IV op. 96	1850	1851

1. *Nachtlied* (Goethe). 2. *Schneeglöckchen* (Anon.). 3. *Ihre Stimme* (Platen). 4. *Gesungen!* (von der Neun). 5. *Himmel und Erde* (von der Neun).

Lieder und Gesänge op. 127	1850, 1851	1854

1. *Sängers Trost* (Kerner). 2. *Dein Angesicht* (Heine). 3. *Es leuchtet meine Liebe* (Heine). 4. *Mein altes Ross* (Strachwitz). 5. *Schlusslied des Narren* (Shakespeare).

Der Handschuh (Schiller) op. 87	1850?	1850
Sieben Lieder von Kulmann op. 104	1851	1851

1. *Mond, meiner Seele liebling.* 2. *Viel Glück zur Reise.* 3. *Du nennst mich armes Mädchen.* 4. *Der Zeisig.* 5. *Reich' mir die Hand.* 6. *Die letzten Blumen starben.* 7. *Gekämpft hat meine Barke.*

Vier Husarenlieder von Lenau op. 117	1851	1852

1. *Der Husar.* 2. *Der leidige Frieden.* 3. *Den grünen Zeigern.* 4. *Da liegt der Feinde gestreckte Schar.*

Drei Gedichte von Pfarrius op. 119	1851	1853

1. *Die Hütte.* 2. *Warnung.* 3. *Der Bräutigam und die Birke.*

Fünf heitere Gesänge op. 125	1851	1853

1. *Der Meerfee* (Buddeus). 2. *Husarenabzug* (Candidus). 3. *Jung Volkers Lied* (Mörike). 4. *Frühlingslied* (Braun). 5. *Frühlingslust* (Anon.).

Sechs Gesänge op. 107	1851–52	1852

1. *Herzeleid* (Ullrich). 2. *Die Fensterscheibe*

358 · APPENDIX B

(Ullrich). 3. *Der Gärtner* (Mörike). 4. *Die Spinnerin* (Heyse). 5. *Im Wald* (Wolfgang Müller). 6. *Abendlied* (Kinkel).

Gedichte der Königin Maria Stuart op. 135   1852   1855
    1. *Abschied von Frankreich*. 2. *Nach der Geburt ihres Sohnes*. 3. *An die Königin Elisabeth*. 4. *Abschied von der Welt*. 5. *Gebet*.

Vier Gesänge op. 142   1852   1858
    1. *Trost im Gesang* (Kerner). 2. *Lehn' deine Wang'* (Heine). 3. *Mädchen-Schwermut* (Anon.). 4. *Mein Wagen rollet langsam* (Heine).

b. Works for Declamation

Schön Hedwig (Hebbel) op. 106   1849   1853
Zwei Balladen op. 122   1852, 1853   1853
    1. *Ballade vom Haideknaben* (Hebbel). 2. *Die Flüchtlinge* (Shelley).

c. Mixed Voices or Chorus

Drei Gedichte von Geibel op. 29   1840   1841
    1. *Ländliches Lied* (duet). 2. *Lied* (trio). 3. *Zigeunerleben* (quartet).

Sechs Lieder op. 33   1840   1842
    (for male chorus)
    1. *Der träumende See* (Mosen). 2. *Die Minnesänger* (Heine). 3. *Die Lotosblume* (Heine). 4. *Der Zecher als Doctrinair* (Mosen). 5. *Rastlose Liebe* (Goethe). 6. *Frühlingsglocken* (Reinick).

Vier Duette op. 34   1840   1841
    1. *Liebesgarten* (Reinick). 2. *Liebhabers Ständchen* (Burns). 3. *Unter'm Fenster* (Burns). 4. *Familien-Gemälde* (Grün).

Drei zweistimmige Lieder op. 43   1840   1844
    1. *Wenn ich ein Vöglein wär'* (Anon.). 2. *Herbstlied* (Mahlmann). 3. *Schön Blümelein* (Reinick).

Fünf Lieder von Burns op. 55   1846   1847
    (for mixed chorus)
    1. *Das Hochlandmädchen*. 2. *Zahnweh*. 3. *Mich zieht es nach dem Dörfchen hin*. 4. *Die alte gute Zeit*. 5. *Hochlandbursch*.

Vier Gesänge op. 59   1846   1848
    (for mixed chorus)
    1. *Nord oder Süd* (Lappe). 2. *Am Bodensee*

(Platen). 3. *Jägerlied* (Mörike). 4. *Gute Nacht* (Rückert).		
"Hirtenknaben" (Droste-Hülshoff; for op. 59) WoO 18 (2 S. & 2 T.)	1846	1930
Drei Gesänge op. 62 (for male chorus) 1. *Der Eidgenossen Nachtwache* (Eichendorff). 2. *Freiheitslied* (Rückert). 3. *Schlachtgesang* (Klopstock).	1847	1848
Ritornelle von Rückert op. 65 (for male chorus) 1. *Die Rose.* 2. *Lasst Lautenspiel.* 3. *Blüt' oder Schnee.* 4. *Gebt mir zu trinken!* 5. *Zürne nicht.* 6. *Im Sommertagen.* 7. *In Meeres Mitten.*	1847	1849
Beim Abschied zu singen (Feuchtersleben) op. 84 (for mixed chorus and wind ensemble)	1847	1850
Canon für Männerstimme (Rückert) WoO 12	1847	1906
"Mache deinem Meister Ehre" (Rückert) WoO 17 (for male chorus)	1847	1928
"Schwarze-Rot-Gold" (Freiligrath) WoO 13 (for male chorus)	1848	1913
"Zu den Waffen" (Ullrich) WoO 14 (for male chorus)	1848	1914
"Deutsche Freiheitsgesang" (Fürst) WoO 15 (for male chorus)	1848	1914
Romanzen und Balladen, Heft I op. 67 (for mixed chorus) 1. *Der König von Thule* (Goethe). 2. *Schön Rohtraut* (Mörike). 3. *Heidenröslein* (Goethe). 4. *Ungewitter* (Chamisso). 5. *John Anderson* (Burns).	1849	1849
Romanzen, Heft I op. 69 (for female chorus; piano ad lib. accompaniment) 1. *Tamburinschlägerin* (Eichendorff). 2. *Waldmädchen* (Eichendorff). 3. *Klosterfräulein* (Kerner). 4. *Soldatenbraut* (Mörike). 5. *Meerfey* (Eichendorff). 6. *Die Capelle* (Uhland).	1849	1849
Spanisches Liederspiel (Geibel) op. 74 (includes 3 solo songs) 1. *Erste Begegnung* (S.A.). 2. *Intermezzo* (T.B.).	1849	1849

3. *Liebesgram* (S.A.). 4. *In der Nacht* (S.T.).
5. *Es ist verraten* (S.A.T.B.). 6. *Melancholie* (S.).
7. *Geständnis* (T.). 8. *Botschaft* (S.A.). 9. *Ich bin geliebt* (S.A.T.B.). 10. *Der Contrabandiste* (B.)

Romanzen und Balladen, Heft II op. 75   1849   1850
(for mixed chorus)
1. *Schnitter Tod* (Anon.). 2. *Im Walde* (Eichendorff). 3. *Der traurige Jäger* (Eichendorff).
4. *Der Rekrut* (Burns). 5. *Vom verwundeten Knaben* (Anon.).

Vier Duette op. 78   1849   1850
1. *Tanzlied* (Rückert). 2. *Er und sie* (Kerner).
3. *Ich denke dein* (Goethe). 4. *Wiegenlied* (Hebbel).

Romanzen, Heft II op. 91   1849   1851
(for female chorus; piano ad lib. accompaniment)
1. *Rosmarin* (Anon.). 2. *Jäger Wohlgemut* (from *Des Knaben Wunderhorn*). 3. *Der Wassermann* (Kerner). 4. *Das verlassene Mägdelein* (Mörike). 5. *Der Bleicherin Nachtlied* (Reinick).
6. *In Meeres Mitten* (Rückert).

Minnespiel (Rückert) op. 101   1849   1852
(includes four solo songs)
1. *Lied* (T.). 2. *Gesang* (S.). 3. *Duett* (A.B.).
4. *Lied* (T.). 5. *Quartett* (S.A.T.B.). 6. *Lied* (A.). 7. *Duett* (S.T.). 8. *Quartett* (S.A.T.B.).

Jagdlieder (Laube) op. 137   1849   1857
(for male chorus; four horns ad lib. accompaniment)
1. *Zur hohen Jagd*. 2. *Habet acht*. 3. *Jagdmorgen*.
4. *Frühe*. 5. *Bei der Flasche*.

Spanische Liebeslieder (Geibel) op. 138   1849   1857
(includes four solo songs; piano 4-hands accompaniment)
1. *Vorspiel* (Pf.). 2. *Lied* (S.). 3. *Lied* (T.).
4. *Duett* (S.A.). 5. *Romanze* (B.). 6. *Intermezzo* (Pf.). 7. *Lied* (T.). 8. *Lied* (A.). 9. *Duett* (T.B.).
10. *Quartett* (S.A.T.B.).

Vier doppelchörige Gesänge op. 141   1849   1858
1. *An die Sterne* (Rückert). 2. *Ungewisses Licht* (Zedlitz). 3. *Zuversicht* (Zedlitz). 4. *Talismane* (Goethe).

Romanzen und Balladen, Heft III op. 145   1849   1860
(for mixed chorus)
1. *Der Schmidt* (Uhland). 2. *Die Nonne* (Anon.). 3. *Der Sänger* (Uhland). 4. *John An-*

derson (Burns). 5. *Romanze vom Gänsebuben* (Malsburg).

Romanzen und Balladen, Heft IV op. 146 (for mixed chorus) 1. *Brautgesang* (Uhland). 2. *Bänkelsänger Willie* (Burns). 3. *Der Traum* (Uhland). 4. *Sommerlied* (Rückert). 5. *Das Schifflein* (Uhland).	1849	1860
"Sommerruh" (Schad) WoO 9 (duet with piano accompaniment)	1849	1890
Mädchenlieder von Kulmann op. 103 (duets) 1. *Mailied*. 2. *Frühlingslied*. 3. *An die Nachtigall*. 4. *An den Abendstern*.	1851	1851
Drei Lieder op. 114 (trios for female voices) 1. *Nänie* (Bechstein). 2. *Triolett* (L'Egru). 3. *Spruch* (Rückert).	1853?	1853

d. Soloists, chorus, and orchestra

Requiem für Mignon op. 98b	1849	1851
Nachtlied von Hebbel op. 108 (chorus and orchestra)	1849	1852
Neujahrslied von Rückert op. 144 (chorus and orchestra)	1849, 1850	1861
Der Königssohn op. 116	1851	1853
Des Sängers Fluch op. 139	1852	1858
Vom Pagen und der Königstochter op. 140	1852	1857
Fest-Ouvertüre ("Rheinweinlied") op. 123 (chorus and orchestra)	1852–53	1854
Das Glück von Edenhall op. 143	1853	1860

3. Chamber Compositions

Piano Quartet in C minor WoO 32	1829	1979
Three String Quartets op. 41	1842	1843
Piano Quintet op. 44	1842	1843
Piano Quartet op. 47	1842	1845
Fantasiestücke (piano trio) op. 88	1842	1850
Andante und Variationen op. 46 (two pianos)	1843	1844
Andante und Variationen op. 46 WoO 10a (original version for two pianos, two cellos, and horn)	1843	1893
Piano Trio No. 1 op. 63	1847	1848
Piano Trio No. 2 op. 80	1847	1849
Adagio und Allegro (horn and piano) op. 70	1849	1849

Fantasiestücke (clarinet and piano) op. 73	1849	1849
Drei Romanzen (oboe and piano) op. 94	1849	1851
Fünf Stücke im Volkston (cello and piano) op. 102	1849	1851
Violin Sonata No. 1 op. 105	1851	1852
Piano Trio No. 3 op. 110	1851	1852
Märchenbilder (viola and piano) op. 113	1851	1852
Violin Sonata No. 2 op. 121	1851	1853
Piano accompaniment for Bach's Violin Sonatas WoO 2	1852, 1853	1853
Märchenerzählungen (clarinet, viola, and piano) op. 132	1853	1854
Violin Sonata No. 3 WoO 27	1853	1956
Piano accompaniments to selected Caprices of Paganini WoO 25	1853	1941
Piano accompaniments to Bach's Cello Suites	1853	1986

4. Compositions for Solo Instrument and Orchestra

Concertsatz (piano; reconstruction)	1839	1988
Piano Concerto op. 54	1841, 1845	1846
Konzertstück (four French horns) op. 86	1849	1851
Introduction und Allegro appassionato (piano) op. 92	1849	1852
Cello Concerto op. 129	1850	1854
Phantasie (violin) op. 131	1853	1854
Koncert-Allegro mit Introduction (piano) op. 134	1853	1855
Violin Concerto WoO 23	1853	1937
Arrangement for violin of the Cello Concerto op. 129	1853	1987

5. Orchestral Compositions

Symphony in G minor WoO 29	1832, 1833	1972
Symphony No. 1 op. 38	1841	1853
Overture, Scherzo, and Finale op. 52	1841	1846
Symphony No. 4 op. 120	1841, 1851	1853
Symphony No. 2 op. 61	1845–46	1847
Symphony No. 3 op. 97	1850	1851
Ouvertüre zu Schillers Braut von Messina op. 100	1850–51	1851
Ouvertüre zu Shakespeares Julius Cäsar op. 128	1851	1854
Ouvertüre zu Goethes Hermann und Dorothea op. 136	1851	1857

6. Oratorios, Stage Works, and Religious Compositions

a. Oratorios

Das Paradies und die Peri op. 50	1843	1844
Szenen aus Goethes Faust WoO 3	1844–53	1858
Der Rose Pilgerfahrt op. 112	1851	1852

b. Stage Works

Der Corsär (fragments)	1844	1983
Genoveva op. 81	1847–48	1850
Manfred op. 115	1848–49	1852

c. Religious Compositions

Adventlied von Rückert op. 71 (soprano, chorus, and orchestra)	1848	1849
Motette "Verzweifle nicht" (Rückert) op. 93 (double chorus and orchestra)	1849	1851
Mass op. 147	1852	1862
Requiem op. 148	1852	1864

APPENDIX C

Personalia

Alkan, Charles Henri Valentin (1813–88), French pianist and composer. Alkan was the greatest virtuoso of his age but, because of his reclusive nature, performed infrequently. His works are distinctive and original. Unfortunately, Schumann was familiar only with a few of his salon pieces.

Arnim, Bettina von (1785–1859), writer and composer. Sister of Clemens Brentano and wife of Ludwig Achim von Arnim. She wrote reminiscences of Beethoven and Goethe, which were criticized for their flights of fancy. Outspoken and idealistic, she championed women's rights and defiantly opposed discrimination against minorities (including Jews and the mentally ill).

Arnim, Ludwig Achim von (1781–1831), poet, novelist, dramatist, and critic. Coeditor of *The Youth's Magic Horn*, and creator of fiction of great imagination. Husband of Bettina and close friend of her brother, the poet Clemens Brentano.

Bennett, William Sterndale (1816–75), English pianist, composer, and teacher. Mendelssohn served as his mentor. Conductor of the London Philharmonic from 1856 to 1866, and professor of music at Cambridge University from 1856 until his death.

Berwald, Franz (1796–1868), Swedish composer, active in Germany and Austria. Little regarded during his lifetime, his chamber compositions and four symphonies are among the most innovative of the 1840s and 1850s.

Brendel, Franz (1811–68), editor of the *Neue Zeitschrift für Musik* from 1845. Teacher at the Leipzig Conservatory, and friend of Schumann. He became a strong advocate of Wagner and Liszt.

Brentano, Clemens (1778–1842), poet, novelist, and dramatist. Editor with Arnim of *The Youth's Magic Horn*. In later years, he became a devout Catholic, and lamented the frivolity of his earlier work.

Burgmüller, Norbert (1810–36), one of the most gifted composers of his generation. Among his most notable compositions are two symphonies, four string quartets, and a piano sonata. Schumann was a great champion of his music, and orchestrated part of Burgmüller's unfinished Symphony No. 2.

Chamisso, Adelbert von (1781–1838), poet, naturalist, and novelist. Best known for his creation of Peter Schlemihl, the unfortunate man who sold his shadow. Like Schumann, he had a wife considerably younger than himself. The poems that he wrote in her honor—*Frauenliebe und Leben*—were set by Schumann as his op. 42.

Cherubini, Luigi (1760–1842), Italian composer and teacher. Beethoven admired his work. Director of the Paris Conservatory from 1822, he was regarded as one of the foremost contrapuntists of his day.

David, Ferdinand (1810–73), violinist and composer. A good friend of Mendelssohn, he became concertmaster of the Gewandhaus Orchestra and professor at the Leipzig Conservatory.

Dorn, Heinrich (1804–92), composer, teacher, and conductor. Like Mendelssohn, he was a student of Zelter. Unlike Schumann (whom he briefly taught), Dorn moved well in official music circles. He was director of the Royal Opera in Berlin from 1849 to 1868.

Field, John (1782–1837), Irish pianist and composer. Creator of the nocturne, he was greatly esteemed for his expressive playing. Much of his life was spent in Russia. Both Wieck and Chopin were admirers of his work.

Franz, Robert (1815–92), composer and editor of Baroque music. Known for his nearly three hundred lieder, he was an early supporter of Schumann's compositions.

Gade, Niels (1817–90), Danish composer. A friend of both Mendelssohn and Schumann, his Symphony No. 1 op. 5 (1843) established his reputation in Germany. In 1861, he was appointed Kapellmeister in Copenhagen.

Hauptmann, Moritz (1792–1868), violinist, composer, and theorist. A conservative musician, he was professor of counterpoint and composition at the Leipzig Conservatory. A good friend of Spohr, he found Schumann's earlier work to be baffling.

Heller, Stephen (1814–88), pianist and composer. Settled in Paris in 1838. An infrequent performer, he was best known for his piano miniatures. He and Schumann shared an infatuation with Jean Paul.

Henselt, Adolf (1814–89), German pianist and composer. Despite his great virtuosity, he was plagued by stage fright and performed rarely. He settled in St Petersburg and helped the Schumanns during their Russian journey.

Herz, Henri (1806–88), Austrian composer and pianist. Settled in Paris in 1818. Popular and prolific, his facile style epitomized for Schumann the low musical standards of the day.

Hiller, Ferdinand (1811–85), pianist and composer. A pupil of Hummel, Hiller was unusually active in the musical life of his day (and counted among his friends Berlioz, Chopin, Mendelssohn, and Schumann). He was Schumann's predecessor in Düsseldorf, and recommended him for the post. Conductor at Cologne from 1850.

Hummel, Johann Nepomuk (1778–1837), piano virtuoso, composer, and teacher. Student of Mozart. In 1820, he was appointed Kapellmeister in Weimar. Although aware of his conservative reputation, for a time Schumann hoped to become his student.

Joachim, Joseph (1831–1907), violinist and composer. Studied and performed in Leipzig from 1843 to 1850. Schumann was enthralled with his virtuosity. Concertmaster at Hanover from 1853 to 1866, at which time he established a close friendship with Brahms. From 1868, he was director of the royal Hochschule für Musik in Berlin.

Kalkbrenner, Friedrich (1788–1849), German pianist and composer who settled in Paris. One of the most famous teachers of his time; Schuncke studied with him. Chopin briefly considered becoming his student.

Lind, Jenny (1820–87), singer. Known as the "Swedish Nightingale," she was famed for her unpretentious nature and the beauty of her voice (particularly the upper register). She appeared at several concerts with the Schumanns, and he was much taken with her musical ability and selflessness.

Louis Ferdinand, Prince (1772–1806), distinguished pianist and composer. Student of Dussek and nephew of Frederick the Great, he was one of the most promising composers of his generation. He was killed at the battle of Saalfeld.

Marschner, Heinrich (1795–1861), leading composer of opera in the 1820s and 1830s. Kapellmeister at Hanover from 1831 to 1859. His most popular operas dealt with the supernatural and were representative of the contemporary fascination with "Gothick" terror.

Meyerbeer, Giacomo (1791–1864), most popular composer of opera of his day (dating from the Paris production in 1831 of *Robert le diable*). Meyerbeer composed little, but attempted to make an unforgettable spectacle of each of his productions. Schumann was convinced that Meyerbeer was more concerned with fame and money than with dedication and service to Art.

Moscheles, Ignaz (1794–1870), piano virtuoso and composer. Active in English musical life, beginning with his first appearance with the London Philharmonic in 1821. He was a good friend of Mendelssohn. Schumann, in his youth, hoped to become Moscheles's pupil.

Novalis (1772–1801), pseudonym for Friedrich Leopold von Hardenberg. Poet and novelist, best known for the melancholy "Hymns to the Night," and the symbol of the unattainable blue flower (found in his novel *Heinrich von Ofterdingen*).

Reinick, Robert (1805–52), poet and painter. Schumann set many of his poems to music, and turned to him for assistance in the creation of *Genoveva*.

Rellstab, Ludwig (1799–1860), music critic and pianist. Student of Ludwig Berger. Founder in 1830 of *Iris im Gebiet der Tonkunst*, and long a major figure in German music criticism.

Rethel, Alfred (1816–59), artist. Active in many genres, including historical painting and book illustration. Best known for his macabre series of wood engravings, *Another Dance of Death*. Rethel went insane and, like Schumann, spent time in Endenich.

Richter, Johann Paul Friedrich, known as Jean Paul (1763–1825), prolific German novelist. Major works include *Hesperus* (1795), *Titan* (1803), and *Flegeljahre* (*Walt and Vult*) (1805). Jean Paul's writings are fanciful, poetic, and distinctive. Schumann was fascinated by them, and during the 1830s used several as a source of inspiration for his music.

Richter, Ludwig (1803–84), artist. Known for his painting, especially landscapes and imaginative themes (*St Genevieve in the Forest*), as well as book illustrations. Schumann became a good friend and for a time taught composition to Richter's son.

Rietz, Julius (1812–77), cellist, composer, and conductor. Director of the Gewandhaus Orchestra from 1848 to 1861. He preceded Hiller as music director in Düsseldorf.

Schuncke, Ludwig (1810–34), pianist and composer. He was a child prodigy, and traveled to Paris, where he became a student of Kalkbrenner. Although they knew one another for only about a year, he was perhaps Schumann's closest friend.

Spohr, Ludwig (1784–1859), violinist and composer. Appointed Kapellmeister in Kassel in 1822. His operas (especially *Faust* and *Jessonda*) and nine symphonies were highly regarded. Schumann was eager to gain his support, but Spohr found much of Schumann's music too unconventional.

Thibaut, Anton Friedrich Justus (1774–1840), professor of law at Heidelberg University. A distinguished musical amateur, his love of early music inspired his book *Purity in Music*. Schumann read it several times and held it in high esteem.

APPENDIX D

Select Bibliography

Thematic Catalogue and Listing of First Editions

Hofmann, Kurt. *Die Erstdrucke der Werke von Robert Schumann.* Tutzing: Hans Schneider, 1979.

Hofmann, Kurt and Keil, Siegmar. *Robert Schumann: Thematisches Verzeichnis sämtlichen im Druck erschienen musikalischen Werke.* 5th ed. Hamburg: Schuberth, 1982.

Correspondence, Diaries, and Writings by Schumann

Erler, Hermann. *Robert Schumann's Leben: Aus seinen Briefen geschildert.* 2 vols. Berlin: Ries & Erler, 1887.

Holde, Artur. "Suppressed Passages in the Brahms-Joachim Correspondence Published for the First Time," *The Musical Quarterly* XLV (1959), pp. 312–24.

Jansen, F. Gustav. "Briefwechsel zwischen Robert Franz und Robert Schumann," *Die Musik* VIII (1908/09), pp. 280–91; 346–59.

Kross, Siegfried, ed. *Briefe und Notizen Robert und Clara Schumanns.* 2nd ed. Bonn: Bouvier Verlag, 1982.

Schumann, Clara and Schumann, Robert. *Briefwechsel: Kritische Gesamtausgabe*, ed. Eva Weissweiler. 2 vols. Frankfurt am Main: Stroemfeld/Roter Stern, 1984-.

Schumann, Clara and Schumann, Robert. *The Complete Correspondence of Clara and Robert Schumann*, ed. Eva Weissweiler. Trans. Hildegard Fritscht and Ronald L. Crawford. 2 vols. New York: Lang, 1994-.

Schumann, Clara and Schumann, Robert. *The Marriage Diaries*, trans. P. Ostwald. Boston: Northeastern University Press, 1993.

Schumann, Robert. *Briefe. Neue Folge*, ed. F. Gustav Jansen. Leipzig: Breitkopf und Härtel, 1904.

Schumann, Robert. *Briefe und Gedichte aus dem Album Robert und Clara Schumanns*, ed. Wolfgang Boetticher. Leipzig: VEB Deutscher Verlag für Musik, 1981.

Schumann, Robert. *Gesammelte Schriften über Musik und Musiker*, ed. Martin Kreisig. 2 vols. Leipzig: Breitkopf & Härtel, 1914.

Schumann, Robert. *Haushaltbücher, 1837–1856*, ed. Gerd Nauhaus. 2 vols. Leipzig: VEB Deutscher Verlag für Musik, 1982.

Schumann, Robert. *Jugendbriefe*, ed. Clara Schumann. Leipzig: Breitkopf & Härtel, 1886.
Schumann, Robert. *Der junge Schumann: Dichtungen und Briefe*, ed. Alfred Schumann. Leipzig: Insel-Verlag, 1917.
Schumann, Robert. *Letters*, ed. Karl Storck. Trans. H. Bryant. New York: Blom, 1971 (reprint of 1907 edition).
Schumann, Robert. *Manuskripte—Briefe—Schumanniana—Katalog Nr. 188*. Tutzing: Musikantiquariat Hans Schneider, 1974.
Schumann, Robert. *The Musical World of Robert Schumann: A Selection from Schumann's Own Writings*, ed. and trans. Henry Pleasants. London: Gollancz, 1965.
Schumann, Robert. *Tagebücher: 1827–1838*, ed. Georg Eismann. Leipzig: VEB Deutscher Verlag für Musik, 1971.
Schumann, Robert. *Tagebücher: 1836–1854*, ed. Gerd Nauhaus. Leipzig: VEB Deutscher Verlag für Musik, 1987.

Books

Abraham, Gerald, ed. *Schumann: A Symposium*. London: Oxford University Press, 1952.
Bischoff, Bodo. *Monument für Beethoven: Die Entwicklung der Beethoven-Rezeption Robert Schumanns*. Cologne: Verlag Dohr, 1994.
Boetticher, Wolfgang. *Robert Schumanns Klavierwerke: Teil I: Opp. 1–6; Teil II: Opp. 7–13*. 2 vols. Wilhelmshaven: Heinrichshofen's Verlag, 1976, 1984.
Brion, Marcel. *Schumann and the Romantic Age*. Trans. G. Sainsbury. London: Collins, 1956.
Daverio, John. *Robert Schumann: Herald of a "New Poetic Age."* New York: Oxford University Press, 1997.
Eismann, Georg. *Robert Schumann: Ein Quellenwerk über sein Leben und Schaffen*. 2 vols. Leipzig: Breitkopf & Härtel, 1956.
Finson, Jon. *Robert Schumann and the Study of Orchestral Composition: The Genesis of the First Symphony op. 38*. Oxford: Clarendon Press, 1989.
Finson, Jon W. and Todd, R. Larry, eds. *Mendelssohn and Schumann: Essays on Their Music and Its Context*. Durham, NC: Duke University Press, 1984.
Fischer-Dieskau, Dietrich. *Robert Schumann—Words and Music: The Vocal Compositions*. Portland: Amadeus Press, 1988.
Hallmark, Rufus. *The Genesis of Schumann's Dichterliebe*. Ann Arbor: UMI Press, 1976.
Jansen, F. Gustav. *Die Davidsbündler*. Leipzig: Breitkopf & Härtel, 1883.
Kapp, Reinhard. *Studien zum Spätwerk Robert Schumanns*. Tutzing: Hans Schneider, 1984.
Kast, Paul, ed. *Schumanns rheinische Jahre*. Düsseldorf: Droste, 1981.
Litzmann, Berthold. *Clara Schumann—Ein Künstlerleben: Nach Tagebüchern und Briefen*. 3 vols. Hildesheim: Georg Olms, 1971 (reprint of 1908 edition).
Marston, Nicholas. *Schumann: Fantasie Op. 17*. Cambridge, UK: Cambridge University Press, 1992.
Mayeda, Akio. *Robert Schumanns Weg zur Symphonie*. Zürich: Atlantis, 1992.
Niecks, Frederick. *Robert Schumann*. London: J. M. Dent, 1925.
Ostwald, Peter. *Schumann: The Inner Voices of a Musical Genius*. Boston: Northeastern University Press, 1985.
Ozawa, Kazuko. *Quellenstudien zu Robert Schumanns Lieder nach Adelbert von Chamisso*. Frankfurt: Peter Lang, 1989.
Reich, Nancy B. *Clara Schumann: The Artist and the Woman*. Ithaca, NY: Cornell University Press, 1985.
Sams, Eric. *The Songs of Robert Schumann*. 3rd edition. Bloomington, IN: Indiana University Press, 1993.

Schumann, Eugenie. *The Memoirs of Eugenie Schumann*. New York: Dial, 1927.
Schumann, Eugenie. *Robert Schumann: Ein Lebensbild meines Vaters*. Leipzig: Koehler & Amelang, 1931.
Taylor, Ronald. *Robert Schumann: His Life and Work*. New York: Universe Books, 1982.
Todd, R. Larry, ed. *Schumann and His World*. Princeton, NJ: Princeton University Press, 1994.
Walker, Alan, ed. *Robert Schumann: The Man and His Music*. London: Barrie & Jenkins, 1972.
Wasielewski, Wilhelm Joseph von. *Robert Schumann: Eine Biographie*. 4th ed. Leipzig: Breitkopf & Härtel, 1906.

Articles

Abert, Hermann. "Robert Schumann's 'Genoveva'," *Zeitschrift der Internationalen Musikgesellschaft* XI (1910), pp. 277–89.
Abraham, Gerald. "Schumann's Op. II and III," in *Slavonic and Romantic Music*. London: Faber and Faber, 1968, pp. 261–66.
Dadelson, Georg von. "Robert Schumann und die Musik Bachs," *Archiv für Musikwissenschaft* XIV (1957), pp. 46–59.
Deutsch, Otto Erich. "The Discovery of Schubert's Great C-major Symphony: A Story in Fifteen Letters," *The Musical Quarterly* XXXVIII (1952), pp. 528–32.
Draheim, Joachim. "Schumann und Shakespeare," *Neue Zeitschrift für Musik* CXLI (1981), pp. 237–44.
Dusella, Reinhold. "Symphonisches in den Skizzenbüchern Schumanns," in Kross, Siegfried, ed. *Probleme der symphonischen Tradition im 19. Jahrhundert*. Tutzing: Hans Schneider, 1990, pp. 203–24.
Eismann, Georg. "Zu Robert Schumanns letzten Kompositionen," *Beiträge zur Musikwissenschaft* XXVIII (1968), pp. 151–157.
Finson, Jon. "Schumann, Popularity, and the *Ouvertüre, Scherzo, und Finale*, Opus 52," *The Musical Quarterly* LXIX (1983), pp. 1–26.
Finson, Jon W. "Schumann's Mature Style and the *Album of Songs for the Young*," *The Journal of Musicology* VIII (1990), pp. 227–50.
Fiske, Roger. "A Schumann Mystery," *The Musical Times* CV (1964), pp. 574–78.
Gülke, Peter. "Zu Robert Schumanns 'Rheinischer Sinfonie'," *Beiträge zur Musikwissenschaft* XXI (1974), pp. 123–35.
Hallmark, Rufus. "The Rückert Lieder of Robert and Clara Schumann," *19th-Century Music* XIV (1990–91), pp. 3–30.
Jensen, Eric Frederick. "Explicating Jean Paul: Robert Schumann's Program for *Papillons*, Op. 2," *19th-Century Music* XXII (1998–99), pp. 127–44.
Jensen, Eric Frederick. "A New Manuscript of Robert Schumann's *Waldszenen* Op. 82," *The Journal of Musicology* VII (1989), pp. 69–89.
Jensen, Eric Frederick. "Norbert Burgmüller and Robert Schumann," *The Musical Quarterly* LXXIV (1990), pp. 550–65.
Jensen, Eric Frederick. "Schumann at Endenich," *The Musical Times* CXXXIX (1998, March and April), pp. 10–19; 14–24.
Jensen, Eric Frederick. "Schumann, Hummel, and 'The Clarity of a Well-Planned Composition,'" *Studia Musicologica* XL (1999), pp. 59–70.
Kross, Siegfried. "Aus der Frühgeschichte von Robert Schumanns *Neue Zeitschrift für Musik*," *Die Musikforschung* XXXIV (1981), pp. 423–45.
Laux, Karl. " 'Dresden ist doch gar zu schön'—Schumann in der sächsischen Hauptstadt—Eine Ehrenrettung," in Moser, Hans Joachim and Rebling, Eberhard, eds. *Robert Schumann: Aus Anlass seines 100 Todestages*. Leipzig: VEB Verlag, 1956, pp. 25–42.

Lester, Joel. "Robert Schumann and Sonata Forms," *19th-Century Music* XVIII (1994–95), pp. 189–210.
Lippman, Edward A. "Theory and Practice in Schumann's Aesthetics," *Journal of the American Musicological Society* XVII (1964), pp. 310–45.
Mintz, Donald. "Schumann as an Interpreter of Goethe's *Faust*," *Journal of the American Musicological Society* XIV (1961), pp. 235–56.
Myers, Rollo H. "Finding a Lost Schumann Concerto," in Aprahamian, Felix, ed. *Essays on Music: An Anthology from 'The Listener'*. London: Cassell, 1967, pp. 223–27.
Nauhaus, Gerd. "*Der Rose Pilgerfahrt* op. 112: Schumanns Abschied von Oratorium," in Appel, Bernhard R., ed. *Schumann in Düsseldorf: Werke-Texte-Interpretationen*. Mainz: Schott, 1993, pp. 179–99.
Newcomb, Anthony. "Once More 'Between Absolute and Program Music': Schumann's Second Symphony," *Nineteenth-Century Music* VII (1983–84), pp. 233–50.
Roe, Stephen. "The Autograph Manuscript of Schumann's *Piano Concerto*," *The Musical Times* CXXXI (1990), pp. 77–79.
Roesner, Linda Correll. "Schumann's 'Parallel' Forms," *19th-Century Music* XIV (1990–91), pp. 265–78.
Roesner, Linda Correll. "Schumann's Revisions in the First Movement of the Piano Sonata in G Minor, Op. 22," *Nineteenth-Century Music* I (1977–78), pp. 97–109.
Roesner, Linda Correll. "Tonal Strategy and Poetic Content in Schumann's C-major Symphony, Op. 61," in Kross, Siegfried, ed. *Probleme der symphonischen Tradition im 19. Jahrhundert*. Tutzing: Hans Schneider, 1990, pp. 295–306.
Sams, Eric. "Politics, Literature, and People in Schumann's Op. 136," *The Musical Times* CIX (1968), pp. 25–27.
Sams, Eric. "Schumann and Faust," *The Musical Times* CXIII (1972), pp. 543–46.
Schnapp, Friedrich. "Robert Schumann and Heinrich Heine," *The Musical Quarterly* XI (1925), pp. 599–616.
Schoppe, Martin. "Schumanns frühe Texte und Schriften," in Mayeda, Akio and Niemöller, Klaus Wolfgang, eds. *Schumanns Werke: Text und Interpretationen*. Mainz: Schott, 1987, pp. 7–15.
Shitomirski, Daniel. "Schumann in Russland," in *Sammelbände der Robert-Schumann-Gesellschaft*, Vol. I. Leipzig: VEB Deutscher Verlag für Musik, 1961, pp. 19–47.
Siegel, Linda. "A Second Look at Schumann's *Genoveva*," *The Music Review* XXXVI (1975), pp. 17–43.
Sietz, Reinhold. "Zur Textgestaltung von Robert Schumanns 'Genoveva'," *Die Musikforschung* XXIII (1970), pp. 395–410.
Temperley, Nicholas. "Schumann and Sterndale Bennett," *19th-Century Music* XII (1988–89), pp. 207–20.
Truscott, Harold. "The Evolution of Schumann's Last Period," *The Chesterian* XXXI (1957), pp. 76–84, 103–111.
Turchin, Barbara. "Schumann's Conversion to Vocal Music: A Reconsideration," *The Musical Quarterly* LXVII (1981), pp. 392–404.
Wendt, Matthias. "Zu Robert Schumanns Skizzenbüchern," in Mayeda, Akio and Niemöller, Klaus Wolfgang, eds. *Schumanns Werke: Text und Interpretationen*. Mainz: Schott, 1987, pp. 101–14.

Index

Abelard, Pierre, 42
Aeschylus, 43
Alexis, Willibald, 26, 30
Alfieri, Vittorio, 30, 43
Alkan, Charles Henri Valentin, 364
Amsterdam, 135, 274, 278
Anacreon, 9, 43
Andersen, Hans Christian, 45, 192, 299, 341
Aranyi, Jelly d', 308
Arnim, Bettina von, 27, 321, 322, 323, 325, 326, 330, 331, 332, 364
Arnim, Ludwig Achim von, 26, 41, 43, 108, 171, 322, 341, 364
Arts, interrelationship of, 39
Augsburg, 15, 31

Bach, Johann Sebastian, 13, 18, 29, 65, 81, 82, 87, 96, 102, 103, 138, 142, 143, 144, 145, 146, 161, 196, 210, 218, 221, 263, 269, 284, 289, 305, 306, 309
Bargiel, Marianne, 23, 138, 312
Barth, J. A., 112
Bayreuth, 15, 16, 51
Becker, Ernst, 125, 140, 170, 198, 271
Becker, Julius, 107, 236
Becker, Rupert, 271, 277, 278
Beethoven, Ludwig van, 7, 40, 48, 63, 76, 77, 82, 85, 86, 100, 101, 102, 108, 115, 133, 143, 146, 155, 159, 160, 162, 198, 199, 200, 202, 206, 210, 211, 238, 240, 262, 269, 271, 283, 288, 291, 304, 305, 315, 322, 335
Belgium, 136, 178, 263
Bendemann, Eduard, 224, 265, 266
Bennett, William Sterndale, 116, 117, 149, 199, 229, 260, 364
Béranger, Pierre Jean de, 195
Berger, Ludwig, 76
Berlin, 138, 139, 172, 191, 201, 204, 225, 229, 262, 263, 308, 312, 317
Berlioz, Hector, 39, 104, 107, 114, 135, 142, 182, 183, 184, 202, 218, 223

Berwald, Franz, 200, 364
Blanche, Emile, 332
Blechen, Carl, 282, 325
Bockmühl, Robert, 307
Böger, Dr., 278
Bonaparte, Napoleon, 2, 4, 5, 31, 188, 232
Bonaventura, 171
Bonn, 162, 270, 271, 280, 312, 315, 316, 333
Böttger, Adolph, 200, 201, 214
Brahms, Johannes, 153, 208, 271, 275, 301, 307, 309, 310, 311, 312, 316, 317, 318, 319, 320, 321, 322, 324, 325, 333, 334, 344
Breitkopf & Härtel, 17, 80, 133, 183, 221, 227, 230, 231, 261, 267, 273
Brendel, Franz, 30, 175, 189, 197, 215, 241, 364
Brentano, Clemens, 26, 43, 108, 161, 322, 364
Bulwer-Lytton, Lord, Edward, 43
Burgmüller, Norbert, 114, 200, 301, 310, 365
Burns, Robert, 43
Byron, George Gordon, Lord, 4, 43, 81, 130, 183, 222, 229, 237, 238, 254–56, 336

Calderón de la Barca, Pedro, 43, 237
Callot, Jacques, 50
Carlsbad, 7, 190
Carlyle, Thomas, 51, 52
Carus, Agnes, 12, 13, 77, 104
Carus, Carl Gustav, 218–20, 224, 233, 235
Carus, Ernst August, 12, 22, 24, 69, 70, 104
Castelli, Ignaz, 72
Cellini, Benvenuto, 43
Cervantes, Miguel de, 4
Chamisso, Adelbert von, 43, 194, 195, 196, 197, 365
Cherubini, Luigi, 7, 365

Chopin, Frédéric, 60, 65, 67, 77, 85, 88, 109, 110, 114, 117, 128, 151, 159, 171, 184, 199, 223
Christel, 66, 67, 68, 106, 124, 314, 329
Clément, Félix, 282
Cohn, Martin, 278
Colditz, 12, 334
Cologne, 25, 38, 233, 241, 300, 312, 334
Contessa, C. W., 171
Cooper, James Fenimore, 43
Copernicus, 316
Coriolanus, 42, 55
Custine, Astolphe, Marquis de, 187, 188
Czerny, Carl, 7, 103

Dante, 43
David, Félicien, 176
David, Ferdinand, 116, 205, 209, 222, 264, 365
Denmark, 179, 185, 186
Deschamps, Antoni, 332
Dietrich, Albert, 271, 272, 309
Döhner, Hermann, 5
Donizetti, Gaetano, 133
Dorn, Heinrich, 59, 64, 65, 72, 81, 104, 112, 117, 138, 144, 148, 190, 192, 224, 287, 365
Dresden, 2, 9, 18, 69, 123, 128, 139, 178, 185, 190, 191, 204, 217, 218, 219, 220, 222, 223, 224, 225, 226, 227, 232, 233, 234, 235, 241, 245, 260, 262, 265, 283, 287, 295, 299, 336, 339
Dreyschock, Alexander, 114
Droste-Hülshoff, Annette von, 43
Dufourd, Claudine, 134
Durante, Francesco, 29
Dürer, Albrecht, 238
Düsseldorf, 178, 204, 226, 227, 233, 234, 235, 257, 259–63, 268, 270, 271, 274, 276, 301, 304, 305, 306, 312, 318, 319, 322, 333

Ehlert, Louis, 176, 210
Eichendorff, Josef von, 43, 44, 45, 161, 194, 341
Einert, Wilhelm, 138
Endenich, 280, 282, 310, 312, 313, 314, 315, 316, 317, 319, 320, 321, 322, 323, 324, 325, 326, 330, 331, 332, 334, 335, 344
England, 9, 27, 136, 179, 212, 260, 261, 318, 333

Ernst, Heinrich Wilhelm, 33, 34, 38
Euripides, 43

Fétis, François-Joseph, 104
Field, John, 60, 62, 365
Fielding, Henry, 43
Fink, Gottfried Wilhelm, 104
Flechsig, Emil, 1, 4, 11, 12, 13, 14, 18, 19, 24, 26, 28, 47, 53, 66, 73, 212
Forcellini, Egidio, 9
Forkel, Johann Nicolaus, 143–44
Frankenberg, Adolph, 339
Franz, Robert, 206, 220, 365
Fricken, Ernestine von, 66, 118, 119, 120, 121, 122, 123, 127, 129, 134, 148, 149, 161, 314
Friedrich, Caspar David, 219
Froebel, Friedrich, 335, 338, 339

Gade, Niels, 153, 182, 184, 191, 257, 340, 365
Geibel, Emanuel, 43, 194, 294, 295, 340
Genelli, Bonaventura, 157, 158
Gerold, Carl, 130
Goethe, J. W. von, 7, 43, 80, 98, 108, 166, 167, 183, 188, 194, 222, 239–42, 254, 255, 256, 304, 316, 322, 336, 340
Goldschmidt, M., 141
Goldsmith, Oliver, 43
Gontard, Susette, 310
Görres, Joseph von, 26
Grabbe, Christian Dietrich, 46, 47
Grillparzer, Franz, 43
Grimm, Jacob and Wilhelm, 99
Grimm, Julius Otto, 275, 315, 316
Grosse, Carl Friedrich, 41
Günderrode, Caroline von, 325
Gutzkow, Karl, 43

Hallé, Charles, 172
Hamburg, 204, 234, 271, 317
Handel, George Frederic, 29
Hanover, 275, 308, 317, 319
Hanslick, Eduard, 324
Häring, Wilhelm. See Alexis, Willibald
Härtel, Hermann, 158, 234, 313
Hartmann, C. H. F., 111, 112
Hartmann, Mathilde, 315
Hasenklever, Richard, 278, 312
Haslinger, Tobias, 130, 131, 132, 149
Hauff, Wilhelm, 43

Hauptmann, Moritz, 148, 160, 204, 211, 215–16, 221, 272, 365
Haydn, Franz Joseph, 6, 7, 13, 206, 207, 210, 211, 283
Hazlitt, William, 39, 281, 309
Hebbel, Friedrich, 45, 46, 243, 244, 245, 246, 247, 250, 295, 299
Heidelberg, 12, 15, 25, 26, 27, 28, 30, 31, 32, 33, 36, 46, 61, 65, 69, 83, 84, 85, 87, 88, 89, 108, 263
Heine, Heinrich, 15, 44, 46, 47, 135, 194, 195
Heinse, Gottlob Heinrich, 3
Heinse, Wilhelm, 43
Helbig, Carl G., 220, 226
Heller, Stephen, 54, 55, 105, 107, 112, 117, 135, 334, 365
Heloise, and Abelard, 42
Henselt, Adolph, 117, 137, 186, 187, 287, 365
Herlossohn, K. G. R., 110
Hertel, Gottfried 9
Herwegh, Georg, 43
Herz, Henri, 7, 13, 114, 365
Hesse, Hermann, 106
Hiller, Ferdinand, 176, 191, 223, 226, 227, 228, 229, 233, 234, 235, 241, 242, 244, 259, 268, 269, 334, 365–66
Hirschbach, Hermann, 160, 193, 210
Hoffmann, E.T.A., 22, 23, 41, 43, 48, 49, 74, 78, 109, 166, 168, 169, 171, 222, 236, 237, 247, 299, 341
Hoffmann von Fallersleben, 340
Hofmeister, Friedrich, 17, 101, 110, 205
Hölderlin, Friedrich, 11, 47, 282, 310, 325
Holland, 136, 178, 179, 263, 268, 274, 276, 319
Homer, 43, 336
Horace, 43
Horn, Moritz, 270, 342, 343
Hübner, Rudolf, 224
Hugo, Victor, 43, 184, 269
Humboldt, Alexander von, 43
Hummel, Johann Nepomuk, 7, 24, 25, 36, 43, 59, 60, 61, 62, 63, 85, 107, 118, 206, 366
Hunt, Leigh, 174
Hünten, Franz, 114
Huth, Louis, 243

Immermann, Karl, 43, 47, 239
Irving, Washington, 43
Italy, 30, 31, 35

Jacobi, J. G., 80
Jena, 56
Joachim, Joseph, 184, 270, 271, 272, 274, 275, 276, 277, 307, 308, 309, 310, 312, 318, 319, 320, 321, 324, 325, 331, 332, 334, 366

Kafka, Franz, 131
Kahlert, August, 220
Kalkbrenner, Friedrich, 7, 366
Kassel, 201, 204
Kerner, Justinus, 43, 80, 194
Kistner, Friedrich, 94, 152, 158, 307
Kleist, Heinrich von, 47, 48, 257
Knorr, Julius, 111, 112
Kohl, Robert, 339
Kossmaly, Carl, 132, 181, 212, 238
Krahe, Carl, 15
Kreischa, 232, 336
Kulmann, Elisabeth, 344
Kuntsch, Johann Gottfried, 5, 6, 7, 38, 65, 100, 144, 226, 235
Kurrer, Heinrich Wilhelm von, 15, 31

Laidlaw, Anna Robena, 172
Laube, Heinrich, 295
Laurens, Jean-Joseph-Bonaventure, 270
Leipzig, 2, 3, 4, 12, 14, 15, 16, 17, 18, 21, 22, 23, 24, 25, 30, 31, 32, 33, 34, 35, 36, 38, 45, 46, 50, 73, 76, 101, 108, 115, 118, 123, 125, 128, 131, 138, 139, 140, 178, 179, 182, 184, 188, 189, 191, 201, 215, 217, 218, 223, 224, 227, 232, 234, 235, 241, 245, 253, 266, 268, 275, 288, 313, 317, 326
Leipzig Theater, 18, 64
Lenau, Nikolaus, 47, 48, 235, 282, 297, 299
Leo, Leonardo, 29
Leonardo da Vinci, 31
Lind, Jenny, 225, 234, 366
List, Emilie, 135, 136, 137
Liszt, Franz, 39, 96, 97, 128, 129, 140, 159, 162, 172, 183, 186, 202, 210, 218, 223, 228, 229, 235, 236, 255, 287, 304, 316, 317, 318, 337, 339
Loewe, Carl, 197, 213
London, 63, 131, 135
Lorenz, Oswald, 131, 189
Louis Ferdinand, Prince, 24, 32, 42, 84, 85, 144, 207, 366
Luther, Martin, 257, 261

Lvov, A. F., 189
Lyser, Johann Peter, 96, 112

Macaulay, Thomas Babington, 43
Mahler, Gustav, 202
Marbach, Oswald, 238
Marcello, Benedetto, 29
Märchen, 49, 299, 341, 342, 343, 344
Marpurg, Friedrich Wilhelm, 65, 98
Marschner, Heinrich, 149, 237, 239, 255, 366
Mayer, Charles, 103
Méhul, Etienne, 7
Mendelssohn, Felix, ix, 76, 114, 115, 116, 133, 139, 143, 182, 184, 185, 186, 191, 200, 205, 207, 211, 218, 219, 223, 224, 226, 227, 228, 229, 233, 253, 254, 259, 260, 276, 277, 287, 288, 296, 304, 306, 335, 336
Metternich, Prince Clemens Wenzel von, 130
Meyerbeer, Giacomo, ix, 114, 135, 228, 234, 238, 245, 304, 366
Mittermaier, Karl Joseph, 28
Montalti, family of, 42
Moore, Thomas, 43, 212, 213, 214, 237
Mörike, Eduard, 43
Moscheles, Ignaz, 7, 25, 32, 35, 36, 63, 68, 88, 94, 116, 124, 142, 150, 155, 157, 158, 159, 366
Moscow, 42, 186, 187, 188
Mozart, Wolfgang Amadeus, 7, 13, 39, 46, 49, 60, 107, 160, 200, 206, 210, 211, 218, 255, 283, 288, 335
Müller, Christian, 72
Müller, Maler, 243
Murat, Joachim, 26

Napoleon I. *See* Bonaparte, Napoleon
Naubert, Christiane Benedicte, 41
Nerval, Gérard de, 332
Neue Zeitschrift für Musik, x, 42, 47, 48, 49, 54, 56, 110, 111, 112, 113, 114, 115, 116, 117, 124, 127, 129, 130, 131, 132, 133, 137, 151, 158, 165, 167, 168, 175, 178, 181, 182, 183, 185, 189, 190, 210, 217, 227, 239, 271, 276, 296, 317, 318, 339
Noel, Richard, 278
Nottebohm, Gustav, 297
Novalis, 40, 43, 78, 337, 341, 342, 366
Novello, Clara, 166

Ortlepp, Ernst, 103, 111
Ossian, 257
Otto, Franz, 107, 110

Paganini, Niccolò, 33, 43, 61, 62, 86, 95, 96, 97, 107, 126, 151, 218, 320, 321
Palestrina, Giovanni Pierluigi da, 29
Paris, 44, 61, 68, 76, 86, 90, 131, 133, 134, 135, 136, 138, 153, 172, 178, 183, 184, 223, 229
Pasta, Giuditta, 31
Pellico, Sylvio, 43, 312
Pestalozzi, Heinrich, 338
Peters, Dr., 313, 314, 315, 316, 317
Petrarch, 30, 43
Platen, August von, 43
Pleyel, Ignaz, 7, 13
Pohl, Richard, 257, 262, 267
Ponsard, François, 43
Program music 39, 40

Quincey, Thomas de, 26

Rachel, Elisa, 153
Racine, Jean, 43
Rakemann, Louis, 129
Raphael, 39
Reinick, Robert, 194, 242, 243, 244, 367
Reinecke, Carl, 185, 242
Reissiger, Carl, 223, 224
Reissmann, August, 282
Rellstab, Ludwig, 57, 74, 90, 91, 103, 104, 337, 367
Rethel, Alfred, 282, 326, 367
Reuter, Moritz, 71, 75
Rhineland, 25, 26, 54, 234, 263, 267
Richarz, Franz, 313, 314, 316, 323, 324, 325, 326, 327, 328, 329, 330, 331, 332, 333
Richter, Jean Paul, 4, 13, 14, 15, 16, 19, 30, 33, 40, 41, 42, 48, 50, 51, 52, 53, 54, 55, 57, 74, 80, 81, 82, 83, 87, 88, 89, 90, 94, 99, 105, 108, 113, 117, 130, 143, 146, 150, 152, 153, 160, 161, 171, 177, 283, 335, 337, 338, 367
    Flegeljahre 19, 51, 53, 55, 90, 91, 92, 93, 94, 108, 150, 151
Richter, Ludwig, 224, 230, 245, 340, 367
Ries, Ferdinand, 7
Rietschel, Ernst, 224
Rietz, Julius, 233, 246, 276, 296, 367

Righini, Vincenzo, 7
Röller, Eduard, 73
Romanticism, ix, 32, 44, 55, 200
Rosen, Gisbert, 15, 16, 18, 25, 26, 27, 38, 47
Rossini, Gioacchino, 31, 86
Rousseau, Jean-Jacques, 43
Rubens, Peter Paul, 263
Rückert, Friedrich, 43, 194, 295, 306
Rudel, Gottlob, 19, 22, 35, 37
Rufinatscha, Johann, 297
Runge, Philipp Otto, 337
Russia, 2, 68, 153, 186, 187, 189, 190, 239

Sand, George, 43, 184
Schäffer, Julius, 206
Schiller, Friedrich, 4, 42, 43, 222, 304, 316, 340
Schlegel, August Wilhelm, 43, 55
Schlegel, Friedrich, 43, 152, 163
Schneeberg, 72, 73, 101
Schneider, Friedrich 7
Schröder-Devrient, Wilhelmine, 223
Schubert, Franz, 13, 24, 30, 32, 40, 63, 81, 83, 85, 114, 133, 196, 200, 201, 277, 295
Schuberth, Julius, 230
Schulze, Ernst, 43
Schumann, August, 2, 3, 4, 5, 9, 10, 15, 21, 37, 41, 43, 50, 53, 61, 75, 137
Schumann, Carl, 5, 14, 27, 38, 74, 75, 124, 186, 229, 232
Schumann, Clara, x, 22, 23, 43, 55, 61, 64, 70, 72, 75, 77, 78, 104, 106, 109, 119, 120, 121, 122, 123, 141, 142, 143, 146, 151, 153, 154, 155, 157, 159, 161, 162, 163, 164, 166, 168, 169, 170, 172, 173, 183, 185, 190, 193, 194, 197, 198, 205, 209, 210, 217, 218, 219, 220, 221, 224, 225, 228, 229, 232, 233, 235, 236, 260, 263, 265, 268, 270, 272, 273, 275, 278, 282, 291, 301, 308, 311, 329, 335, 336, 337, 338, 340
  Accounts of Schumann's final illness, 276, 277, 278, 279
  Compositions, 82, 102, 155, 157, 158, 163, 165, 167, 171, 291
  Courtship, 122–40
  Endenich, 312–26, 330, 333, 334
  Married life, 174–81
  Russian tour, 186–89
Schumann, Eduard, 5, 14, 30, 111, 124, 125, 132, 137, 172

Schumann, Elise, 177, 225, 338, 339
Schumann, Emil, 222, 225, 226, 336
Schumann, Emilie, 5, 10, 11, 75
Schumann, Eugenie, 260, 308, 334, 340
Schumann, Ferdinand, 222
Schumann, Friedrich, 4
Schumann, Johanne Christiane Schnabel, 3, 4, 5, 11, 14, 19, 25, 27, 30, 34, 35, 36, 37, 38, 40, 58, 59, 62, 63, 65, 68, 69, 73, 75, 78, 79, 83, 104, 111, 118, 119, 123, 234
Schumann, Julie, 222, 339
Schumann, Julius, 5, 74, 75
Schumann, Ludwig, 222, 334
Schumann, Marie, 177, 185, 225, 229, 232, 279, 280, 335, 338, 339, 340
Schumann, Robert,
  As conductor, 227–28, 259–60, 262–65, 268, 272–74
  Financial concerns, 180–82, 190, 229, 231
  Hand injury, 69–71, 83
  Improvisation, 7, 8, 61, 83
  Interest in cipher, 152–55
  Instrumentation, 101, 202–04, 242, 301
  Mental illness, 11, 74, 75, 129, 189–91, 219–21, 270, 277–79, 282, 315–16, 319, 323, 326–32
  Musical sketches, 56, 77, 84, 85, 86, 98, 99, 100, 102, 194, 210, 211, 245
  On education, 336, 338–39
  Operatic projects, 180, 222, 236–39, 256, 304
  Personality, 73, 74, 175–76, 265, 266
  Role in Dresden revolt, 232–33
  View of program music, 142–43
  Writings 8, 9, 14, 40, 41, 42, 43, 57, 100, 107, 110, 113, 114, 115, 151, 188, 221, 267, 269, 271, 275

Compositions

Abegg Variations op. 1, 32, 62, 72, 82, 86, 87, 88, 89, 100, 101, 104, 108, 118
Accompaniments to Bach's Partitas, Sonatas, and Suites, 269, 306
Adagio and Allegro op. 70, 231
Adventlied op. 71, 306
Albumblätter op. 124, 86, 103, 267
Album for the Young op. 68, 229–30, 231, 294, 335, 340
Allegro op. 8, 72, 86, 94, 95, 97, 119
Andante and Variations op. 46, 188, 206, 207, 225

Schumann, Robert (*continued*)
  Arabesque op. 18, 133, 146, 170, 181
  Ballszenen op. 109, 299
  Belsatzar op. 57, 194
  Bilder aus dem Östen op. 66, 44, 294
  Blumenstück op.19, 133, 146, 170, 181
  Bride of Messina Overture op. 100, 261, 282, 304
  Bünte Blätter op. 99, 199
  Canon on "*An Alexis*" WoO 4, 84
  Carnaval op.9, xiii, 82, 119, 142, 147, 149, 150, 151, 152, 155, 159, 172, 173, 230
  Cello Concerto op. 129, 307, 309
    Violin arrangement, 307
  Concert-Allegro op. 134, 270, 274, 307, 309
  Concerto for Four Horns op. 86, 295, 296
  Concert sans orchestre (Piano Sonata No. 3) op. 14, 128, 130, 147, 148, 149, 156, 157, 172
  The Corsair, 238, 240, 242
  Davidsbündlertänze op. 6, 107, 128, 165, 167
  Dichterliebe op. 48, 44, 194, 195, 223
  Drei Fantasiestücke op. 111, 261, 299
  Drei Gesänge op. 31, 195
  Drei Gesänge op. 62, 227, 295
  Drei Klaviersonaten für die Jugend op. 118, 270, 341
  Drei Romanzen op. 28, 170, 171, 181
  Drei Romanzen op. 94, 294
  Early Lieder, 80, 81, 98, 159
  Etudes on the Allegretto from Beethoven's Symphony No. 7 WoO 31, 85, 86, 102
  Etudes symphoniques op. 13, 119, 125, 130, 145, 148, 149, 155
  Fantasie op. 17, 40, 128, 147, 155, 161, 162, 163, 164, 165, 198, 230, 291
  Fantasiestücke op. 12, 50, 77, 128, 165, 166, 172, 173
  Fantasiestücke op. 73, 231, 294
  Fantasiestücke op. 88, 180–81, 206, 207
  Fantasy for Violin op. 131, 270, 275
  Faschingsschwank aus Wien op. 26, 133, 156, 157, 169,
  First Piano Sonata op. 11, 85, 107, 123, 128, 147, 155, 156, 157, 158, 159, 160, 161
  Four Duets op. 34, 182
  Four Fugues op. 72, 171, 222, 284
  Four Marches op. 76, 233, 282, 295
  Four Pieces for Piano op. 32, 133, 144, 170
  Five Songs by Robert Burns op. 55, 227, 294, 295
  Frauenliebe und Leben op. 42, 196, 197, 198, 207, 291
  Fünf Lieder op. 40, 45
  Fünf Stücke im Volkston op. 102, 294
  Genoveva op. 81, 44, 46, 213, 225, 229, 231, 232, 234, 235, 243, 244, 256, 258, 281, 294, 297, 317, 343
  Gesänge der Frühe op. 133, 270, 309, 310, 311
  Hermann and Dorothea Overture op. 136, 261, 282, 304
  Humoreske op. 20, 133, 170, 171
  Impromptus op. 5, 73, 78, 86, 101, 102, 104, 128, 144
  Intermezzi op. 4, 72, 82, 86, 97, 98, 99, 100, 101, 104, 147, 155, 165
  Introduction and Allegro op. 92, 295, 296, 307
  Jagdlieder op. 137, 295
  Julius Caesar Overture op. 128, 56, 261, 268, 282, 304
  Kinderball op. 130, 270, 341
  Kinderszenen op. 15, 77, 128, 168, 186, 337, 338
  The King's Son op. 116, 257, 258, 261, 282
  Kreisleriana op. 16, 49, 50, 128, 130, 146, 168, 169, 173, 207, 275
  Lieder op. 98a, 256, 305
  Liederkreis op. 24, 44, 194, 195
  Liederkreis op. 39, 44, 194, 196, 293
  Lieder und Gesänge op. 127, 56
  The Luck of Edenhall op. 143, 257, 268
  Mädchenlieder op. 103, 261, 344
  Manfred op. 115, 213, 229, 254–56, 266, 281, 295, 299
  Märchenbilder op. 113, 299, 342
  Märchenerzählungen op. 132, 270, 299, 309, 342
  Mass op. 147, 266, 305, 306
  Minnespiel op.101, 295
  The Minstrel's Curse op. 139, 257, 258, 266, 282, 305
  Nachtlied op. 108, 46, 295
  Nachtstücke op. 22, 50, 133, 170, 171, 172
  Novelletten op. 21, 56, 128, 166, 167, 168, 173
  Overture, Scherzo, and Finale op. 52, 180, 204, 205, 301
  Paganini accompaniments, 320, 324
  Paganini Etudes op. 3, 72, 86, 95, 96, 104, 172
  Paganini Etudes op. 10, 86, 97, 172

Papillons op. 2, xii, 32, 62, 63, 82, 86, 89, 90, 91, 92, 93, 94, 97, 98, 99, 103, 104,105, 150, 151
Paradise and the Peri op. 50, 180, 181, 185, 212–16, 225, 230, 231, 237, 242, 251, 260, 262, 264, 275, 343
Piano Concerto op. 54, 180, 204, 205, 206, 213, 222, 225, 226, 234, 268, 287, 296, 307, 309
Piano Concerto in C minor, 85
Piano Concerto in D minor, 133, 170, 287
Piano Concerto in E flat major, 13, 85
Piano Concerto in F major, 61, 84, 85, 94, 101
Piano Quartet op. 47, 180, 206, 207, 212
Piano Quartet WoO 32, 25, 32, 84, 100, 101
Piano Quintet op. 44, 180, 183, 188, 189, 206, 207, 212, 225, 228
Piano Trio No. 1 op.63, 225, 293, 294
Piano Trio No. 2 op. 80, 225, 293
Piano Trio No. 3 op. 110, 261, 266, 305
The Pilgrimage of the Rose op. 112, 213, 261, 266, 274, 278, 342, 343
Polonaises WoO 20, 83, 89
The Princess and the Page op. 140, 257, 258, 266, 305
Proposed *Klavierschule*, 137
Psalm 150, 8, 80
Requiem op. 148, 266, 305, 306
Requiem for Mignon op. 98b, 213, 256, 305
Ritornelle op. 65, 228
Romances op. 69, 228
Romances op. 91, 228
Romances and Ballads op. 49, 195
Romances and Ballads op. 67, 228, 294
Romances and Ballads op. 75, 294
Romances for Cello, 309, 310
Scenes from Goethe's *Faust* WoO 3, 189, 191, 213, 220, 229, 239–42, 251, 254, 255, 268–69, 281, 291, 295, 307, 309, 343
Schön Hedwig op. 106, 299
Sechs Gedichte und Requiem op. 90, 48, 235, 297, 298
Sechs Gesänge op. 89, 297
Sechs Gesänge op. 107, 297
Second Piano Sonata op. 22, 128, 147, 156, 157, 159, 173
Seven Pieces in the Form of Fughettas op. 126, 269, 307
Sieben Lieder op. 104, 261, 344

Six Fugues on the Name "Bach" op. 60, 144, 222, 284, 289
Sketches for Pedal Piano op. 58, 284, 285
Sonata in F minor, 156
Song Album for the Young op. 79, 231, 294, 340
Spanische Liebeslieder op. 138, 295
Spanisches Liederspiel op. 74, 231, 294
String Quartets op. 41, 180, 182, 183, 188, 206, 209–212, 227, 230
Studies for Pedal Piano op. 56, 144, 222, 284, 285, 287
Symphony in C minor, 180, 199, 200
Symphony in G minor WoO 29, 56, 72, 73, 78, 100, 101
Symphony No. 1 op. 38, 133, 179, 180, 181, 182, 187, 188, 200–05, 207, 213, 214, 225, 230, 328
Symphony No. 2 op. 61, 204, 222, 224, 226, 287–93
Symphony No. 3 op. 97, 182, 261, 266, 282, 300, 301
Symphony No. 4 op. 120, 180, 205, 261, 268, 301–04
Theme in E flat WoO 24, 277, 280, 310, 311
Toccata op. 7, 32, 84, 86, 103, 173
Variations on Chopin's Nocturne op. 15 no. 3, 85
Verzweifle nicht op. 93, 306
Vier Duette op. 78, 294
Vier Gesänge op. 59, 294
Vier Husarenlieder op. 117, 261, 299
Violin Concerto WoO 23, 270, 307, 308, 309, 310
Violin Fantasy op. 131, 270, 275, 307, 308, 309
Violin Sonata No. 1 op. 105, 261, 266, 305
Violin Sonata No. 2 op. 121, 261, 305
Violin Sonata No. 3 WoO 27, 309
Waldszenen op. 82, 46, 341
Zwei Balladen op. 122, 299
Zwölf Gedichte op. 35, 44, 181, 196
Zwölf Gedichte op. 37, 44
Zwölf vierhändige Klavierstücke für kleine und grosse Kinder op. 85, 340–41
Schumann, Rosalie, 74, 75, 76, 125, 314
Schumann, Therese, 30, 125
Schuncke, Ludwig, 76, 103, 111, 112, 138, 226, 367
Scott, Walter, 4, 26, 43, 149, 239
Sechter, Simon, 297

Sedlnitzsky, Count Joseph, 130, 131
Semmel, Moritz, 19, 30
Shakespeare, William, 55, 56, 57, 122, 168, 177, 183, 236, 237, 256, 269, 336
Shelley, Percy Bysshe, 43, 217, 222
Sire, Simonin de, 70, 128
Slowacki, Julius, 237
Sobolewski, J. F. E., 158, 165
Sonnenberg, Franz Anton, 11
Sophocles, 43, 336
Spohr, Ludwig, ix, 200, 201, 204, 211–12, 238, 239, 367
St. Petersburg, 178, 186, 187, 188
Stegmayer, Ferdinand, 111
Stern, Julius, 263
Sterne, Laurence, 52
Stowe, Harriet Beecher, 43
Strindberg, August, 58
Sue, Eugène, 43
Switzerland, 30, 35, 263

Tausch, Julius, 260, 261, 264, 266, 268, 272, 273
Thackeray, William Makepiece, 17
Thalberg, Sigismond, 126, 179
Thibaut, Anton Friedrich Justus, 28, 29, 30, 34, 46, 367
Tieck, Ludwig, 41, 43, 45, 55, 108, 171, 243, 244, 245, 246, 247, 250, 299, 341
Töpken, Theodor, 69, 83, 87, 88, 89, 95, 97, 103, 112, 117

Uhland, Johann Ludwig, 43, 340
United States of America, 135, 179, 187

Verhulst, Johann, 177, 207
Vienna, 34, 48, 63, 69, 76, 126, 129, 130, 131, 132, 133, 135, 137, 156, 170, 172, 173, 204, 225, 229, 262, 287, 317, 338
Vigenère, Blaise de, 152
Vittoria, Tomaso de, 29

Vogler, Abbé, 114
Voigt, Carl, 76
Voigt, Henriette, 76, 77, 89, 94, 112, 118, 119, 138, 149, 157, 207, 337
Volkmann, Robert, 216
Vulpius, Christian August, 41

Wackenroder, Heinrich, 238, 337
Wagner, Richard, ix, 39, 199, 202, 218, 223, 224, 227, 228, 232, 233, 239, 251, 253, 254
Wasielewski, Wilhelm Joseph von, 2, 10, 74, 220, 241, 254, 260, 262, 264, 269, 271, 282, 288, 300, 306, 312, 326
Weber, Bernhard Anselm, 7
Weber, Carl Maria von, 7, 9, 10, 39, 86, 88, 114, 223, 239, 251, 255
Weber, Gottfried, 65, 72, 95, 103
Weimar, 59, 60, 229, 241, 317
Wenzel, Ernst Ferdinand, 137
Wettig, Carl, 296, 297
Whistling, Friedrich, 295
Wieck, Alwin, 64
Wieck, Friedrich, 22, 23, 24, 31, 35, 36, 37, 38, 40, 43, 58, 59, 60, 61, 62, 63, 64, 65, 66, 68, 69, 70, 71, 78, 84, 101, 104, 106, 108, 111, 118, 142, 159, 169, 172, 175, 182, 185, 190, 191, 217, 236
  Opposes Clara's marriage, 122–27, 129, 130, 131, 133–40
Wiedebein, Gottlob, 20, 21, 80, 98, 108, 192, 296
Wielhorski, Count Michail, 187, 189
Wolf, Hugo, 282

Young, Edward, 3

Zschokke, Heinrich, 41
Zumsteeg, Johann Rudolf, 166
Zwickau, 1, 2, 4, 5, 6, 9, 16, 17, 18, 19, 25, 38, 40, 72, 75, 78, 101, 130, 131, 226